Studies in the Social and Economic History of the Witwatersrand 1886–1914

Volume 2
New Nineveh

By the same author

Chibaro: African Mine Labour in Southern Rhodesia, 1900–1933 (London, 1976)
Studies in the History of African Mine Labour in Colonial Zimbabwe (Gwelo, 1978), with I. R. Phimister
Studies in the Social and Economic History of the Witwatersrand, 1886–*1914*. *Volume 1, New Babylon* (London, 1982)

Charles van Onselen

Studies in the Social and Economic History of the Witwatersrand 1886–1914

Volume 2
New Nineveh

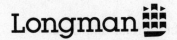

Longman Group Ltd.,
Longman House, Burnt Mill,
Harlow, Essex CM20 2JE

Published in the United States of
America by Longman Inc., New York

Associated companies, branches and representatives
throughout the world

First published 1982

British Library Cataloguing in Publication Data

Van Onselen, C.
    Studies in the social and economic
    history of the Witwatersrand 1886–1914.
    Vol. 2: New Nineveh
    1. Witwatersrand, South Africa – History
    – Social aspects   2. Witwatersrand,
    South Africa – History – Economic aspects
    I. Title
    330.9682'204   DT848.W/

ISBN 0-582-64384-8
ISBN 0-582-64385-6   Pbk

Library of Congress Cataloging in Publication Data

Van Onselen, Charles.
    Studies in the social and economic history of
Witwatersrand, 1886–1914.

    Bibliography: v. 2, p.
    Includes indexes.
    Contents: v. 1. New Babylon – v. 2. New Nineveh.
    1. Witwatersrand (South Africa) – Economic
conditions. 2. Witwatersrand (South Africa) – Social
conditions. I. Title.
HC905.Z7W558   330.9682'2   82-15361
ISBN 0-582-64382-1 (v. 1   AACR2
ISBN 0-582-64383-X (pbk.: v. 1)
ISBN 0-582-64384-8 (v. 2)
ISBN 0-582-64385-6 (pbk.: 2)

Printed in Great Britain by Butler & Tanner Ltd, Frome and London

To Belinda, Gareth and Jessica

Ancient Nineveh and Babylon have been revived. Johannesburg is their twentieth century prototype. It is a city of unbridled squander and unfathomable squalor. Living is more costly than one's wildest dreams. All the necessaries of life are impudently dear. Miners of England and Australia, however poor may be your lot, however dark your present prospects, let no man tempt you to South Africa with tales of the wages that are paid upon the Rand! The wages are high indeed, but the price the workers pay for them is paid in suffering and blood.

A. Pratt, *The Real South Africa* (1913)

Contents

List of tables and illustrations

Tables

Maps and diagrams

Photographs

Abbreviations

B.W.E.A.	British Women's Emigration Association
C.A.J.	Cabmen's Association of Johannesburg
C.D.U.	Cab Drivers' Union
E.D.N.L.A.	Employers' Domestic Native Labour Association
I.L.P.	Independent Labour Party
M.L.A.	Member of the Legislative Assembly
N.Z.A.S.M.	Netherlands South Africa Railway Company
R.U.I.C.	Rand Unemployed Investigation Committee
S.A.C.S.	South African Colonisation Society
S.A.E.C.	South African Expansion Committee
S. & D.N.	Standard and Diggers' News
S.L.C.	Special Liquor Committee
T.M.A.	Transvaal Miners' Association
W.L.V.A.	Witwatersrand Licensed Victuallers' Association
W.N.L.A.	Witwatersrand Native Labour Association
Y.M.C.A.	Young Men's Christian Association
Z.A.R.	Zuid Afrikaansche Republiek
Zarp	Zuid Afrikaansche Republiekeinsche Polisie

CHAPTER ONE

The Witches of Suburbia

Domestic service on the Witwatersrand, 1890–1914

> Perhaps it is not always easy for the white mistress to decide on the best
> treatment for her native servant ... The rules are not easily laid down,
> but they form an ethical code, an unwritten law, which it is quite clear
> enough for her who runs a house to read.
>
> *Imperial Colonist*, November 1911

Viewed historically, the South African labour market has always been
dominated by three major sectors of employment – mining, agriculture and
domestic service. The twentieth-century emergence and rise of secondary
industry as an employer of labour has supplemented rather than restructured
this pattern. In the 1980s, as well as the 1880s, domestic service remains one of
the most important sectors of a rapidly developing capitalist economy. Yet,
despite this, it is largely in vain that one scans the literature for any reflection of
this reality. With the notable exception of Jacklyn Cock's thorough
examination of *Maids and Madams*, there is little beyond a few local surveys by
anthropologists to break the monotony of the bleak academic landscape.[1]

 This neglect may be more pronounced in southern African studies, but
it is certainly not confined to it. As late as 1909 domestic servants constituted
the largest occupational grouping in England – being larger than agriculture,
mining or even engineering – yet it is only relatively recently that these
neglected workers have received the more widespread attention from scholars
that they clearly deserve. Although we now have David Katzman's suggestive
work, we still do not have an exhaustive study of domestic service in the United
States of America.[2] In this latter context, however, we do have the great
advantage of a powerful novel – Richard Wright's *Native Son*, which had such
a significant effect on the subsequent writings of Frantz Fanon. Whilst there
are also literary works that explore similar themes in Africa, notably by Doris
Lessing, there is as yet no scholarly account of domestic service in the changing
colonial context.

 There seem to be two sets of related reasons behind this academic
apathy, and both ultimately derive from the nature of domestic service itself.
First, domestic servants serve, they do not produce. Not being commodity
producers, their labour is difficult to evaluate in capitalist terms – which is why
economists relegate their role to a discussion about the problems of national
accounting. In addition, most servants live and labour in isolation. Well away
from the production lines of factories, or the more easily recognisable haunts

and culture of the working class, they are fragmented as a group – features which do not readily earn them the curiosity of sociologists. Secondly, and largely because of these reasons, it is difficult to generate data about them. What is required, ideally, are the personal records and observations of those within the house itself – the employers and the servants. Thus a historian of 'The Domestic Servant Class in Eighteenth Century England' finds it easy to write about using 'the usual quarries of the social historian: diaries, memoirs, letters, magazines, newspapers, the accounts of travellers, and literary works'.[3] No such simple solution exists for the social historian of the colonies, where problems of class, colour and literacy combine to place diaries, memoirs and letters of employers and servants at a premium.

Undoubtedly these are formidable problems, and in the South African case there are elements of them that are insurmountable. To do justice to all the subtleties and complexities that a history of domestic servants on the Witwatersrand demands is virtually impossible. But the questions and issues that remain are so important and insistent that they deserve even the most tentative of answers. How and why did domestic service manage to remain such a large and viable sector of the economy at a time when the demands of a powerful mining industry for labour seemed insatiable? What role did the state play in relation to this problem? How did white middle and working-class wives, often finding themselves for the first time in the position of being employers of domestic labour, control black male workers in the vulnerable intimacy of their homes? How did the first generation of African men, newly off the land as independent pastoralists, peasants and family-heads in their own right cope with roles which they considered to be largely female, in situations which sought to colonise them as 'boys'? What was the response of white female servants from a metropolitan background who found themselves plunged into a colonial nexus where they had to work side-by-side with black male servants? How, in Bertram Doyle's words, was 'the etiquette of race relations' forged in such a new and potentially explosive situation?[4]

This study will explore four broad areas in an attempt to answer some of these questions. First, it will examine the position of domestic service within the Witwatersrand labour market. Secondly, it will offer an outline of the roles, duties and conditions of service for servants. Thirdly, it will attempt to specify some of the ways in which the state and employers sought to control domestic servants. Finally, it will attempt to analyse some of the responses of those who found themselves in domestic service.

Domestic service in the Witwatersrand labour market

The period before the South African War, 1887–1899

In 1887 the Witwatersrand produced gold valued at £81,000. By 1899 that production had increased to a value of about £15,000,000 per annum. At the core of the Rand, Johannesburg, a mining camp with a population of about 3,000 of all races in 1887, was transformed to a mining metropolis of 100,000 inhabitants by 1899. Although it is difficult to document, it can be assumed that within that urban core a service sector developed with a demand for labour that at least matched this spectacular growth. What *is* known, is that when a census was taken within a three-mile radius of Market square in 1896, it revealed that central Johannesburg was served by: 3,253 domestic servants (largely black), 3,054 servants (white and coloured), 402 cooks (white), 345 laundresses (coloured), 341 waiters (white), 235 housekeepers (white), 219 nurses, 165 grooms, 146 'houseboys', 106 'kitchenboys', 84 coachmen (black and white), 8 stable-keepers, 5 charwomen, 5 stewards, 4 mother's helps, 3 valets and 1 page.[5]

This rather stark statistical skeleton provided by the 1896 census is a reasonable departure point for a more detailed study of the domestic service sector prior to 1899. For within it lie several clues as to the particular life-style and class composition of white Johannesburg in the pre-war period. This is in turn necessary in order to develop a more sophisticated understanding of the particular patterns of demand for domestic servants.

At the apex of the town's social pyramid stood members of the haute bourgeoisie and their wives. The families of these merchant and mining capitalists were served by small numbers of specialist white servants such as stewards, valets and cooks, and larger numbers of white, black or coloured laundresses, waiters and general servants. It would not be uncommon for such privileged households to have between four and six servants.

Below this small upper class came the more swollen ranks of the petty-bourgeois families and amongst these would number the 1,074 'wives' (as opposed to the 5,350 'housewives') noted in the census. The men of this class were predominantly drawn from the trading, shop-keeping and commercial world of the mining town. Depending on their income and social standing, which could vary enormously, these middle-class families would employ one or more white specialist servants. Most frequently this would be a cook or a housemaid, or in the case of a respectable unmarried man of middle age, a housekeeper. Almost invariably such a white servant would be assisted by one or more black general servants. The greatest of all petty-bourgeois employers of white servants, however, were the hotel and boarding-house keepers. It was essentially this group of entrepreneurs who catered for the needs of the bulk of the male working population who were without the services of their wives and daughters – the immigrant miners. As employers, it was they who gave work to the majority of white cooks, waiters, housekeepers, laundresses and housemaids. Here again the battery of white specialist servants was assisted by an army of black general servants.

The base of the pyramid was formed by the working-class households. Such households could assume one of two major forms. First, there were those cases where a group of four or six immigrant miners combined to collectively hire and occupy a house. In the better-off of such houses a housekeeper would occasionally be employed and assisted by a black general servant. More frequently, however, the miners' domestic chores would simply be undertaken by an African 'houseboy'. Secondly, there would be the less common case where a full working-class family occupied a home. Here the wives and daughters of the artisans, shop assistants, municipal workers or miners would undertake much of the domestic work with the assistance of a black general servant. In such homes it was also not uncommon for the family to take in a 'lodger' in order to supplement its income in an expensive city.

From this broad profile it is clear that, outside working-class homes, there was a fairly widespread general demand for white female labour through much of the 1890s. More particularly, there was a call for labour in the boarding-houses – the 1896 Johannesburg census listed 62 boarding-house keepers whilst in the same year the Witwatersrand Boarding-House Keepers' Protection Association claimed a membership of 90.[6] At the same time white women were in demand to serve as cooks, housemaids and nurses in the homes of the upper and middle classes. In both these cases, however, the demand was particularly pronounced in the early 1890s; that is, before the railways reached Johannesburg, and in the boom period that preceded the Jameson Raid of 1895. In the recession years, following the Raid and leading up to the outbreak of the South African War, there was a noticeable slackening-off in the demand for white female labour although the general level remained high. As late as 1899, it was noted that: 'Good white servants are not plentiful here, and the law of supply and demand has to be taken into consideration, and pretty seriously too.'[7]

Wage rates were tied to this slightly changing pattern in demand, remaining firm through the early 1890s, peaking slightly toward 1895–6 and then easing between 1897 and 1899. White nurses and housemaids commanded cash wages ranging between £4 and £5 per month, plus meals and a room in the house that were worth an additional £2 to £5 a month.[8] Most European women appear to have been acceptable as nurses but English, Irish and Scottish girls were 'always preferred as housemaids because they are smarter in appearance and work than their continental cousins'.[9] German women were widely sought as cooks, and at one stage around 1896 commanded cash wages of up to £10 per month in addition to meals and a room in the house. By 1898–9, however, their wages had been reduced to between £5 and £7 per month and some were reported to be 'glad to work at almost whatever is offered, since a situation means a home as well'.[10] On the rare occasions when a black or coloured woman was available for service in one of the above roles she would usually be offered the job, minus the offer of a room, and at a lower wage rate.[11]

Viewed from one of the South African coastal towns, or even England, these wage rates must have appeared most attractive to female domestics. In England, in 1895, for example, a woman of between 20 and 25 years of age working in a middle or upper-class family could still only look to an annual cash wage of between £15 and £18.[12] Johannesburg, however, was a town with a notoriously high cost of living, and moreover, one with such a marked imbalance in the sex ratios that no working-class woman ventured there lightly. Under these circumstances it is worth enquiring where this labour market was supplied from.

One source of supply was the employment bureau of the day that specialised in domestic servants – the registry office. In return for fees obtained from either party, these offices would place employers and work-seekers in contact with each other. Such registry offices had long been a feature of places like Durban, Cape Town and Port Elizabeth, and either placed local workers or arranged for the 'importation' of suitable European domestic servants. In Johannesburg, the firm of Simpson Moncrieff was established as a registry office in January 1891, and by 1899 had been joined by a second agency, the

South African Employment Bureau. Acting independently, or indirectly benefiting from the earlier efforts of the coastal agencies, these registry offices played a limited part in meeting Johannesburg's needs for specialist servants. But the overall scale of the problem was clearly beyond the capacities of the registries.[13] When servants' wages rose particularly rapidly in 1896 Richard Porter, Secretary of the Witwatersrand Boarding-House Keepers' Protection Association, was sent directly to London in an attempt to recruit labour – an attempt which naturally met with strenuous local opposition from service workers.[14] In addition, because of the fees involved, the registry offices were usually the final resort of the frustrated employer or work-seeker. Thus both parties continued to place a great deal of trust in 'market forces'.

To the extent that employers looked to within the country for a growing supply of white female labour, their trust in 'market forces' was largely misplaced. It is true that in the worst recessions, such as that of 1890–2, some working-class families, with considerable misgivings, placed their daughters in domestic service.[15] It was also true that there were cases of young Afrikaner women going into service in the city. Martharina Christina van Wyk, for example, a nineteen year old girl from the Orange Free State, bound herself to a two-year contract with Mr Bekker of Hillbrow because her parents 'were too poor to support her'.[16] In both cases, however, the numbers involved must have been small. Full immigrant working-class families were the exception rather than the rule, and in town and country alike poor Afrikaner women were notoriously averse to going into service. It was partly for this reason that it was sourly noted in a Johannesburg newspaper in 1899 that 'Dutch girls as a rule know more about Paardekraal and inspanning a team of oxen than about domesticity.'[17]

In other ways, however, 'market forces' did not completely disappoint employers – although it hardly satisfied them either. Many foreign women who had made their way to Johannesburg independently to make a living or seek a fortune were willing to work as domestic servants for brief periods. For the large part composed of tough individualists drawn from the lumpen-proletariat, these women were hardly suitable material for moulding into a docile servant class. They drifted in and out of domestic service between jobs as tea-room waitresses, barmaids or prostitutes.[18] With some justification then they were 'regarded with a certain amount of suspicion' or as being of essentially 'doubtful character'.[19]

With such volatile groups and uncertain sources of supply it can be appreciated why the demand for white female domestic labour in Johannesburg remained at a relatively high level throughout the 1890s. This, coupled with the fact that white women were considered to be unsuited to the rougher elements of housework in a sub-tropical climate also helps explain why it was that there was a steadily increasing demand for the labour of the largest group of servants of all on the Witwatersrand – African men.

The demand for black men as domestic servants in Johannesburg arrived at the same time as the first waggons of the 'Rand pioneers' trundled into the mining camp. Indeed, some of the small group of women involved had been far-sighted enough to foresee a 'servant problem' in their new environment and to take precautionary measures. Mrs Willie Rockey who arrived in 1886, for example, brought at least one domestic servant with her from the Cape Colony. For several years, however, women such as Mrs Rockey had to undertake a large proportion of the household chores personally.[20] When Archibald Colquhoun (later of Mashonaland) passed through Johannesburg in 1890 he noted:

> Service was almost unprocurable. Raw Kaffirs, who till a few months before had never seen the inside of a house, were pressed into service for which they had no natural bent, and the best one could hope for was an inferior type of Cape boy.[21]

This situation improved somewhat in the early 1890s, but demand again started to peak after 1893, reaching a high point in 1896. Even in the recession following the Jameson Raid, however, the general level of demand for black male domestic servants remained high – a trend that was no doubt aggravated by the employers' strategy of cutting back on white female domestics between 1897 and 1899.

The concomitant of this demand level was steadily rising wages. It would appear that between 1887 and 1892 the wage of an untrained 'houseboy' ranged between £3 and £4 with the monthly average being about £3 10s 0d. As their rudimentary skills developed, and as demand for their services increased after 1893, however, so 'houseboys' demanded higher wages. From 1892 to 1896 the range of wages widened to between £3 and £6 with a monthly average of about £4, a situation that remained relatively unchanged until the outbreak of the South African War in 1899.[22]

But, as in the case of white female domestic servants, 'houseboys' did not only receive cash wages – there were also other emoluments that had to be taken into consideration when attempting to assess their income. 'Here in Johannesburg', noted the irritated leader-writer of the *Standard and Diggers' News* in 1898, 'the swarthy savage condescends to be taught the minimum of service for £4 per month with food, quarters, and gifts of clothing . . .'[23] These steadily rising real wages incorporating the payments in kind were, in many cases, exaggerated out of all proportion in the minds of the employers. Nevertheless, there was an increase in wages which annoyed white householders, the more so since the increases continued into a period when their own cash incomes were falling, and when 'market forces' should have been reducing servants' wages. In an editorial in 1897, *The Star* surveyed 'Houseboy's Wages', and noted sadly that neither the advent of the railways, nor a series of rural disasters in the shape of droughts, locusts and cattle diseases had been able to bring about an immediate and marked reduction in the wages of black servants. The rate of pay for domestic servants, *The Star* concluded, remained at a 'ridiculously high figure'.[24] It was in this context, and in the wake of the Chamber of Mines' successful reduction of African mineworkers' wages in 1896, that employers and public bodies openly debated the virtues of combination in an attempt to reduce 'houseboy' wages.[25] For the first, but not for the last time during a period of recession, Witwatersrand employers of domestic labour toyed with the idea of a Housekeepers' Protection Association. Householders as a group, however, were at least as fragmented as 'houseboys', and the wages held firm.

Cash wages, of course, are never the sole determinants of labour supply, and this is especially true of the colonial situation. But, to the extent that it is possible to separate out this variable, it would appear that the rising wages for domestic servants in Johannesburg were capable of eliciting a steadily increasing flow of labour from the countryside. If this was true for the years before 1895, then it was even more true for the period immediately thereafter when structural changes in town and country manifested themselves in the Witwatersrand labour market.

Prior to 1895 both black miners and 'houseboys' on the Rand had enjoyed rising cash wages but, in 1896, the Chamber of Mines implemented a wage cut for African mineworkers. Almost immediately *The Star* noted that: 'Since the reduction of mine boys' wages there has been a much larger supply of kitchen boys.'[26] After this reduction and over the succeeding years as the collective impact of the rural disasters noted above made itself felt, the domestic service sector must must have become increasingly attractive to the growing numbers of black workers who made their way to the Transvaal. By 1899 a Johannesburg domestic servant could look to a monthly cash wage of 80 shillings, while the black miner, for a similar period of labour earned, on average, 49 shillings and ninepence.[27] When relative conditions of service, health hazards and payments in kind are added to this cash differential, it can readily be appreciated why the domestic service sector must have proved increasingly attractive to many African workers in the late 1890s.

Between 1896 and 1899 this inter-sectoral competition for black labour on the Rand did not seriously threaten the Chamber of Mines, and there were three basic reasons for this. First, the size of the domestic service sector remained relatively small whilst the majority of the white residents were without their families and a settled home life. By 1899 there were probably, at most, 7,500 black domestic servants at work in Johannesburg. Secondly, in the wake of the natural disasters in the countryside during the mid-1890s there was a significant overall increase in the flow of labour to the Rand – enough even to meet the Chamber of Mines' requirements at reduced wages. Between 1895 and 1899 the black labour force on the mines increased from 50,000 to over 96,000 workers. The third reason behind this rather untypical Randlord indifference to competition for labour emerges when the changing composition of the ranks of the 'houseboys' in the 1890s is examined. Who exactly Colquhoun's 'raw kaffirs' of 1890 were is unclear. What is clearer is that, between 1890 and 1895, the 'houseboys' seem to have been more or less equally drawn from Zulus, Zulu speakers from Natal (hereafter collectively but incorrectly termed 'Zulus' for the sake of convenience), Basutos and Shangaans.[28] The twinned impact of wage reductions and rinderpest in 1896–7, however, constituted something of a watershed. Thereafter, for a complex set of reasons, there appears to have been a set of re-adjustments and re-alignments in the labour market which manifested themselves in an increasing degree of ethnic job specialisation on the Witwatersrand.

While the general level of mine wages was reduced in 1896, wages could still cover a monthly range of between 30 and 70 shillings. Within this range, the best wages were paid to the semi-skilled 'drill-boys' who worked on the longest contracts. Before, but more especially after these reductions, Shangaans from the more proletarianised parts of southern Mozambique tended to monopolise these positions. A need and willingness to work for longer periods than most other black migrants, coupled with a previously acquired set of skills meant that these Shangaans came to be systematically favoured by mine managers towards the turn of the century.

Rinderpest for its part struck most powerfully at the comparatively wealthier cattle-keeping people of southern Africa. It was these latter people, especially those drawn from regions geographically adjacent to the Witwatersrand such as Zululand and Natal who were amongst the most anxious to earn cash and re-stock their herds after 1897 – as indeed they were after the turn of the century when a further set of cattle diseases such as lung-sickness and East Coast Fever attacked their herds.[29] It was these people without previously developed mining skills who were drawn to the position of 'houseboy'. Even food and quarters of bad quality, when combined with relatively high cash wages, offered migrants the prospect of being able to save. Moreover, and at least as important, was the fact that the position of the 'houseboy' was governed by a monthly engagement under the Masters and Servants' legislation as opposed to the longer fixed-term contracts of the mining industry. This meant – to the considerable annoyance of employers over the ensuing decade – that the 'houseboy' could move fairly freely, and that labour turnover consequently remained at a relatively high level.[30] It also meant that this pool of migrant labourers was not particularly attractive to mine managers at that time, and thus likely to receive proportionately lower wages as mineworkers. For a combination of these reasons, the 'Zulus' made the position of 'houseboy' on the Witwatersrand their very own to an increasing extent after 1897. By the outbreak of the war the words 'houseboy' and 'Zulu' had become almost synonymous on the Rand labour market.

It was under this very special set of circumstances that a gracious mining industry was willing to tolerate the growing inter-sectoral competition for labour and allow white Johannesburg its quota of 'houseboys' – a situation in marked contrast to the post-South African War period.

Reconstruction and the period thereafter, 1902–1914

With the outbreak of war in 1899 the thousands of domestic servants in Johannesburg, along with their employers and other inhabitants of the city, joined the throng wishing to leave the Transvaal. The exit was not universally simple or painless. Several hundred 'Zulu' 'kitchen boys' were left stranded without money when their employers summarily decamped without paying them their wages. A minority of these were forced to stay on in the city, but the majority managed to join the march back to Natal and Zululand under the guidance of J. S. Marwick.[31] During the remaining years of the war many of these men worked for the Imperial army at rates that were significantly higher than any previously ruling in southern Africa. The housekeepers, cooks and housemaids for the most part boarded the trains for the Cape – not always an uneventful trip since drunken refugees tended to force their attentions on coloured servant women making the journey south.[32] Many of the employers spent the duration of the war in Cape Town, or if more opulent, in England.

Employers and servants alike returned to a Witwatersrand that was economically, politically, and socially transformed between 1902 and 1914. At the centre of these transforming processes lay a rapidly developing mining industry, and the successive administrations of the British, Transvaal, and Union governments. In Johannesburg, however, these changes manifested themselves in ways other than simply the economic or political. As it had regularly done before 1899, the city once again more than doubled in size. From a population of about 109,000 of all races in 1902, the city grew to a point where by 1914 it had over 250,000 inhabitants of all races. But this time the change in Johannesburg – and indeed in other Reef towns – was more than demographic: it involved a fundamental change in the social composition of the city.[33]

In 1897, only 12 per cent of the white employees of the Witwatersrand gold mines were married and had their families resident with them in the Transvaal; by 1902 this figure had risen to 20 per cent, and by 1912 it was up to 42 per cent.[34] In the post-war period members of the working class for the first time, like the white middle and upper classes before them, could enjoy the privilege of family life in significant numbers. Put another way, this meant that between 1902 and 1914 there was a decline in the number of miners sharing accommodation or living in boarding-houses, and a marked increase in the number of working-class homes. This structural change affected the domestic service sector in at least two important ways.

First, the decline in collective working-class accommodation in one form or another brought about a reduction in the need for white specialist servants – a feature that was especially noticeable after 1906 when the boarding-house business had contracted somewhat, and wives had done much to replace cooks and housekeepers. This trend was compounded when the service needs of middle and upper-class families, whose family structure had remained fairly constant, grew relatively slowly – demand being only in proportion to their limited size in the society as a whole. Secondly, the growth in the number of white working-class homes led to a marked increase in the overall demand for black domestic servants. It is these large-scale trends that form the backdrop against which we should seek a more detailed understanding of demand, supply and wages of servants between 1902 and 1914.

Measures taken during the South African War did much to shape the domestic service sector of the Witwatersrand labour market in the immediate post-war period and the years leading up to the depression of 1906–8. Some members of the middle and upper classes returning to their northern suburbs homes from Cape Town, or England, took the precaution of taking along contract-bound white servants with them.[35] Others, however, placed their trust in the market and were bitterly disappointed. In April 1902, the demand for white female domestic labour in Johannesburg was described as being 'immense', and while the situation improved somewhat in the following years, demand easily kept abreast of supply until at least the end of 1905.[36] Wages for European servants reflected this demand by retaining their late-1890s level, and then rising slightly. By the end of 1905, a housemaid earned cash wages of between £4 and £5 per month, while a cook or 'cook-general' earned between £6 and £8 per month.[37]

The demand for black domestic servants after the war was no less pronounced. In this case the problem of a faltering supply was made worse by the continuing demands of the army, and the military authorities' insistence on issuing a permit before a servant could be recruited from a neighbouring colony. Initially this procedure did much to impede the inflow of 'Zulus' who by now constituted the most natural reservoir of 'houseboys'. But the problem also went beyond this since even those Africans who managed to get into the city apparently held aloof from domestic service in the first months after the war.[38] This was hardly surprising since the £2 10s 0d to £3 10s 0d cash wages that employers were offering was below the pre-war level, and substantially below the erstwhile domestic servants' wartime earnings. But such was the demand for their services that wages were gradually forced back to the level of the late 1890s. By the onset of the depression in 1906, Johannesburg's 25,000 to 30,000 'houseboys' were once again earning cash wages of between £4 and £5 per month – a rate 30 per cent to 50 per cent higher than anywhere else in South Africa.[39]

White householders, however, were not the only ones to experience a serious shortage of labour after the war, nor were they the most important employers in the Transvaal. The Chamber of Mines, too, found itself faced with a 'shortage' of labour after the mines were re-opened in 1901, and for reasons that were not entirely unfamiliar. In an effort to reduce costs the mine owners cut the wages of black workers, and then discovered to their chagrin that a continuous supply of African labour was not forthcoming. But, unlike the weak and less organised householders, the Randlords were able to make their economic initiative hold. In 1904, with the aid and support of the government, they were able to secure vital supplies of indentured labour from China. This partial solution to their immediate problem, however, did not prevent the mine owners from continually casting covetous glances at other sectors of the Rand labour market that were better served by African labour. Neither did it prevent them from scouring the countryside for all available workers. Nor did it stop them from continuing to complain loudly about the 'shortage' of black labour.

All of these vociferous demands for cheap black labour were ultimately directed at the new British administration which was already beset with the problem of how best to politically stabilise and anglicise the Transvaal. The Milner administration undertook piecemeal solutions as best it could. In May 1902 a scheme was devised by which, for several months, black female domestic servants were provided to the citizens of Johannesburg from the military refugee camps.[40] Milner, with all the fervour of imperialism, however, was not really interested in piecemeal problem solving. What was required was a more imaginative and radical solution, and in this he was assisted by an Englishman, Sir John Ardagh.

In June 1902 Ardagh wrote to the Colonial Office pointing out how in southern Africa the number of males had always outnumbered the white females, and that this imbalance in the sex ratio was likely to be exacerbated by the number of soldiers settling in the Transvaal after the war. What was required to offset this, and at the same time help ease the domestic British 'problem' of a 'surplus' of women, was a system of female emigration to the colonies.[41] Milner seized on this idea for within it he saw the seeds of a solution to some of the most pressing problems he was confronted with. For if female domestic servants and other wage-earning women from Britain could be encouraged to emigrate to South Africa, then they would assist in achieving several objectives. First, they could help ease the demand for domestic labour on the Rand. Secondly, if white female domestic servants went in sufficient numbers they could replace the black male 'houseboys' who would then be available as workers for the gold mines. Thirdly, if these women married and settled down they would contribute to the development of a stable and loyal British working class in the Transvaal.

What made these ideas even more appealing was the fact that the infrastructure for such a scheme had already been laid by the British Women's Emigration Association (B.W.E.A.). Flushed with the success of the imperial war, and partly financed by Rhodes and Rothschild, the B.W.E.A. had, in April 1902, set up a South African Expansion Committee (S.A.E.C.) in London which, in turn, was assisted by a branch in Johannesburg. The London Committee, under the patronage of Milner and Chamberlain, numbered amongst others as its members Lady Knightley of Fawsley, Mrs C. S. Goldmann and Mrs Lionel Phillips. The Johannesburg branch operated under the aegis of an 'advisory council' which included amongst its members Sir Percy FitzPatrick (President), F. H. P. Creswell (Sec.), R. W. Schumacher, J. Wybergh, W. Windham, Mrs Drummond Chaplin, Mrs Sidney Jennings and Mrs Harold Strange. Its day-to-day operations, however, were run by an executive committee composed of Mesdames Jennings, FitzPatrick, Marx, Matthews and Emrys Evans.[42] Neither of these committees could be accused of being unmindful of the interests of mining capital.

What Milner first did to put his scheme into operation was to create a 'Women's Immigration Department' in the Transvaal, and then to incorporate these various committees into his administration by granting them official recognition and financial assistance. In mid-1903, the London-based S.A.E.C. became independent of its parent body (the B.W.E.A.) under a new name – the South African Colonisation Society. As an advisory committee to what was by now the 'Transvaal Immigration Department', the Colonisation Society, amongst other things, vetted the applications received from potential immigrants, and then selected and forwarded suitable domestic servants to the new colony. The Johannesburg branch of the Colonisation Society, also in its capacity as an officially recognised advisory committee, received and vetted applications from would-be employers, and then in turn arranged for the reception of the immigrant domestic servants.[43]

Middle and upper-class Johannesburg at first embraced Milner's scheme with alacrity. The prospect of patriotism and parlour-maids at palatable prices smacked of a middle-class millennium. Along with lady helps, laundry-maids and even a few dairy-maids, Irish housemaids were requisitioned since they were considered to be 'generally stronger and less liable to illness than Scotch or English girls'.[44] Amongst members of the middle class in particular, however, the greatest demand of all was for that rare servant who would cook and undertake general household duties as well, the so-called 'cook-general'. At rates ranging between £48 and £72 per year (cash wages), plus the cost of a steamship passage for the servant (£12–£15), hundreds of applications were received from would-be employers. This demand is shown in Table 1 below.[45]

Table 1. Demand and supply of European female domestic servants during the reconstruction era

Period	No. of applications from employers	No. of servants supplied
1/7/02 to 30/6/03	1,200	502
1/7/03 to 30/6/04	866	367
1/7/04 to 30/6/05	565	173
Total	2,631	1,042

It is estimated that in the decade between 1902 and 1912 the S.A.C.S. introduced a total of about 1,500 white female domestic servants to the Witwatersrand. What is also clearly evident from these figures, however, is the fact that there was a marked decline in the Society's activities after 1905. During the depression of 1906–8 the demand for white servants fell even more rapidly than it did before that, and when Premier Botha's *Het Volk* assumed office in 1907, it cut the subsidy to the Colonisation Society, since, for obvious reasons the new nationalist government saw no reason to assist English immigration to the Transvaal. Despite further generous financial assistance from various Rand mining companies after Union, the Colonisation Society was virtually moribund by 1912.[46]

There were, however, also more deep-seated social and economic reasons behind the failure of the Milner scheme – and reasons that lay both in Britain and on the Witwatersrand. During the crucial first three years of the scheme the Colonisation Society failed to supply both the quantity and quality of servant demanded in Johannesburg. The Colonisation Society attempted to recruit servants in Britain in precisely the decade during which women, in large numbers, were deserting the long hours, low wages and lonely labour of domestic service for work in industry.[47] Moreover, to a greater or lesser degree British servants tended to be specialists, and they thus viewed the more 'general' type of work being offered them in the Transvaal with suspicion, even though it held out the prospect of employment at considerably higher wages. The problem was well put in the *Annual Report* of the Colonisation Society in 1903:

> The great difficulty in the selection of girls of the servant class is chiefly the fact that the servant most in demand in the Transvaal is not known in England. What is required is a cook-general, but the English general servant is not, as a rule, a sufficiently good cook to fulfil the duties required, and those who are good enough cooks will not turn their hands to all the other work expected of them.[48]

It was largely in vain that the Society continually pointed out that 'All servants in the colonies are expected to be able to lend a hand to do anything that is wanted.'[49]

On the Witwatersrand a not entirely dissimilar set of factors also went some way to undermining the short and long-term viability of the scheme. The basic constraints imposed by labour in domestic service did not differ fundamentally in Johannesburg and London. Thus, the supply of immigrant servants was constantly diminished as women left paid household labour to seek a more independent and satisfying life elsewhere. While the Rand could not boast a well-developed sector of secondary industry, there was a keen demand for the cheap labour of women as waitresses in tea-rooms, assistants in shops or as clerical workers in offices or, to a lesser extent, in small factories.[50] Before 1906 several cooks were quick to spot that they could put their specialised skills to more profitable commercial use, and they promptly left private service to open their own boarding-houses.[51] But, in a society where men outnumbered women, marriage proved to be the greatest social and economic escape hatch of all from domestic service. Whilst such marriages might have contributed to Milner's policy of anglicisation, they certainly did not appeal to the servant-seeking middle class who came to refer to the Colonisation Society in derisive terms as a 'matrimonial agency'.[52]

The single greatest problem of all, however, made itself felt almost as soon as the immigrant servants set foot in the colony. It took white domestics no time at all to realise that in South Africa hard physical labour at low wages was first and foremost the province of the black man. 'The consequence', *The Star* noted in retrospect, 'was that householders who engaged white domestic servants invariably had a male native to do what women term the rough work of a house.' This was all 'very well for people who could afford a staff of servants' but not for those of more modest means. In practice it meant that the white woman in service was 'not a domestic' but 'more of an administration official'.[53] The middle class simply could not afford the additional expense of a servant who was only willing to 'administer'.

This colonial reality destroyed the scheme insofar as it was designed to help reduce the overall demand for servants. Far from easing the situation, it in many cases actually exacerbated the problem since immigrant white domestics who went into the boarding-house business, or who set up their own homes, became employers of black labour in their own right. A young Scottish servant might still write home in mid-1903 that 'Lord Milner is trying to get the black boys back to the mines and out of service', but the Imperial overlord himself and the mine owners must have known already that the scheme was failing.[54] As active and enthusiastic partners in the immigration scheme they watched in dismay as black men continued to swell the domestic service sector while the mines experienced a 'labour crisis'. By 1904 – the very year in which the Imperial overlord and the Randlords were forced to turn to China for labour – there were 20,000 'kitchen boys' in Johannesburg alone, while the Witwatersrand mine compounds between them could only muster 68,000 black workers. This fact, when allied to the mounting inadequacy of the immigration scheme must have proved exceedingly irksome to Milner and the mine owners, but they were not yet willing to acknowledge defeat.

The idea that an organised effort should be made to reduce the wages of Africans in domestic service was not a new one. Indeed, it had been around in one form or another on the Rand for the better part of a decade. Whenever such ideas had been mooted in the past, however, they had been advocated by relatively unorganised middle-class elements who sought to profit directly from a reduction in their servants' wages. Furthermore these middle-class sponsored schemes had been articulated at times when black labour supplies in the mining industry were increasing, and they had thus received no real support from the state, the Randlords or their allies. This lukewarm reception by other parties was not surprising since such middle-class schemes did not have as a primary objective an increase in the supply of mine labour, although a drastic reduction in wages may, indirectly, have produced such a result. All of this, however, was very different from the efforts made to enforce a wage reduction during the reconstruction era.

In the second half of 1904 incomes in several sectors of the Witwatersrand economy fell markedly as the post-war recession deepened. The resultant shortage of cash made itself felt in white working-class homes where there had been wage reductions, whilst the reduced turnover in commerce caused considerable concern amongst middle-class traders. At such times white employers across a wide class spectrum must have been more than ordinarily resentful of paying wages – let alone wages that were still rising – to African domestic servants.[55] In addition, the 'shortage' of black mine labour was as acute as ever. This, then, was a singularly propitious moment for employers to cooperate in an effort to reduce 'kitchen boy' wages. When the Milner administration at the behest of its Native Affairs Department cut the wages of black government employees late in the year the mining capitalists seized their opportunity. On 23 November 1904, E. P. Rathbone, long-time ideologue for the Chamber of Mines and editor of the journal *South African Mines, Commerce and Industry* wrote to *The Star* with the encouragement of 'many industrial and representative parties' suggesting that it was 'absolutely monstrous that, through want of a little firm combination, the ridiculous wages paid to coloured domestic servants should not be reduced'.[56]

Over the next fourteen days Rathbone, with the generous assistance and strong editorial support of *The Star*, proceeded to expand on what his notion of 'a little firm combination' was. He, Major H. M. Downes, F. Drake, G. Kent and others proposed to float a registered limited liability company to be called the Employers' Domestic Native Labour Association (E.D.N.L.A.). Like the mine owners' recruiting organisation, the Witwatersrand Native Labour Association on which it was modelled, E.D.N.L.A. would eventually constitute a monopsony, all employers agreeing to employ 'houseboys' only at the newly reduced wage rate which was to be decided upon. E.D.N.L.A. was to have a capital of £600 made up of £1 shares of which only ten shillings would be paid on subscription. The promoters calculated that a minimum of 1,000 householders would have to join E.D.N.L.A. in order to make the scheme viable. In addition to fixing the wages of African domestic servants, E.D.N.L.A. would also undertake to keep a register of information on the efficiency, honesty and sobriety of servants thus enabling it to 'black-list' any undesirable 'houseboys'.[57]

But Christmas, 'kitchen boys' and companies apparently did not mix. Despite vigorous prodding by *The Star* and Rathbone the majority of white householders seemed to remain apathetic. Whether it was simply the festive season generally, or the fact that money was even tighter than usual at Christmas in 1904 is unclear, but few people yeemed willing to subscribe to E.D.N.L.A. shares. Rathbone soon discovered, as he put it, that 'what is everybody's business is usually nobody's business'. In late December he made one last attempt to salvage the scheme by appealing to the women's organisations in the suburbs to become involved, but again to no avail. The last stand of all in this great battle against the 'kitchen boys' and their wages was left to Rathbone's colleague – the redoubtable Major Downes. In late January 1905 the Major unsuccessfully attempted to revive the scheme as a 'Mutual Benefit Society' which required a mere half-a-crown as a subscription fee.[58]

White Johannesburg need not have despaired, however, for what the Major could not give them in a recession, the 'market' in a depression would. Just as 1896–7 had marked a watershed in the domestic service sector of the local economy in the 1890s, so the depression of 1906–8 constituted a landmark in the first decade of the twentieth century. In both cases structural changes in the labour market were inaugurated by a series of complex economic and political changes that took place in the town as well as the countryside, and in both cases they heralded the advent of a new period in which increasing supplies of labour produced a steady decline in the wages of domestic workers.

The scalpel of economic depression made its first cuts in the most predictable place – where labour was highest paid and least 'productive'. White female domestics, and especially the cooks-general, found that their services were amongst the first to be dispensed with by the middle classes. Although more skilled and competent than many black servants, they did less of the essential 'rough work' around the house, and were thus more vulnerable to dismissal. If these largely English-speaking women were the first fired, then they were also amongst the last to be re-hired in what became a relatively cluttered labour market, and this process in turn had a depressing effect on wages. From cash wages of between £6 and £8 per month in 1905, wages for cooks-general fell to between £3 10s 0d and £5 in 1907. A further sign of the times was the fact that the South African Colonisation Society – which had previously insisted on a minimum cash wage of £4 per month for an immigrant servant – reduced the figure to £3 per month in 1907.[59]

If, however, the depression forced certain middle-class elements to forego the luxury of a semi-skilled 'cook-general', it did not make them abandon the idea of having a white servant. Showing a willingness to cut according to the new cloth, inhabitants of the predominantly English-speaking northern suburbs now cast around for white labour that was cheaper still. In this search their eyes came to rest, not for the first time, on the pools of urban poverty and largely Afrikaner distress in Fordsburg, Vrededorp and Newlands. Consciously adhering to the constructs of the dominant British ideology of the time, at least one middle-class woman of standing advocated that the wives and daughters of the less fortunate should be sent to the workhouse to qualify as white servants, and that charity should be avoided since it only tended to further degrade the poor.[60] The Star, always aspiring to subtlety, was content to chant a variation on a theme from Milner. Its leader writer suggested that Emily Hobhouse could best use her considerable influence amongst Afrikaners if she would persuade them to allow their daughters to enter domestic service and, by doing so, 'compel the Kaffir "boy" to seek employment for which he is naturally endowed'.[61] To their bewilderment and considerable annoyance, however, the middle and ruling-classes uncovered that basic social fact that each of its generations has to rediscover for itself – namely, that during the severest of depressions and distress the poor prefer the communality of collective suffering to individual life-saving labour amongst alien classes. Afrikaner women, always reluctant to enter domestic service, were now more unwilling than ever to abandon their children, families and homes to work for their conquerors.[62]

But if the depression could not deliver urban Afrikaner women into service, then it did at least partly compensate the middle classes by producing an alternative supply of female labour from rural areas. Between 1906 and 1908 droughts, cattle diseases, the depression and an African rebellion in Natal and Zululand all combined to produce a new wave of proletarianisation that surged through the countryside and deposited thousands of African females in the cities. This influx of black women into Johannesburg was perceived by its white citizens partly in horror, and partly in hope. On the one hand many of these women – none of whom were subject to the pass laws – found their way to the notorious 'mine locations' in the city where they lived by prostitution, hawking, or beer brewing. On the other, however, there was the redeeming feature that a 'good number' – albeit without passes – entered into domestic service. The first signs of this new development in the labour market came as early as March 1906, when Martin's Agency indicated that it was ready to receive applications for a second 'batch' of 'Zulu Servant Girls' who were willing to serve under a twelve-month contract.[63]

The white middle class considered this arrival of a significant number of African women in the city to be hopeful for other reasons as well. The depression had brought with it one of the recurrent waves of 'black peril' scares to Johannesburg. This state of near collective hysteria invariably manifested itself in a flood of accusations by white women – some with reason but for the most part without justification – that black men had, or had attempted to, sexually assault them. Leading middle-class elements now reasoned, as they did again in the subsequent scare of 1912–3, that if they could train this new pool of African female labour for service, then they could replace the 'houseboy' and so dispel the potential danger that lurked behind every kitchen cupboard. This outlook was further rationalised by the addition of familiar ideological notions which suggested that women were in any case 'naturally' more suited to this type of labour than men.[64]

The initiative in these matters was taken by the Church of England Mission. By February 1908, its Native Girls' Industrial School Committee had acquired a small cottage in Doornfontein where black women were instructed 'in all branches of housework, cooking and laundry work'. This Sherwell street school started with only two pupils but within ten months there were so many applications for admission that the Committee had to make more ambitious arrangements. With the aid of Church funds, donations and money collected from Africans in the countryside and local mine compounds, a new property was acquired in Rosettenville in 1909, where the expanded St Agnes Native Girls' Industrial School could accommodate forty pupils. Showing every sign of becoming a successful and worthwhile venture, the new institution now gained indirect state and mining house approval when it received the enthusiastic support of, amongst others, Lady Selborne, Mrs R. W. Schumacher and Mrs Albu.[65]

The St Agnes School started off promisingly enough with 37 pupils ranging in age from six to nineteen years being under the guidance of Deaconess Julia. It would appear that the majority of these girls were drawn from the mine locations since Deaconess Julia assured her public audiences that it was 'largely from this source that the girl domestic of the future would be drawn'. But despite the fact that the state provided bursaries for some of its pupils, the School did not prosper as was hoped. The three-year course must have sapped the financial resources of black parents, and most pupils left to seek work well before the course was completed. By late 1911 the School had produced a mere 20 graduates, and its intake had declined to 25 pupils.[66]

From this it is clear that the depression and its immediate aftermath hardly produced an adequate supply of trained black housemaids. Neither did it bring about a radical change in the composition of the labour market in this respect – and that despite the fact that a 'good number' of untrained African women entered into domestic service. For although poverty might have brought thousands of black women into the city, only a minority of them ended up working in white households. The social and economic reasons for this lay with both prospective employees and employers.

African fathers, mothers and husbands had the most rooted objection to their female kin entering into domestic service during the first decade of the twentieth century. They believed, with good reason, that many women entering service would be seduced by white men and ultimately become immoral.[67] The black women themselves appear to have favoured making an independent legal or illegal living in the locations rather than sacrifice their working lives to the white masters and mistresses of the suburbs.[68]

The white mistresses for their part had good reasons for not wanting to employ black women as domestic servants. They believed African women to be 'ignorant', and more 'difficult to manage' than the black men to whom they were accustomed. One of their real fears, however, remained largely unstated or, at best, was stated in highly ideological form. White women were deeply disturbed by the possibility that black housemaids would develop sexual liaisons with their husbands. Unable or unwilling to confront their husbands directly, they stated instead that black females were grossly 'immoral'. Their fears were also shared by others. In 1908 the leader writer of *The Star* suggested that one cogent reason against the appointment of 'Kaffir Housemaids' was the fact that it increased the risk of a 'bastard population'.[69] Important as these reservations undoubtedly were, they were augmented by an equally persuasive economic argument – the fact that African women were simply no cheaper to employ than black men. Despite the depression, black women sought virtually the same wages from employers as other groups of servants on the Rand. Thus, while they introduced a new and growing element into the labour market they did not initially re-structure it.[70] Some of the more significant re-structuring that did take place during the depression came from other quarters. More especially it came from the state, and the employment of juvenile labour in domestic service.

Young African boys – 'piccanins' – had been employed as domestic servants in small Transvaal towns such as Middelburg since at least the turn of the century. Between 1902 and 1908, however, these Pedi tribesmen suffered a particularly severe set of rural disasters. In the years that their cattle were not struck by East Coast Fever, their crops were devastated by droughts and locusts.[71] These agricultural reverses significantly increased the supply of labour from this part of the country, and many more black boys made their way to the towns and cities in order to make a living. On the Rand, state-licensed labour agents were quick to spot this new flow of labour, and capitalise on it. Particularly from the advent of the depression, in 1906, firms such as B. G. Shepperson, P. D. de Villiers and Ross's systematically recruited 'piccanins' of between ten and fifteen years of age in the Pietersburg district of the northern Transvaal. These firms then supplied householders who, in exchange for a capitation fee of £2 and a train fare, acquired the services of a 'piccanin' who was bound by contract to them by cash wages of between ten and twenty shillings per month 'according to size'.[72]

During the earliest months of the depression the government was content to allow this 'natural' functioning of the labour market to operate at its own pace. But when the Liberal government in Britain prevented the further recruitment of Chinese indentured labour for the Rand mining industry in November 1906, there was a new and urgent reason to facilitate this influx of juvenile labour from the northern Transvaal. Just as in the immediate post-war period it was believed that white female immigrant labour would release the 'Zulus' for work underground, it was now hoped that the influx of cheaper still 'piccanin' labour would help displace the 'houseboys' into the mine compounds. To achieve this objective, the government appointed H. M. Taberer as Director of the Government Native Labour Bureau in 1907.[73]

In mid-January 1908 Taberer announced to the Witwatersrand public that the labour bureau was willing to undertake some of the role of a registry office by supplying 'piccanins' for domestic service. Like the labour agents, the state obtained the bulk of these African boys from the Pietersburg district, and then forwarded them to a compound in Germiston where employers made their 'selection' – probably also 'according to size'. Unlike the independent agents, however, the bureau attempted to run its business with a slightly more responsible attitude. As far as was possible it attempted to recruit only those youths who were over fourteen years of age – so that they could come under the control of the pass laws. This mixed blessing at least afforded some of the older lads a measure of legal protection that was denied to the ten- to fourteen-year-olds.[74]

The state scheme operated successfully enough for three weeks, and during this period it supplied householders with at least 150 'piccanins'. By mid-February, however, the scheme started to run into difficulties. The labour agents, and Shepperson in particular, complained that the state was destroying their delicate enterprises. In addition to this, the government started having reservations of its own. It found that the state had to charge a higher capitation fee than the agents to keep Taberer's scheme viable, and that it therefore tended to experience greater difficulty in placing its 'piccanins' than the independent agents. For both of these reasons Government Native Labour Bureau recruitment was stopped on 13 February 1908. Thereafter the administration was again content to resort to the cheaper workings of the 'market place'. The government instructed its native commissioners to 'encourage' youths to enlist for domestic service, while it once more allowed the independent state-licensed agents the undisputed right to supply the Witwatersrand market.[75] Although Taberer's formal scheme had failed, the latter arrangement continued to operate with government approval long after the depression.[76]

The influx of Pedi 'piccanins', the availability of a growing number of African women, the continuing arrival of black men from the countryside, the presence of a pool of unemployed European cooks-general, and the curtailment of demand for servants during a depression all left their mark on the service sector of the Rand labour market. From late 1907 through to 1909 there were indications of growing distress amongst the ranks of the 'houseboys' as suburban residents complained about an increase in petty theft by domestic servants. White householders constantly grumbled about the fact that their servant usually had some 'brother or sister' living in the back yard at 'their expense'. These and other tell-tale signs also showed that the market was becoming over-supplied. Gangs of African boys and older men roamed the streets in search of work. Labour agents who found that they could not dispose of their 'piccanins' quickly enough were forced into the unusual practice of having to advertise. Perhaps most significant of all, however, was the fact that in the winter of 1909, for the first time, there was no marked seasonal fluctuation in the labour supply to the domestic service sector.[77]

Employers took the opportunity presented by a swollen labour supply to make a series of complex substitutions which varied with their fears, prejudices and class position. Invariably, however, the consequence of such a labour substitution was cheaper service for the householder. White women were replaced by black men or coloured women, while both of these could in turn be replaced by black women. All adult servants in their turn were liable to replacement by the cheapest labour of all – that of the 'piccanins'. Under these circumstances the wages of the single largest group of servants, the 'houseboys', could only move in one direction – down. What Milner, Rathbone and the Botha government between them could not achieve over eight years, the depression and a progressively underdeveloped countryside delivered in 24 months. Cash wages for 'houseboys' fell from a monthly average of 90 shillings in 1905 to 60 shillings in 1907, and then 50 shillings in 1908 – an overall reduction in their cash income of 46 per cent.[78]

As always, the realities of a depression lingered and helped to shape the post-depression era, 1909–14. Some of this continuing influence can be detected in the demand for white female domestic servants. After 1909, many of the middle classes again aspired to the services of a white servant but after their labour substitution experiences of the depression they were unwilling to revert to the pre-1906 wage rates. Their reduced offers were hardly capable of eliciting the much-prized cooks-general and, more often than not, such employers found that their wages tended to attract 'generals' rather than 'cooks'. By the time the recession of 1913–14 set in, these white female domestic servants were earning cash wages of between £2 10s 0d and £5 per month. At these wages it was hardly surprising to find that such women were in short supply.[79]

But if many in the middle class got the 'generals', then the remaining upper echelons of this and the ruling class got the 'cooks'. In the homes of the rich there was a strong and continuing demand for the genuine cook-general or the more specialist skills of a cook. In this case demand kept abreast of supply, and wages firmed in the post-depression period. From their all-time low of between £3 10s 0d and £5 during the depression of 1906–8, cash wages for cooks or cooks-general rallied to between £5 15s 0d and £7 per month in 1913.[80]

WAGE RATES OF DOMESTIC SERVANTS ON THE WITWATERSRAND 1890-1914

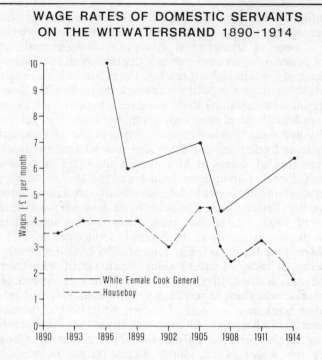

Just as many of the more privileged members of society wanted their white servants back after 1908, so too the lower-middle and working-class whites sought to recover their 'Zulu' servants in the post-depression period. From the summer of 1909 onwards the demand for 'houseboys' continued to firm through 1910 to 1912. This call for the black man's labour was most pronounced during 1911 and early 1912, and the resulting competition reflected itself in two public debates that arose during this period.

First, the 'kitchen boys'' oldest enemies – the state and the mining industry – reared their heads. From 1907 to 1910 the mining industry had managed to increase its black labour complement by approximately 20,000 workers each year. Between 1910 and 1911, however, it had only acquired an additional 6,000 workers – a mere thirty per cent of the annual increase that it had sustained ever since the recruiting of Chinese labour had been stopped. Under these circumstances the Randlords and their allies invariably became nervous, and when they became nervous they had a habit of peering through the kitchen windows of Witwatersrand homes.

In October 1911 H. C. Hull, Treasurer in the new Union government, raised the issue in public when he questioned the large-scale unproductive use of black labour in domestic employment at a political gathering. Hull estimated that in the Witwatersrand–Pretoria area alone there were close on 150,000 'houseboys', and suggested that their employers should compensate the state for keeping this labour tied up at a time when industry needed all available African workers. He therefore proposed that householders should pay a labour tax of £3 per month for the privilege of keeping an adult male in domestic service. Although Hull's comments were made at a meeting in a rural area – and thus stated for the benefit of farm as much as mine owners – his proposals gave Rand householders a nasty shock and produced some heated responses. In the end, however, nothing came of these proposals.[81]

The second debate, which centred around domestic labour and technology, did not frighten Johannesburg citizens nearly as much as did the Union Treasurer. From mid-1911 onwards, retailers, the Johannesburg City Council and the press drew increasing attention to the possibilities offered by modern electric household appliances. The *Rand Daily Mail* spelt out part of its vision of the future in an editorial in May 1912:

> In New York the difficulty of securing domestic help has led to a wonderful extension of all labour-saving appliances, so that the house-wife can without any great hardship, do the work of the house, or flat, herself. Electric heaters and cookers, special methods for removing refuse, the provision of hot and cold water in every bedroom, and other inventions, lighten the usual household task so considerably that the absence of a servant is hardly felt. We feel convinced that much may be done along these lines to render the help of the male Kaffir unnecessary.[82]

But despite the great hope placed in the cooker-oven in particular, the Witwatersrand could not be recast in the mould of American capital so easily. In a society where domestic labour was cheap, household appliances were considered expensive, and thus South Africa continued to assume its own distinctive capitalist profile.[83]

Household appliances and the proposed Hull Tax thus left the 'houseboys' unscathed while the economy continued to gain strength between 1909 and 1912. From 1912 to 1914, however, the 'houseboys' once again found themselves under attack. In 1912 the Rand experienced its worst ever 'black peril' scare, and this was followed by a recession that continued until the outbreak of war. Yet another disastrous drought, this time in 1911, drove thousands more African women and children to the cities in search of a living.[84] On this occasion, however, black women came in such numbers that most of them appear to have been willing to accept lower rates for domestic employment than their male counterparts. Thus, for a combination of the old reasons of part-prejudice and part-economy, the 'houseboys' were again liable to substitution by cheaper labour and this showed itself in the changing cash wage rates. From the 50 shillings per month that they were earning at the end of the depression in 1908, 'houseboys'' wages rose to between 60 and 70 shillings by 1911–2. In the recession that followed, however, earnings fell back to between 40 and 60 shillings per month. When the Chamber of Mines undertook a survey of white working-class households in 1913, it found that black domestic servants were paid an average monthly cash wage of 37 shillings and sixpence.[85]

In this survey of the domestic service sector of the Rand labour market between 1890 and 1914, several noteworthy features emerge. First, it is striking to what extent the sector reflected the changing class composition and structure of a city in a maturing capitalist system. This can be seen particularly clearly in the changing demand for white and black servants. The demand for white servants was at its highest when the bulk of the population, the working class, was unable or unwilling to reproduce itself at the point of production – i.e. while 'single' migratory males lived in boarding-houses. Once the working-class family constituted itself in its classic nuclear form with wives and daughters after the South African War, there was an overall decline in the demand for white servants, although this trend was offset by the continuing aspiration of the middle classes to a European domestic servant. In a colonial society, however, even the white working class demanded servants and it is this factor that was largely responsible for the overall growth of the sector and the predominance of black servants.

In South Africa then, the white proletariat built the price of a black servant into the cost of reproducing itself, and this brings us to the second noteworthy feature– the marked conflict between the capitalists and the white proletarian's black servant during the mining industry's period of initial development. Mining capitalists had two good fundamental reasons for being resentful of black domestic servants between 1890 and 1914.

(a) As long as the white working class insisted on the employment of a black domestic servant as a condition of its reproducing itself, so long would the necessary means of subsistence of the most skilled part of the working class be 'artificially' high. It was for precisely this reason that the Chamber of Mines and its allies invariably drew attention to the wages of black domestic servants whenever the high 'cost of living' on the Witwatersrand was discussed.[86] Crudely put, the mine owners reasoned that if they could reduce the wages paid to black servants, they would ultimately be able to reduce the wage bill for the white working class, increase profits and thus benefit capital.

(b) The extremely competitive wages paid to black domestic servants, especially in the early years, increased the price of African labour and threatened labour supplies to the primary industry in the state. Mine owners resented this competition for unskilled adult male labour from a sector that was ultimately funded by themselves! This contradiction in capitalist development hampered profits, and the mine owners and the state consequently lost no opportunity to render the sector more unattractive, or to replace black men with the cheaper labour of women or children.

The third feature that emerges clearly from this survey is the long-term decline in the wages of black domestic servants. Since 'houseboy' wages were ultimately linked to the earnings of the white working class, they tended to reflect the changing wages of white miners. This was particularly clear during periods of recession or depression, when the wages of white workers and domestic servants fell sympathetically. Growing proletarianisation in the countryside, coupled with increasing vulnerability to labour substitution by members of the opposite sex or other age groups meant, however, that 'houseboy' wages never recovered as much in periods of prosperity as they had lost in periods of recession. The fact that growing numbers of 'houseboys' were willing to work for declining cash wages points to both the conditions of service in household labour during this period, and black South Africans' greater dislike of mine labour at wages that were also declining.

Roles, duties and conditions of service for domestic servants

A formidable number of variables in almost infinite permutations and combinations makes it rather difficult to generalise about this aspect of domestic service on the Witwatersrand between 1890 and 1914. The class of employer, the size and location of his or her house, the number of servants the family was willing to employ, the presence or absence of children and the individual fears, foibles and prejudices of the employer could all affect the duties of a servant. In addition, the class, colour, tribe, sex, age, experience and education of a domestic servant could all help determine the conditions of service he or she was employed under. These differencs are important and they should not be minimised. They should not, however, be allowed to obscure such general patterns as do emerge in this area. In the following section an attempt will be made to explore the duties and conditions of service of some of the more important categories of domestic servants to be found on the Rand during this period.

House/parlour maid

Leading members of Johannesburg's commercial, financial and industrial bourgeoisie could afford to maintain a sizeable staff of specialist servants between 1890 and 1914 and no doubt thereafter as well. J. W. Quinn, baker, benefactor and town councillor, employed a cook, nurse and coachman in addition to several black servants in 1896. The financier, S. J. Cohen, kept a similar establishment in 1903 – only he employed a housemaid instead of a nurse. Max Epstein, a noted member of the Stock Exchange, kept a similar staff to his financier colleague but went one further by employing a 'companion' for his allegedly neurotic wife. Amongst the largest complements of all, however, was that at 'Northwards' in Parktown, the home of Col. J. Dale Lace, mining magnate, town councillor and social patron *par excellence* of ruling-class society. In 1905, the staff at 'Northwards' comprised six white servants (cook, butler, coachman and three housemaids), and twice as many black servants to take charge of the 'rough' domestic work, stables and gardens.[87] In the homes of the Randlords, like the Ecksteins, a racially mixed staff of as many as twenty servants was not unusual.

In such establishments the role of 'housemaid' or 'slavey' was one of the lowest positions in the domestic hierarchy which a white female could occupy. Not only were the incumbents required to live in a modest room on the premises, but they also received amongst the lowest cash wages on the property. In the large and well-off Dale Lace residence, for example, the housemaids, in addition to their uniforms and 'beer money' of fourteen shillings, received cash wages of between £4 and £5 per month. These wages were similar – and in some cases less – than those received by black servants in the same establishment and elsewhere in the city. This, coupled with the nature of the duties attached to the post, meant that there was never a ready supply of white housemaids on the Witwatersrand. For this reason employers invariably sought such labour from either the registry offices or the South African Colonisation Society. The immigrant housemaids, however, were as quick as any other Europeans to appreciate that in South Africa hard labour at low wages was considered to be 'kaffir work' and thus turnover in this category of employment remained at a consistently high level.[88]

The housemaid's routine duties involved a daily round of cleaning, sweeping, polishing, tidying and dusting. Johannesburg, which was notorious for its dust and dirt during the early years, ensured that these tasks were both demanding and time consuming. In several of her chores, however, the housemaid was assisted by a black man – the making of beds, for example, appears to have been a commonly shared task. Other very demanding work, such as the cleaning of stoves or grates, was done largely by the black man with the assistance of the housemaid. It was usually at this point that the mistress of the house started to experience difficulties with her staff since what frequently started out as a joint housemaid–'houseboy' chore soon degenerated into a task involving only housemaid 'supervision'. This had the undesirable consequence of leaving the housemaid 'idle' and of generating considerable animosity between white female and black male servants. In addition to the chores outlined above it was also the housemaid's duty to assist in serving the family at meal times. Although it is difficult to be precise, it would appear that all of these duties made for a lengthy working day. Anna Herrmann, who was employed by the very demanding Cohen family, claimed that a normal working day started at 6 a.m. and ended at 10.30 p.m. Her case, however, does not appear to be typical since she was given added duties which housemaids were not normally expected to perform, and in the end she and a hard-worked cook both deserted the Cohen household to seek more congenial work elsewhere.[89]

Leisure-time activities posed difficulties for young female domestics in Johannesburg and this was particularly true between 1895 and 1908. A well developed 'white slave' traffic in women and organised prostitution on a substantial scale were only two of the dangers that confronted the unwary. Equally menacing in its own way, however, were the low wages paid to housemaids in a city where there was a considerable preponderence of males over females. All of these factors combined to make the threat of lax moral behaviour and part-time prostitution on the part of the housemaids a matter of real concern to certain elements within the ruling classes. Thus, at different times the employers, the church and the state all undertook to organise activities which would steer female domestic servants clear of these dangers.

In 1898 Miss Plunkett's Club was set up in the city to help keep respectable young women out of trouble. After the war, the Women's Immigration Department and the South African Colonisation Society placed great emphasis on moral qualities in their selection of domestic servants for the Rand – a fact which pointed to the existence of similar problems in England. These organisations also made substantial efforts to ensure the welfare of these women once they had reached Johannesburg. Despite their precautions, however, 15 out of 500 such servants turned out to be 'morally unsatisfactory' between 1902 and 1904. The Church of England chose to make its effort through an organisation that had traditionally dominated domestic servants at 'Home' – the Girls' Friendly Society; the major objective of the Society being 'to raise the standard of true, pure womanhood throughout the Empire'.[90]

The majority of the housemaids, however, seem to have followed the orthodox leisure-time activities of their class. On their Thursday afternoons off they would often visit their friends who were in service elsewhere in the city. As for the rest, they appear to have had their heads turned by the usual things that appeal to any younger generation. Paternalistic employers were concerned that they 'wasted' their time and money on pretty dresses, 'giddy' visits to the fortune-teller or on reading 'trashy novels'.[91]

The cook-general

In Johannesburg it was only the very rich who could afford the services of a fully qualified cook who, by 1905, could earn as much as £12 per month. The majority of the lower-bourgeois and upper-middle-class families therefore had to be content with the services of a cook-general and a relatively modest staff of black servants. In such homes the cook-general was frequently the only white servant employed, but the family would also enjoy the services of between three and five African male servants. The cook-general was thus likely to find herself at least partly in charge of, and responsible for, the work of the 'houseboy', 'garden boy', 'kitchen boy' and black 'coachman'.

The role and status of the cook-general as the only white servant in a staff of mixed races within the household was riddled with ambiguities and tension. Broadly conceived, there were two basic patterns of relationships that could develop, and each was enmeshed in its own problems. First, the employing family could perceive the cook-general primarily as a fellow *white* and only secondarily as a servant. If this happened the cook-general could often become a 'valued personal friend of both master and mistress'. It was vital that if the relationship was to be managed in this way, however, then the initiative for it should come from the mistress rather than the maid. For, if the cook-general of her own accord pushed too far and too strongly in this direction, then she was in danger of disregarding her servant status altogether and transgressing the class boundaries between herself and her employers. When this happened employers invariably became resentful and accused the maid of 'putting on airs' or of getting 'beyond her station'.[92]

Secondly, the employing family could choose to perceive the cook-general primarily as a *servant* rather than as a fellow white. This managerial style in effect left the white female domestic 'relegated to the society of black men'. If the first pattern of relationships had the danger of producing employer-based resentment, then the latter gave rise to employee hostility. Annoyed at having been pushed back into their class category with other black servants, the cooks-general tended to strike back by accusing the employers of not knowing how to treat them as *white* servants. These accusations they made all the more effective by pointing out that the *nouveau riche* middle classes of Johannesburg lacked the domestic managerial experience of the English ruling class to which they were accustomed. With biting accuracy they pointed to the recent and rapid class mobility of their employers by referring to them as a 'mushroom' or 'veld aristocracy'. As one shocked cook-general put it:

> Judge of my surprise on arrival at my new home when I recognised my lord and master as an ex-publican from Birmingham and my lady as the daughter of a well-known butcher to whose establishment I had often been on errands in the same neighbourhood.[93]

Clearly, class and class-consciousness partly forged in the old metropole could not always be effortlessly incorporated into the new colonial social structure.

These ambiguities in determining the exact status of the white servant also revealed themselves in other areas. Cooks-general who were fortunate enough to develop close relationships with economically privileged and liberal employers no doubt ate well enough, getting their share of what appeared on the family table. Other European servants, however, found that they were given a diet of special meat and second-rate vegetables with the result that they claimed to be 'nearly starving' for want of decent nourishment.[94]

In the question of accommodation the same range of possibilities opened up and ultimately a combination of employer's income, status considerations and employee's wishes determined whether or not the cook-general lived on the premises. In Johannesburg, middle-class homes were not designed to accommodate white servants and thus many cooks-general who did live in often had to make do with the smallest and least comfortable room in the house. Lower-middle-class employers found that they simply did not have the space to offer their white servants a room at all. In such cases the cook-general would hire a room in a 'respectable' working class suburb, or in one of the racially integrated slum areas of older Johannesburg where she would then live with workers and servants of all colours.[95]

In theory, the cook-general had an awesome range of duties to fulfil. All the cooking and cleaning in the home were her responsibility and in addition she could be called upon to assist with the mending of clothes or doing of other 'needlework'. In some homes she would also be expected to do the washing and ironing, but this was a small minority of cases since most domestic servants – black as well as white – refused to undertake this hard specialised work in addition to their other duties. For washing and ironing then, the mistress had to look beyond the cook-general to the local steam laundries, Cape coloured laundresses, or the Zulu craft guild that undertook much of the washing in the city.[96]

In practice, however, all the old ambiguities came into play to bedevil the problem of allocating duties to the cook-general. White women considered it to be 'undignified' to do 'such work as scrubbing floors, cleaning windows, washing up' and a score of other household tasks. This resistance or refusal to do hard unpleasant work produced considerable tension between mistress and maid, and the problem was only partially resolved by the employment of additional black servants to undertake such chores. Once the black men were employed, however, the cook-general would frequently fall prey to the temptation of delegating not only the 'rough work' to the 'houseboy' but an increasing proportion of her other duties as well. This in turn would spark off a new round of tensions between mistress and maid, and between the cook-general and an increasingly hard-worked and resentful 'houseboy'.[97]

But regardless of whether they actually performed their duties or merely supervised them, the cooks-general appear to have worked lengthy hours. This was at least partly due to the fact that they were responsible for meals and thus had to be on duty most evenings. The majority of these women started work between 5 and 7 a.m. and finished at some time between 9 p.m. and midnight. These were long hours and if they lived on the premises, and there were tensions in the household, they could also be lonely hours. In a talk on 'Servants and their treatment' in 1912, Mrs W. F. Lance pointed out that she felt:

> ... in sympathy with the young woman who went into a household where perhaps only one white maid was kept, where she had no one to speak to all day long, and her evenings were also spent alone.[98]

It was hardly surprising then, continued Mrs Lance, that women deserted domestic service for the comparative warmth and independence offered by working-class life in a factory.

Cooks-general appear to have spent their occasional evenings and afternoons off in much the same way as the housemaids although, being somewhat older than the latter, they were less frequently accused of 'wasting' their time or money. A popular haunt for the immigrant cook-general was the South African Colonisation Society Hostel in central Johannesburg where they would gather on a Thursday afternoon to collect their mail or meet their countrywomen.[99]

Children's nurse

In a mature capitalist system one of the major functions of the family, and more especially of its female members, is to socialise children. Precisely because the Witwatersrand did *not* constitute a mature capitalist system between 1890 and 1914 this family function could not be easily or simply fulfilled. There were three basic reasons for this. First, as we have seen, the sexual composition of the white proletariat was only gradually transformed to the point where it could reproduce itself. Secondly, this meant that there was a comparative shortage of white mothers, daughters, aunts and grandmothers to assist in the process of child-rearing and socialisation. Thirdly, not even surrogate socialisation by a female domestic servant was a real possibility since, for a complex set of reasons, the historical process of proletarianisation had initially yielded a male-dominated service sector. Thus, when the predominant amount of child-rearing and socialisation was not directly undertaken by the mother, it was usually done by a black *male* servant. This delegation of responsibility for the child's socialisation, in a society deeply ridden with fear and race prejudice, produced a measure of guilt in the white family – and this was more especially the case where the child happened to be female. From the early 1890s until the outbreak of the South African War the overwhelming majority of 'nurses' in Johannesburg were 'Zulu' males and, so it was reported, most of them performed their duties in an 'excellent' manner. During this period the overall economic dominance of this sector by the 'Zulus', like that of their counterparts the 'kitchen boys', was not in question. Perhaps equally significant is the fact that while there was no serious alternative to this male labour there was no major ideological onslaught on their dominance of this role either.[100]

Immediately after the war, however, there was a sharp increase in the number of white wives and mothers in the Witwatersrand population. Now, for the first time, there was a significant and keen demand amongst the better-off families for the services of a professional child's nurse. The lower-bourgeois and upper-middle classes, however, found it hard to fill these positions with Europeans since the wages they offered were so low and since they expected nursemaids to undertake many 'housemaid' duties in addition to those of child-minding.[101] Thus while a small number of families managed to acquire the full-time services of a nanny, the majority had to continue to rely on their 'Zulu' nurses until at least 1908 and in some cases until very much later.

Between 1906 and 1908 the Witwatersrand experienced its first wave of really serious post-war 'black peril' scares. On this occasion there were also a small number of sexual assaults on very young white girls which contributed to the spreading hysteria. 'Black peril', the availability of the first limited number of black females in the service sector and a new attempt by the state and the Randlords to get the black man into the mining compounds combined to give weight to an ideological attack on the role of the 'Zulu' nurse. From late 1906 it was reported that there was a growing feeling that 'the Kaffir is not the person to be placed in charge of young children'. When *The Star* ran an editorial on 'The Servant Problem' to promote the use of 'piccanin' domestic labour in January 1908, it skilfully combined a growing public prejudice which it had helped foster as well as mining house interest, by suggesting that the 'kaffir' should be compelled to 'change the perambulator for the pick'.[102] In the wake of these events a growing number of black women found employment as 'nurses' between 1908 and 1909. After the second wave of 'black peril' scares in 1912–3 there was a renewed demand for white nursemaids but such substitution as there was on this occasion usually involved black rather than white women. Right up to 1914, however, there were very many black males in employment as 'nurses' in Johannesburg homes.[103]

This gradual and incomplete process of substituting black females for male 'Zulu' 'nurses' between 1908 and 1914 was accompanied by its own particular brand of strident racist ideology. This was perhaps to be seen in its clearest and most bizarre form in the letters which a noted public correspondent, Philip Hammond, wrote to the press in 1909. Hammond assured his Johannesburg readers that if the appointment of a black nurse to a white child did not 'end in death' then it would certainly 'end in disfigurement'. 'The child', wrote Hammond, 'will absorb some of the attributes of the coloured nurse. It will develop a cloudy and oily skin, often a blotchy face, and in many ways puzzle both mother and doctor . . .'.[104] The effect of this 'extreme' form of racist ideology on its audience was interesting.

On the one hand it was clear that very few people subscribed to Hammond's crude notion of the physical contamination of white children by black nurses. On the other, however, nobody dismissed his ideas as being totally unfounded or insane since the 'over-stated' or 'extremist' views of the public correspondent simply revealed, in purer crystallised form, many of the shapeless ideas that floated freely and fully in the minds of most white South Africans. After all, it was only a year later that Sir Matthew Nathan, in a public address to the South African Colonisation Society noted in the course of some remarks on the black nurse that: 'Just as the natives had a peculiar exterior so they had a peculiar character, and it was obvious that the British colonist did not want his child imbued with the ideas of a lower civilisation.'[105]

It was this latter and relatively subtle idea – that there were ultimately social prices to be paid for allowing one's children to be reared by people from another culture – that really concerned Witwatersrand mothers. Filled with guilt and prejudice, however, these white women removed their reservations from a *cultural* nexus and instead made them colour their *racist* perceptions. As a 'Housewife' noted in 1907:

> Many mothers have remarked the change for the worse in their sons' characters, never for a moment suspecting the freedom and close intimacy that there is between the lads and the native servants. Unconsciously the lads imbibe the loose ideas of morals from the natives, and these, unhappily, colour all their actions, to the distress of their parents and friends.[106]

It was for these reasons, amongst others, that the mothers wanted the black male servants removed as 'nurses' – wishing to replace them with the selfsame black females whom they considered to be too 'immoral' to associate with their husbands.

The 'houseboy'

While the rich had their cooks and specialist staff, and the middle classes enjoyed the services of their cooks-general and other black staff, the bulk of the white population – the lower-middle and working classes – made do with the services of the ubiquitous 'houseboy'. Above all others, it was this solitary general domestic servant who undertook the bulk of the domestic labour on the Witwatersrand between 1890 and 1914. Throughout these years the 'houseboy' was under close public scrutiny and even the most critical of observers, during the most stressful of circumstances, were fulsome in their praises of his attributes.

In the 1890s the first generation of Johannesburg 'houseboys' were considered to be noteworthy for their 'ignorance, but also for their amiable nature, general trustworthiness and especially for their capacity for hard work'.[107] As peasants newly off the land they were understandably untrained and 'ignorant' of European customs but sympathetic observers were quick to place these deficiencies in their correct perspective:

> A kafir properly trained makes a capital servant, quick to learn,

obedient, faithful, and apparently conscientious, if such a word may be used in this context. You would not take a man or woman from the country districts of England, Scotland or Ireland, and turn them into waiters, cooks and house-servants in a week or two.[108]

In retrospect, it would appear that it took about six or seven years for the Witwatersrand to acquire a pool of basically trained 'houseboys'.

After the South African War, once the 'houseboys' had acquired the most necessary domestic skills, the charge of 'ignorance' was seldom if ever raised and Mrs Lionel Phillips probably spoke for many when she praised these servants as 'an invaluable asset'. The Minister of Native Affairs was even more forthcoming. In 1912, at the height of the 'black peril' hysteria, he told white South Africans that 'rightly handled' the 'houseboys' were 'perhaps the best domestic servants in the world'. In the following year his words were echoed by a government commission of enquiry which found that 'as a rule, the native houseboy is an excellent servant, and frequently performs long and faithful service'.[109]

It is difficult to generalise about the duties of a 'houseboy' since, as we have seen before, duties tended to vary according to the class of the employer, the size and age of the family, the number of staff kept and the individual experience and attributes of the servant himself. In most homes, however, the 'houseboys' were responsible for the making of fires, cleaning stoves, sweeping, washing dishes, preparing morning and afternoon tea, keeping the yard clean, and doing such routine garden work as weeding and watering.[110] If the overwhelming majority of these duties were unskilled and centred on the kitchen, then the servant could be accorded the slightly lower status of 'kitchen boy'. In a significant number of homes, however, the 'houseboys' would assist in the preparation of meals or undertake the actual cooking of everyday meals for the family. In these latter cases the 'houseboy' was in fact no less than a regular black cook-general and, like the cook-general, would undertake to do the full range of household duties with the possible exception of washing and ironing.

In several Johannesburg middle-class families the 'houseboy' was also called upon to perform other tasks, such as acting as 'coachman' when the occasion demanded. Since it was an offence under the municipal by-laws to leave a horse and trap unattended in the streets, many mistresses made a practice of taking the 'houseboy' along with them on shopping trips so that he might play the role of coachman when necessary. In Johannesburg, a white woman out shopping with her 'houseboy', or sitting beside a black 'coachman', was a frequent enough sight to raise squeals of protest from articulate racists or unemployed white coachmen.[111]

But the 'houseboy's' duties did not end there. In many middle and some working-class homes he was also called upon to perform some of the more intimate functions of a body servant. Not only did they help their masters to dress and undress but, in the privacy of the house they undertook tasks for the mistress which many Europeans felt should only be performed by a white female servant. Trusted 'houseboys' served early morning coffee in the bedroom, sometimes assisted the mistress with the more difficult items of clothing while dressing, drew her bath and, on at least one occasion which

An African 'houseboy'

Sol. T. Plaatje recorded in his famous essay *The Mote and the Beam*, sponged her back.[112]

The execution of these various duties brought the 'houseboys' into close contact with European women for a large part of their working day. 'White women', Mrs Lance pointed out in her talk in 1912, 'in many cases worked side by side with the boys from morning to night'. The nature and extent of this complementary labour, however, could vary according to the class of employer and the personalities of the parties involved. In working-class homes, where he was the only servant employed, the 'houseboy' would often work directly alongside the mistress of the house, but in lower-middle-class homes he might find himself working with either the mistress, or the cook-general, or both.

In many cases these working relationships were tolerably paternalistic or even amicable. Very many more, however, were characterised by friction and hostility or conscious disputes that arose from the unfair allocation of household chores. Depending on which of these patterns developed, and whether or not there were other black servants present, the life of a 'houseboy' – like that of a cook-general – could be more or less lonely and isolated.[113] In addition, and again like their cooks-general counterparts, the 'houseboys' worked long hours with the average day starting between 5 and 7 a.m. and finishing at some time between 6 and 9 p.m.[114]

The 'houseboy's' remuneration for these long hours and varied duties was a cash wage and – as the employers never failed to point out – 'board and lodging'. In most cases the staple diet consisted of a daily ration of 'mealie meal' for porridge, occasional issues of cheap cuts of meat and whatever happened to be left over from the family table. Although it is difficult to be certain, it would appear that when cash wages declined after the South African War, 'houseboys' often demanded – and got – a slightly more varied diet with more frequent issues of meat.[115] Once again, however, this general pattern has to be offset against that ever present minority of employers who appear to have fed their black servants particularly well.

The 'lodgings' which employers offered their black servants were, in the first instance, more for the convenience of the white family than for the comfort of the 'houseboy'. In fact, in many modest working-class homes before the First World War the 'houseboy' did not have a room at all but simply slept on the kitchen floor at night. In other homes the 'houseboy's' room' was in reality part of the stables. On the majority of properties, however, there was usually a small single room without ablution facilities set aside in the back yard, and it was here that the majority of the black male servants on the Witwatersrand lived. The quality of this accommodation varied according to the usual factors, but with the average being somewhat closer to a hovel than a habitable room.[116]

The primary purpose of the servants' rooms, however, was to exercise control over the black domestics – and the 'houseboys' knew this only too well and resented it deeply. Thus in 1902, when the 'houseboys' returned to the Rand with some ready cash and new expectations after the war, a significant number of them refused to re-occupy the old hovels in the back yard. Knowing just how great the demand for their services was, the 'houseboys' pushed the employers into allowing them to live off the premises. What they then did was to club together and collectively rent a house within a Johannesburg suburb like Ophirton or Doornfontein, and live there free from the scrutiny of their employers. Yet others hired a room in a slum yard in old Jeppe or Doornfontein, or lodged themselves in the location.[117] Elements of this new pattern of independence in Johannesburg persisted right up to 1914, but never again on the scale of that immediate post-war period. Growing proletarianisation, but above all the declining cash wages for 'houseboys', progressively undermined these black servants' independence and ultimately drove them back to the employers' property.

In another area, however, the 'houseboys'' battle for independence never ceased and that was in their quest for adequate leisure time. To the considerable annoyance of many white families, the 'houseboys' insisted on having Sundays off and any employer invasion of this time was both deeply resented and strongly resisted. In addition, many 'houseboys' demanded a couple of hours off each afternoon in order to enjoy a meal and recover from a working day that had already seen about eight hours of labour.[118]

The importance of this leisure time to black male domestic servants who often worked in stringent isolation, in a culturally alien environment and under conditions of considerable tension cannot be overstressed. 'Houseboys' relaxed either by entertaining friends in their 'rooms', or by going to the slum yards or mine locations where they spent their time drinking, card-playing or whoring. Once these more basic needs had been met, however, they also took the opportunity to express and re-assert themselves in the props of the invading culture that so relentlessly attempted to relegate them to the one-dimensional status of 'boy'. Outraged and threatened whites complained about the sights in Jeppe on a Sunday afternoon when domestic servants, 'attired in the most up-to-date costumes, and carrying canes and sticks', could be seen 'swaggering along using English language of the most appalling description'.[119]

The 'houseboys' however, were not merely taken with the form of 'western civilisation', they also looked for substance. In particular, they longed to be educated in the hours when they were not at work. When the 'Transvaal Native Association' was formed after the war it received aid and support from two men who were thoroughly familiar with 'houseboys' and their aspirations – James Bold and John Parker, the partners in Parker's Registry Office. It was these men, and especially Parker as 'Honorary President' who, in 1905–6, encouraged the Native Association in its efforts to establish a meeting hall, library and night school for Johannesburg's black workers. Although this venture does not appear to have come to much, the 'houseboys' continued their struggle to become educated. In 1908 somebody else who was well acquainted with domestic servants, Miss M. C. Bruce, of the St Agnes Native Girls' Industrial School, noted that: 'During the past half dozen years the Kaffir has been educating himself in his little tin shanty in our back yards to a degree that might astonish the average Johannesburger did he think about it.' Yet another observer, Ambrose Pratt, confirmed this during his visit to South Africa in 1910. Pratt was struck by what he termed as the black man's 'intense desire' for education, and noted that: 'The vast majority of natives in domestic employment have books in their possession with which they are continually attempting to instruct themselves.'[120] Clearly, Johannesburg might have been 'the university of crime', as John X. Merriman once called it, but for many 'houseboys' it was also a valued educational institution of another sort.

The control of domestic servants

The state

As we have seen above, the demand for white female domestic servants was at its most pronounced during Milner's reconstruction era. It was also during most of this period, between 1902–5, that the wages for European servants were rising. Under these circumstances it is perhaps predictable that employees would seek maximum mobility and that employers would do their utmost to prevent it. Invariably, such struggles are mediated through the law, and in most capitalist societies it is the masters rather than the servants who make the law. South Africa, however, was not merely a developing capitalist society, but also a colonial one, and for this reason it is of more than usual interest to see what role the state played in the attempt to control both black and white servants.

Between 1902 and 1905 several leading bourgeois families recruited their specialist domestic servants directly from England, and so too did the South African Colonisation Society. In return for forwarding the passage money for the journey to South Africa, the masters expected these servants to sign a contract of up to a year during which period the loan was wholly or partially repayable to the employer. This arrangement already contained the seeds of contradiction within it, as the Colonisation Society pointed out:

> ... for the women who are most suitable for emigration by independence of character, and love of enterprise and adventure, are precisely those who are most reluctant to bind themselves to an unknown employer in a strange country.[121]

Once these servants got to Johannesburg and found that they were required to do work that was considered to be socially unacceptable for a white woman, that the cash wages did not go as far as they thought they would, or that there were higher wages to be got elsewhere, they ignored their contracts and deserted.

On 12 March 1902 Elizabeth Knowles summarily left service at 'Northwards' after a disagreement with Mrs Dale Lace. Colonel J. Dale Lace had little hesitation in having her prosecuted for what he believed to be a breach of contract. The magistrate, however, ruled that a contract signed outside the country was not binding in the Transvaal unless approved by magistrate and registered within two months of the servant's arrival. Instead, he found Miss Knowles guilty under the Masters' and Servants' Act and gave her the nominal sentence of a £1 fine or two days' hard labour.[122] This decision, at exactly the time that the South African Colonisation Society scheme for large-scale immigrant labour had been launched, alarmed the employers considerably. *The Star* was quick to spot the danger and in an editorial appealed for a 'reform' of the law which would make such contracts binding.[123]

The law did not change, and the employers apparently did not learn from the Knowles decision. On 16 January 1903 the following notice appeared in the local press.

> Two German Servant Girls viz.:–
> ANNA HERRMANN and
> EMMA HOORMAN
> have deserted my service, being
> indentured to me for two years.
> All persons are hereby warned
> against harbouring them. If
> whereabouts are known please
> communicate with Criminal
> Investigation Department,
> Johannesburg. Siegfried J. Cohen

Anna Herrmann was subsequently found working for Mrs Hermann Eckstein and prosecuted on 29 January 1903. Again the magistrate refused to uphold the contract and felt obliged to give Mr Cohen a lecture on the evils of lengthy contracts for white servants. This time the nominal sentence under the Masters' and Servants' Act was ten shillings and two days' imprisonment.[124]

But even this second decision was not enough for the richest, most stubborn and uncompromising employers of all. In September 1905 the Dale Laces once again brought out several servants from England under contract. Within three months all but one of these servants had left 'Northwards' for more tolerable conditions or higher wages elsewhere. When the last servant, a housemaid named Alice Shurville, gave notice of her intention to leave in January 1906, the Colonel refused to accept it, and withheld wages that were due to her. Undaunted, Miss Shurville took her eminent employer to court, while he in turn attempted to defend the action on the basis of the contract. The magistrate awarded the housemaid her wages, a small amount for damages, and the cost of the proceedings.[125]

By the time that this second Dale Lace case was decided upon the Colonisation Society's scheme for immigrant servants was virtually dead. Significantly enough, *The Star* did not make an appeal for the 'reform' of the law on this occasion. Instead it contented itself with the smug warning to employers that they had themselves to blame if they did not register their contracts with white servants in the Transvaal.[126] It was also clear by this time, from the remarks made by magistrates and the nominal sentences they imposed on European deserters, that the state was reluctant to deliver white servants into the hands of their employers. But if the state disappointed the employers in regard to a small number of white servants, then it more than compensated by harshly controlling the majority of servants that really made the system function – the black 'houseboys'.

From 1896 to 1914 the major mechanism which the state employed to control black labour on the Witwatersrand and elsewhere was, of course, the pass laws. The primary purpose of this repressive legislation was to channel black workers to the most important capitalist industry – the mines – and to ensure that they stayed on as cheap labour for the duration of their contracts. It was precisely for these reasons that the introduction and modification of pass law legislation invariably took place in periods of marked economic stress in the capitalist system. Thus, the first pass laws were introduced to the Rand in the wake of the Jameson Raid and the recession which it heralded. The black labour crisis in the post-war period, however, prompted the major revision, extension and sophistication of the pass laws by the Milner administration. Thereafter, the system was up-dated and modified whenever conditions demanded it – as for example during the depression in the wake of the departure of the Chinese labourers from the Rand in 1908.

Although these laws were primarily directed at industrial workers, they also applied to domestic servants. But since they were intended for the benefit of the former rather than the latter, they earned some hostility from the employers of domestic labour, and the universal hatred of black workers. James Bold, of Parker's Registry Office, probably spoke for many in the service sector in 1906 when he said that:

> ... there can be no doubt that the native pass laws were framed to prevent the townspeople from obtaining domestic servants, or to render their employment so irksome to employers as to be prohibitory. Personally, I have no doubt that they are framed solely in the interests of the capitalists.[127]

A survey of the labour market reveals that the thrust of Bold's observation was close to the mark.

An important secondary purpose of the pass laws was to control the movement of black workers within the cities. In addition to a monthly pass to show that he was in regular employment, any African male who wished to proceed beyond the bounds of the municipality, or to travel outside prescribed hours, had to produce a 'special pass' signed by his employer. These laws thus severely restricted the free movement of blacks and, in the case of 'houseboys', must have markedly increased their feelings of isolation by tending to confine them to the suburbs. To make matters worse, these passes were constantly demanded by black policemen – men whom a commission of enquiry in 1913 found to be largely 'ignorant' and 'illiterate'.[128]

But the pass laws did not only isolate Africans, they also helped – albeit partly unintentionally – to humiliate them. In 1914, for example, a journalist with a keen eye noted how a stylishly dressed black man made his way through Joubert Park in a rather conspicuous manner until such time as he was accosted by a policeman.

> 'Where's your pass?' said the constable. All the rise and 'swank' taken out of him; the native humbly felt in his pockets for his pass, and after the constable was satisfied about it, he was allowed to proceed. But his step had lost its spring and lightness, and his eye its brightness too. He was a crushed and fallen man.[129]

The pass laws etched themselves deeply into the psyches of urban African men. Who then can wonder why they sometimes unleashed such deep, passionate and destructive urges in the men who were called 'boys'?

The remaining important control function which the passes served more directly, was to provide a record of the 'character' of the black worker. When, for one or another reason the worker's contract came to an end, the employer would indicate his 'character' in the appropriate place on the pass. This white assessment of black performance was important to all African workers, but it was of special importance to the 'houseboy' who was in search not of cheap unskilled labour, but of semi-skilled employment at better wages in the intimacy of a European household. No doubt many employers gave their ex-servants adequate, fair or even excellent references. A great many others, however, deliberately spoilt their 'houseboy's' pass through the addition of spiteful or malicious comments. These gratuitous remarks had the effect of pegging or reducing the worker's subsequent wages, or of jeopardising his chances of getting other employment altogether.[130] Again this was potent fuel for the hatred that burnt in many a 'houseboy' heart.

The employers

One of the most pervasive and successful ways in which householders attempted to control their domestic servants was through the manipulation of wage payments. In the years prior to the rinderpest, relatively independent 'Zulu houseboys' appear to have favoured a system of weekly cash wage payments. In an unstable mining camp with many unscrupulous employers who did not hesitate to defraud their employees of their wages, the advantages of this system to what were essentially short-term domestic servants was obvious. By 1896–7, when the process of proletarianisation in the countryside was more advanced, however, many Rand householders shifted to what they called the 'Natal system' – viz., paying their servants on a monthly basis. This meant, as an employer told his colleagues at a meeting of the Johannesburg Mercantile Association, that: 'The boys kept far more sober, they had a better hold on them, and they stayed longer.' After the South African War the monthly payment system appears to have become almost universal. But not even this was enough for some employers who further extended and 'refined' the system. As a matter of policy they kept 'houseboy' wages in arrears by anything from two to four weeks as a form of 'insurance' against instant departure by their domestic servants.[131]

In an equally deliberate attempt to defraud their employees of their wages, a significant number of employers also sought to provoke a mid-month confrontation with their servants. It is 'a common practice' for people to engage servants in Johannesburg, alleged a cook-general in 1905, 'and then to find the means to dispense with them before the month is up, for no other reason than to swindle the poor unfortunate women out of their pay'. A thousand and one 'houseboys' could have echoed these words in chorus, and there was no other single employer practice that produced a greater sense of injustice, or provoked a more violent response from black male domestic servants, than this one.[132]

Whilst the primary purpose of this employer stratagem might have been to refine robbery, it also had the indirect beneficial consequence of enhancing control over servants between pay-days. Servants, who were certainly aware of this employer-tactic, would have had to be abnormally passive and unusually restrained under provocation if they wished to get the chance of obtaining the wages due to them. Even total passivity, however, did not always guarantee the 'houseboy' his wages. The commission of enquiry in the wake of the great 'black peril' scare of 1912 found that in a significant number of cases employers had simply trumped up charges of sexual assault against their 'houseboys' in order to defraud them of their wages.[133]

More direct, but at least as crude, were some of the methods that employers used to control servants within their homes. We know from Jan Note – the founder of the most notorious black criminal gang on the Witwatersrand during this period – that when he went to be a 'kitchen boy' in Johannesburg in 1887 his employers threatened him with a revolver while giving him his instructions. Since his employers eventually transpired to be highway robbers this behaviour was perhaps not surprising. What *is* surprising, however, is how ready ordinary householders, including women, were to threaten 'houseboys' with guns.[134] In addition, not a few mistresses and their white female domestic servants appear to have been willing to strike or *sjambok* 'houseboys' who did not perform their duties adequately, or quickly enough for their employers' liking.[135] Needless to say, such assaults did nothing to reduce the tension in what was already a highly charged atmosphere.

Employer control, however, also extended beyond the immediate work situation into the servant's 'private life'. This extension, as we have already noted in passing, was made possible largely through the manner in which domestic servants were accommodated. Male, but more especially female domestic servants, found that their sexual relationships were under the close, critical and constant scrutiny of their employers. This was particularly so in the case of white women who had a bedroom within the house itself – although it also applied to black and coloured women who happened to occupy a room in the back yard of the premises. For obvious reasons this was yet another cause of friction and Mrs Lance, in her talk on the treatment of servants, made a point of suggesting that if householders gave their cooks-general a private sitting-room in addition to a bedroom in which to entertain their male friends, then employer–employee relationships would improve.[136] In addition to this moral surveillance, employers of all classes did not hesitate to invade and inspect their servants' rooms and goods if they suspected them of theft or any other misdemeanour.[137] Servants were always visible to their employers – in work or leisure hours alike.

Besides these cruder cudgels, employers also possessed a selection of more subtle instruments with which to control their black servants, and perhaps one of the most striking of these was to be found in the field of communication. With masters and mistresses unable to speak Zulu, and servants as yet unable to speak English, urban households gave rise to a jargon which one observer aptly termed an 'emergency language'. This 'language', which later as *fanakalo* – 'do it like this' – became the industrial *lingua franca* of southern Africa, was at the time almost universally known by the socially more significant name of 'Kitchen Kaffir'.

It was this Zulu-based jargon, interspersed with English and Afrikaans words, that served as the basic medium of communication between white mistresses and black servants in Johannesburg households. While this 'Esperanto of South Africa' might have made simple commands possible it denied more subtle or complex communication, and as such it was the basis of much misunderstanding and conflict. Invariably, however, the onus and responsibility for this lack of understanding was made to rest with the servant rather than the master or mistress, and the 'houseboy' was frequently chastised for 'not knowing his own language'. In addition, many Europeans felt threatened by Africans who spoke or attempted to speak English as this implied creeping equality, and thus insisted on blacks speaking 'Kitchen Kaffir'. Unable to communicate in their first language and saddled instead with a brittle and bastard tongue, black servants had their dependent and colonised status perpetually reinforced through appearing to be stupid, inarticulate and incoherent. The 'language' might have been conceived in a kitchen, but it was also *kaffir* – with all that that implied for white South Africans.[138]

If the element of control in the use of 'Kitchen Kaffir' was largely an unconscious by-product in the use of language, then the same surely cannot be said of the names which many white employers gave their black servants. Like their Victorian predecessors who did not hesitate to change 'their servants'' names arbitrarily if they happened to clash with those of the 'family', European employers were quick to rename their 'Zulu' employees. In part, this was no doubt simply due to the difficulties which whites experienced with the pronunciation of Zulu names, and some of the new names like 'New One' or 'Long One' were relatively innocent. But, whereas Victorian masters simply gave their servants other randomly chosen Christian names to distance themselves from their employees, many Witwatersrand householders gave their servants the names of commodities or objects. Names such as 'Saucepan', 'Shilling', 'Brandy', 'Sixpence' or 'Matches' not only distanced servants from employers, they also humiliated them, and ultimately denied their humanity altogether.[139] Being a 'boy' must have hurt a man's pride, being a boy-commodity must have crushed much of his remaining human dignity in what was already a servile position.

One of the remaining ways in which employers controlled their servants – white as well as black – but especially the 'houseboys', was through gifts of cast-off clothing in an era when the use of servants' uniforms was anything but widespread. This practice, however, was beset with difficulties and produced a deep-seated ambivalence within the minds of European employers. On the one hand, employers made capital out of their gifts of second-hand clothing to servants by using it as an ideological device with which to justify low cash wages.[140] It also had the largely unconscious, but nevertheless desirable consequence of increasing the dependency of the servant.[141] Both of these procedures ultimately facilitated employer control, although in different ways.

On the other hand, however, black servants who dressed like their masters – indeed, in what was, until very recently, the master's own clothing – were modelling themselves on Europeans, and this had implications of aspirant if not actual equality. Between 1890 and 1914, when the Witwatersrand social structure was changing particularly rapidly, and when personal class distinctions between workers and the petty bourgeoisie were not as visible or marked as they were in later years, nothing threatened Europeans more than this practice of blacks wearing 'white' clothes.[142] It was therefore predictable that one of the later proposals for dealing with the 'houseboy' 'black peril' threat was that:

> No native should be allowed to wear ordinary European dress during working hours, and employers should combine to this end. European dress gives him an inflated sense of importance and equality.[143]

When, very much later, 'houseboy' uniforms were introduced to the Witwatersrand, they doubtlessly served more than a simple utilitarian purpose.

The colonial master and mistresses' ideology

In the colonies, at least as much as in the metropolis, masters and mistresses spent an endless amount of time talking about their servants – and not infrequently such discussions took place in the presence of an apparently deaf-mute 'houseboy'. On the Witwatersrand, employers also addressed volumes of letters to the press on some or other recent dimension of the 'servant problem'. Here again the notions of the employers were subjected to the scrutiny of the cooks-general and the 'houseboys' and, on occasion, produced vigorous clashes in the correspondence columns of the local press. While it is difficult, if not impossible to assess to what extent these notions of the employing classes were internalised by the servants, it is important to have an idea of what some of these ideological constructs were. But since much of this ground has already been covered in passing, the discussion here will be necessarily brief.

'If the Kaffir is brother to anything', wrote one Charles O'Hara in 1912, 'it is to the anthropoid ape.' This view of Africans being more akin to animals than humans was not restricted to the lunatic fringe of racists in Witwatersrand society. In 1897 the pretentiously opinionated and self-styled 'progressive' newspaper *The Star* had run an editorial in which it claimed that: 'In South Africa in general the Kaffir is a mere naked savage, with not much more intelligence than a baboon, and not much more ambition.' On this, as on other occasions, it was left to the pro-Kruger and allegedly backward *Standard and Diggers' News* to defend the black 'houseboy' with some sane and well reasoned perspectives. Partly because of these animal-cum-savage origins, African men were supposed to be highly sexed and uninhibited, and therefore constituted 'one of the most lustful savage races on earth'.[144]

It was considered, however, that if the 'noble savage' could be obtained immediately after his 'wild' youthful stage then he could be turned into 'a natural servant' since 'the instinct of the race makes for absolute obedience to their employers'. The problem with this was that it was all too difficult to obtain a 'kaffir' whose mind was *tabula rasa*. Usually he had already been interfered with before he entered service – most notably by the missionaries who gave him dangerous ideas of equality. Obviously then, the 'mission kaffir' made the worst possible type of servant.[145]

The best way of dealing with a black servant was as with a 'child' – firmly and fairly. In Johannesburg very cruel or brutal methods were perceived as being backveld or 'Boer', and unsuited to a modern city. With the passage of time, however, several citizens looked back with nostalgia to what they saw as the 'good old days' of servant control and discovered that they were, after all, 'Boer'-inspired. Mrs J. L. Robinson's letter to General Louis Botha on the 'houseboy' problems in 1907 is not untypical:

> I have been in Jo'burg for the last fifteen years, and under the rule of the late President Kruger, we had nothing of this kind of thing to contend with. Then these Kaffirs were kept in their proper place, not allowed to strut about, dressed up to imitate the white man, nor to ride about in cabs, rickshaws and bicycles. They were not allowed to be insolent, and ask what wages they liked. It was the same in the Free State and other places.[146]

As so often in South Africa, English speakers helped forge and fashion an oppressive present and then, in retrospect, attributed it to an Afrikaner past.

Given the fairly consistent shortage of white female servants on the Rand before the First World War, it is understandable that mistresses were sorely perplexed by what they perceived as 'reasonless objections to "domestic service" '. These were all the more puzzling since it was said of housework that:

> ... there is hardly any work so much admired: it has the power which no other work within women's ken has, to hold homes together, to make lives happy, and almost to reconstruct the nation or spoil it. A woman who is a good housekeeper gets praise from thousands, and blame from none.[147]

Who was suited to such work? Well, 'a woman of no extraordinary amount of intellect' but 'with a well ordered mind and capable womanly hands'! As with all servants, such women should be well disciplined since it was well known that the 'weakness of a ruler makes bad subjects'. But a mistress who took an interest in her employees, and who ensured fair and considerate treatment would never be in want of good servants.

On the Witwatersrand, however, the mistresses had an additional ideological task to perform – they had to tell the white housemaids, especially those newly arrived from 'home', how they should behave towards the 'houseboy':

> They should be civil and kind, not dictatorial or imperious; but they should never allow any familiarity. They should not touch their hands, or sit in a room where there are boys, or do anything whereby an insolent native may take liberties. A girl is often inclined to think of a native boy as a 'thing', a 'machine', an 'animal', not as a man, and if she never rouses any feeling he will usually do his work mechanically and never think of molesting her.[148]

Clearly, the 'etiquette of race relations' between servants had to be taught at least as much as it was 'naturally' acquired in a racist society. White householders taught well, but as we shall see, not all their pupils were willing to understand the lesson, and 'feelings' were certainly aroused.

The response of domestic servants and the resistance of blacks to colonisation

Universal patterns

In many cases white and black servants responded to the basic state instruments that respectively bound them to their employers – the contract and pass laws – by ignoring them, and deserting from service. This drastic action, however, was seldom taken lightly, and the fact that servants were willing to make considerable financial sacrifices rather than stay with their employers, testifies to the depth of their feelings. Anna Herrmann attempted to borrow 1,000 German marks in order to free herself from her contract with Siegfried Cohen before she finally deserted, and both she and the cook told the coachman that 'they would rather drown themselves than stop at the place'. Black male servants could be no less determined. In the mid-1890s, an observer of Johannesburg life noted that masters would occasionally get a minor financial windfall since 'houseboys' tended 'to disappear one evening, not even taking the trouble to ask for their money' – money that was theirs, that sometimes included their savings as well as the wages that were due to them.[149]

But if these responses were driven by desperation, then there is abundant evidence to show that black servants also responded to the state's instruments of control in a variety of other ways. Those who were more passive, or perhaps it was simply that they had more faith in the law and money, paid shady lawyers or legal agents to help them negotiate thorny legal paths. Virtually from the moment that the pass laws were introduced, however, others, through poverty, ingenuity or a sense of injustice, challenged the system in a more vigorous way. Black friends forged passes for one another – the literate helped the illiterate. Those who were not fortunate enough to have an obliging friend were forced into more contractual relationships in order to get their passes or 'characters' altered. In 1906, for a fee of half-a-crown, the Honorary President of the 'Transvaal Native Association' or his business partner at Parker's Domestic Registry Office, would alter an unsuitable 'character' on a 'houseboy's' pass. No doubt for a slightly larger fee, lumpenproletarian elements in the city were willing to undertake the same task, or compose an entirely false testimonial for a 'houseboy'.[150]

A good number of servants could certainly have done with false testimonials. Housemaids and 'houseboys' alike appear to have indulged in their fair share of petty thieving, regularly taking food, clothing or alcohol from their employers.[151] While little can or should be read into these actions, these thefts do suggest a shortage of ready cash and, at very least, the value which servants attached to these positions in domestic employment. In a different category entirely, were those cases in which 'houseboys' deliberately burgled the homes of ex-employers who had withheld their wages or 'spoilt' their passes.[152] Here was a single, clear and unequivocal statement about the chances of justice being obtained through the orthodox channels of the law, and of the need for swift and full compensation.

Other, and more oblique statements, were made by the 'houseboys' in the day-to-day work situation – as expressed through their attitude towards their employers and work. It was a constant theme in employer ideology that black servants were becoming more 'cheeky' or 'insolent' and, since such arguments were invariably used instrumentally in an attempt to secure greater control over the 'houseboys', such statements should be viewed with a very critical eye. But, having noted this, the employer's objections should not be dismissed out of hand since there are two additionally noteworthy features about such complaints.

First, it is striking just how constant such complaints were; and it should be remembered that ideology feeds on a diet of fact as well as fiction. It is probable that a first generation of black domestic workers who were losing their base of rural independence, and labouring for cash wages that experienced an overall decline, *were* increasingly resentful of the situation in which they found themselves. Secondly, it is equally noteworthy how the volume of such employer complaints increased at periods of structural stress within the system – in particular, in 1896–7, 1902, 1906–8 and 1912–4.[153]

Thus it was in Heidelberg, in 1902, that it was alleged that teachings of 'social equality' by an 'Ethiopian Methodist' minister were at the base of 'some disobedience on the part of native servants'.[154] Again, in the depression year of 1906, at exactly the time that black domestic workers' wages were falling most rapidly and their home districts were being disrupted by the Bambatha rebellion, 'houseboys' were noted as being more truculent and difficult to manage. The *Transvaal Leader* recorded this unrest amongst 'a section of the Kaffir servants of the community' and further noted that only 'Zulu' and not Pedi or Shangaan 'houseboys' were affected.[155]

Essentially the same syndrome is to be detected where black attitudes crystallised and hardened into an outright refusal to work, or, at least, to undertake certain tasks. By the very structuring of the roles, conditions of service and the allocating of work in Witwatersrand homes, such incidents were always liable to occur. What is again noteworthy, however, is the apparent frequency with which such incidents occurred during periods of more general crisis.[156] There thus appear to be more prosecutions of black domestic servants for refusal to work during the miners' strikes of 1913, and perhaps it is significant that the local press chose precisely the same moment to draw attention to the unease amongst white employers about the 'absolute disrespect' and 'insolence of native houseboys'.[157] *Prima facie* there is good reason to believe that the changing material conditions of rural and urban life helped shape and pulse the consciousness of 'houseboys' at least as much as any other group of migrant workers in the city. From other, more organised responses, it would also appear that it was the urban rather than rural milieu that became increasingly dominant in that process between 1890 and 1914. One pattern of rural and urban 'houseboy' response which did not undergo much change during this period was the rather more direct and unambiguous procedure of administering poison to a much hated employer. Usually such attempted murders – for they seldom succeeded – carried all the hallmarks of individual and hastily conceived schemes that were triggered by 'last straw' provocative actions on the part of the intended victim. Household disinfectant or fly poison were added to the tea or coffee of white women who had insulted, assaulted or dismissed 'houseboys'.[158]

On at least one occasion, however, employers believed that there were more organised plans afoot by their 'houseboys' to murder them. In late 1898, in lower Doornfontein, a mistress became 'violently ill' after drinking tea made by her 'houseboy'. Subsequent observations and enquiries produced the rumour that a 'witch doctor' had instructed all his fellow tribesmen to poison their mistresses in this manner, with herbs which he provided. This story caused 'considerable alarm' in the racially mixed community, and a reporter sent to investigate the matter noted at the time that 'The ladies of the neighbourhood are now strongly inclined to make tea for themselves.'[159] Regardless of the truth of these allegations, it is clear that relations between black domestic workers and white mistresses were bad enough to sustain such a rumour, and that employers were conscious of the fact that 'houseboys', if sufficiently provoked, could resist in ways that might well prove fatal.

'Houseboy' resistance, however, was not confined to the cities – as was to be expected with flows of migrant labour, it also spilled over into the countryside. Workers on the Witwatersrand, including domestic servants, constantly added new symbols, ideas and attitudes to their store of conceptual baggage which they then carried back to the rural areas and redistributed amongst their kinsmen.[160] Whilst it is not intended to explore these fascinating linkages in any depth here, the recounting of a single incident can help to re-alert us to the importance of the city's contribution to the struggle in the countryside.

During the depression, in 1908, a Morolong 'kitchen boy', calling himself John Whitesun, left his employment in Johannesburg and made his way back to his home district of Mafeking. There, armed with a bullock's horn, a 'Queen's banner' with a coat-of-arms and with what were alleged to be 'Ethiopian' teachings, he joined forces with a Makwena herdsman named Cross Degomaile. From there, he and Degomaile – the latter now modestly renamed 'Jesus Christ' – proceeded to make their way first to Kanye, and then ultimately to Taungs.

Preaching enthusiastically in the countryside, the pair of prophets soon attracted the attention of the white and black authorities in the region. They also found, however, that their prestige increased enormously when they were first arrested by the administration, and then subsequently released as supposedly harmless lunatics. From then on, an increasingly radical millenarian message attracted a growing number of supporters who were distinguished by the red cloth badges which they wore.

Events eventually came to a head when the prophets addressed a meeting of between 1,000 and 1,500 followers at Taungs on 24 July 1909. 'Jesus Christ' and his assistant told their black followers – in English, Dutch and Sechuana – that they 'remembered the rinderpest' and that Victoria had imposed a tax on them 'and that God was cross about it, and that was why the Queen died'. For the benefit of those who had worked in the old South African Republic, Whitesun also thought it worth mentioning that 'Paul Kruger used to give them 25 (lashes) and he was now getting 25 elsewhere (hell)'. Then, most spectacularly of all, that the people 'were tired of the white man's rule', that there 'was going to be a bloody war', and that by sunset there would not be a single European left alive in Taungs. These prophecies did the nerves of the local whites of the district no good at all. Whitesun and 'Jesus' were promptly arrested, and subsequently sentenced to four and a half and five years' imprisonment with hard labour respectively. In his summing up at the trial, the Judge expressed the hope that 'when they come out of gaol they would discontinue preaching the Gospel'.[161]

In itself there is nothing startling about this rural protest movement – indeed it has many features in common with other such movements which developed during the colonial era. Neither is the fact that there were linkages between the town and the countryside in itself novel – this too was a common feature of such movements. Nevertheless, it is interesting to trace what is specifically 'Witwatersrand' in the origin of this movement, to consider what it tells us about the consciousness of 'houseboys', and to speculate about what cross-fertilisation of ideas there might have been in its development. At least three noteworthy features seem to emerge.

First, Whitesun, as the leader of the movement stated categorically that 'He had learned his theology at Johannesburg'. If this was so, and there is no reason to doubt it, then if offers us further evidence about the important influence which the Bible had in shaping the consciousness of black men on the Rand during this period. Indeed, what is striking is how this biblical message appealed to Africans across the class spectrum – ranging from independent ministers to 'houseboys', and even through to the leader of a criminal gang like the Ninevites.[162]

Secondly, Whitesun, like those 'disobedient native servants' at Heidelberg after the war was, moved by 'Ethiopian' teachings about 'social equality'. Whereas the rural prophet Degomaile was largely concerned about misfortune in the countryside, like tax and rinderpest, Whitesun was more interested in the towns and keener to ask that 'the white people and black become united and drink from the same vessel, as they had one God'. Here surely was the imagery and concern of a 'houseboy', rather than that of a herdsman. If this and events at Heidelberg are considered, then it would appear that servile status imposed by race did not settle easily on 'houseboys', and that they registered their ideological objections to it.

The third feature of the Whitesun movement which commands attention is the red cloth badges which he encouraged his followers to wear. It is probably true that the use of this colour drew on some symbolism deeply embedded in the culture of the African resistance. At the trial of the prophets a hostile witness – Chief Molala of the Batlapin – said that: 'He did not know what the badges meant, but they were worn in the early days by the fighting men'. But, whatever the truth of this may have been, Whitesun would have seen the selfsame tokens used in very different surroundings shortly before he left Johannesburg for the countryside. In 1907, red handkerchiefs and neckties – the colours of organised labour – were to be seen everywhere as trade unionists sported their symbols during the mineworkers' strike. If, however, Whitesun had failed to spot the tokens and their significance then, he could hardly also have missed the red cloth badges of the 'houseboy' gangs that so frightened the whites of Johannesburg in 1908 – the *Amalaita*. Red might have started and ended as the colour of rebellion for Africans in the countryside but, for any 'houseboy' on the Rand between 1906 and 1908, it would always have new overlays and a special depth of meaning.

The 'black peril'

Between 1890 and 1914 the Witwatersrand – and Johannesburg in particular – were swept by periodic waves of collective sexual hysteria. During these violent storms of social tension, sometimes branded as the 'social curse' but more frequently simply known as the 'black peril', white women, on an unprecedented scale, alleged that they had been sexually molested or assaulted by black men. At the very eye of these storms lay the European household, and within it relationships between black and white servants on the one hand, and 'houseboys' and mistresses on the other. Nothing so embittered 'race relations' in urban South Africa before the First World War as these 'black peril' scares, and nothing has been so little studied. To understand and place the 'black peril' in perspective, however, it is first necessary to scrutinise the lull before and between the social storms.

Relationships between 'houseboys' and white female domestic servants on the Witwatersrand were, for reasons that have already been explored above, frequently marked by tension and conflict. While this pattern was, on balance, probably the dominant one, it was far from being exclusive. Employers like Sir Matthew Nathan were cognisant of a second, and subordinate pattern of relationships. In a talk to the South African Colonisation Society in 1910, he noted that: 'If the staff was mixed there was a tendency for the white servants to become too familiar with the family or the native servants', and, he pointedly added, 'of these two the latter was less desirable'.[163]

That this secondary pattern of relationships should develop at all, and that when it did so that it should run along essentially class-determined lines, is hardly surprising. In bourgeois and upper-middle-class homes, domestic servants laboured for long hours in splendid isolation. In such homes, servants who were kept socially distant from the employing family and given limited access to outside society, were constantly thrown into each others' company. It was perfectly understandable therefore, that a degree of 'familiarity' should develop between the sexes, and that this should be reinforced by the age and status of most domestic servants who were single and between the ages of 18 and 35. Elsewhere in the city, where there were few African women, the social structure also forced black workers to turn their attention to the only other group of females of their own class that were present in significant numbers – the white domestic servants.

It is difficult to recount cases of such class-bound romances across the colour line partly because it involved behaviour that was by its very nature private, and partly because white society frowned on such relationships. Where, for one reason or another, however, such relationships soured and produced open conflict, or where they became too visible in an intolerant society, then they eventually also surfaced in the law courts. It is to these latter cases that we have to turn if we want a glimpse into this aspect of relations between domestic servants.

In 1895, Jim Hloywa courted Jessie McTavish, a 'comely' housemaid in service with a manager of a Johannesburg branch of the Standard Bank, Mr Shotter. Jim pursued an allegedly reluctant Jessie through a series of letters which he confidently signed, and which he had delivered to the Shotter household via a fellow servant. When, for reasons that are unclear, he threatened Jessie and the relationship became unmanageable, he wrote her a final letter in which he took his reluctant leave. 'Yes, I better just good-bye', he wrote, 'But I really wanted to be engaged with you'. 'I am a Kaffir', he concluded, 'but my money is as much as of a white man.' 'I winned in the sweep last year £10,000.'[164] Similar correspondence initiated by an African can be traced to one of the city's tea-rooms where white and black served together as waiter and waitress.[165] Such letters – as Jim Hloywa who received six months' imprisonment and 25 lashes with the 'cat' could testify – produced brutal sentences.

When such letters came from the white servants rather than black men, however, they tended to produce shock or outrage, but seldom court cases or tough sentences. In 1898, one 'Joseph' promptly and permanently brought his trial for 'indecent behaviour' to a close when he announced to a startled court that he was ready to produce a series of letters from house-keeper Edith Simpson, in which she invited him to 'come round and see her'.[166] Again such correspondence was not unique. In 1913 a master was 'shocked' when he found a letter by a white woman addressed to 'My Dear Thomas' – his 'houseboy'. Rather innocently the enclosed note simply enquired of Thomas: 'Can't you come and see me one day, if you can get off?'. To prove the authenticity of the note, the outraged master offered to make the letter available for public inspection.[167] It is possible that such snippets of correspondence simply reveal the tip of the proverbial iceberg. What is slightly clearer, is that at least some of these relationships produced a depth of feeling and a sense of commitment that went beyond casual sexual encounters.

In 1904 Marcus Matopa and Caroline Dyer both entered domestic service in a Johannesburg household. From this there developed a relationship which culminated in the housemaid's pregnancy. The couple then left service, and went to live at the 'houseboy's kraal' at Waterval North near Pretoria. Here the two remained until they were discovered by a missionary who obligingly reported their presence to local government officals. The court refused to sentence the couple but 'warned' them, and then ordered Caroline back to service with her former employer in Johannesburg.[168] Once more the story is not without a later parallel. In 1914, a 'Zulu' and a white 'nursemaid' were found living together in a room in Doornfontein. The couple informed the magistrate that it was their wish to leave for Kimberley and get married, but the court separated the couple and placed the woman on probation.[169]

This evidence alone suggests that if the development of intimate sexual relationships between domestic servants in Rand homes was not a common occurrence, than it was not an entirely novel one either. The strongest support for this contention comes from the government enquiry that was set up to investigate the last major 'black peril' scare shortly before the First World War – the commission appointed to enquire into assaults on women. The commission, which sat in 1913, was of the opinion that 'serious consideration' would have to be given to 'the danger of natives working in close contact with white female servants, especially those that have been imported from Europe'. In the emasculating manner of the colonist, the male-dominated commission smugly contented itself with the opinion that where sexual intercourse had taken place between servants, 'the facts seem to point to sexual perversion on the part of the female'. Apparently this 'perversion' was widespread enough, however, for it to recommend that 'European servants should be taught how to treat the native; they should not touch or allow themselves to be touched by the latter'.[170] Clearly, amongst new arrivals in the kitchen, the realities of physical proximity and class affinity pulled the sexes together almost as strongly as acquired colour prejudice pulled them apart.

Just as servants were drawn together in the homes of the more wealthy, so 'houseboys' and mistresses were pushed into each other's company in lower-middle and working-class homes – and for many of the same reasons. Long hours of more or less collective labour in relative isolation forged bonds of common humanity which the crass racism of a prejudiced society could not always overcome. But, despite this similarity between the two situations, the development of a 'houseboy'/mistress relationship was, in the end, always more difficult to develop and sustain than its white servant/black servant counterpart. Again the reasons for this were largely class-determined. Whereas relationships between domestic servants were ultimately relationships of *equality* between fellow workers and peers, that between 'houseboy' and mistress remained inherently unequal since it was also – in the final analysis – a relationship between employer and employee. In turn it was precisely because the latter relationships were fundamentally unequal that the initiatives for establishing such liaisons differed. Whereas in the servant/servant relationship either party appeared to have been willing to take the initiative, in the 'houseboy'/mistress relationship the employer seems to have been more willing and able to take the initiative.

There is strongly suggestive evidence of such mistress-initiated relationships even before the South African War.[171] What is clearer from more reliable observers, however, is that after the war such relationships were far more frequent. In 1911, many Witwatersrand whites were shocked when it was suggested publicly that mistresses encouraged black servants to sleep with them. Not so the ministers attached to the South African Mission to the Compounds and the Interior. In an editorial in their magazine, the clergymen said that they knew such allegations 'to be true from instances that have come under [our] own observation from confessions made to us by converts'. The 1913 commission of enqury also admitted that there were instances to support such an allegation, but that the charge was 'baseless in regard to the majority or even a large number of cases'. But if the commissioners had difficulty in finding cases where 'the native was as Joseph and the white woman as Potiphar's wife', then perhaps it was because they failed to consult the black author and journalist Sol T. Plaatje. He 'could fill a book on such first hand information about the vicissitudes of houseboys', but, in his work *The Mote and the Beam*, chose to 'select only one story illustrative of the unenviable lot of this class of worker, especially in Johannesburg'.[172]

But while female initiatives in such relationships appear to have been predominant, they were again certainly not exclusive. Black servants occasionally admitted to the affections that they had developed for their mistresses, as well as to the sexual advances that they made to them. These confessions, made under the gravest of possible circumstances, required exceptional courage, which is perhaps why they appear to be relatively infrequent. In 1912, for example, one such case occurred in which a 'houseboy' who 'caught hold' of his mistress by the hand and told her that 'he liked her very much', was sentenced to four months' imprisonment with hard labour and five lashes for 'assault'.[173]

Other black servants, however, were probably consciously or unconsciously inhibited from making direct approaches to their white mistresses by the strength of the class barriers that existed between themselves and their employers. In order to overcome these barriers, the domestic servants made indirect attempts to secure the sexual favours of their European mistresses – significantly enough, a procedure that seems to be wholly absent from their interaction with other white servants. Some 'houseboys' turned to shady white or Asian traders for various concoctions, or for reputed aphrodisiacs like cantharides, 'Spanish Fly'. Yet others placed their faith in traditional love potions obtained from 'witch doctors', or in acquiring so-called 'Malay Tricks' or charms. A favoured procedure seems to have been to put such potions or *muti* into the mistress's tea – something which perhaps casts light on the great Doornfontein tea-drinking scare of 1898 from another angle. In any event, at least some of these ploys appear to have been successful since the 1913 commission reported that there had been instances involving white women, where consent to sexual intercourse had been 'extorted' 'by superstitious dread of pretended occult powers on the part of the offender'.[174]

Looking back at the period between 1890 and 1914 then, at least three general observations can be made about the sexual relationships that developed between white women and the black male domestic servants. First, such relationships seem to have developed most readily along class lines – those between 'houseboys' and white female servants being relatively prominent. Secondly, such relationships could be initiated by either partner where servants were involved, but were more frequently at the instigation of the employer in the case of a mistress/'houseboy' relationship. Thirdly, while such relationships were never openly tolerated or considered to be 'normal', they did nevertheless occur on a substantial scale. Given this, it remains to be considered when these developed clandestine relationships or their latent equivalents broke down on a significant scale, and why they should do so.

The first really noteworthy 'black peril' scare in Johannesburg appears to have occurred during spring of 1893. In early September of that year one of the morning newspapers drew the attention of its readers to a series of attempted rapes by trusted black servants who were considered by whites to be 'almost part of the family'. 'Beware of your "houseboy" ', cautioned the editorial, 'for under the innocent front may be lurking and lying latent the passions of the panther, and worse!'[175]

This early squall was followed by four years of relative tranquility during which there was no marked public outcry about such alleged offences. This calm, however, was in marked contrast to the storm that followed. On 3 July 1897 Mrs Anne Lightfoot was raped and then severely assaulted by her 'kitchen boy', Louis, after a dispute over his wages. This notable attack of sexual brutality was followed by widespread hysteria during which the virtues of public hanging for such offenders was vigorously debated.[176] Once the storm had passed, however, it was followed by a lengthy period of calm which lasted until a few years after the South African War.

In 1904, but more especially from late 1905 onwards, there were familiar social rustlings when sporadic cases of 'black peril' were reported in Johannesburg.[177] These stirrings picked up markedly in volume during 1906, and then finally the winds of panic blew relentlessly throughout 1907 and 1908. The height of public concern during this storm appears to have been reached in mid-1907 when the 'Associated Women's Organisations of the Transvaal' approached the government with a plea that, amongst other moves, social segregation be implemented in an attempt to cope with the curse of the 'black peril'.[178]

This time the storm was followed by a brief period of calm, only to be disturbed by a most unexpected and violent gust during 1911. On 2 February 1911, a 'governess' was out cycling beyond Orange Grove when she was attacked and raped by an unknown assailant who spoke 'kitchen kaffir'. This attack, which became known as the 'Lyndhurst Outrage', was given sensational coverage in the local press and it really unleashed a storm of acute European anxiety. It was followed by a massive police pass-drive against 'houseboys' and a public meeting which, amongst other measures, demanded a mandatory death sentence for attempted rape by black men.[179] This time, however, the city never really settled down and when yet another sensational rape occurred fourteen months later, the full impact of gale-force white fury tore through Johannesburg.

At about midnight on 12 April 1912, Mrs W. Harrison was attacked and raped by one or more black men while sleeping in her Turffontein home with two small children. This savage attack, in the middle of a solidly working-class district, produced an immediate white male backlash. Within days a series of meetings was held where revolver-brandishing southern suburbs residents organised themselves into vigilante groups. These groups, barely under the control of the local police, swept through the suburban streets at night checking on passes, and assaulting several Africans they happened to come across. On 23 April, 'someone hanged an effigy of a native from the headgear of one of the southern mines'. 'The dummy could be seen for many miles around and was mistaken [by many blacks] for the real genuine article.' In white eyes these acts of aggression were further justified when, three days later Mrs Harrison died – from, as it later transpired, an incorrectly self-administered dose of chloride of mercury.[180]

As the embers of racial hatred continued to flicker in late April and early May 1912, so they were fanned into fuller profile by the sensationalist local press. When it soon became clear that the government and others were less than enthusiastic about what they considered to be an undignified and unnecessary over-reaction by Johannesburg citizens, the *Rand Daily Mail* stepped in to force the state's hand. It organised the largest ever political petition on the Witwatersrand, and on 9 May 1912 handed over 51,925 signatures to parliament in a demand for government action on the 'black peril'. It was largely this pressure that gave rise to the subsequent commission of enquiry.[181]

Since some of these events were expressly designed to ensure continued interest in such offences, the public's temperature did not readily cool. In late June 1912, one 'John Jacobs' appeared in court charged with the rape of the unfortunate Mrs Harrison. After a protracted trial, Jacobs was eventually found not guilty and discharged.[182] Throughout the remainder of the year, however, there were continued reports of 'black peril' cases and it was only early in the following year, 1913, when such offences were eclipsed by more dramatic political events, that anything approaching 'normality' could be detected in public discussions about such events. Even then, however, the storm had not completely blown itself out. There was a brief, and less serious, resurgance of 'black peril' hysteria in late 1913, which soon gave way to the more demanding fear of impending war.[183] Such statistical foundations as there were to these waves of mass hysteria before the First World War are to be found in Table 2 below.

In re-surveying these periodic 'black peril' scares that occurred between 1890 and 1914 for their underlying causes then, one outstanding feature seems to

Table 2. Sexual assaults in the Transvaal 1901–12

Year	Rape	Attempted rape	Indecent assault	Total convic- tions	Number of charges
1901	0	0	3	3	3
1902	0	1	3	4	5
1903	1	1	2	4	4
1904	1	3	7	11	11
1905	1	4	7	12	16
1906	3	6	8	17	21
1907	3	5	11	19	26
1908	4	5	13	22	30
1909	3	5	5	13	25
1910	0	6	18	24	33
1911	3	12	22	37	46
1912	3	10	20	33	51

Data extracted from *Report of Commission on Assaults on Women 1913*, para. 28

emerge. It is clear that the majority of such attacks of public hysteria coincided with periods of stress or acute tension within the political economy of the Witwatersrand as a whole. This broadly observable trend, in itself not particularly helpful in enhancing our understanding, comes into sharper focus and assumes a more meaningful dimension when we examine the context of each of these 'black peril' waves more closely.

The least pronounced of these scares was that of 1893. Significantly enough, it came towards the end of a fairly lengthy period of economic uncertainty on the Rand but at a moment during which Johannesburg itself was still within the clutches of a marked recession. Indeed, on the very day that the *Standard and Diggers' News* printed its 'passions of the panther' editorial on 'houseboys', it ran a second leader in which it commented on the bad times, and noted how many working men had been forced to send their wives and children away to live at cheaper centres away from the Witwatersrand.[184]

What was perhaps still shadowy in 1893 became clearer during the next scare, which was in the aftermath of the Jameson Raid and the recession which that incursion had helped to precipitate. The Lightfoot rape which lay at the centre of the 1897 scare occurred not only in generally unsettled times, but in the immediate wake of manifestly dramatic events. In the six to eight weeks preceding the attack, the Rand had seen a unilateral reduction in the wages of black miners, the formation of a white mineworkers' union and a series of strikes by both European and African mineworkers.

The syndrome of recession–political uncertainty–industrial action, was also to be detected in the following 'black peril' scare between 1906 and 1908. Most of this wave of public hysteria was located in the midst of a serious economic depression, and at a time when the British reconstruction administration was handing over power to Botha's Het Volk government. More specifically still, it is noteworthy how the crest of public concern in May/June 1907 yet again coincided with a time when the white miners were out on strike.

All of these familiar ingredients, although in much less clearly crystallised form, were also to be found in the final outbreak of 'black peril' hysteria before the First World War. In 1911–2, through 1913 and into 1914 the economy gradually wound its way down into the pre-war recession. Again this period, which followed on Union and led up to the outbreak of the First World War was hardly characterised by its political stability – something that was more especially true of the Transvaal. Finally, the tail end of this 'black peril' scare yet again coincided with a period when Witwatersrand miners were out on strike.

This underlying 'black peril' syndrome was most important because of its direct and specific linkages with the household economies of the Witwatersrand. It meant that the major 'black peril' scare occurred at times when the incomes of white middle and working-class families were falling generally. This in turn meant that much of the hysteria was firmly rooted in periods when the wages of domestic servants were falling. But not only were the incomes of employing families generally falling, in the case of many working-class homes incomes actually dried up completely during the strikes of 1897, 1907 and 1913. In consequence, there was an inherently greater risk of the employers defaulting on wage payment due to domestic servants during these periods. In large part then, it is to these underlying structural reasons that we have to turn if we wish to understand many of the so-called 'black peril' cases.

In several cases these economic pressures manifested themselves openly in 'black peril' conflict between mistresses and 'houseboys', and for obvious reasons this was more especially so in working-class homes where these parties most frequently came into direct contact with each other. Although it in itself hardly qualified as a 'scare', it will be remembered that the Lightfoot case of 1897 was triggered off by a dispute about the 'kitchen boy's' wages. In other cases there is also ample evidence to suggest that the actual dismissal, or impending dismissal, of the 'houseboy', was an important contributing factor to the alleged assault. Under such circumstances, it would have been a convenient ploy for a mistress to suggest that she had been sexually assaulted. That white women were consciously capable of resorting to such cynical stratagems was confirmed by the 1913 commission which reported how, in a significant number of cases, 'black peril' charges had, and were being trumped up by employers in order to defraud their 'houseboys' of their wages.[185]

But if 'black peril' charges were sometimes consciously manipulated to achieve immediate economic objectives in working-class homes, then it also seems possible that they were more subtly, perhaps even unconsciously used to similar instrumental ends in middle-class homes. It was in these latter situations, where there was a multi-racial staff, that the large majority of sexual offences by 'houseboys' against white female domestic servants allegedly took place.

Given the generally more relaxed and familiar relationships that existed between servants, it is perfectly feasible that black men *did* in fact make more frequent and direct sexual approaches to their fellow female workers. During 'normal' times, when incomes were steady and jobs not at stake, such 'houseboy' advances were no doubt more or less resented, and considered to be one of the 'hazards' of the job.[186] In periods of recession, however, the wages of white domestics fell to what they considered to be 'kaffir' levels, thus further reducing the economic distance between groups that were already socially proximate. In addition, such recessionary periods constantly held out the danger of staff retrenchment, and often it was the white servant that was the first to go. Under these more antagonistic circumstances there were obvious benefits for the white servant if she could succeed in getting the 'houseboy' dismissed first – and a charge of 'black peril' was singularly well suited to this end. The 'houseboy's' dismissal eased pressure on the household's limited available funds for wages, and that – together with the gaining of the white family's sympathy through the use of a highly emotive charge – probably secured the European servant her job for some time to come. While it is impossible to prove such a hypothesis conclusively, further weight is lent to it by the fact that 'black peril' charges appear to be totally absent from those households marked by economic stability and security – the homes of the bourgeoisie.[187]

But, although such economic motives can be found to underlie most 'black peril' allegations, they certainly cannot be made to account directly for all such cases. It seems clear that in a significant minority of cases such allegations were used as rationalisations in order to avoid acute personal embarrassment or for other, more complex, psychological reasons. Again it would appear that the complainants in such cases could have been more or less conscious of their motivations. As we have already noted in passing, there were instances in which white women, for any one of a number of reasons, used 'black peril' allegations as a way of ending relationships with a 'houseboy' that had become unmanageable.[188] Yet other cases seem to hinge around either the vague, or explicitly sensational accusations of adolescent girls within the household – a group that was likely to be particularly sensitive to 'sexual' behaviour.[189] Many other instances simply derived from women of an extremely nervous disposition who became frightened, or who over-reacted to what would possibly have passed as a minor occurrence in more stable times.[190] But, when all this has been said about a minority of individual 'black peril' cases, it still remains that these complex human fears and anxieties chose to surface collectively under the very distinctive social and economic conditions outlined above. It was as if at certain times there were witches at loose in suburbia – black witches which a tense and neurotic white society sought to exorcise from its midst.

In part, it was the task of the 1913 commission on assaults to 'smell out' those witches, and this it attempted to do. In the manner of some traditional practitioner it sought to isolate the culprit – in this case the 'houseboy' – and then have him excluded from the community. The 'local segregation of natives in urban areas', the commission concluded in its report, 'is highly desirable'. This powerful proposal was designed to get the 'houseboy' out of the employer's back yard and into a highly regulated system of municipal locations. In addition, the commission also made other suggestions for improved police protection and social control which were designed to cope with the 'problem' of the black male domestic worker.[191]

In the end, however, the 'black peril' commission turned out to be more of an ideological fountain than a political stream capable of cutting new channels of control within urban society. It simply threw up existing ideas into new patterns which interested parties could then point to when seeking justification for behaviour that was ultimately based on economic and political self-interest.[192] The real erosion of the 'houseboy's' position on the Rand came not so much through the commission, but through the deeper and more powerful currents of proletarianisation at work in the countryside. Ultimately it was these latter processes which swept new and cheaper labour supplies into the cities, and which dislodged the 'houseboy' from back yard and domestic service sector alike.

For their part, African leaders appear to have been fully aware of the fact that the cry of 'black peril' and the commission which it provoked, could be used to achieve and justify more oppressive measures against blacks. Selby Msimang curtly dismissed the white catchword of the day as a 'political term', while Sol Plaatje drew attention to the fact that it was being used in part to provide ideological justification for the Native Land Act. R. V. Selope Thema and Lerothodi Ntyweyi were equally quick to point out that discussions about the 'black peril' could carry no weight in African circles until such time as they were broadened to include the 'white peril' – the problem of white men seducing black women.[193]

Much of this political in-fighting passed the 'houseboys' by since they were occupied with more pressing problems. During the worst 'black peril' scares, such as those of 1911–2, many of them stayed indoors for fear of being arrested under the pass laws. The 'houseboys'' most anxious moments of all, however, came after the Harrison rape in Turffontein. Then, in the face of the 'Kaffir Drives' led by the armed white vigilantes, many voted with their feet, fleeing the city for the comparative sanity of the countryside.[194]

But not all of the 'houseboys' were content simply to retreat or defend in the face of white society's various onslaughts. At least some of them must have stayed on to sing an old African work song:

> Be damn the whites, they call us Jim.
> Be damn the whites, they call us Jim.
> In spite of the fact that they despise us,
> some of their women love us,
> In spite of the fact that they despise us,
> some of their women love us.[195]

For many more, however, singing was not enough. At night, and over the week-ends they met and organised themselves into armed 'houseboy' gangs. Then, replete with new identities, they poured into the streets of suburbia singing, chanting and openly challenging the society that sought to oppress them. The 'houseboys' were no more. These were the men of the *Amalaita*.

The Amalaita

The origins of organised activity by black domestic servants on the Witwatersrand stretch back directly to the 1890s, and indirectly to the very year of Johannesburg's establishment. During the early 1890s, the most important black organisation within the city was a 'secret society' of criminals and robbers known as the *izigebengu* or Ninevites. This 'Zulu'-dominated gang was largely the product of a man who himself had been a 'houseboy' in Jeppe in 1886 and later at Turffontein – Jan Note.[196] While the thrust of later Ninevite activity was clearly of the orthodox criminal variety, it would appear that during the mid-1890s members of the gang were also willing to undertake 'work' in conjunction with, or on behalf of, their 'houseboy' brothers.

In June 1896 a country correspondent of the *Natal Witness* reported certain conversations which he had had with 'natives' who had worked in Johannesburg, 'either at the mines or among resident families'. He reported that the izigebengu had been formed by black men to protect their interests 'without recourse to a law court', since the latter procedure could only bring down 'punishment on Kaffirs'. The correspondent then proceeded to recount an example of Ninevite activity which he had been supplied with by his informants:

> When a man has a wrong to redress as, for instance when his master has 'done him' out of his wages, he makes his grievance known to the Izigebengu, some of the members of which are thereupon told off to knock the offending master on the head. These watch their opportunity, and in due course carry out their orders. Reports say that the favourite method is to knock at the door of the former master at night, and if he opens it himself, he is there and then 'settled'. Should someone else open the door, an excuse is made . . . and another occasion is awaited . . . '*Ba gwenza*', a man of some standing said, '*ngoba ngu muzi onge na 'mteto*' – They do it because it is a town without law.[197]

Examples of such assaults, as well as of burglaries involving 'houseboys' and the izigebengu can certainly be found for early Johannesburg.[198] From this it would seem that at least before 1899 the Ninevites performed more of a social banditry function than they have hitherto been given credit for, and that 'Zulu' 'houseboys' figured quite prominently in this movement.

In 1899, however, the outbreak of the South African War forced the izigebengu and the 'Zulu' 'houseboys' back to the towns and rural areas of Natal. Many of these men gained employment with the Imperial army, but a large number of the younger domestic servants sought work as 'houseboys' in the larger urban centres. By late 1900 these izigebengu or *izigelegele* – brigands, as they were sometimes also known – had started to regroup in the suburbs of Durban. In May 1901 the Superintendent of Police, R. C. Alexander, reported that it was becoming 'a nightly occurrence all over the borough for native lads and young men to parade the streets and roads to the annoyance of everyone', and that they made 'filthy remarks' at passers-by.[199]

These ex-Johannesburg elements soon became a conspicuous part of the Durban scene – a departure which contrasted sharply with the more secretive practices of the older parent gang. The new groups dressed in distinctive wide-bottomed trousers of many colours and paraded through the streets playing music that was 'generally a strange combination of complicated Dutch, English and Native' tunes. The instrument most favoured for this new and vital black music of the cities and the one invariably associated with the gangs, was the mouth-organ. Rival groups from within the city met and regularly challenged each other to organised fights. In addition, many of these gangs went in for organised robbery – usually, but not always, choosing fellow Africans as their victims. As a local newspaper correspondent pointed out, this meant that: 'A white employer might have a kitchen boy or a coachman to work for him during the day while the same individual might prove his assailant, under masque, at night'. It was also thought that it was these exploits which earned the gangs their name – *Olaita*.

The word *olaita*, suggested *Ipepa lo Hlanga* in 1903, presumably came:

> from the fact that when they 'hold up' anyone, they ask him to 'light' or *'kanyisa'* – a very familiar term much in use amongst native quack-doctors when asking for *'ugxa'* or retaining.fee which is usually paid by the patient before any medical treatment is commenced . . . . These native desperadoes . . . whenever they meet a person, they ask him to 'light' his way by putting his whole purse at their disposal . . . . If he succeeds in paying up he is said to have 'lighted' his way and is allowed to pass on unmolested.[200]

But while the derivation of the word may be in dispute, it is beyond doubt that the Amalaita gangs were already in existence in Durban between 1901 and 1904, and that they presented a challenge to authority – more particularly to the local black police whose endless demands for passes they vigorously resisted.

It comes as rather a surprise therefore to learn that the first Amalaita gangs to appear on the Witwatersrand after the South African War were entirely devoid of 'Zulu' members. On second thoughts, however, this is less puzzling than appears at first glance. 'Zulus' returning to Johannesburg in the immediate post-war period appear to have rejoined branches of the older Ninevite organisation rather than incur the displeasure of its well-established leadership by founding new rival gangs.[201] Thus, such elements of Amalaita culture as the 'Zulus' did bring to the Rand with them after 1901, were primarily used to re-fertilise the parent gang in its various forms. What other black groups within Johannesburg saw and imitated after the war then, was essentially the old izigebengu structure overlaid with the features of the new coastal culture.

One of the first such non-Zulu groups to experiment with Amalaita organisation appeared in the eastern suburbs of Johannesburg in 1906. On Sundays, groups of Sotho adolescents, said to be 'church-going boys', staged military-style parades through the streets of that part of the city. It was later claimed that these rather spectacular activities soon attracted the attention and additional support of members of other ethnic groups. Unlike the more respectable northerners, however, these later members, including a few 'Zulus', were considered to have been of a 'very low type'.[202]

But no sooner had this ethnically diverse nucleus established itself than it in turn was overrun by a massive new membership. It was these new devotees, the Pedi, and particularly those young men and 'piccanins' that the 1906–8 depression had brought to the cities, that made the Rand Amalaita gangs their very own. Thus it was at about this time that gang leaders ceased giving commands in English and changed to Sesotho and by 1908 a Johannesburg magistrate was forced to notice that: 'It was a strange thing that almost all the "Amalaita boys" came from Pietersburg.'[203] If the Amalaita had started as a hybrid outgrowth of Nguni society, then it was subsequently infused with elements of Northern Sotho culture – and Pedi youth culture in particular.[204]

These new gangs drew on earlier and older patterns, and then modified or extended them to meet their own requirements. The leader of the Amalaita was entitled *Morena* or 'prince', and he was assisted by his captains and sergeants who administered the oath of allegiance to the new recruits – the corporals. The various ranks were signified by means of coloured patches which the Amalaita wore on their distinctive 'knickerbocker' trousers. In addition to this, every member wore some or other form of special hat or helmet and a coloured knotted handkerchief around the neck which indicated the particular gang of which he was a member. Finally, each Amalaita wore the universal sign of the movement – the red cloth badge. Whistles, mouth-organs, piano accordians, sticks and battle axes forged from modified saddlers' knives rounded off the requirements of a fully equipped Amalaita gang which consisted of between 50 and 100 members.[205]

Not all members of the Amalaita, however, wore this uniform since there was a further feature to this new youth movement on the Witwatersrand which distinguished it from its coastal predecessor – the fact that it sometimes accommodated both sexes. While it is true that the 1906–8 depression brought the 'piccanins' to town, it was equally noteworthy for the fact that it had pushed the first significant numbers of black women into the Transvaal cities. Many of these young women, aged fifteen or more, were drawn to the Amalaita and at least some of the gangs – probably composed of age-related sets drawn from Pedi society – readily incorporated them. These women wore their own distinctive matching uniforms made up of a *kop doek* of a colour appropriate to the gang, low-necked blouses, a short 'accordion-pleated' skirt called Scot's *rokkies*, black stockings, and high-heeled shoes. Never really equal in number or status to their male counterparts in the movement, the Amalaita 'girls' nevertheless formed a significant part of the gangs based in the suburbs or in the more notorious urban locations such as that at the George Goch Mine.[206]

It was also during the depression, and to a lesser extent during the next five years, that the Amalaita gangs developed particularly rapidly and spread over the larger part of the Witwatersrand. In Johannesburg, the gangs were most strongly in evidence on the eastern and southern fringes of the city – in white working-class suburbs such as Kensington, Bezuidenhout Valley, Ophirton and Turffontein. On the West Rand they were equally conspicuous in the other working-class strongholds of Roodepoort and Krugersdorp.[207] These patterns of distribution and periods of greatest Amalaita growth are important because they point to the nature and function of the movement on the Rand.

First, they mean that the Amalaita were largely recruited from amongst the most poorly paid 'houseboys', something which, especially between 1906 and 1908, was also a strongly age-related factor. It also means, however, that the ranks of the Amalaita were frequently swollen by the many unemployed of the period, and there is certainly evidence to support this.[208] With these

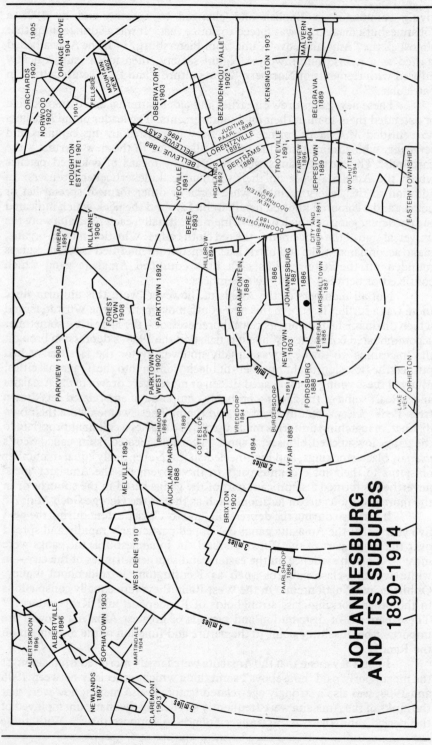

JOHANNESBURG AND ITS SUBURBS 1890–1914

features in mind it is easier to understand why it was that the Amalaita gangs were so consistently involved in petty crime. It also helps explain why the Amalaita were such noted pass forgers, and why in turn there was particularly marked conflict between them and the police.[209] As young men who had lost the battle against poverty in the countryside, the Amalaita were always likely to make a more determined stand against the passes and the police which sought to cleanse the cities of the black unemployed.

Secondly, these patterns mean that Amalaita activity was at its height during periods when 'houseboy' wages were falling most rapidly – times that were hardly characterised by good relations between employers and employees. In addition, it is noteworthy how the year of the greatest Amalaita activity of all, 1908, came in the wake of one of the more serious 'black peril' crises – that is in a period when black men in general, and 'houseboys' in particular were on the psychological retreat. Given this, the upsurge and form of Amalaita activity between September and December of 1908 is less than completely puzzling. In the working-class suburbs of Johannesburg they singled out their immediate employers and perceived oppressors, the white women, jostled them off the side-walks, insulted them, and generally subjected them to a barrage of intimidatory remarks.[210] Similarly, when they came across isolated and unarmed policemen on the beat they surrounded them and sang their war-cry – *Ingoma ya malaita*, 'Song of the Amalaita' – or, more pointedly still, *Wholo makhoa*, 'Down with the Whites'.[211]

From these activities it seems clearer as to what some of the major functions of the Amalaita movement on the Witwatersrand were between 1906 and 1914. In essence it was a movement of young black domestic servants and their unemployed peers born out of hard times in a new and harsh environment. It drew country cousins of both sexes together in unfamiliar urban surroundings by drawing on better-known forms of rural behaviour, and at least one police officer saw in this the original creative function of the Amalaita.[212] It was also, however, a movement which sought to give its members who laboured in alienated colonised isolation a sense of purpose and dignity – in short, it transformed 'Saucepan' into a 'Sergeant' in the army of the people. Hardly surprising then that some of the 'worst' Amalaita had the best references testifying to the fact that they were 'excellent houseboys'.[213] It was precisely *because* he was such a 'good', 'polite', and servile 'boy' during the day that 'Saucepan' had to become that virile, manly, aggressive 'Sergeant' of the night. It is in this latter light that the Amalaita should be seen as the 'houseboys'' liberation army fighting to reassert its decolonised manhood during one of the first major waves of South African proletarianisation. And, as in all struggles involving the deepest of human emotions, the individual battles could be bloody and brutal.

On the night of 12 April 1912 the Amalaita 'Chief' of Turffontein, a man named 'Roma' who hailed from the Pietersburg district, rounded up about a dozen male members of his gang and briefed them on their mission. From their meeting place the Amalaita proceeded to the back yards of several European households where they called out a further eight female membes of the gang – including the 'Chief's' appointed 'Queen', Jokaby. At this point each member of the Amalaita had his or her face blackened with soot, and they then marched off under the leadership of Roma to do the night's work.

The gang was brought to a halt outside the Turffontein home of a woman whose husband was away at work on the night shift – Mrs W. Harrison. On being asked by one of the female members of the gang why they had been brought there, Amalaita lieutenant Marseliba replied:

We have come to this house on the complaint of a person who complains that he is not being properly treated by the 'missus'.[214]

Then, the women and all but three of the Amalaita were posted to act as look-outs. Roma, John and Daniel then forced the bedroom window of the house, entered, and in full view of several members of the gang took turns to hold and rape Mrs Harrison. After equally pointed threats and warnings about the need for secrecy, the platoon of 'houseboys' disbanded.[215]

It was this single act of savagery that did more to unleash the hounds of racial hatred in the suburbs than any other incident before the First World War. It was the Harrison rape that directly gave rise to the white vigilantes, and indirectly to the Commission of Enquiry into Assaults on Women in the following year. Yet, for all that, there was not a word about Roma or Amalaita gangs when the commission issued its report in 1913. How could there be when the security of the domestic servants' organisation was so strong? It took two full years of police detection including the infiltration of the Amalaita and the cynical seduction of some of the female members of Roma's gang before the perpetrators of this crime became known in 1914. In the meantime the white vigilantes of the southern suburbs and the Amalaita frequently passed each other by – both parties, in their differing ways, scouring the streets for the witches of suburbia. It is one of modern South Africa's many tragedies that skin colour in the streets has always been easier to recognise than class in the kitchen.

Notes

1 J. Cock, *Maids and Madams: A Study in the Politics of Exploitation* (Johannesburg 1980). The two most accessible of the surveys are: E. Preston-Whyte, 'Race Attitudes and Behaviour: The Case of Domestic Employment in White South African Homes', *African Studies*, 35, 2, 1976, pp. 71–89, and M. G. Whisson and W. Weil, *Domestic Servants* (Johannesburg 1971).

2 D. Katzman, *Seven Days a Week* (New York 1978). Amongst other works relating to domestic service in England, the following were found to be useful: J. Burnett, *Useful Toil* (London 1974), L. Davidoff, *The Best Circles: Society, Etiquette and the Season* (London 1973), P. Horn, *The Rise and Fall of the Victorian Domestic Servant* (Dublin 1975), and of course, F. Thompson, *Lark Rise to Candleford* (London 1973).

3 J. Jean Hecht, *The Domestic Servant Class in Eighteenth-Century England* (London 1956), p. xi.

4 B. Doyle, *The Etiquette of Race Relations: A Study in Social Control* (New York 1971).

5 *Johannesburg Census* 1896, Order IV, p. 38.

6 *Ibid*. See also *The Star*, 9 January 1897, and *Longland's Johannesburg and District Directory 1899*, pp. 262–263.

7 *The Star*, 27 January 1897.
8 For an indication of a base line of wages see 'Hotel Employees' in the *Standard and Diggers' News*, 27 February 1897 (hereafter abbreviated to *S. & D.N.*). More generally, see the excellent article on 'The Cost of Living – The Servant Problem', in *The Star*, 27 January 1899.
9 *Ibid.*
10 *Ibid.*
11 In 1896 there were 553 black women in employment in domestic service in Johannesburg. See J. J. Fourie, 'Die Koms van die Bantoe na die Rand en hulle posisie aldaar, 1886–1899', M.A. thesis, Randse Afrikaanse Universiteit, December 1976, p. 141. See also, *S. & D.N.*, 27 March 1896. For coloured women in domestic service see, for example, *S. & D.N.*, 14 September 1898, or *The Star*, 27 January 1899.
12 L. Davidoff and R. Hawthorn, *A Day in the Life of a Victorian Domestic Servant* (London 1976), p. 81.
13 For the origin of registry offices see J. Jean Hecht, *The Domestic Servant Class*, p. 19. In Johannesburg, see *Census* 1896, Order IV, p. 38, and *Longland's Johannesburg and District Directory*, 1899.
14 See *S. & D.N.* of 9 January 1897, 27 February 1897 and 25 March 1897.
15 See, for example, the letter to the Editor of *The Press* (Pretoria) by the labour leader J. T. Bain, reproduced in *S. & D.N.*, 1 February 1894.
16 *S. & D.N.*, 16 August 1898.
17 *The Star*, 27 January 1899. See also *S. & D.N.*, 28 August 1897.
18 Thus Martharina van Wyk (see 16 above) deserted from service in order to become a waitress in Pretoria. Mrs C. M. Venn, a 'Rand Pioneer', brought a German maid with her from the coast in the 1880s. 'But "Matilda" was soon spirited away by a barkeeper with the offer of a handsome salary'. 'Lady Pioneers on the Rand', *South African Lady's Pictorial*, 2, 13, September 1911, p. 45. For an example of a housemaid-cum-prostitute in Johannesburg, see the case of Mathilde Young in Cape Archives Depot, Attorney General's papers, Vol A.G. 1026, German Consul General to Attorney General, 31 July 1903. This combination of servant and prostitute was not, of course, confined to mining towns. See also P. Horn, *The Victorian Servant*, pp. 133–135.
19 *The Star*, 27 January 1899 and Mrs Lionel Phillips, *Some South African Recollections* (London 1899), p. 116.
20 'Lady Pioneers on the Rand', *South African Lady's Pictorial*, 2, 20, April 1912, p. 18.
21 A. R. Colquhoun, *Dan to Beersheba* (London 1908), p. 268.
22 This pattern of wage trends has been established from widely scattered fragments of newspaper and other material throughout the period. Some of the more helpful items include: H. Lionel Tangye, *In New South Africa* (London 1896), p. 88; 'Native Wages Question' in the *Johannesburg Weekly Times*, 26 December 1896; 'Hotel Employees' in *S. & D.N.*, 27 February 1897; 'Houseboys' Wages' in *The Star*, 3 May 1897; and 'Kaffir Domestics' in the *S. & D.N.*, 25 October 1898.
23 *Ibid.*
24 *The Star*, 3 May 1897.
25 See, for example, *Johannesburg Weekly Times*, 26 December 1896; 'Nil Desperandum' to the Editor, *The Star*, 13 July 1898 and 'R.E.D.' to the Editor, *S. & D.N.*, 27 October 1898.
26 *The Star*, 3 May 1897.
27 *Command 1895, Further Correspondence relating to the Affairs of the Transvaal and Orange River Colonies* (H.M.S.O. London 1904), Appendix 1, p. 342.
28 Again, this information is culled from a wide variety of sources containing fragments of evidence. Amongst the more helpful were 'At the Street Corner' in *S.*

& *D.N.*, 23 October 1895 and 'Kaffir Domestics' in *S. & D.N.*, 25 October 1898.

29 S. Marks, *Reluctant Rebellion* (Oxford 1970), pp. 128–130.

30 For employers' complaints about the high turnover of labour see 'Kaffir Domestics' in *S. & D.N.*, 25 October 1898, and several letters addressed to the Editor of *The Star*, 6 December 1904.

31 See 'Moneyless Kitchen Boys', *S. & D.N.*, 9 October 1899.

32 For example, see *S. & D.N.*, 12 October 1899.

33 See 'Female Emigration' in *The Star*, 30 April 1902. Predictably enough this influx led to a shortage of cheap labour in domestic service in Cape Town in the post-war period. See 'The Servant Problem' in *The Star*, 5 December 1904.

34 *Report of the Small Holdings Commission (Transvaal) 1913* (U.G. 51–13), p. 12. For the expansion in the demand for domestic servants which this engendered in white working-class homes, see, for example, Madelaine Alston, *At Home on the Veld* (London 1906), p. 69.

35 For examples, see *The Star* of 15 March 1902, 17 April 1902 and 18 September 1902.

36 See 'Women's Immigration' in *The Star*, 28 April 1902, and 'The Needs of South Africa' in *The Star*, 30 April 1902. See also Transvaal Archives Depot (T.A.D.) Gov., Vol. 146, Enclosure No. 2 in Transvaal Despatch No. 102 of 12 February 1902 and T.A.D. Gov., Vol. 150, Acting Sec., Tvl. Immigration Office to Private Sec., H.E. The Governor, 11 May 1904.

37 See 'Women's Affairs' in *The Star*, 18 February 1905. Also, Lady Knightley of Fawsley, 'The Terms and Conditions of Domestic Service in England and South Africa', *Imperial Colonist*, Vol. IV, No. 48, December 1905, p. 139.

38 For example, see 'Householders' to Editor, *The Star*, 19 July 1902. More importantly, see 'Loafing Kafirs – The House Boy Question' in *The Star*, 16 August 1902.

39 For 'houseboy' wages between 1902 and 1906, see T.A.D. Gov., Vol. 150, Acting Sec., Tvl. Immigration Office to Private Sec. H.E. The Governor, 11 May 1904, p. 2, and *The Star*, 29 November 1904, 1 December 1904, and 21 December 1906. For estimates of the number of 'houseboys' in employment in Johannesburg in 1905–6, see W. H. Vivian, 'The Cost of Living in Johannesburg', *Imperial Colonist*, IV, 39, March 1905, p. 27, and Philip Hammond to Editor of *The Star*, 20 December 1906. In a talk on 'Natives as House Servants' in February 1909, A. R. Hands gave 30,000 as an 'official' estimate – see University of the Witwatersrand Archives, C.P.S.A., A.B. 767, Diocesan Board of Mission Minutes 1905–21. In an election speech in 1911, the Treasurer of the Union Government suggested that there were 150,000 'houseboys' employed in Johannesburg and Pretoria. See *The Star*, 18 October 1911. *The Report of the Commission Appointed to Enquire into Assaults on Women in 1913* (U.G. 34–13), however, estimated that there were about 90,000 domestic servants employed on the Rand, para. 42, p. 14.

40 T.A.D., S.N.A., File N.A. 1008/02, Major H.J.A. Eyre to all Camp Superintendents, Circular No. 46, 30 April 1902.

41 M. Streak, *Lord Milner's Immigration Policy for the Transvaal 1897–1905* (Rand Afrikaans University Publication, Series B1, January 1969), pp. 44–45. In 1903, it was estimated in an article in the *Quarterly Review* that there were 43,000 more men than women in the Transvaal – see report in *The Star*, 14 August 1903.

42 This paragraph is based on: 'Women's Immigration', *The Star*, 18 April 1902; 'S. African Emigration', *The Star*, 21 April 1902; 'Women's Immigration – South African Expansion Committee', *The Star*, 28 April 1902; and 'The Needs of South Africa', *The Star*, 30 April 1902. Also, *Transvaal Administration Reports for 1905*, Immigration Dept., pp. J1–J7.

43 *Ibid.*, and Streak, *Milner's Immigration Policy*, p. 44–45.

44 *Imperial Colonist*, II, 5 May 1903, p. 54. For this Irish preference see also *The Star*, 30 December 1913.

45 Table constructed from the following sources: T.A.D. Gov., Vol. 146, 'Extract from Report by the Secretary of the Transvaal Immigration Office', Johannesburg, dated 29 January 1904; T.A.D. Gov., Vol. 150, Acting Sec., Tvl. Immigration Office to Private Sec., H.E. The Governor, 11 May 1904, p. 1; and *Transvaal Administration Reports 1905*, Immigration Dept., p. J4.

46 Evidence of Mrs Marian Logan (S.A.C.S.) to *Transvaal Indigency Commission 1906–08* (T.G. 13–1908), para. 8571 and 8597, and *Imperial Colonist*, IX, No. 114, June 1911. See also 'Imported English Girls' in *The Star*, 14 January 1910.

47 See P. Horn, *The Rise and Fall of the Victorian Domestic Servant*, pp. 23–5, or L. Davidoff and R. Hawthorn, *Victorian Domestic Servant*, p. 77. This 'exporting' of domestic servants thus met with English resistance; see Mrs Evelyn Cecil, 'The Needs of South Africa', *The Star*, 30 April 1902. For distaste of domestic service in South Africa amongst white women, see Lady Knightley of Fawsley, 'The Terms and Conditions of Domestic Service in England and South Africa', p. 137, or *Transvaal Indigency Commission 1906–08*, para. 1743.

48 City of London Polytechnic, Fawcett Library, Mss Vol. 41, *South African Colonisation Society Reports 1903*, p. 52. See also *Imperial Colonist*, 11, 6 June 1903, p. 66.

49 Countess of Selborne, 'Demand for White Nurses in the Transvaal', *Imperial Colonist*, X, 127, July 1912, p. 119.

50 T.A.D. Gov., Vol. 150, Acting Sec. Tvl. Immigration Office to Private Sec., H.E. The Governor, 11 May 1904, p. 2, and *Transvaal Indigency Commission 1906–08*, para. 1948 and statement by Dr T. B. Gilchrist, p. 240. By W.W.I. secondary industry was already sufficiently advanced for authorities to despair of successfully 'importing' white female domestics; see *Report of the Commission appointed to Enquire into Assaults on Women 1913* (U.G. 39–13), para. 123.

51 Fawcett Library, Mss Vol. 41, *South African Colonisation Society Report 1904*, p. 80.

52 See, for example, 'Notes and Comments' in *The Star*, 14 December 1908 and Miss C. Nina Boyle on 'The White Servant Question' to Editor, *The Star*, 18 December 1908. It was estimated that within the first five years of the scheme, one in three immigrant domestics got married. See evidence of Mrs Marian Logan (S.A.C.S.) to *Transvaal Indigency Commission 1906–08*, paras 8576–8577. The problem, of course, pre-dated the S.A.C.S. On 27 January 1899, *The Star* noted of the white female domestic servant: 'If she is at all good looking she had no trouble in getting a husband, and as a rule one who can give her a much more exalted position than she could ever dream of in the Old Country.'

53 *The Star*, 18 October 1911. It was also for this reason that advertisements for white servants in the 'Situations Vacant' column were frequently forced to carry the reassuring phrase 'boy kept' if they wished to attract respondents. See examples in *The Star* of 29 August 1903, 7 December 1903 or 28 January 1904.

54 See 'J.D.'s' letter to 'Lady C.', reproduced in the *Imperial Colonist*, II, 6, June 1903, p. 69.

55 See H. M. Downes to Editor, *The Star*, 3 December 1904 and two other letters to the Editor in *The Star*, 6 December 1904. Clearest of all, however, is M. Wilkinson to Editor, *The Star*, 8 December 1904.

56 Edgar P. Rathbone to Editor, *The Star*, 23 November 1904. Also, 'Native Servant Question' by Rathbone in *The Star*, 8 December 1904.

57 Central events in the E.D.N.L.A. scheme are recorded in the following newspaper accounts: E. P. Rathbone to Editor, *The Star*, 23 November 1904, H. M. Downes to Editor, *The Star*, 3 December 1904, and E. P. Rathbone to Editor, *The Star*, 8 December 1904. See also editorials of *The Star* in the following issues: 5 December

1904, 7 December 1904, 9 December 1904 and 27 December 1904. The full prospectus of the E.D.N.L.A. was published in *The Star*, 8 December 1904.

58 For the decline of the scheme, see E. P. Rathbone to Editor, in *The Star* of 15 and 27 December 1904. Also, 'Native Domestic Servants' in *The Star*, 24 January 1905.

59 This paragraph is largely based on the following reports in *The Star*: 'White Domestic Servants', 5 March 1907; 'Unemployed Women', 14 March 1907; and 'Women's Problem – The Domestic Servant', 17 October 1907.

60 Nina Boyle, a noted middle-class activist, thus wrote to the Editor of *The Star* on 18 December 1908: 'My own scheme, that legislation should be introduced for the compulsory training and employment, as in workhouses at Home, of the children of those who habitually live on charity, seems to me a reasonable and satisfactory one, though neither original nor sensational. It would ensure a supply of white women servants, would spur many chronic idlers to effort, and would lift a large class from degradation into decency.' For an excellent analysis of how these ideas operated in contemporary England, see Gareth Stedman-Jones, *Outcast London* (Oxford 1971).

61 'Notes and Comments', *The Star*, 8 October 1908.

62 See, for example, *Transvaal Indigency Commission 1906–08*, paras. 1761–1768.

63 *The Star*, 10 March 1906. See also 'Transvaaler' to Editor, *The Star*, 7 April 1909.

64 For this pattern of reasoning, see the report on a public meeting entitled 'Black Peril' in *The Star*, 2 July 1908. For specific connections with domestic training, see M. C. Bruce (Sec. Native Girls' Industrial School Committee) to Editor, *The Star*, 10 December 1908, and later, *Report of the Commission appointed to Enquire into Assaults on Women 1913*, para. 138.

65 For information on the Church Industrial Schools, see University of the Witwatersrand Archives, C.P.S.A. A.B. 767, Diocesan Board of Mission Minutes 1905–21, 'Natives as House Servants', talk given by A. R. Hands at meeting held on 4 February 1909. This is supplemented by information drawn from the following items in *The Star*: M. C. Bruce to Editor, 2 July 1908; 'Kaffir Housemaids', 11 December 1908; 'Native Women – The New Movement', 17 March 1909; 'Native Women', 20 March 1909; and 'The Hull Tax', 18 October 1911.

66 *Ibid*. See also, however, D. Gaitskell, ' "Christian Compounds for Girls": Church Hostels for African Women in Johannesburg, 1907–1970', *Journal of Southern African Studies*, 6, 1, 1979, pp. 44–69. For a black perspective on the scheme and some of the other reasons that lay behind its failure, see the leading article on 'Domestic Service' in *Ilanga Lase Natal*, 24 November 1911.

67 'Do you think that the majority of young Native females who come to work get ruined by white men? Yes, very nearly all of them; very few escape – not more than ten per cent.' R. C. Alexander, Superintendent of Police, Durban, in evidence to *South African Native Affairs Commission 1903–05*, 111, para. 23,292, p. 647. In the Transvaal, see the opinions of William Letseleba (Chairman of Transvaal Native Union) as expressed in his correspondence with the Governor-General and reproduced in *The Star*, 24 October 1911. Most specific of all, however, is S. T. Plaatje on 'Miscegenation' (*Pretoria News*, 30 January 1911), reprinted in T. J. Couzens and B. Willan (eds.), *English in Africa* (Grahamstown), 3, 2, September 1976, p. 83. Plaatje's contention that white male employers – and especially those of British descent – seduced black servants while their wives were away from home for various reasons, was subsequently confirmed by a later enquiry. See, *Report of the Commission appointed to Enquire into Assaults on Women 1913*, para. 18.

68 For an account of some of these attitudes and activities, see, for example, 'Krugersdorp' in *The Star*, 16 November 1908.

69 For the full range of these attitudes, see the following items in *The Star*: M. C.

Bruce to the Editor, 10 December 1908.; 'Kaffir Housemaids', 11 December 1908; M. Wyndham to Editor, 18 December 1908; and several letters to the Editor, 13 February 1908.

70 See 'The Servant Problem' and 'Kaffir Housemaids', in *The Star* of 23 January 1908 and 11 December 1908.

71 See Carole Cooper, 'Land and Labour in the Transvaal c. 1900', M.A. African Studies, University of London, September 1974, pp. 27–34.

72 For general information on these firms, see T.A.D., S.N.A., Vol. 82, 371/08 and S.N.A. File No. 2259/08. Also, *The Star*, 24 November 1908.

73 See 'The Servant Problem', 'Piccanins for Domestic Service', and 'Piccanins – The Government Registry', all in *The Star*, 23 January 1908.

74 See T.A.D., S.N.A. File 2259/08, H. Payne, Inspector Native Affairs Dept., to Director, Govt. Native Labour Bureau, 27 August 1908. Also, *The Star*, 29 January 1908.

75 'Piccanins', *The Star*, 13 February 1908.

76 See, for example, 'Piccanin House Boys', in *The Star*, 3 February 1909.

77 This paragraph is based on the following items drawn from *The Star*: 'Native Domestic Labour', 2 November 1907; 'Piccanins', 23 January 1908; Henry Adler to Editor, 11 April 1908; 'Piccaninies', 24 November 1908; and the item 'House and Shop Natives' in the weekly 'Commercial Affairs' column of 17 July 1909.

78 Drawn from the following items in *The Star*: H. W. Hartland on 'The Wages Question' to Editor, 31 October 1907, and 'House and Shop Natives', 17 July 1909. See also, T.A.D., S.N.A., N.A. 4199/07, Mrs J. L. Robinson to Gen. Louis Botha, 9 December 1907.

79 Paragraph based on the following items from *The Star*: 'Common Sense' to Editor, 6 February 1911; 'Town and Reef', 8 August 1911; 'Disheartened' to Editor, 8 May 1912, and 'Black Peril', 30 December 1913. The wage rate is drawn from *Report of the Small Holdings Commission (Transvaal) 1913*.

80 *Ibid.*

81 See 'Labour Problem' and 'The Hull Tax' in *The Star* of 17 and 18 October 1911.

82 'Abolish the Houseboy?', *Rand Daily Mail*, 1 May 1912.

83 In 1911 it was estimated that it would cost £40 to fully equip a house with electric applicances of a wide range. See 'Household Electricity' and 'Commercial Affairs' in *The Star*, 15 July 1911. The prognosis for the electric cooker can be found in 'Solving the Servant Problem', *The Star*, 18 March 1912. Public consumption of electricity continued to lag, however, and in late 1912 the city council was forced to spend £140 in a campaign to advertise the benefits of domestic electricity, see *The Star*, 8 August 1912. For several decades, however, white South Africans were extremely slow to switch to electric appliances.

84 See Carole Cooper, 'Land and Labour in the Transvaal c. 1900', M.A. thesis, p. 27. See also, *Report of the Commission appointed to Enquire into Assaults on Women 1913*, para. 105 and paras 131–138.

85 See the following items in *The Star*: 'House and Shop Natives', 17 July 1909; 'Englishwoman' to the Editor, 4 February 1911; and 'The Cost of Living', 27 January 1914. Also *Report of the Economic Commission* (U.G. 12 of 1914), para. 24.

86 *Ibid.* In its editorial on 27 January 1914, *The Star* noted: 'Another item that differentiates Rand habits from English is the extent to which natives are employed as servants by the families of artisans ... We are strongly convinced that it is to local production, coupled to some extent with a *change in the habits of the working classes*, that we must look for a real and permanent cheapening in the cost of living.' (Author's emphasis.)

87 Paragraph based on the following items: 'Doings at Darnaway – High Life Below Stairs', *S. & D.N.*, 1 July 1896; 'White Servants' Contracts', *Rand Daily Mail*, 30 January 1903; 'Situations Vacant', *The Star*, 12 August 1903 and 8 March 1904;

'Master and Servant', *The Star*, 2 March 1906; and 'Epstein Divorce', in *The Star*, 21 and 24 August 1906.

88 *Ibid.* See also the following items in *The Star*: 'The Cost of Living', 27 January 1899; 'Immigration of British Women', 5 February 1903; and 'Town and Reef', 8 August 1911. For an example of an employment profile of a Rand housemaid, see Annie Walkman's evidence in the 'Epstein Divorce' in *The Star*, 21 August 1906.

89 Paragraph based on: 'Charge of Assault', *S. & D.N.*, 4 March 1899; 'White Servants' Contracts', *Rand Daily Mail*, 30 January 1903; 'Johannesburg Housekeepers', *The Star*, 20 October 1903; and 'Servants: How to Treat Them', *The Star*, 29 November 1912.

90 These two paras based on: 'Girls on the Rand', *Diamond Fields' Advertiser*, 31 March 1898 and T.A.D., Gov., Vol. 146, 'Extract from Report by the Sec. of the Tvl. Immigration Office', Johannesburg, 29 January 1904. In the same file see also 'Distress in South Africa', an extract from the *Edinburgh Evening News*, 16 December 1903. Also, 'Girls' Friendly Society', *The Star*, 25 November 1905. For background to the Society see Horn, *The Rise and Fall of the Victorian Servant*, pp. 106–7.

91 See the letters by 'J.H.C.' and 'J.D.' reproduced in the *Imperial Colonist*, II, 6, June 1903, pp. 68–9. Also, 'Housewife' and 'Observant' to Editor, *The Star*, on 18 October 1907 and 1 July 1910.

92 The problem of 'Jack being as good as his master (of a similar colour)', was an old one in the colonies. See, for example, the article on 'The Domestic Servant' in *S. & D.N.*, 8 May 1891. For a clear statement of the two possible patterns of relationships, see Sir Matthew Nathan's comments in the *Imperial Colonist*, VIII, 102, June 1910, p. 84. Also Mrs Phillip's, 'A Three Months' View of Women's Opportunities and Work in South Africa' in *Imperial Colonist*, IV, 37, January 1905, p. 6. For an example of employer resentment of servant transgression of class boundaries, see 'Housewife' to Editor, *The Star*, 18 October 1907.

93 See especially the superb letter from 'May Ann' to Editor, *The Star*, 21 October 1907. Also, 'Disheartened' to Editor, *The Star*, 8 May 1912.

94 See, for example, 'Women's Affairs – Mistresses and Maids', *The Star*, 18 February 1905.

95 For some accounts of accommodation of white female domestics see: 'Housing the Women', *The Star*, 13 March 1902; 'Immigration of British Women', *The Star*, 5 February 1903; 'Abolish the Houseboy?', *Rand Daily Mail*, 1 May 1912; 'Servants: How to Treat Them', *The Star*, 29 November 1912; *Report of the Commission appointed to Enquire into Assaults on Women 1913*, para. 98; and 'Did not Know it was a Crime', *Transvaal Leader*, 18 July 1914.

96 On the duties of a cook-general see: 'Women's Immigration 11' and 'Mistress' to Editor in *The Star* of 18 April 1902 and 22 October 1907. For an account of some of the problems of laundry work in the Johannesburg household see: 'The Cost of Living', *The Star*, 27 January 1899; 'Johannesburg Housekeepers', *The Star*, 20 October 1903; 'Women's Affairs', *The Star*, 18 February 1905; and 'A Question of Colour' in *Transvaal Leader*, 30 December 1908.

97 Paragraph based on: Lady Knightley of Fawsley, 'The Terms and Conditions of Domestic Service in England and South Africa' in *Imperial Colonist*, IV, 48, December 1905, p. 138; 'Housewife' to Editor, *The Star*, 18 October 1907; and 'A Mistress' to Editor, *The Star*, 22 October 1907.

98 'Servants: How to Treat Them', *The Star*, 29 November 1912. Loneliness was not, of course, simply a product of the South African situation – it was, in part, inherent to the job. See P. Horn, *The Rise and Fall of the Victorian Servant*, pp. 105–6.

99 See *Transvaal Administration Reports for 1905*, Immigration Dept., Annex. 8, p. J6. Also, 'J.C. to Lady C.', reproduced in *Imperial Colonist*, II, 6, June 1903, pp. 59–60.

100 See, for example, H. Lionel Tangye, *In New South Africa* (London 1896), p. 88, or Mr Diamond in *The Sun*, quoted in *S. & D.N.*, 5 December 1896.

101 For white nursemaids and their duties, see the following items drawn from *The Star*: 'The Cost of Living', 27 January 1899; 'Situations Vacant', 12 August 1903 and 28 January 1904. See also, *Imperial Colonist*, V, 60, December 1906, p. 175, and 'Letter to Lady Knox' in *ibid.*, X, 124, April 1912, pp. 70–1.

102 *The Star*, 23 January 1908.

103 Latter half of para. based on: 'Jan and the Nurse Girl', *The Star*, 13 October 1908; 'Transvaaler' to Editor, *The Star*, 7 April 1909; The Countess of Selborne, 'Demand for White Nurses in the Transvaal', *Imperial Colonist*, X, 127, July 1912, pp. 118–19. See also the letter from 'A Mother' reproduced in *Ilanga lase Natal*, 3 November 1911.

104 Philip Hammond to Editor, *The Star*, 11 March 1909. For earlier Hammond views on the same subject, see his letter to the Editor, *The Star*, 20 December 1906.

105 *Imperial Colonist*, VIII, 102, June 1910, p. 84.

106 'Housewife' to Editor, *The Star*, 2 November 1907. For further problems associated with the socialisation of children, see Mrs H. H. Oldroyd on the 'Servant Question' in *The Star*, 1 May 1912, and *Imperial Colonist*, X, 127, July 1912, pp. 118–19.

107 See the following: 'Nemesis' to Editor, *S. & D.N.*, 23 August 1897; H. Lionel Tangye, *In New South Africa* (London 1896), p. 88; and Adele le Bourgeois Chapin, *Their Trackless Ways* (London 1931), p. 115.

108 Editorial on 'The Kaffir Problem', *S. & D.N.*, 13 October 1897.

109 Para. based on: 'Housewife' to Editor, *The Star*, 9 February 1911; 'Mr Burton's Statement', *The Star*, 24 April 1912; and *Report of the Commission appointed to Enquire into Assaults on Women 1913*, para. 109.

110 For some accounts of the 'houseboy's' duties see, for example, Lady Knightley of Fawsley, 'The Terms and Conditions of Domestic Service in England and South Africa', p. 138 and Philip Hammond to Editor, *The Star*, 30 December 1906.

111 This para. based on: 'The "Laita" Gangs', *Ipepa lo Hlanga*, 20 November 1903; A. Scott to Editor, *The Star*, 24 February 1908; 'Tonight's Meeting', *The Star*, 7 February 1911; *Imperial Colonist*, IX, 19, November 1911, p. 26; and 'Vrededorp's Views', *Rand Daily Mail*, 1 May 1912.

112 This para. based on: 'Assault on a Woman', *The Star*, 22 February 1902; C. M. Dantu (Sec., Jhb. Branch A.P.O.) to Editor, *Transvaal Leader*, 7 February 1911; Sybil Cormack Smith, 'The Wrong Way to Manage Black Servants', *Imperial Colonist*, IX, 19, November 1911, p. 25; *Report of the Commission appointed to Enquire into Assaults on Women 1913*, paras 110 and 111; and S. T. Plaatje, 'The Mote and the Beam' (1921) *in* T. J. Couzens and B. Willan (eds.), *English in Africa*, *op. cit.*, pp. 90–1.

113 For further information on these relationships see below, section on 'The Black Peril'.

114 See 'Nemesis' to Editor, *S. & D.N.*, 23 August 1897; 'Kaffir Domestics', *S. & D.N.*, 28 October 1898; and 'An Englishwoman' to Editor, *The Star*, 5 March 1907.

115 See *S. & D.N.*, 11 September 1895; 'Another Suffering Householder' to Editor, *The Star*, 1 December 1904; and 'Fit Via Vi' to Editor, *The Star*, 9 May 1912.

116 See 'A Bibulous Burglar', *S. & D.N.*, 26 January 1899, 'Charge against a Native', *The Star*, 9 September 1905; Mrs J. Roberts to Editor, *The Star*, 1 September 1908; and 'Abolish the Houseboy?', *Rand Daily Mail*, 1 May 1912.

117 See especially the excellent descriptions in 'Loafing Kaffirs – The Houseboy Question' in *The Star*, 16 August 1902. Also, *Report on the Commission appointed to Enquire into Assaults on Women 1913*, para. 98 and para. 152.

118 See 'At the Street Corner', *S. & D.N.*, 23 October 1895; 'Housewife' to Editor,

The Star, 2 November 1907; T.A.D., S.N.A., N.A. 4199/07, Mrs J. L. Robinson to General Louis Botha, 9 December 1907; and J. J. Yates to Editor, *The Star*, 4 September 1912.

119 Para. based on the following items drawn from *The Star*: Mrs J. Roberts to the Editor, 1 September 1908; 'Native Women', 20 March 1909; and Bertie C. Simes to the Editor, 8 May 1912.

120 Para. based on: 'Another of the Same', *The Star*, 3 February 1906; J. Bold to Editor, *The Star*, 6 February 1906; M. C. Bruce to Editor, *The Star*, 10 December 1908; and Ambrose Pratt, *The Real South Africa* (London 1913), pp. 8, 17–18 and 53.

121 Fawcett Library, Mss Vol. 41, *South African Colonisation Society Reports 1903*, p. 25.

122 'Yesterday's Trials', *The Star*, 15 March 1902.

123 'Women's Immigration', *The Star*, 28 April 1902.

124 For the Anna Herrmann case, see: 'Notice', *The Star*, 16 January 1903; 'Master and Servant', *The Star*, 30 January 1903; and 'White Servants' Contracts', *Rand Daily Mail*, 30 January 1903.

125 'Master and Servant', *The Star*, 2 March 1906; and 'Master and Servant', *The Star*, 6 March 1906.

126 'Notes and Comments', *The Star*, 7 March 1906.

127 J. Bold to Editor, *The Star*, 6 February 1906. For earlier examples of complaints by employers, see 'A Grievance', *S. & D.N.*, 2 October 1896; and 'Sufferer', *S. & D.N.*, 21 January 1897.

128 See especially William Letseleba (Chairman, Tvl. Native Union) to Governor General, reprinted in *The Star*, 24 October 1911, and *Report of the Commission appointed to Enquire into Assaults on Women 1913*, para. 142.

129 *The Star*, 23 February 1914.

130 For examples, see the following items drawn from *The Star*: 'Attempted Murder at Boksburg', 4 April 1902; 'The Pass Law Case', 1 February 1906; and 'Mark it "Good" ', 17 January 1913.

131 Para. based on, amongst other fragments: 'Native Wages Question', *Johannesburg Weekly Times*, 26 December 1896, and 'X.Y.Z.' to Editor, *The Star*, 17 November 1908.

132 For black male servants see, for examples: 'He Helped Himself', *S. & D.N.*, 10 August 1895; 'Attack on Mr Webb', *S. & D.N.*, 16 August 1895; and especially 'Izigebengu', *The Star*, 16 June 1896; and 'Native Violence', *The Star*, 17 June 1896. The comments of the cook-general are taken from 'Women's Affairs – Mistresses and Maids', *The Star*, 18 February 1903.

133 *Report of the Commission appointed to Enquire into Assaults on Women 1913*, para. 120.

134 Even before the South African War some employers gave their white female servants revolvers to protect themselves against the 'black peril', see Mrs Lionel Phillips, *Some South African Recollections* (London 1899), p. 50. For other examples, see: 'Jan Note's Life and Introduction to Crime' in S.A. *Department of Justice Annual Report 1912*, pp. 238–40; 'Insolent Native', *The Star*, 10 January 1912; and 'Charge against a Native', *The Star*, 14 March 1912.

135 For examples of assaults on domestic servants see: 'The Kafir Problem', *S. & D.N.*, 13 October 1897; also the following items drawn from *The Star*: 'Police Court Cases', 7 February 1902; 'Guilty: Yet Not Guilty', 16 October 1907; 'Lashes Awarded', 13 March 1912; and 'Attacked his Employer', 22 December 1913.

136 Para. based on the following items drawn from *The Star*: Mrs J. Roberts to the Editor, 1 September 1908; 'Employers' Responsibilities', 18 November 1908; and 'Servants: How to Treat Them', 29 November 1912.

137 See, for example, 'Alleged Theft by a Servant', and 'Connoisseur in Smokes', in

The Star of 17 August 1902 and 9 November 1911.

138 'Fanakalo' is one of the many great unexplored areas in South African social history. However, for a few observations, see ' "Kitchen Kaffir" – The Esperanto of South Africa', by 'Umlungu', in *The Star*, 18 July 1913, and C. van Onselen, *Chibaro* (London 1976), p. 152.

139 For Victorian naming practices, see P. Horn, *The Victorian Servant*, p. 113. In *The Star* of 4 July 1912 a journalist gave a short list of some of the African 'names' that appeared on the court roll of the Criminal Sessions and commented: 'The names betray a high range of intellectuality on the part of the white people who christened the boys'.

140 For examples, see: 'Kafir Domestics', *S. & D.N.*, 25 October 1898; or 'One of the Suffering Householders' to Editor, *The Star*, 8 December 1904. For gifts of clothing to white servants, see, for example: 'Charge against a Lady's Maid', *The Star*, 18 July 1903.

141 This, and other points, are well made in M. G. Whisson and W. Weil, *Domestic Servants* (Johannesburg 1971), pp. 40–3.

142 See, for example, the great editorial battle between *The Star* and the *Standard and Diggers' News* in *S. & D.N.*, 'The Kafir Problem', 13 October 1897. For other examples of European resentment of blacks' dress see: 'Nil Desperandum' to Editor, *The Star*, 13 July 1898; 'Loafing Kafirs', *The Star*, 16 August 1902; T.A.D., S.N.A., N.A. 4199/07; Mrs J. L. Robinson to·Gen. Louis Botha, 9 December 1907; or 'As Others See Us' to Editor, *The Star*, 30 April 1912.

143 'Chatelaine' to Editor, *The Star*, 16 February 1911.

144 This para. based on: 'The Kafir Problem', *S. & D.N.*, 13 October 1897; 'The "Black Peril" ', *Transvaal Leader*, 22 September 1908; Charles O'Hara to Editor, *The Star*, 30 April 1912; and 'A Shop Window Evil', *Rand Daily Mail*, 7 January 1914.

145 Para. largely based on: 'The Kafir Problem', *S. & D.N.*, 13 October 1897; 'A Mother' to Editor, *The Star*, 1 November 1907; and T.A.D., S.N.A., N.A. 4199/07, Mrs J. L. Robinson to Gen. Louis Botha, 9 December 1907.

146 T.A.D., S.N.A., N.A. 4199/07, Mrs J. L. Robinson to Gen. Louis Botha, 9 December 1907. Remainder of the para. based on: 'The Kafir Problem', *S. & D.N.*, 13 October 1897; 'The Native Question', *The Star*, 23 January 1902; and Mrs J. Roberts to Editor, *The Star*, 1 September 1908.

147 'Women's Affairs – The Domestic Bogey', *The Star*, 17 February 1906. The remainder of the para. based on: 'Women's Immigration', *The Star*, 28 April 1902; 'Women's Problem – The Domestic Servant', *The Star*, 17 October 1907; 'Householder' to Editor, *The Star*, 24 October 1907; and 'To be Mistress of the House', *The Star*, 21 September 1910.

148 *The Imperial Colonist*, II, 5, May 1903, p. 54.

149 See: H. Lionel Tangye, *In New South Africa* (London 1896), p. 86; 'White Servants' Contracts', *Rand Daily Mail*, 30 January 1903; and 'Women's Affairs', *The Star*, 18 February 1905.

150 Para. based on: H. F. Hunt Phillips to Editor, *The Star*, 17 June 1896; 'A Grievance', *S. & D.N.*, 2 October 1896; 'The Pass Law Case', *The Star*, 1 February 1906; Mrs J. Roberts to Editor, *The Star*, 1 September 1908; and *Report of the Commission of Enquiry appointed to Enquire into Assaults on Women 1913*, para. 92. This problem of a suitable 'character' – and its solution – was not restricted to the Transvaal. See P. Horn, *The Victorian Servant*, p. 45.

151 For examples see: 'The Domestic Servant Question', *S. & D.N.*, 5 December 1896; 'Yesterday's Trials', *The Star*, 17 April 1902; 'Charge against a Lady's Maid', *The Star*, 18 July 1903; and 'Connoisseur in Smokes', *The Star*, 9 November 1911. Again, of course, this practice is not confined to servants in the colonial situation. See P. Horn, *The Victorian Servant*, pp. 138 and 146.

152 See, for example, 'He Helped Himself', *S. & D.N.*, 10 August 1895, or
    'Attempted Murder and Robbery', *The Star*, 4 April 1902. See also the final section
    of this essay on the Amalaita.
153 For complaints about black 'insolence' see: 'Pay the Boys by the Month',
    Johannesburg Weekly Times, 26 December 1896; 'The Kafir Problem', *S. & D.N.*,
    13 October 1897; 'Householders' to Editor, *The Star*, 19 July 1902; 'Loafing
    Kafirs', *The Star*, 16 August 1902; and 'A Mother' to Editor, *The Star*, 1
    November 1907. The evidence in note 156 below also pertains to this problem.
154 'The Rev. C. A. Lane and the Coloured People', *The Star*, 25 October 1904.
155 *Transvaal Leader*, 12 July 1906. On the Zululand disturbances, see S. Marks,
    Reluctant Rebellion (Oxford 1970).
156 For examples, see the following items drawn from *The Star*: 'Police Court Cases', 7
    February 1902; 'Time to Reflect', 25 November 1909; 'Trouble with Houseboy', 3
    April 1911; 'Mark it "Good" ', 17 January 1913; 'Struck a Woman', 25 August
    1913; and 'With a Table Knife', 2 December 1913.
157 'Native Crime', *The Star*, 27 December 1913.
158 For rural cases, see, for example, 'A Would-be Poisoner', in *The Star* of 22 October
    1904 and 9 December 1904. For Witwatersrand cases see the following items in
    The Star: 'Alleged Attempted Murder', 14 August 1903; 'Mistress and Servant', 23
    August 1907; 'Guilty: Yet Not Guilty', 16 October 1907; and 'House Boy in
    Trouble', 26 November 1907.
159 'Kafir Servants and Witch Doctors', *S. & D.N.*, 6 December 1898.
160 For some examples of this drawn from Natal see *South African Native Affairs
    Commission 1903–5*, III, paras 20,089, 20,174, 23,722, 24,630, 26,783, 29,944
    and 31,907.
161 As yet I have been unable to trace the original High Court proceedings of this case.
    All quotes from the movement here, and in subsequent paragraphs are taken from
    the following reports in *The Star*: 'Native Fanatics', 12 August 1909; 'The Taungs
    Incident', 13 August 1909; 'Ethiopianism', 14 August 1909, and 'The Bechuana
    Prophets', 9 November 1909.
162 See below, Chapter 4, 'The Regiment of the Hill', p. 175.
163 *Imperial Colonist*, VIII, No. 102, June 1910, p. 84.
164 See reports in the *S. & D.N.*, 12 October 1895, and 'Jim loved the White Girl', 14
    October 1895.
165 Waiter 'Joe', with the assistance of friend 'John', wrote as follows to an unmarried
    fellow waitress: 'Oh my dear friend, I am sore for you. I like your hand so dearly. I
    love you very much. I do not know what to do with you because I love you.' This
    letter was worth a fine of £3 or one month's imprisonment. See, 'Native Insolence',
    The Star, 22 August 1913. Predictably enough the 'tea-rooms' had their fair share
    of 'black peril' scares. See, for example, 'Native and White Girls', *The Star*, 23
    August 1911. (See also note 50 above and text.)
166 'A Peculiar Case', *S. & D.N.*, 19 July 1898.
167 'Colonist' to Editor, *The Star*, 8 February 1913.
168 See following items in *The Star*: 'Black and White', 23 August 1904; 'Black and
    White', 21 September 1904; and 'Under the Morality Law', 27 October 1904. See
    also reports in the *Pretoria News* of 24 August and 29 October 1904.
169 'White Woman and Native', *The Star*, 17 July 1914, and 'Did not know it was a
    Crime', *Transvaal Leader*, 18 July 1914.
170 *Report of the Commission appointed to Enquire into Assaults on Women 1913*, paras
    112–13 and 139. (Hereafter, *Commission on Assaults on Women 1913*.)
171 See, for example, 'A Shocking Scandal', in *S. & D.N.* of 22 and 23 June 1898.
172 See *Africa's Golden Harvests*, March 1911, p. 8; *Commission on Assaults on Women
    1913*, para. 112; and S. T. Plaatje, 'The Mote and the Beam', p. 90.
173 'Impudent Native', *The Star*, 27 August 1912. See also 'Woman's Screams', *The*

Star, 2 October 1912.

174 This para. based on: 'Selling Love Philtres', *The Star*, 24 September 1902; 'Pretended Love Medicine', *The Star*, 19 April 1907; *Africa's Golden Harvests*, April 1907, p. 14; 'The Black Peril', *Transvaal Leader*, 26 May 1908 and 27 May 1908; 'Story of Witchcraft', *The Star*, 29 May 1908; 'Love Potion Trick', *The Star*, 16 September 1908; 'A "Medicine" Case', *The Star*, 16 September 1908; 'The Black Peril', *Transvaal Leader*, 22 September 1908; and *Commission on Assaults on Women 1913*, paras 40 and 198.

175 *S. & D.N.*, 15 September 1893.

176 For the Lightfoot case and some of the subsequent developments, see the following items drawn from the *S. & D.N.*: 'Hanging too Lenient', 30 July 1897; 'Hanging too Merciful', 30 July 1897; 'Public Hanging', 20 August 1897; and 'Public Hanging', 23 August 1897.

177 For some examples reported in *The Star* see 'A Night Intruder', 27 May 1904; 'Charge against a Native', 9 September 1905; or 'Charge against a Kaffir', 19 September 1905.

178 For an extract of the A.W.O.T. petition, see T.A.D., S.N.A., N.A. 1924/07. For some of the background to this see the following items in *The Star*: 'Guild of Loyal Women', 19 April 1907; and 'The Black Peril', 7 June 1907.

179 For these events see, amongst other items in *The Star*, the following: 'The Black Peril', 3 February 1911; 'Views of the Workers', 4 February 1911; 'The Mass Meeting', 7 February 1911; 'Vigilance of the Police', 7 February 1911; and 'The Voice of the Rand', 8 February 1911.

180 For this and other events see: *The Star*, 13 April 1912; 'Black Peril', *The Star*, 20 April 1912; 'Black Peril', *Rand Daily Mail*, 20 April 1912; 'Black Peril', *The Star*, 23 April 1912; 'The Turffontein Drive', *Rand Daily Mail*, 24 April 1912; 'Mrs Harrison's Death', *The Star*, 13 June 1913; and 'Turffontein Outrage', *Transvaal Leader*, 3 May 1914.

181 See, amongst other items, the following drawn from the *Rand Daily Mail*: 'The Public and the "Black Peril" ', 26 April 1912; 'Only a Few Days More', 1 May 1912; 'Kaffir Drives', 2 May 1912; and 'The Petition and After', 9 May 1912. See also 'Something Achieved', *The Star*, 10 May 1912. On the role of the press during these crises, see *Commission on Assaults on Women 1913*, para. 26.

182 See the following items drawn from *The Star*: 'Black Peril', 2 May 1912; 'Turffontein Outrage', 13 January 1912; and 'Turffontein Case', 23 August 1912.

183 For the late 1913 scare, see, amongst others, the following items drawn from *The Star*: 'Father's Fight', 2 December 1913; 'Is "Mushla" Insulting?', 5 December 1913; 'Native at the Door', 22 December 1913; 'Attacked his Employer', 22 December 1913; and 'Native Crime', 27 December 1913.

184 'Hanging too Lenient', *S. & D.N.*, 30 July 1897.

185 *Ibid.* The remainder of this para. is based on material drawn from the following items in *The Star*: 'The Black Peril', 24 June 1907; 'The Black Peril', 27 April 1908; 'White Woman Attacked', 29 April 1908; and 'Is "Mushla" Insulting?', 5 December 1913. Also *Commission on Assaults on Women 1913*, para. 120. This interpretation, however, has been criticised for being 'functionalist' – see T. Keegan, 'Black Peril, Lapsed Whites and Moral Peril: A Study of Ideological Crisis in Early Twentieth Century South Africa', unpublished paper, January 1980. It remains unclear, however, how Keegan's remarks, which are based on a study of rural 'black peril' on Orange Free State *farms*, helps us to understand urban 'black peril' cases in white working-class Witwatersrand homes.

186 Thus white domestics did not always instantly draw the attention of their employers or the police to what they considered to be minor sexual advances. For examples of such approaches and delays in reporting them, see: 'The Social Pest', *S. & D.N.*, 27 August 1897; 'The Black Peril', *The Star*, 24 June 1907; 'Kitchen

Boy Again', *The Star*, 2 September 1907; and 'Alleged Assault', *The Star*, 1 October 1907.

187 For examples of 'black peril' cases involving white and black servants, see *ibid.*, and 'A Night Intruder', *The Star*, 27 May 1904; 'Charge against a Native', *The Star*, 9 September 1905; 'Black Peril Again', *Rand Daily Mail*, 15 September 1908; 'White Woman's Complaints', *The Star*, 2 November 1908; 'Servant Girl's Complaint', *The Star*, 18 May 1911; and 'Lashes Awarded', *The Star*, 13 March 1912.

188 See notes 164 and 166 above, and 'Assaulting a Lady', *The Star*, 8 May 1912. Also S. T. Plaatje, 'The Mote and the Beam', p. 91.

189 See 'Charge of Assault', *S. & D.N.*, 4 March 1899 and the following items drawn from *The Star*: 'Servant Girl's Complaint', 18 May 1911; 'Lashes for Native', 26 November 1912; 'House Broken Into', 16 October 1913; 'Early Morning Alarm', 13 July 1914; and 'Black Peril', 21 July 1914.

190 A good example of this is to be found in the letter from 'An Unprotected Daughter' to Editor, *The Star*, 30 November 1911. The author recounted her morning journey to work: 'I looked at the passing people, white and black, and my eyes caught those of a big black man, who in an instant gave me a wicked laugh, and, drawing his thick black lips into a round, thrust out the tip of his red tongue at me, and passed on!' One does not have to be a psychologist to guess at the sort of fear being expressed here. For a further example, see 'Houseboy Sentenced', *The Star*, 2 December 1913. More generally on this problem, see *Commission on Assaults on Women 1913*, para. 26.

191 *Commission on Assaults on Women 1913*, paras 140–161.

192 Such as the Randlords, for example. R. W. Schumacher consistently made use of the later 'Black Peril' scares to try to cope with another recession activity – the illicit selling of liquor to African workers. See, for example, 'The Curse of the Rand', *The Star*, 14 May 1912. Since the Chamber of Mines saw to it that it was well represented on the enquiry into the 'black peril', Schumacher's concern was also driven home in the report. See, *Commission on Assaults on Women 1913*, paras 51–9 and 80–5.

193 Para. based on: H. Selby Msimang to Editor, *Evening Chronicle*, 2 October 1913; S. T. Plaatje, 'The Mote and the Beam', p. 92. R. V. Selope-Thema to Editor, *Transvaal Leader*, 12 June 1912; and J. J. Lerothodi Ntyweyi's correspondence on 'Whites and Blacks', published in *The Star*, 15 September 1911.

194 See, for example, 'Vigilance of the Police', *The Star*, 7 February 1911, and 'The Turffontein Drive', *Rand Daily Mail*, 24 April 1912.

195 From T. Makiwane, 'African Work Songs' in L. Hughes (ed.), *An African Tragedy* (New York 1974), p. 99.

196 See below, Chapter 4, 'The Regiment of the Hills', p. 173.

197 'Izigebengu – A Native Secret Society', *The Star*, 16 June 1896.

198 See especially the attack on J. N. Webb reported in *S. & D.N.*, 16 August 1895, and 'Native Violence', *The Star*, 17 June 1896. For a remarkable court confession by an ex-'Houseboy' izigebenga, see 'Attempted Murder and Robbery', *The Star*, 4 April 1902.

199 'Native Labour', *Ipepa lo Hlanga*, 24 May 1901.

200 See 'The Laita Gangs or Native Brigands', *Ipepa lo Hlanga*, 20 November 1903, and 'Native Hooligans at Durban', *The Star*, 26 October 1904. Jeff Guy, however, has drawn my attention to Harriette Colenso's suggestion that the Amalaitas might have considered themselves to be 'all-right-ers'. See National Archives, Pietermaritzburg, Colenso Collection, Box 76, Harriette E. Colenso to Aunt Eliza (Bunyon), 13 September 1911. This suggestion is made all the more forceful by the fact that Harriette Colenso was basing her observation on her visit to Pretoria.

201 See below, Chapter 4, 'The Regiment of the Hills', p. 177–9.

202 'The Growth of the Amalaita', *Rand Daily Mail*, 11 September 1908.

203 *Ibid.*, and 'Passless Natives – A Strange Coincidence', *The Star*, 22 September 1908. See also, however, E. Mphahlele, *Down Second Avenue* (London 1959), pp. 100–1.

204 Many Amalaita activities such as fighting, music playing, petty thieving and age-solidarity are elements taught and experienced in Pedi initiation schools. In this sense it seems likely that the Amalaita gangs partly performed an important social function for Pedi youngsters who, during the recession, lost access to the traditional initiation schools. See G. M. Pitje, 'Traditional Systems of Male Education among Pedi and Cognate Tribes', *African Studies*, 9, 2 and 3, June and September 1950, especially pp. 71–2 and 107–9.

205 Para. based on: 'The Growth of the Amalaita', *Rand Daily Mail*, 11 September 1908; 'Native Hooligans', *The Star*, 29 September 1908; 'Amalaita at La Rochelle', *The Star*, 23 November 1908; and 'Rand Police Courts', *Rand Daily Mail*, 10 May 1914.

206 For female Amalaitas, see: 'The Growth of the Amalaita', *Rand Daily Mail*, 11 September 1908; 'Amalaita', *The Star*, 18 November 1908; 'Native Women', *The Star*, 20 March 1909; and 'Magistrate's Cases', *Transvaal Leader*, 6 May 1914. The idea that these were possibly age-related sets comes from comments made by the Rev. Porches. See 'Missionary Conference – Amalaita and Native Girls', *The Star*, 5 August 1910.

207 See 'Native Hooligans', *The Star*, 7 September 1908; 'Rand Police Courts', *Rand Daily Mail*, 10 September 1908; 'The Amalaita', *Rand Daily Mail*, 12 September 1908; 'A Native Gathering', *The Star*, 21 September 1908; 'Amalaita Gangs', *The Star*, 4 November 1908 and *The Star*, 16 November 1908.

208 See, for example, 'Amalaita Again', *The Star*, 15 July 1910.

209 See: 'The Growth of the Amalaita', *Rand Daily Mail*, 11 September 1908; 'Amalaita at La Rochelle', *Rand Daily Mail*, 23 November 1908; and R. V. Selope Thema to Editor, *Transvaal Leader*, 10 October 1913.

210 See especially: 'Native Hooligans', *The Star*, 7 September 1908; 'Native Hooligans', *Transvaal Leader*, 8 September 1908; and 'The Native Trouble', *The Star*, 16 November 1908.

211 'Growth of the Amalaita', *Rand Daily Mail*, 11 September 1908, and 'Amalaita at La Rochelle', *Rand Daily Mail*, 23 November 1908.

212 'Amalaita – Functions of the Society', *The Star*, 18 November 1908.

213 See, for example, 'The Amalaita', *The Star*, 23 April 1909, and evidence led in the Harrison case, note 215 below.

214 'Rand Police Courts – Amalaita Outrage', *Rand Daily Mail*, 16 May 1914, and 'Magistrate's Cases', *Transvaal Leader*, 10 May 1914.

215 The full story of the Harrison rape case can be pieced together from the following accounts: 'Turffontein Case', *The Star*, 4 May 1914; 'Magistrate's Cases', *Transvaal Leader*, 5 May 1914; 'Turffontein Case', *The Star*, 5 May 1914; 'Magistrate's Cases', *Transvaal Leader*, 6 May 1914; 'Turffontein Outrage: Native Detective's Evidence', *Transvaal Leader*, 8 May 1914; 'Magistrate's Cases', *Transvaal Leader*, 10 May 1914; 'Rand Police Courts – Amalaita Outrage', *Rand Daily Mail* 16 May 1914; and 'Turffontein Case', *Transvaal Leader*, 30 May 1914.

CHAPTER TWO

AmaWasha

The Zulu washermen's guild of the Witwatersrand, 1890–1914

Amongst others, there are two aspects to the development of capitalism in southern Africa which immediately capture the interest of the historian who seeks to understand the processes of social and economic transformation that accompany an industrial revolution. The first of these is the very rapidity with which this change was brought about in South Africa. From the time that diamonds were first discovered in the late 1860s, up to the First World War – by which time the foundations of a modern capitalist state had been firmly laid – a little more than half a century had elapsed. Compared with the several centuries that it took for a similar transformation to take place in Europe, these five decades constitute a very brief moment – albeit a crucially important one – in our history. The second is how, during this transition to a modern industrial state, most black South Africans were systematically denied access to alternative means of earning an independent livelihood until the point was reached where they had only their labour to sell, and so came to form the largest part of the working class in the new society.

The social historian of the Witwatersrand in general, and of Johannesburg in particular, is constantly reminded of these two themes as he conducts his research, if for no other reason than the fact that the city cannot be artificially divorced from these large-scale processes which helped first to transform the economic system as a whole, and then to shape its society. It is not enough, however, to see in the new urban areas the apotheosis of an all-conquering capitalism and to eulogise it accordingly – as do most of the popular historians who see in the story of Johannesburg only the technological triumph of the mining industry or the 'romance' of the Randlords. But neither is it enough for other historians to challenge this vision by presenting a simple picture of 'radical pessimism' which seeks only to highlight the one-way march of Africans or Afrikaners into the working class. The South African transition to capitalism – like that elsewhere – was fraught with contradictions and conflicts and its cities were thus capable of opening as well as closing economic avenues, and there certainly was always more than one route into or out of the working class. Perhaps one of the better illustrations of these complexities is afforded by a study of those black washermen who played a central part in the social and economic life of much of the Witwatersrand between 1890 and 1914 – the *AmaWasha* or Zulu washermen's guild.

For most of the period between 1890 and 1906 the Zulu washermen's guild of the Witwatersrand, not unlike its medieval European equivalents, constituted 'an industrial corporation enjoying the monopoly of practising a particular profession, in accordance with regulations sanctioned by public authority'.[1] This recognition of the AmaWasha, which entailed an exemption from the provisions of the Masters and Servants' Law, served to place this group of self-employed businessmen at the forefront of privileged blacks in an industrialising state which usually sought to confine African economic activity to wage labour in the employ of whites. In addition to being freed from the pass system, members of the guild were also exempted from a local by-law which prevented blacks from carrying weapons, and were further entitled to wear the distinctive turban and uniform of their trade. Finally, in yet another uncharacteristic concession, the authorities allowed the AmaWasha to brew as much beer as they required for their own consumption.[2]

The Zulu washermen's guild, again like the earlier European craft guilds, both restricted entry into its ranks and determined the prices charged for its services – powers which gave its members rather distinctive opportunities to accumulate capital. But, despite the fact that many of the guild's members did manage to make considerable cash savings, none of them chose to convert their businesses to employ the mechanised processing techniques of the modern laundryman. Looking back to the countryside from where they had come, rather than ahead to the growing urban areas into which they had temporarily been pushed, the washermen chose to invest their savings in land and cattle rather than in plant and equipment. In a period otherwise characterised by growing African proletarianisation, however, even this form of re-investment was enough to ensure the washermen a significant measure of economic protection and in parts of rural Natal the AmaWasha came to constitute a conspicuously successful stratum in black society. As such, the washermen and their children largely avoided the direct mass march into the working class of the new South Africa which so many of their peers were forced to undertake.

The rise of the washermen's guild, 1890–1896

In many societies, but possibly most clearly of all on the Asian subcontinent, there are close links between notions of purity and pollution on the one hand, and that of occupation or profession on the other. Amongst the Hindus of India these perceptions are vividly reflected in the caste structure of society which – amidst countless other examples – ordains a special place for those washermen who undertake to clean the soiled linen of other members of the community.[3] When the first large-scale movement of Indians from the subcontinent to the east coast of southern Africa took place from 1860 onwards, members of that lowly washermen's caste, the *Dhobis*, were amongst the emigrants.

It would appear that Dhobis who had emigrated to Natal independently as so-called 'passenger Indians', or who had managed to buy their way out of indentured labour on the sugar plantations, turned to their traditional profession at some stage during the early 1870s. Present-day African informants claim that it was at about this time that Zulu speakers first noticed the turbanned Dhobis undertaking the commercial washing of clothes in the Umgeni river. The same informants claim that the Zulus soon noted that there were insufficient Dhobis to meet the needs of all the white inhabitants of Durban, and that blacks therefore quickly adopted the turban and entered the business for themselves.[4] What is known with greater certainty, however, is that by 1878 many blacks in Durban were already undertaking the commercial washing of clothing since the Togt Law of that year sought to peg their earnings at two shillings and sixpence per day.[5] Furthermore, it is clear that from the late 1880s onwards the Durban Corporation regularly issued 'washermen's permits' to blacks.[6] Thus, by the last quarter of the nineteenth century many Africans in Natal and Zululand were already aware of the Dhobis and, more importantly, of the income that could be generated through the washing of clothes in the urban areas.

This knowledge of new opportunities to earn cash in the cities came at an important time for Africans since it coincided with a period of accelerated proletarianisation in Zululand and the Natal interior. In many areas, but perhaps more particularly within the triangular region situated between Dundee, Ladysmith and Greytown, the extension of white stock-farming activities, dwindling access to land, a series of cattle diseases and increased taxation combined to force blacks to sell their labour in growing numbers during this period.[7] Up to the mid-1880s, the sluggish growth and modest size of the urban areas that were most accessible to Africans drawn from within the region must have seriously limited the possibilities for would-be washermen. Once gold was discovered in 1886, however, and the rapid and sustained development of the Witwatersrand followed, an exciting new opportunity presented itself to these Africans.

From 1890 onwards Kanyile, Vilakazi, Sithole, Mchunu and Buthelezi clansmen from within this Natal triangle started to peel off the land, and to undertake the long march to the Witwatersrand in order to become washermen. Some of these middle-aged tribesmen, who were accompanied by their younger sons, were drawn from the Umsinga district where a system of communal land tenure pertained. Many others however, amongst them the Mchunus and Buthelezis who appear to have dominated the ranks of the AmaWasha, came from the families of labour tenants located on white farms in the Weenen district.[8] Once on the Witwatersrand itself, these tribesmen were joined by a smaller number of Hindu Dhobis who were also fleeing a political and economic climate that was becoming increasingly hostile to Asians during the early 1890s.

It was not only the demand generated by a mushrooming white population along the line of the Reef, however, that made Johannesburg an obvious target for Dhobis and AmaWasha alike; there were qualitative as well as quantitative features to the new market which made the town uniquely well suited to the dramatic growth of a washermen's corps.[9] First, as an inland town without the advantage of being sited on a large river, Johannesburg was without any major system of natural drainage which would allow for the ready removal of effluent. For reasons of public health, therefore, the domestic washing of clothing and the tipping of slops into the streets was prohibited early on. Indeed, it was only some twenty years after the town was started, in 1906, that the first professionally engineered extensive drainage system came into operation. This in turn meant that for many years the legal washing of clothing was restricted to those streams on the outskirts of the mining town –

an inconvenient, tedious and time-consuming practice.[10] Secondly, until some time after the South African War, the bulk of the town's white population was composed of male migrant workers of varying degrees of permanence. These miners, single or separated from their families in Cornwall and elsewhere, were thus without recourse to that female labour which normally undertook the washing and ironing of their clothes.[11]

The economic space created by these distinctly favourable conditions was rapidly filled by the incoming tide of Zulu washermen, and by 1890 there were already a couple of hundred AmaWasha at work in the Braamfontein spruit to the north of the mining camp. By October 1893, when an outbreak of smallpox first occasioned the licensing of the washermen and a slight shifting of their sites, their numbers had risen to over seven hundred. The elapse of two more years saw the growth of the guild outstrip the capacity of the spruit, and by 1895 the AmaWasha had extended their operations to four major locations spread around the town. The vast majority of the washermen continued to cluster to the north of the town where the Braamfontein Estate (Sans Souci), Lady Dunbar, Landau and Eastwood sites converged to form what was, in effect, a single Braamfontein–Auckland Park complex. East of the town there was a smaller site at Elandsfontein, while two still smaller sites at Booysens and Concordia served the southern suburbs. In October 1896 an all-time record number of over 1,200 washermen located at eight or more sites paid the shilling licence fee that was necessary to register with the town's health authorities each month.[12]

While the immigrant miners of Johannesburg watched this dramatic increase in the numbers of washermen with a feeling approaching resignation – since there was no real alternative to the service provided by the guild – other Europeans unreservedly welcomed the growth of the new black industry on

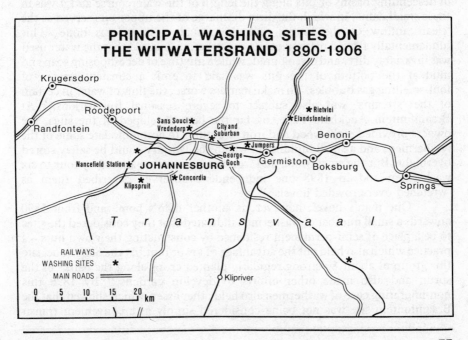

PRINCIPAL WASHING SITES ON
THE WITWATERSRAND 1890-1906

Krugersdorp
Roodepoort
Randfontein
Sans Souci
Vrededorp
City and Suburban
Rietvlei
Elandsfontein
Benoni
Jumpers
George
Goch
Germiston
Boksburg
Nancefield Station
JOHANNESBURG
Concordia
Klipspruit
Springs

Transvaal

RAILWAYS
WASHING SITES ★
MAIN ROADS

0 5 10 15 20 km

Klipriver

the Rand. Throughout the 1890s landowners fortunate enough to have streams on their property found that their assets appreciated significantly more rapidly than those of their neighbours. Instead of waiting patiently for the speculative profits that could be realised by the sale of land to the fast encroaching town, these owners found that they could also look forward to the handsome cash income that could be reaped from rent paid by the washermen during the interim. Louw Geldenhuis, for example, a farm owner and local representative in the *Volksraad* let a small portion of the stream on his property to Lady Drummond Dunbar – the wife of a local health official – at £100 per annum. The formidable Lady Dunbar, however, recovered more than three times that amount through sub-letting the property to the Zulu washermen. More substantial still was the £350 a year which the Concordia Mining Company obtained from the rental of its property to black washermen during the mid-1890s. Throughout the decade before the South African War, however, it was the coffers of the Braamfontein Estate Company which benefitted most from the new industry. By 1895 that Company could afford to pay for the services of a full-time manager, as well as for the upkeep of all the plantations on its estate from the £2400 which it received in rent from the AmaWasha.[13] In return for these sizeable sums in rent, the property owners provided the washermen with access to the basic facilities which the AmaWasha required to follow their profession. Each washerman paid two shillings and sixpence per week for the right to use the stream, and a further five shillings a week for the privilege of living in a hut on the property.[14] While on the surface of things this monthly rental of approximately thirty shillings from each washerman perhaps did not appear unreasonable, in practice the 'facilities' often turned out to be less than satisfactory.

At each site where laundry was undertaken, the AmaWasha cut a series of descending basins or pits along the length of the watercourse and it was in these small dams, in which the dirty discharge of the upper pits served as the 'clean' inflow of the lower, that the actual washing was done. This fundamentally flawed method of site construction ensured that the water used was invariably dirty and discoloured, while a mixture of decomposing soap and mud at the bottom of the pits was said to emit a constant stream of foul-smelling gas bubbles. To make matters worse, the flow of water in certain of the 'streams' was also subject to severe seasonal fluctuations.[15] At Braamfontein–Auckland Park, by far the best developed of the sites, the owners provided eight wood and iron structures to accommodate some of the washermen, and a small building in which the laundry could be safely stored overnight. But the small wood and iron huts were often shared by four to six washermen and in 1898 one independent observer described them as 'wretched over-crowded hovels'.[16]

One man's hovel, however, is another man's home and from 1890 onwards a small number of washermen indicated that they considered the sites to be a place of semi-permanent residence by constructing their own huts – a practice which also held out the advantage of lower rent. At the Sans Souci site this group of about 80-strong regularly planted crops along the banks of the spruit and also made other efforts to develop gardens.[17] By 1896 this non-migrating core of washermen also held other assets which showed that the Braamfontein site was not being considered simply as a convenient transit camp on a rural–urban–rural journey. In addition to scores of dogs, and small numbers of pigs and cattle, the community around Sans Souci also laid claim to fourteen horses and four carts. Perhaps even more significantly, the same census showed that besides the 546 Zulu washermen and fourteen Dhobis, there were also four Indian females and 64 black women resident on the site in 1896.[18] Thus, by the mid-1890s, some of the washing sites were already in the process of transforming themselves into the more familiar type of black 'location' communities to be found elsewhere in and around Johannesburg.

But even this broadening social base could not detract from the fact that in essence these remained AmaWasha communities, and this in turn meant that much of the social and economic life on the sites was pulsed and regulated by Nguni custom. What makes the AmaWasha of particular interest in this respect, however, is the fascinating manner in which elements of the older Zulu social structure were incorporated into the new urban business community of the washermen's guild. At each site, it was said, an induna of 'high rank' and 'comparative wealth' was in firm control of a corps of washermen, and it was he who organised the watch to ensure that the clothes lying around to dry were not stolen from the site. More importantly, it was the induna who saw to the 'recruiting of all his own men' and who had the power to fill 'all vacancies'.[19] As the guild grew and the number of places at the most favoured sites declined during the mid-nineties, so the role of induna must have assumed increasing importance. Without an induna who was willing to act as broker with the site-owner and the municipal authorities, the would-be washerman had little prospect of success. Thus it was after a typical four-month spell of work at the sites in 1895/6 that George Buthelezi, with his induna's prior approval, arranged for his kinsman, Khona Mchunu, to take over from him for a while and 'keep his place warm' until he returned.[20]

Since such alternates or replacements were frequently related, often of a similar age and usually drawn from the same rural areas, it is possible that vestiges of the Zulu regimental system were woven into the fabric of the washermen's guild. An observant journalist noted that when the indunas of the various washing sites marched their men into town once a month in order to get their municipal licences renewed, they kept 'perfect time' and proudly sang the songs of their old regiments.[21] It was at these same monthly gatherings on the Market square that the AmaWasha from all the sites around Johannesburg met to discuss their collective business, and to pay their respects to the leader of the guild, the formidable Kwaaiman.[22] From 1890 to 1895, Kwaaiman and the senior indunas presided over an expanding AmaWasha empire which, with the possible exception of the inconvenience caused by the smallpox outbreak in 1893 and the more regular licensing procedure which followed this event, experienced few major upheavals. Much of this changed, however, when the summer rains failed to materialise in 1895 and from then onwards the washermen had growing cause for concern.

While the pits at the crowded washing sites were always somewhat contaminated, their condition became truly disgusting during a drought, and by late October 1895 the local health inspectors had ordered a temporary closure of the main Braamfontein–Auckland Park sites until such time as the pits had been thoroughly cleaned. As drastic was the recommendation that the number of washermen at the Concordia, Booysens and Elandsfontein sites be reduced by half, and that no further licences whatsoever be issued for the two latter sites until the water levels there had improved considerably.[23] This unsatisfactory position, which threatened both the public health and the income of about 150 washermen, persisted throughout the dry summer of 1895. When autumn came, in March 1896, the Johannesburg Sanitary Board saw the need to plan for a longer-term and more radical solution to the problem of the washing sites and duly appointed a sub-committee to examine the question. Once the committee was appointed there was immediate speculation that the washermen would be permanently removed from the town outskirts to a more distant site with a more reliable supply of water.[24] But while such talk might have dampened the spirits of the AmaWasha it proved to be much less disconcerting news to at least two other parties – capitalists with an interest in establishing steam laundries, and land speculators with an alternative site to offer the Sanitary Board.

In fact, the first steam laundry in Johannesburg appears to have been founded before the drought and washing crisis of 1895/6. In the summer of 1894, one August Fossati opened a steam laundry on the banks of the Fordsburg spruit – a venture which operated with seemingly indifferent success for a year or two.[25] It was in late October 1895, however, that an American named William B. Hall made the first really serious attempt at running such an industry along modern lines when he floated the Crystal Steam Laundry Company. Hall's scheme, which made provision for the importation of some of the best available plant and equipment from the United States, soon captured the enthusiastic support of several of the town's leading mining and other capitalists. Amongst some of the more prominent shareholders in the 'American Laundry', as it was popularly known, were Otto Beit, Hennan Jennings, Otto Lenz, F. O. Nelson, G. Reunert, E. M. Sheppard, and G. E. Webber.[26] Eleven months later – in September 1896 – the Crystal Steam Laundry was in operation next to Lady Dunbar's leasehold property on the Richmond Estate: that is, at the very heart of the territory that had previously been exclusively occupied by the washermen's guild.

But, as the Zulu washermen discovered, bad news seldom travels unaccompanied and no sooner was the idea of the 'American Laundry' mooted than prominent members of the local French and Italian communities proposed the establishment of a rival 'French Laundry'. It is likely that the promoters of this latter scheme drew on the advice of Oreste Nannucci – the managing director of the largest laundry in Cape Town, who also had business interests in Johannesburg[27] – as well as that of the less successful August Fossati. Be that as it may, in June 1896 the promoters who had well-developed financial and commercial interests in the young mining town floated the Auckland Park Steam Laundry Company with a registered capital of £12,500. Amongst the more prominent members of this company were Georges Aubert (French Consul in Johannesburg), W. E. Desplaud, Henri Duval (of the *Banque Francaise de l'Afrique du Sud*), Fernand Pagny, and M. A. Zoccola (Managing Director of the Grand National Hotel).[28] Yet again this laundry was sited on the Richmond Estate during the latter part of 1896, and this issued the AmaWasha with their second direct challenge.

The flurry of financial activity in the mid-1890s, however, was not confined to those associated with the two new steam laundries. Well before it was made officially known that there was to be a search for a single consolidated site for all the washermen some of those in public office, and others with access to privileged information, sought to benefit from the situation. Some time before March 1896 the mining magnate George Goch, assisted by two members of the Sanitary Board – Edward Hancock and H. G. Filmer – sought to ensure that the washermen's guild would eventually be moved to one of the smaller sites which he owned on the eastern outskirts of the town. Predictably, this manoeuvre soon attracted hostile comment and failed, not least of all because it lacked subtlety. Edward Hancock, besides being the Chairman of the Sanitary Board at the time, was also George Goch's brother-in-law, while the other member – Henry Filmer – was the mine owner's attorney.[29] Likewise, it was also at some stage before the more public discussion of March 1896 that representatives from the Concordia Mining Company sought to persuade certain members of the Sanitary Board that their site was most suited to the needs of the AmaWasha. Again, some of Johannesburg's less charitable observers would not have failed to have noticed that Edward Hancock was a leading shareholder in the Concordia Mining Company.[30]

When tenders for the new washing site were eventually submitted to a full meeting of the Sanitary Board in April 1896, however, it was three other proposals that were considered. Of these, only one, Mr Dell's offer of a site to accommodate 1,500 washermen at the farm 'Witbank' on the Klip river, was thought of as a serious proposition; but even then there were serious obstacles to overcome before this proposal could be accepted. Not only was the suggested rental for the new site excessive, but the farm itself was a full two and a half hour rail journey from Johannesburg. This time out of more public-spirited motives, Edward Hancock delayed proceedings, bargained for better terms, and in August 1896 the Sanitary Board eventually approved a modified offer from Dell.[31]

All of these developments – the advent of the steam laundries and the proposed removal of the guild members to Witbank – deeply distressed the AmaWasha. On 9 September 1896, while the Dell offer was still awaiting final approval in Pretoria, Kwaaiman took the initiative and informed the Sanitary Board that he and his colleagues strongly objected to any site that was too distant from the town. The Board 'noted' but otherwise ignored this protest, and then proceeded to put great pressure on the Zulu washermen to accept the inevitability of the move to Klip river. Four weeks later the Sanitary Board's health officers refused to issue the washermen with licences that would allow them to operate at the established Johannesburg sites during November. For obvious reasons this action further fuelled AmaWasha discontent, and many of the washermen were heard to state openly that they would abandon their profession rather than undertake the move to Witbank.[32]

On 8 November 1896 the members of the guild held a mass meeting on the Market square, and once again instructed Kwaaiman to put their objections to the authorities – this time to A. H. Smithers, the Sanitary Board's 'Inspector of Natives'. This meeting proved to be no more succesful than the earlier one. Smithers curtly informed the leader of the guild that once his members' current licences had expired, all the washermen would wash at the Klip river site, or not at all. The news of the ultimatum from the authorities immediately raised a deep and serious division within the ranks of the AmaWasha. Within three days of the meeting, however, a small contingent of washermen made the first rail journey to Witbank. The Inspector of Natives, misreading the extent of the rift within the guild, took this as a sign that the majority of the washermen would soon follow and make their way to the Klip river site without further protest.[33]

Between 30 November and 2 December several hundred AmaWasha left their old and familiar workplaces, informing the site owners that they no longer wished to be involved in the washing business. Of this large number a few succeeded in obtaining positions as domestic servants, but the vast majority proceeded directly to their homes in the rural areas of Natal.[34] Within twelve hours white Johannesburg lost the services of nearly forty per cent of the black washermen's corps that usually met its laundry needs. The extent of that loss is reflected in Table 3.[35]

Table 3. Number of washing licences issued monthly by the Johannesburg Sanitary Board/Town

	1893	1894	1895	1896	1897	1898	1900	1904
Jan		605			500	521		
Feb		556			513	388		
Mar		507			569	458	66	
Apr		654		845				
May				923		546		
June				939		316		429
July				1036				
Aug		683		1043		233		
Sep		524					120	220
Oct	729	591		1222				
Nov	635			892		650		
Dec	556	511	821	498		535		

The swift exodus of such a large part of the washermen's guild soon frustrated many of the town's white residents who now turned to the remaining Zulu laundrymen for help. From 2 December, however, and for a full week thereafter, the overwhelming majority of the remaining AmaWasha stayed on at their old central site but went on 'strike', and refused to take in any new work. To make matters worse, the 100-strong contingent of washermen who had moved to the new site at Witbank seized the moment to double the charge for their services. By the end of the week Europeans were either starting to wash their own clothing at home illegally, or reluctantly paying the 100 per cent increase to meet the weekly laundry bill.[36]

Then, just when the defiant washermen's action appeared to be seriously inconveniencing the white community, the AmaWasha's resistance started to collapse. From about 8 December 1896 onwards, growing numbers of washermen capitulated and defected to the distant Klip river site.[37] Lack of leadership, the need for cash, the presence of the new steam laundries, and 'scabs' at Witbank all combined to undermine the morale of the AmaWasha, and by the last week of 1896 most of the washermen's guild was at work in the Klip river.

The AmaWasha on the defensive, 1897–1906

There were several obvious reasons behind the AmaWasha's objection to being moved out to Witbank in late 1896, and of these the most fundamental was the desire to maintain cheap and ready access to their customers of long standing. It was this commonsense consideration which lay at the base of the washermen's unsuccessful protest, and in order to more fully appreciate the reasons behind their resistance it is helpful to consider how the move to Klip river threatened their economic well-being.

While still situated on the immediate outskirts of Johannesburg, the Zulu washermen enjoyed a working week with a predictable rhythm to it. The first day of the week was usually devoted to the collection and delivery of bundles of washing. While a half-dozen or so washermen made use of their horses and carts for this purpose, the majority of guild members simply slung the large bundles over their sticks and made the two to five mile journey into town once or twice on foot. Monday was also usually the day on which the AmaWasha collected their fees from their customers. The remainder of the working week – from early Tuesday morning until late Saturday afternoon – was spent on the actual laundering operations; a routine that was only broken by the occasional mid-week special afternoon delivery. Sunday, invariably a day of rest or leisure, rounded off a strenuous week.[38]

Working within this pattern, an average washerman processed three bundles of clothing a day or about eighteen bundles per week, and since the charge for a load of washing varied between four and five shillings, this usually generated a weekly income of about three pounds. This gave each washerman a monthly average income of twelve pounds which, during the prevailing four-monthly spell of migrant labour, yielded a gross income of about forty-eight pounds. Against this, however, the washermen had to offset certain unavoidable costs which, over the same four-month cycle, came to a little more than seven pounds.[39] Thus, after a typical tour of duty on the Witwatersrand, a returning member of the washermen's guild could look back on a gross profit of about forty-eight pounds. An outline of these transactions is shown in Table 4.

Table 4. Income and expenditure of a Zulu washerman over a four-month period between 1890 and 1896

Income		Expenditure	
Income		*Expenditure*	
60 bundles of washing per month at 4/- per bundle for four months		Initial Sanitary Board registration fee	1s 6d
		4 licences at 1/- per month	4s 0d
	£48 0s 0d	Hut rental at £1 per month	£4 0s 0d
		Site hire at 2/6 per week	£2 0s 0d
		1/3 pass exemption fee at £3 per year	£1 0s 0d
	£48 0s 0d		£7 5s 6d

These gross figures, however, provide no more than a mere outline since they do not take into account some of the other more tangential 'business' transactions which did much to raise the washermen's real income. Throughout the years the AmaWasha occupied the 'locations' close to the town sites, they and the women who lived with them derived a considerable income from the illegal sale of beer which they, as members of the guild, were permitted to brew for their own consumption but not to market commercially.[40] An additional source of income, in cash or kind, was the spoil that accrued to less scrupulous washermen who stole or sold their customers' clothing.

From mid-1894 A. H. Smithers, the Sanitary Board official responsible for the AmaWasha, was constantly beset with complaints by Europeans about the loss of their laundry. By late 1895 these complaints reached such a volume – well over 100 a month – that the Inspector of Natives recommended the appointment of a full-time official to deal with all such cases. While many of these losses could be attributed to individual thefts by washermen, there were also occasions when it was clearly undertaken on a more systematic basis – as when, in 1894, Smithers recovered no less than ten 'missing' bundles of clothing during a single surprise inspection at a washing site. Most organised of all, however, was the regular selling of clothing to a gang of 'Peruvians' – Russian or Polish Jews – in 1895. Since the peddling and second-hand clothing trade in the town was firmly in the hands of East European immigrants, these 'Peruvians' would have been well placed to dispose of large quantities of clothing in the retail trade. It was quite conceivable, therefore, that a white miner who had sent his laundry for washing with the guild would end up having to repurchase his own garments from a second-hand clothing dealer in the city centre![41]

While it is difficult to estimate how much additional revenue a washerman could raise through the sale of beer or second-hand clothing, there are clear indications that this involvement in 'informal sector' opportunities was becoming increasingly important prior to the move to Klip river. But here again, this income had to be offset against necessary overhead expenditure – such as the cost of food while at the working sites, and, after 1895, the cost of rail transport between Natal and the Transvaal. Even when all these factors are taken into account, however, it would still appear that before 1896 a washerman could reasonably be expected to have a net income of between forty and fifty pounds after four months' labour on the Witwatersrand. Since most members of the guild undertook two such spells of labour each year, it meant that each washerman could take back cash savings of between eighty and one hundred pounds to the rural areas every twelve months. Incomes of this order placed the AmaWasha in a rather exceptional socio-economic category and not surprisingly their children, when subsequently questioned about their fathers' position in rural society, deemed the washermen to be 'wealthy'.[42]

But much of this changed rapidly once the guild was forced to move to the Klip river site in 1896. The move significantly increased the washermen's overhead costs, seriously disrupted their work rhythm and badly undermined their sources of supplementary income. Above all else, however, it was the Netherlands South Africa Railway Company, the N.Z.A.S.M., and the cost of transport which threatened to financially cripple the AmaWasha. Washermen now had to meet the cost of rail transport for the two and a half hour journey between the Witbank site and their customers, and this necessitated a substantial cash outlay. In addition to this the guild members were, for some months, also obliged to pay a charge for all bundles of laundry exceeding 50 lbs in weight. Undoubtedly it was the direct costs incurred in this manner that did most to keep the AmaWasha away from the new site. The Sanitary Board readily acknowledged this problem and consistently put pressure on the railway company to reduce its charges. When the N.Z.A.S.M. did eventually agree to reduce its prices there was an immediate, albeit modest increase in the numbers of washermen willing to make use of the Klip river site.[43]

It was not only the direct cost of N.Z.A.S.M. transport which adversely affected the fortunes of the washermen's guild, however, it was also the quality and frequency of the service provided by the railway company which did much to undermine the washermen's productivity. For several weeks an indifferent N.Z.A.S.M. management was content to allow the AmaWasha and their bundles to be carried in empty coal trucks – a somewhat cynical and inappropriate service for those engaged in the laundry industry. More serious still was the manner in which an infrequent rail service disrupted the washermen's work and business rhythm. During the first two months at Witbank there was only a twice-weekly service between the new site and Johannesburg and even when this did improve to a more regular and reliable daily service, in March 1897, it still did not fully meet the guild's needs.[44] The railway company's time-table made it simply impossible for a washerman to make a return journey to the site, as well as undertake all his deliveries and collections within the town in a single day. In short, the AmaWasha had to spend a great deal more time travelling and less time working, and ultimately this reflected itself in much reduced turnover.

But in addition to the above, there were at least three other formidable disadvantages to be faced by the washermen who made the move to the Klip river site. First, once at Witbank the washermen for a variety of reasons could no longer plant crops or keep the gardens to which they had become accustomed at the old sites and this, coupled with the fact that they now had to make most of their purchases at a local store which could not offer competitive urban prices, meant that they were forced to spend more money on food than had previously been the case.[45] Secondly, since their 'location' was now well beyond the town and cut off from the normal weekend influx of visitors and customers, beer-selling ceased to be a profitable side-line. Indeed, the appearance of a white-owned canteen at the new washing site meant that the AmaWasha were reduced from being small-scale producers of alcohol to simple consumers.[46] Thirdly, the Witbank site was isolated, centralised, and under the direct supervision of four black policemen and a much-feared Constable Botha of the Z.A.R. police.[47] This greatly reduced the chance of any sustained involvement in the illegal second-hand clothes trade.

Thus, caught in the economic scissors of increased costs and falling revenue, the members of the guild responded like any orthodox businessmen and increased their prices. From the first week in December 1896 the washermen put up their prices from four shillings to eight shillings for a bundle of washing in an attempt to cope with the new cost structure that had been imposed upon them – a one hundred per cent increase. From that point on, the AmaWasha's regular clients found that their laundry needs were being less efficiently dealt with, by a smaller number of washermen, at prices substantially higher than anything they had been called upon to pay before. This was a situation that was ripe for exploitation by those who possessed the necessary capital to acquire machinery for modern mass processing techniques. Thus, although the Rand generally was in a state of economic recession after the Jameson Raid, this part of the service sector continued to expand. Whereas there were only two steam laundries in Johannesburg in late 1896, by April 1898 there were at least half a dozen in operation. While the black laundrymen were away, the white capitalists seized the chance to play.

One of the first of the new enterprises, the Melrose Steam Laundry, was opened to the north of the town on the banks of the Jukskei river in April 1897. The promoters of this company realised, as did others at the time, that while capital might be harder to find during a recession, the same was not true of labour. They thus set about recruiting workers from amongst those Dhobis who were making their way to the Witwatersrand in increasing numbers after 1895.[48] Through offering these east coast Asian immigrants accommodation, rations and a small cash wage, the laundry owners soon acquired a stabilised labour force for their new venture.

While the Dhobis at Melrose were undoubtedly poor they were, however, far from being totally demoralised by their vulnerable economic position. Within weeks of the laundry opening the workers came out on an unsuccessful strike against what they considered to be an exploitative piece-work system that had been introduced by the management.[49] After this unsteady start, the laundry continued to make slow but steady progress. By 1899 its workers were sufficiently settled for them to ask the owners to grant them a site on which they could construct a Hindu temple so that their religious needs could be met. This request was granted, and the temple-cum-school no doubt further assisted the stabilisation of the work-force.[50] The Melrose Laundry continued to operate right up to the depression in the 1920s, while the small corrugated-iron Siva Subramanian Temple still stands today amidst the rather incongruous surroundings of the city's opulent northern suburbs.

But in the Johannesburg of 1897 poverty and bitter distress were not confined to the Asian or African communities – something of which several white charities were only too well aware. The Johannesburg Relief Committee, like most of its Victorian counterparts, however, was reluctant to 'pauperise' the unemployed by simply providing charity to the needy. It therefore cast about for a scheme which would avoid the moral pitfalls associated with 'indiscriminate relief' and at the same time offer help to some of the many destitute Afrikaner families in the western suburbs of Burgersdorp and Vrededorp. Noting the absence of the AmaWasha from nearby Braamfontein, the Committee struck upon the idea of establishing a laundry which, while running on a non-profit basis, would offer some employment for urban poor whites.[51]

In mid-1897 the members of the Johannesburg Relief Committee therefore approached the Kruger government for a site on which to locate the laundry which it hoped would employ indigent Afrikaner women. The State President and his colleagues viewed the project with some sympathy, granted the necessary site in Vrededorp and – in September of the same year – set up the *Maatschappy tot nut van het Algemeen* to act as the governing body of this charitable institution.[52] The Committee, however, was particularly slow in pushing ahead with the scheme and when the South African War broke out two years later the land granted by the Kruger government had still not been utilised.[53] But despite the failure of the Relief Committee to provide Afrikaner women with more formal employment, many other women – some of them white, many others coloured and black – took up the hand-washing of clothing as a means of earning a living from 1897 onwards.[54]

As if somehow to add insult to the absent Zulu washermen's economic injury, however, the most important developments of all continued to take place on the Richmond Estate at the very centre of their old Braamfontein–Auckland Park washing site. Here, the rudimentary industrial complex established during the booming business climate of 1895/6 was severely shaken by the 1897 recession but nevertheless survived to make further headway. The Crystal Steam Laundry only remained in business in 1897 through being able to secure an additional loan of £1,500 from the American-linked firm of Chaplin and Manion Ltd.[55] Thereafter, under the guidance of F. O. Nelson, the laundry recovered to make steady progress right up to the outbreak of war.

Next door the Crystal Laundry's sister factory, the Auckland Park Steam Laundry, was rather less fortunate. By late 1897 the 'French Company' was in serious trouble with its property being firmly bonded to a Parisian financier.[56] Then, just when all seemed lost, the Company found buyers to take over the venture as a going concern. In January 1898 the Auckland Park Steam Laundry was refloated as the Palace Steam Laundry Limited with a major part of the new company's capital of £8,000 being provided by two local men – A. C. Reich and Edmund Fordtran. But here too at least some of the new capital appears to have been raised in the United States since the de Boer family of Illinois were reported as holding shares to the value of £1,500 in the new company.[57] Under its new lease of economic life the Palace Steam Laundry made steady progress and functioned until at least 1920.

At about the same time that these developments were taking place at the Richmond Estate, however, the two steam laundries were joined by a third enterprise of a related sort – a soap factory. In February 1897, the Kruger government granted a butcher, H. Woolf, and others, a concession to process tallow obtained from Transvaal animals into household and other soap. On the strength of this, Woolf floated the Transvaal Soap Company with a nominal capital of £10,000 but since finance was hard to raise during a recession, the company was restructured in November 1897 in such a way as to allow it to operate with a more modest working capital of £4,000.[58] Unfortunately for Woolf and his partners the rinderpest epidemic in the same year prevented the company from readily obtaining all the tallow it required. Despite this difficult start, the company went into production in 1898, and manufactured increasing quantities of soap during the next ten years. In 1908, the Transvaal Soap Company was again restructured, and in 1912 the factory at Richmond was acquired by the international giant, Lever Brothers.[59]

The members of the washermen's guild, viewing these developments from the splendid isolation of Witbank in 1897, had good reason to be distressed. Despite the prevailing uncertain economic conditions the two large steam laundries, three or four other medium-sized enterprises and a small number of hand-washing establishments run by members of the Cantonese community were all making significant inroads into a market that had previously been overwhelmingly dominated by the Zulu washermen.[60] But while developments at the Richmond Estate undoubtedly depressed the AmaWasha, it was also true that such hope and optimism as they retained for a return to the town also emanated from the old Braamfontein–Auckland Park complex. For right from the time of the expulsion of the guild from the town a small number of defiant washermen had stayed on at one of the old sites at Richmond. It was this splinter group of the guild, aided and abetted by the site-owners, who fought the Sanitary Board, undermined the viability of the Klip river establishment and who were ultimately responsible for the restoration of much of the old order.

In December 1896, when the vast majority of the AmaWasha were making the move to Witbank, Lady Drummond Dunbar persuaded sixty washermen hiring a site from her to remain on the property. While the economic advantage of such a stay obviously appealed to the washermen, they were less confident about the legal consequences which would follow if they should follow their old profession without the necessary Sanitary Board licence. Lady Dunbar, however, promised that she would ensure their legal protection provided that they agreed to take out passes under the law that was generally applicable to Africans. This the washermen agreed to and, abandoning their privileged position as pass-exempt guild members, they duly enrolled as Lady Dunbar's 'servants' and continued to follow their calling.[61]

The Sanitary Board was quick to take up this challenge and immediately prosecuted those washermen operating without the necessary licence. Lady Dunbar and the site-owners, however, struck back by contesting the legal right of the Board to withhold licences, and by organising a public petition for the return of the AmaWasha and the cheaper laundry service which they provided.[62] Over the next six months a series of intermittent skirmishes between the Sanitary Board and Lady Dunbar took place in the courts. Then, a decisive legal battle was fought when the case of two of Lady Dunbar's 'servants' – Stephanus and Inzonda – was referred to the High Court for a final decision.[63] On 8 July 1897 the High Court ruled in Lady Dunbar's favour, and immediately the site-owners put out the word that the AmaWasha would be safe and welcome to return to their old places for work. Within four weeks so many of the washermen had left the Klip river site that the store there was forced to close down for want of business. By early September there was not a single washerman left at Witbank.[64]

The Zulu washermen returned to Johannesburg with undisguised pleasure in 1897 and at once reverted to charging their formerly competitive price of three to four shillings per bundle of washing. The majority of the washermen found their way back to their favourite sites at Braamfontein–Auckland Park which were now conveniently – if not hygienically – supplied with warm soapy water discharged from the plants of the Crystal and Palace Steam laundries. Others, including yet more Dhobis who had arrived from the east coast, went elsewhere or made their way to new sites that now developed at Langlaagte and near the Jumpers mine.[65]

Yet, for all their delight at being back in their old haunts, the washermen found that certain important changes had taken place during their absence at Witbank – changes that greatly weakened their economic position.

By 1898 the washermen's corps had been reduced to half of its size in 1896, and this – as well as the fact that there were now no less than six laundries in town undertaking the washing and ironing of clothing at four shillings per dozen items – in large part reflected the damage inflicted by the move to Klip river.[66] There had also been a series of other developments, however, which in the long run proved to be at least as serious for the washermen. The move to Witbank had split the ranks of the AmaWasha and badly undermined the unity of the guild, and it was really only once they had returned to Johannesburg that it became apparent just how much of their former cohesiveness and discipline the washermen had lost. The guild members no longer enjoyed the benefits of having an undisputed leader such as Kwaaiman, with the result that their frequent collective marches into Market square and the meetings to which they gave rise declined, and this in turn made for a more isolated existence at the various washing locations. This loss of internal control manifested itself in the growing number of reports of theft, gambling, drinking and violence that came from the washing sites between 1897 and the outbreak of war.[67]

The Johannesburg Sanitary Board and its successor in late 1897, the Town Council, viewed these deteriorating conditions at the old washing sites with some dismay. It was not so much the decay in the social conditions within these black communities which disturbed the white authorities, however, as the fact that the washing pits themselves remained as disgusting and unhygienic as ever.[68] But, still smarting from the legal blows inflicted on it by Lady Dunbar's lawyers, the Council was powerless to effectively control the sites and it was thus forced into formulating a new set of by-laws in September 1897. This set of by-laws extended the Council's jurisdiction to cover washing sites 'adjoining' the town as well as those within it – a manoeuvre which would allow the municipality to control independent washermen as well as those employed as 'servants' by site-owners. In addition, the new regulations reinforced an earlier provision which required a washerman to wear a numbered brass badge on his left arm, and increased the cost of a washing licence from one shilling to two shillings and sixpence per month. It was only in late 1898, however, that the Executive Committee of the Volksraad got around to approving these draft regulations, and it was only in April 1899 that they were eventually published in the *Government Gazette* and became legally binding.[69] With such belated legal backing, it was hardly surprising that A. H. Smithers complained bitterly about his inability to control the washermen in the period leading up to the outbreak of the war.[70]

When war was declared in October 1899 the large majority of AmaWasha left the sites for their rural homes in Natal and in many cases sought, and found, work with the invading British forces.[71] A non-migratory core of about 120 washermen, however, stayed on at the washing sites where they were joined by other black men and women stranded by the war. This heterogeneous population which, in addition to the working washermen, now included several professional liquor-sellers and prostitutes, became increasingly difficult to control between 1899 and 1902.[72] Not only were there the by now normal allegations of theft, gambling and immorality, but once the mines reopened with a seriously depleted African mine labour supply, there were also bitter complaints that washing locations adjacent to mines – such as those of George Goch, Jumpers and Concordia – offered a refuge for drunken black miners.[73]

After the British occupation of Johannesburg in May 1900, the incoming administration at once addressed itself to the problem of urban African communities in general, and to the question of the washermen and the washing sites in particular. In this regard, it would appear that the new authorities set themselves the task of achieving three overlapping objectives between 1900 and 1904. First, as a matter of some urgency, they set out to 'clean up' the washing locations by expelling the beer-brewers and liquor-sellers who significantly reduced the productivity of the black labour force on adjacent mines. Secondly, they sought to establish effective legal control over the washermen themselves, as well as the washing sites. Thirdly, and in the longer term, they desired to enhance control and segregation by attempting to get all urban Africans to live in a single consolidated location.

In October 1900, a proclamation signed by the Military Governor decreed all washing sites to be within municipal jurisdiction, and empowered the authorities to remove all persons other than registered washermen from the sites and place them in the location that had been established near Vrededorp during the pre-war years.[74] It seems possible that these powers contributed to the closure of the Jumpers and George Goch washing sites shortly thereafter. What is known with greater certainty is that it only took the municipality and the government a further twelve months to move in and destroy the oldest, and by now most central of all the washing sites in Johannesburg – that at Sans Souci in the Braamfontein–Auckland Park complex.[75]

Towards the end of 1901 the Sans Souci washermen were informed that no further licences would be issued for their site, and that they should immediately remove themselves to the old 'Kaffir Location'. This announcement was accompanied by the news that the new British pass law – unlike the old Republican legislation – did not make provision for a pass-exemption for 'those coloured persons earning their living independently of a white master'.[76] These measures threatened to remove some of the remaining independent AmaWasha from their competitive central site in the town and arbitrarily reduce them to the menial status of 'servants' in the new economy. In February 1902 induna Mahlangu and others – on behalf of the Sans Souci washermen – petitioned the Commissioner of Native Affairs, Sir Godfrey Lagden, for relief from these oppressive measures. The petitioners pointed out to Lagden that they had occupied the site in question since 1890, that many of them had erected houses and lived there permanently, that the cheap service which they provided was favoured by a significant section of the white population, that their crops were still ripening in the ground and that any move would expose them to considerable hardship.[77] The Commissioner of Native Affairs allowed the washermen to reap their crops. In April 1902 the Sans Souci AmaWasha moved from their central site – not to the 'Kaffir Location' as Lagden had hoped, but to the notorious washing location at Concordia.[78]

This partially successful act of evasion by the Sans Souci washermen was made possible by certain legal loopholes that continued to exist during the transition from a military to a civil administration in the city. From late 1902 onwards, however, the Milner administration steadily prepared the way for local government authorities to further regulate the activities of any

AmaWasha. In August 1903 representatives from the Government and the Johannesburg and Pretoria town councils held a conference to draft yet another special set of by-laws to deal with, amongst other issues, washermen, locations and steam laundries. Finally, in October 1903, these regulations were approved, and the municipal authorities were fully empowered to deal with the 'problem' of the washermen and their 'private locations'.[79]

Early in 1904, before these regulations could be effectively enforced, Johannesburg was struck by an outbreak of plague and as a precaution against the spread of the disease the Plague Committee ordered that the largest part of the old 'Kaffir Location' be razed to the ground. It was in response to this measure and the immediate problems which it created that the municipality hastily acquired the farm Klipspruit some thirteen miles from town.[80] Urban blacks were deeply distressed by these developments, and further alarmed by the rumour that the imposition of a strict quarantine would confine them to the Witwatersrand even after they had completed their labour contracts.

This sense of unease, through a combination of chance and design, transformed the usual Sunday afternoon gathering of blacks and others at the Market square into what the press termed a 'Native Mass Meeting' on 27 March 1904. As a group who had already experienced the effects of one expulsion from the town in 1896, and as small businessmen who stood to lose at least as much as black workers from any new move, the turbanned AmaWasha figured prominently at this meeting – leading the crowd in chanting and singing at a venue where they had gathered many times before. After the meeting had been addressed in Zulu by J. S. Marwick, the crowd, somewhat reassured by the general tenor of his remarks, quietly dispersed.[81] The Assistant Secretary for Native Affairs, however, had been very careful to make no promises in his speech and, in May 1904, all the washermen – together with hundreds of other blacks – were sent to the 'emergency camp' at Klipspruit.[82]

Neither the administrative harrassment of the washermen within Johannesburg between 1901 and 1903, nor the evacuation of the remnants of the guild to Klipspruit in 1904 helped to solve one of the city's most basic problems – the continuing need for more satisfactory public laundry facilities. Throughout the period, therefore, there was much criticism of the old washing sites and pressure put on the Council to erect alternate facilities that were cheap, conveniently situated and hygienic.[83] Thus, when the plans for an extensive gravitation sewerage system were formulated in 1902, a scheme for public wash-houses in the working-class suburbs of Burgersdorp and Fordsburg was also mooted.[84] The latter project, however, which in some ways closely resembled the earlier Maatschappy tot nut van het Algemeen, never came to fruition.

For their part, capitalists operating within the service sector of the economy viewed these developments between 1901 and 1904 with some enthusiasm since their net effect was to marginally increase the competitiveness of the more centrally situated steam laundries. Not only were their prices becoming more competitive, but the large influx of whites into Johannesburg in the immediate post-war period left the steam laundries with a much expanded market. In several cases this made for business complacency and some of the laundries were accused of developing a 'take it or leave it' attitude towards customers.[85] For most laundry owners, however, this was the most opportune moment to expand their businesses and between 1901 and 1904 the majority of the larger enterprises extended their premises and acquired new plant and equipment.[86] It was also during the same period that a second specialised laundry complex started to develop in the valley to the immediate east of Doornfontein where there was a plentiful supply of water. Here the Lorentzville Steam Laundry and other smaller enterprises established themselves on a site which is today still dominated by the Johannesburg giant of Advance Steam Laundries.[87]

But once again, the most significant industrial development of all took place at the old Braamfontein–Auckland Park sites. By the end of the war the Crystal or 'American' Laundry, which had previously operated with an extensive credit system, found itself in severe financial difficulties. The majority of shareholders in the company, however, sensing the improved business climate, were most reluctant to wind up the business and place it in liquidation. Instead, the directors suggested that the Company be amalgamated with a smaller laundry owned by F. O. Nelson and then be refloated as a larger consolidated venture. Since Nelson was already a prominent shareholder in the Crystal Laundry there was no insurmountable obstacle to this strategy, and after a shareholders' meeting in July 1902 the new Rand Steam Laundries came into being.[88] As the driving force in the new venture Nelson put the old company's mining connections to good use and systematically secured the mines' boarding-houses and single quarters' laundry contracts for the new venture.[89] Building on this solid foundation of mining-house business the immediate financial future of Rand Steam Laundries was assured, and by late 1902 the company employed over one hundred white and Malay women workers in the main plant at Richmond.[90]

The Zulu washermen, once more viewing the growing strength of city steam laundries from a position of barren economic isolation – this time the Klipspruit camp in June 1904 – could have found little cause for comfort in these developments. But in the weeks that followed they became more optimistic as hundreds of blacks successfully deserted the camp and re-established themselves in the city. The AmaWasha, whose very livelihood depended on a swift return to the urban areas, needed no further prompting and by August 1904 the last of the washermen had left Klipspruit and made the thirteen-mile journey back to Johannesburg. On this occasion, though, their re-entry was less successful than it had been when they returned from the farm Witbank in 1897 since they were now confronted with more sophisticated barriers of urban segregation legislation which effectively denied them access to the oldest and most central washing sites. Thus, most of the new sites which the 220 licensed washermen came to occupy at Claremont, Craighall and Langlaagte between 1904 and 1905 were further away from their white customers than ever before. Of the older sites only one – that at Concordia – was successfully reoccupied during this period.[91]

But the reoccupation of these more peripheral urban sites by the remaining AmaWasha and their families did not perturb the authorities as it might have done, since they knew it to be only a temporary setback in a grander design. At the very moment that urban blacks were deserting the emergency camp and making their way back to Johannesburg, the municipality was laying long-term plans to develop a permanently segregated community at

Zulu washermen at work at Klipspruit municipal laundry

Klipspruit. By June 1904 the Town Engineer had provided the Council's Public Health Committee with detailed estimates for the cost of building a complex which would include a 'Native Location', an 'Asiatic Bazaar' and a separate 'location' and laundry for 460 'washboys'.[92] The small-business component provided for in this scheme pleased the Council since it meant that not only would the venture be largely self-supporting, but that it actually stood the chance of becoming income-generating.[93] The idea of segregation being paid for by the segregated held enormous appeal for white administrators. By early 1906, an ironing-room, a fenced-in drying site and the first of one hundred specially designed concrete wash tubs had been erected at Klipspruit.[94] With blind ruthlessness and staggering cynicism the Council prepared to move the washermen for the last time – this time to an uneconomic washing site that shared its setting with the municipal sewerage works.

The decline of the independent Zulu washermen, 1906–1914

The fragmented clusters of AmaWasha that remained in Johannesburg in 1905 appear to have been less than enthusiastic at the prospect of being moved out to the new municipal sewerage farm with its adjoining well-policed laundry complex,[95] and when the Town Council started to put pressure on the washermen to move to Klipspruit in 1906 many of the more fatalistic amongst them responded as their predecessors had in a somewhat similar situation nearly a decade earlier and simply abandoned their businesses. This time, the departing Zulu washermen also took with them the added burden of anxiety about the Bambatha rebellion that was sweeping through parts of rural Natal.

Others, however, perhaps the surviving members of the old non-migrating core of the guild, chose instead to partly resist the Town Council's pressure to move to Klipspruit. In late 1906 or early 1907, about 75 washermen under the induna Charlie Kanyile made their way to the long deserted washing site to the east of the city on the farm Elandsfontein. This site, on the property of an impecunious farmer named Deyzel, still fell just outside of Johannesburg's newly extended muncipal boundaries. Deyzel, in return for a monthly rental of between £60 and £80, made the washermen welcome on his farm. Kanyile and his cohorts made use of this 'rural' base to tout for business in the city – a practice which the municipal officials were only willing to tolerate while there were insufficient concrete washtubs available at Klipspruit. In time-honoured fashion this group of AmaWasha also supplemented their income by selling beer to the inhabitants of the nearby municipal compound at Rosherville.[96]

In general, however, the overall effect of the enforced move to Klipspruit in 1906 was – as in 1896 – to cause a reduction in the numbers of washermen. Sudden moves out of town, for health-cum-segregation reasons, were shattering blows to small black businessmen whose livelihood depended on providing a cheap service to whites in urban areas. Whereas the municipality had issued a monthly average of 262 washing licences in 1905 while the washermen were still occupying sites adjacent to the city, by the following year, when the first moves to Klipspruit had been effected, this figure had dropped to 199. Thereafter, with the exception of 1907, there was a steady annual decline in the average number of licences issued to the Zulu washermen each month. By 1914, a monthly average of only 93 washing licences was being issued to blacks at work in the Klipspruit municipal laundry. These figures are reflected in Table 5.[97]

Table 5. Washing licences granted at Klipspruit municipal laundry, 1906–14

Year	Total issued	Monthly average	Municipal revenue
1905	3,152	262	£788 0s 6d
1906	2,392	199	£598 19s 6d
1907	2,436	203	£609 11s 0d
1908	2,068	172	£517 0s 0d
1909	2,040	170	£510 0s 0d
1910	1,804	150	£451 0s 0d
1911	1,752	146	£438 0s 0d
1912	1,540	128	£385 0s 0d
1913	1,316	109	£329 0s 0d
1914	1,124	93	£281 0s 0d

Several factors contributed to the gradual demise of the washermen's business after 1906. At the time that the municipality enforced the removal of the washermen from their old sites it also took the opportunity to triple the fee charged for the monthly licence from two shillings and sixpence to seven shillings and sixpence – a move designed to help recoup some of the £3,500 spent on the Klipspruit laundry as swiftly as was possible. Initially the Town Council simply ignored the washermen's complaints about this dramatic increase in price, but once 300 washing bays had been completed in 1907 and it became apparent that the laundry was likely to be permanently saddled with excess capacity, the councillors were forced to rethink the position.[98] After a protracted delay, the Council eventually agreed to reduce the fee to five shillings per month as from July 1908 in the belief that this action alone would be sufficient to coax a further one hundred washermen out of the rural areas and back into their urban businesses.[99]

The washing licence itself, however, was not the single most important factor in a new cost structure that slowly throttled business at Klipspruit. As had been the case at Witbank ten years earlier, it was the absence of cheap and efficient rail transport that did most to ruin the small businessmen who had been relegated to a segregated site miles out of town. Besides having to meet the cost of a return rail fare to Johannesburg, the washermen were once again charged for the bundles of clothing they carried – this time at the rate of sixpence per 100 lbs, with an additional sixpence for every further part thereof.[100] The bill for transport alone thus ran at between ten and fifteen shillings per month, and it was hardly surprising therefore that a spokesman for the washermen could complain in 1907 that 'the railway took all their profits'.[101] In addition to this, the washermen were also called upon to pay for the hire of commercial 'trolleys' to help them transport washing within Johannesburg, and to pay for rickshaw pullers to help them move the heaviest bundles from Nancefield Station to the Klipspruit laundry.[102]

But, also as before, there was another and equally unpleasant side to the washermen's economic plight after 1906 – falling revenue. Some of this could be accounted for by the loss of customers which the washermen suffered as a result of providing a less efficient service. During this period the washermen repeatedly passed on customers' complaints to the authorities about 'spoilt work' that arose from the indiscriminate throwing about of completed laundry by railwaymen, or of losses sustained because of the inadequately protected storage space at Braamfontein Station. More important, though, was the reduction in turnover that was occasioned by an inconvenient railway time-table which seriously eroded the washermen's working hours.[103] Perhaps most important of all, however, was the fact that the removal to Klipspruit took place during the worst period of the economic depression that engulfed the Witwatersrand between 1906 and 1908. The marked decline in white working-class incomes during this period ultimately also affected the prices which the Zulu washermen could charge for their services. Thus, whereas three shillings constituted the minimum charge for a bundle of washing in the years before 1905, by 1909 it constituted a maximum, with charges ranging all the way down to one shilling a bundle.[104]

The Johannesburg Town Council – with the single exception of the small reduction in the licence fee noted above – showed little compassion for the remnants of the washermen's guild that it had bundled out into the economic wilderness in 1906. Having invested the ratepayers money in the Klipspruit laundry, the Council proceeded to behave with the single-minded determination that any ghetto landlord would have been proud of. In October 1907 it put pressure on the remaining washermen at Elandsfontein to make the move to Klipspruit by refusing to renew their licences. When this failed to make Charlie Kanyile and his men undertake the move to the municipal laundry the Town Clerk successfully appealed to the Director of the Government Native Labour Bureau to have the defiant washermen removed from Deyzel's farm under the Squatters Law. Even then about twenty of the washermen continued to resist the authorities by moving even further afield to the farm 'Rietvlei', from where they sought to service the white townships of the East Rand. By December 1907, however, Kanyile and the majority of the group had given up the struggle and reluctantly gone to work at the Klipspruit laundry.[105]

Once the city had been effectively cleared of immediate competition from the AmaWasha there were new opportunities for rival small businessmen and larger capitalists to consolidate their hold over the laundry services within Johannesburg. Amongst the first to benefit from the segregation imposed on the Zulu washermen were members of those 'non-white' ethnic groups not expelled from the inner city. The very act of creating the Klipspruit laundry made it economically possible for poorer members of the Chinese and Asian communities to enter and stay in the laundry business – an ironic development which the Town Council, under pressure from the White League, a racist association of small European traders, could hardly have enjoyed.[106]

Whilst there had been a small Chinese community in Johannesburg since at least the mid-1890s, there was a significant increase in its numbers between 1902 and 1909. Most of the new immigrants were Cantonese speakers who had entered the Transvaal illegally from the Cape and elsewhere in the immediate post-war period.[107] Culturally distinct from their fellow countrymen who laboured underground on the Rand mines during part of the same period, the majority of these 'free' Chinese found their way into the city's retail trade as grocers.[108] A minority, which lacked the necessary capital to enter the retail trade however, chose instead to establish itself in the more demanding laundry business. Significantly, the greatest opportunity for expansion by this latter set of entrepreneurs came only after the Zulu washermen had been pushed out of the city. Whereas there were only about a dozen Chinese laundries in Johannesburg in 1904, by 1907 there were over 40 and as late as 1914 there were still 46 such establishments in the city.[109]

Most of the Chinese laundries were located in the heart of Johannesburg in the older and less affluent suburbs of Fordsburg and Jeppe. Within these central areas they succeeded in providing a relatively cheap service for white workers since they avoided transport costs by refusing to undertake the collection or delivery of laundry.[110] By the time that the most serious phase of the 1906–8 depression had set in, many of these small hand-laundries had already started to make the transition to more substantial businesses employing up to a dozen or more workers.

At least some of the employees in the Chinese laundries were former members of the Zulu washermen's guild – a development which left white Johannesburg largely unmoved.[111] What did distress some elements of the local middle class, though, was the fact that poor white women in the self-same laundries worked side by side with their Chinese employers and fellow black workers. But if the general social proximity distressed them then what truly horrified them were those cases in which such women workers developed intimate relationships with their employers – hardly the most surprising turn of events given the fact that the local Chinese community was almost exclusively male.[112]

It was therefore partly out of racism, and partly out of the desire to dress the open sores of unemployment during an economic depression, that the various schemes for public wash-houses were resuscitated in 1907. The establishment of public laundries in Vrededorp/Fordsburg and Jeppe, so it was reasoned, would simultaneously achieve two socially desirable objectives. First, it would place young white girls beyond the reach of the so-called 'Yellow Peril', and secondly, it would provide badly needed employment for European women and widows in those suburbs where the greatest concentrations of the urban poor were to be found.[113] Yet again these projects – like those mooted earlier – failed to materialise, and the Chinese hand-laundries continued to provide both employment and a service in white working-class areas for several years thereafter.

While the Chinese captured the most central part of the city's laundry market, however, the more peripheral suburbs fell to the Indian washermen. After the establishment of Klipspruit, Dhobis and former steam laundry workers who had managed to accumulate sufficient capital, acquired horses and carts and opened small hand-laundries.[114] Using Newclare in the west and La Rochelle–Rosettenville in the south as bases, these laundrymen successfully toured the outlying white working-class areas in search of business. Between 1906 and 1914, at least twenty, and perhaps as many as fifty such small Indian-owned businesses joined in the struggle to win a share of Johannesburg's laundry market.[115]

The serious competition provided by the new Indian and Chinese laundries within the city cut two ways. While it undoubtedly carved out a sizeable portion of the market previously served by the Klipspruit washermen, it also managed to slice off a hefty chunk of the steam laundries' business – and this was particularly noticeable between 1906 and 1908 when the need for cheap services was at a premium. As the economic climate started to improve in 1909, however, so there were ominous signs that the larger and better capitalised enterprises were set for a further round of expansion which would effectively hold off the challenge from below.[116]

Rand Steam Laundries was yet again in the very forefront of these developments and by 1910 it had thirteen branches spread along the Reef, operated a fleet of 33 delivery vans, and employed a work force of 200 white women and 100 black men at its central Auckland Park works.[117] Signs of expansion were also evident at the rival Lorentzville industrial complex where, between 1910 and 1911, first-generation immigrants from Holland, Germany and Scandinavia floated no less than three new companies – the International, Model and New York steam laundries.[118] By 1912 Johannesburg's steam laundries – after a battle dating back all the way to 1897 – were for the first time in full command of the Rand's laundry market and confident enough to embark on the first of many price-fixing exercises.[119]

Out at Klipspruit, all this urban capitalist and small-business expansion left its collective imprint – perhaps most starkly of all in the declining numbers of Zulu washermen noted above. Unfortunately for the washermen it was not only the rival laundries that increasingly attacked their livelihood in the years before the First World War – they were also undermined by socio-economic changes that occurred within the white working-class home itself. As early as 1902–3, for example, advertisements for rotary washing machines had appeared in the local press under the caption 'No More Wash Boys Needed!'[120] More damaging still was the combined impact that servants and housewives had on domestic labour between 1902 and 1914. Important changes in the white family structure during this period, as well as the declining cost of 'houseboy' services, meant that an increasing number of domestic chores – including the washing of clothes – could be cheaply undertaken within the working-class home, thus rendering paid outside assistance unnecessary.[121]

It was thus a group of already besieged washermen who were relegated to the economic wilderness of Klipspruit in 1906. Although nowhere near as powerful as they had been during the heyday of the guild, the remaining AmaWasha were acutely aware of the fact that they were slowly and certainly being stalked by economic death and in three successive years – 1906, 1907 and 1908 – they complained bitterly to the Johannesburg Town Council about the disadvantages of the new municipal laundry.[122] Virtually all of their objections were ignored. By early 1909 there was substantial discontent amongst the inhabitants of Klipspruit location and amongst those in the very forefront of the ranks of the frustrated stood the turbanned Zulu washermen.[123]

In early June 1909 the AmaWasha and others put pressure on the chairman of the local branch of the Transvaal Native Congress, Kyana, to arrange yet another meeting between the inhabitants of Klipspruit and the authorities; and three weeks later the washermen and other blacks duly met with municipal officials and a senior officer of the Transvaal police. On this occasion, however, the government – concerned about reports emanating from the ghetto – took the precaution of also sending along a representative to the meeting. At this gathering the washermen once more paraded their complaints about rail fares, site charges and the fact that the pervasive smell of sewerage penetrated their laundry and so lost them customers.[124] The government official at the meeting, W. Pritchard of the Native Labour Bureau, took careful note of these objections in order to monitor the municipality's response. A deafening silence ensued.

When the Council did eventually respond five months later, in November 1909, it did so with a provocative arrogance that was breathtaking. Through the Superintendent of the location, Lloyd, the municipality curtly informed the washermen that it intended to *raise* rather than lower the charges for transport between Klipspruit and Johannesburg. With a degree of patience that Job could only aspire to, the washermen yet again set about petitioning the authorities. This time they pointedly avoided the Town Council and directed their appeal to the government.[125]

The government officials assigned the task of enquiring into the long-standing grievances reported back in the clearest terms possible. The 'Complaints Officer' attached to the Native Affairs Department in Johannesburg pointed out that the Zulu washermen 'were forced to live in the location' under conditions that were not only unpleasant, but positively injurious to their health.[126] The Chief Pass Officer in the city, Edward Wilson, while also concerned about considerations of public health at Klipspruit, was equally anxious to establish the deeper reasons underlying the municipal moves against the AmaWasha. Wilson came to the conclusion that the provocative decision to raise rail charges was premeditated, and that the action flowed from a 'white labour policy' which was 'causing the Council deliberately to make conditions impossible for the Zulu washermen'.[127]

On the basis of these very critical reports the Secretary for Native Affairs, W. Windham, wrote to the Town Clerk on 20 November 1909, pointing out the 'very serious nature' of the black grievances and stating that the government felt 'the urgent necessity for breaking up the location at Klipspruit and accommodating the native residents elsewhere'.[128] While the Council felt unable simply to ignore this advice, it was unwilling to undertake the radical steps proposed by Windham. In order to placate the Secretary for Native Affairs and blur the issues, however, the Council arranged instead for the hapless Lloyd to be replaced as the Superintendent of the location and for yet another meeting to be held with the inhabitants of Klipspruit.

This 'absolutely informal meeting' was held in the presence of Windham at the location early in 1910. The washermen and others had yet another opportunity to put their case, while the government officials assured them that – in the future – the Council would listen most carefully to their grievances. If the Council did listen it certainly did not act, and shortly thereafter the Transvaal government officials concerned were absorbed into the Union's new civil service. The noose of segregation around the black laundrymen's necks was never loosened, and the 1910 meeting concluded with the remnants of the Zulu washermen's guild singing their way into economic oblivion to the strains of the national anthem.[129] By 1934 there were a mere fourteen Zulu men at work at the municipal washing site, and in 1953 the City Council finally closed the Klipspruit laundry; content in the knowledge that the capital cost of the segregated facilities had been more than covered by the rentals paid by the washermen over nearly five decades.[130]

Conclusion

There can be little doubt that in the development of a modern industrial state in South Africa one of the clearest, most vivid and deeply traumatic processes evident is that of the proletarianisation of the African population and the creation of a largely black working class. But while this is understandably seen as one of the dominant themes in the economic development of the subcontinent, it should not leave observers insensitive to important variations on the theme, since both the route into the working class and the pace at which the march was conducted could vary significantly.

Some of these variations arose from contradictions that emerged during the period of early capitalist development on the Witwatersrand. Amongst these was the fact that, during the formative era, the mining industry was largely reliant on 'single', or at least unaccompanied European migrant male workers for the bulk of its skilled and semi-skilled labour requirements. This in turn meant that, in a socio-economic system characterised by rapid growth and enormous scale, capitalism was denied one of its central struts – the nuclear family which reproduces the next generation of workers. One of several important consequences of this situation in which men found themselves without women was that a significant market for domestic services developed on the Rand during the two or more decades between the discovery of gold and the First World War.

The possibilities offered by this relatively lucrative and dramatically expanding market for personal services were swiftly appreciated by those blacks experiencing the ravages of proletarianisation in the South African countryside. Zulu-speaking males in nearby Natal were amongst the first to exploit an economic opportunity which allowed them the chance to earn an income without entering the mining industry as unskilled labourers. Partly modelling themselves on the Hindu Dhobis whom they had seen operating on the east coast, and partly drawing on elements of their own social structure, these men bound themselves into the Zulu washermen's guild of the Witwatersrand.

This small economic space which appeared in the cracks of a developing capitalist system offered itself only once as a means of escaping the working class – and then only very briefly since the gap closed up almost as rapidly as it had opened. Yet, within a crucial period of sixteen years between 1890 and 1906, sufficient Zulu males squeezed through this escape hatch into the world of small-scale business for them and their children to avoid subsequent crushing as workers, and for them to constitute a distinctive stratum of the rural society to which they returned. A man like Bhamu Buthelezi, who started life as a labour tenant on a white farm in the Weenen district, subsequently became a washerman on the Rand between 1893 and 1908, accumulated sufficient capital to buy himself land in the Bergville district, and eventually helped to educate his children to the point where they had no need to resort to wage labour in order to earn a living.[131] Bhamu Buthelezi was no exception. On the very farm where he bought land, 'Hambrook', he was joined by at least three other former washermen – a Dhlamini and two Vilakazi brothers – who also managed to acquire property.[132]

Just how different these small black businessmen were from the majority of their fellow countrymen can be illustrated in two ways. First, it can be seen mirrored in the complaint that an AmaWasha spokesman made to the authorities during one of the meetings held at Klipspruit during 1909. At a time when most blacks were being swept *off* the land, the washermen were in the distinguished position of being able to object to being 'unable to pay off any debts on their farms or property in Natal'.[133] More striking still perhaps was the very different 'complaint' registered by a white Bergville farmer some years later. In 1918, George Coventry stated in evidence before the Native Lands Committee that:

'Hambrook' is 811 acres. 22 heads of families bought it. They are not satisfied with that; they are talking to and encouraging all natives around to rent from them at £2 a hut, advising them to stop working on the farms. The head of that farm, Ephraim, has boycotted us for labour. They boycott us unless they get a certain wage. These last two years they had kept labour from going to us. It is registered in the name of a syndicate, but since they have paid for it it has been subdivided and each one has a certain number of acres, and has a number of rent-paying tenants on his piece. A Kraal which has been with me for nearly 30 years is being continually approached to leave and go there. They admit that we have been just and good to them. One or two use fertilisers and copy us and have improved.

Mr Steward then added:

They all use fertilisers and plant in rows and scarify. 'Hambrook' is about the best piece of native cultivated land I have seen. The natives who want to buy land are those who are going to improve.[134]

Clearly, the brief and restricted business opportunity that opened up on the Rand between 1890 and 1914 was capable of producing at least one minor rural wave that ran counter to the dominant tide of proletarianisation in the countryside.

The Zulu washermen, however, were not alone in possessing an eye for the economic chance on the Witwatersrand. Indeed, the very presence and success of the washermen's guild in Johannesburg during the mid-nineties alerted others with greater financial resources to the economic possibilities of the service sector, and led – from 1896 onwards – to the establishment of a growing number of steam laundries within the town. These capitalist enterprises, situated on the very sites at which the guild was most active, at first found it difficult to compete with the cheaper service provided by the washermen. It was during the course of this struggle, however, that laundry owners discovered that, indirectly, their businesses profited from new state policies which were designed to exercise greater control over urban Africans. Immediately after the British occupation of the Transvaal the Milner administration made strenuous efforts to close down the existing washing sites within the city, and to concentrate the activities of the AmaWasha into a single segregated site. This series of administrative measures progressively undermined the washermen's business and in 1906 eventually culminated in the expulsion of the remaining members of the guild to Klipspruit.

It was this removal to Klipspruit which, in the end, did much to hasten the demise of the AmaWasha. But even here capital, class and colour interacted in a way which makes South Africa characteristically complex since the very act of segregating these small black businessmen created residual economic opportunities for other urban ethnic minorities. Once the AmaWasha were tightly bound by the uncompetitive cost structure of a site some thirteen miles out of town, their business fell not only to the large steam laundries but to smaller hand-laundries which sprung up in and around the city. Groups of frustrated Europeans watched, with considerable annoyance, as the economic space forcibly vacated by the Zulu washermen was swiftly filled by Chinese and Indian laundrymen.

While aspirant or existing European tradesmen were angered by the arrival of this set of Chinese and Asian competitors, other whites in the middle classes with less at stake were more deeply disturbed by the inter-racial contact that tended to develop amongst workers of all colours who undertook collective labour in the new establishments. In particular, many Europeans were shocked by the reports of intimate relationships that sometimes developed between poor white women workers and Chinese employers in the city's small hand-laundries. Thus, while the state effectively separated the Zulu washermen from several of their long-time Dhobi colleagues through the creation of Klipspruit in 1906, it was left to the local women's organisations to attempt to remove white women from Chinese laundries during the depression and the years thereafter. To the extent that these efforts enjoyed a measure of success, Johannesburg's working class became further divided along racial and sexual lines between 1906 and 1914.

In conclusion then, it may be noted that Zulu speakers were at least as quick as any other immigrant group on the early Witwatersrand to spot a new economic opportunity and exploit it. The structure which these small black businessmen developed during the early period drew on 'Zulu', and to a lesser extent Indian society, and manifested guild-like characteristics. While the techniques which the AmaWasha employed rendered them increasingly vulnerable to capitalist competition during the years that followed, the decline of the Zulu washermen's guild was greatly hastened by the advent of urban segregation. In South Africa class and colour seldom miss an economic funeral.

Notes

1 H. Pirenne, *The Economy and Society of Medieval Europe* (London 1936), p. 184.
2 For evidence of the washermen's privileged status see: 'The Washboys' Parade', *Standard and Diggers' News* (hereafter *S. & D.N.*), 2 July 1895; 'Wash Boys in Trouble', *S. & D.N.*, 3 August 1895; Johannesburg Public Library (J.P.L.), Johannesburg City Archive (J.C.A.), Box 22, Report of Special Committee chaired by E. Hancock to Chairman and Members of the Sanitary Committee, 15 May 1896; and 'Wash Boys Licences', *S. & D.N.*, 20 June 1896.
3 See, for example, G. S. Ghuyre, *Caste and Class in India* (New York 1952), p. 8 and p. 37; and L. Dumont, *Homo Hierarchicus* (London 1970), pp. 48–49, p. 100 and p. 175.
4 Interview with Mr E. Kaluse, Johannesburg, 11 February 1977. (Tape deposited in the library of the Oral History Project, African Studies Institute, University of the Witwatersrand, Johannesburg. Hereafter, O.H.P., A.S.I., University of Witwatersrand.)
5 *Natal Government Gazette*, 22 July 1878. I am indebted to Prof. M. Swanson for this and the following reference.
6 See Durban, *Mayor's Minutes* covering the period 1890–1913.
7 S. Marks, *Reluctant Rebellion* (Oxford 1970), pp. 15–17.
8 Interview with Mr P. Gumbi, Johannesburg, 16 April 1977; and interviews with Messrs H. Buthelezi and N. Mchunu, Weenen, 25 April 1977. Tapes deposited O.H.P., A.S.I., Univ. of the Witwatersrand. For an indication of the numbers of black males with passes leaving these districts for work in the Transvaal during the mid-1890s see, Pietermaritzburg Archives Depot (P.A.D.), Secretary for Native Affairs (S.N.A.), Confidential Papers 1890–1897, File 668/1895.
9 Including the changing white family structure on the Witwatersrand during this period. For a brief discussion of this aspect see Chapter 1 above, 'The Witches of Suburbia', pp. 9–13.
10 For examples see 'Our Washing', *Johannesburg Weekly Times*, 16 January 1897; and J.P.L., J.C.A., Box 245, 'Washing Regulations', 1897.
11 See Chapter 1 above, 'The Witches of Suburbia', pp. 9–13; and 'Johannesburg's Wash Tub', *The Star*, 20 April 1898.
12 Figure derived from fragmentary data housed in J.P.L., J.C.A., Boxes 220 and 231; and Box 263, Health Officer's Report No. 36 for 1895.
13 Para. based on: J.P.L., J.C.A., Box 217, Manager, Braamfontein Estate Co. Ltd. to Chairman and Members of the Sanitary Board, 12 November 1894; 'The Wash Boys' Parade', *S. & D.N.*, 2 July 1895; 'Concordia Mining Company', *S. & D.N.*, 23 May 1896; Lady Dunbar to the Editor, *The Star*, 31 December 1896; and 'Our Washing', *Johannesburg Weekly Times*, 16 January 1897.
14 See 'The Wash Boys' Parade', *S. & D.N.*, 2 July 1895; and 'Johannesburg's Wash Tub', *The Star*, 20 April 1898.
15 *Ibid*. See also, however: J.P.L., J.C.A., Box 263, J. Smithers to Chairman, Sanitary Board, 27 October 1894 and Health Department, Report No. 36 of 1895; J.P.L., J.C.A., Box 221, Health Inspector's Annual Report for 1895; and 'The Washing Sites', *The Star*, 18 November 1898.
16 *Ibid*.
17 Transvaal Archives Depot (T.A.D.), Secretary for Native Affairs (S.N.A.), File 392/02, Mahlangu and other washermen to Sir Godfrey Lagden, 12 February 1902.
18 Johannesburg, *Census 1896*, Part I, Return 2; and Part IX, Returns 1 and 2.
19 See 'The Wash Boys' Parade', *S. & D.N.*, 2 July 1895; and 'Court Cases', *S. & D.N.*, 3 September 1895. See also P.A.D., S.N.A., File 1/1/216, Johannesburg

Representative's Report for week ended 15 February 1896. I am indebted to Jeff Guy for this reference and others in this series.

20 Interview with Mr R. Buthelezi, Mpungu River, Weenen District, 25 April 1977. Tape deposited O.H.P., A.S.I., Univ. of the Witwatersrand.

21 'The Wash Boys' Parade', *S. & D.N.*, 2 July 1895. See also various reports on 'Kaffir War Dance' in *S. & D.N.*, 8 December 1898.

22 For reports on Kwaaiman see *S. & D.N.* of 3 August 1895 and 9 July 1896. See also, however, P.A.D., S.N.A., File 1/1/216, Johannesburg Representative's Report for week ending 15 February 1896. I am indebted to Jeff Guy for providing me with a copy of this material.

23 J.P.L., J.C.A., Box 263, Report No. 36, T. C. Visser to Chairman and Members of the Sanitary Board, 28 October 1895; and Report No. 43, A. Smithers to Chairman and Members of the Sanitary Board, 28 October 1895. Also, J.P.L., J.C.A., Box 221 'A', L. H. Dunbar to Secretary, Johannesburg Sanitary Board, 6 December 1895.

24 'Health of the Town', *S. & D.N.*, 12 March 1896.

25 J.P.L., J.C.A., Box 219, A. Fossati to Chairman, Sanitary Board, 25 October 1894; and Box 230, A. Fossati to Town Council, 26 April 1898.

26 Registrar of Companies Office (R.C.O.), Pretoria, File on 'Crystal Steam Laundry' (1895); and 'Crystal Steam Laundry', *Johannesburg Weekly Times*, 19 December 1898.

27 See, for example, the advertisement for Nannucci's business in *S. & D.N.*, 4 March 1896. For a confidential report on Nannucci's suitability for the position of Italian Consul in Cape Town, see Cape Archives Depot (C.A.D.), A.G. File 965, Commissioner of Police to J. B. Moffat, Sec. to the Law Dept., Cape Town, 30 May 1902.

28 R.C.O., Pretoria, File T. 1313, 'Auckland Park Steam Laundry Co. Ltd.' (1896). See also G. Aubert, *L'Afrique du Sud* (Paris 1897), p. 237.

29 See, for example, L. Grahame to the Editor, *The Star*, 28 March 1896.

30 'Concordia Mining Company', *S. & D.N.*, 23 May 1896.

31 For the background to the Sanitary Board's acceptance of the Dell offer, see reports of meetings carried in the following: *S. & D.N.*, 12 March 1896; *The Star*, 2 April 1896; *Johannesburg Times*, 1 August 1896; *The Star*, 12 August 1896; and *S. & D.N.*, 13 August 1896. For details of the Sanitary Board's accounting regarding the move to the new site see J.P.L., J.C.A., Box 221, 'Comparative Statement', April 1896.

32 See reports carried in the *S. & D.N.*, 9 September 1896 and 24 October 1896.

33 See items reported in the *S. & D.N.*, 8 November 1896; *The Star*, 16 November 1896; and *The Critic*, 27 November 1896.

34 See *Transvaal Independent*, 2 December 1896; and *Johannesburg Times*, 10 December 1896 and 15 April 1897.

35 Table constructed from fragmentary data contained in J.P.L., J.C.A., Box 201 and Boxes 220–231; and information carried in *Johannesburg Times*, 15 April 1897, and *The Star*, 18 November 1898.

36 'Washboys at Witbank', *S. & D.N.*, 2 December 1896. See also reports in *S. & D.N.*, 3 December 1896; and *The Critic*, 4 December 1896.

37 *Johannesburg Times*, 10 December 1896.

38 Perhaps the best account of the washermen's week is to be found in 'The Washing Site', *The Star*, 18 November 1898.

39 Figures derived from 'Johannesburg's Wash Tub', *The Star*, 20 April 1898, and other scattered sources.

40 'The Wash Boys' Parade', *S. & D.N.*, 2 July 1895; and T.A.D., S.N.A., File 941/02, 'Illicit Liquor Traffic, Summary of Cases November 1901–April 20, 1902'.

41 Para. based on: J.P.L., J.C.A., Box 263, A. H. Smithers to Chairman and Members of the Sanitary Board on 27 June 1894, 18 July 1894, and 1 August 1894. Also items in the *S. & D.N.* of 2 July 1895, 25 October 1895, and 12 March 1896; and *The Star*, 18 November 1898. See also, 'Report of the Superintendent of Locations', Johannesburg, *Mayor's Minute 1905*, p. 171.

42 Interviews with Messrs. H. and R. Buthelezi, Weenen, 25 April 1977. Tapes deposited O.H.P., A.S.I., University of the Witwatersrand.

43 See *Johannesburg Weekly Times*, 26 December 1896; 'The Washing Site Bogy', *Johannesburg Times*, 15 April 1897; *The Star*, 15 April 1897; and 'Drought and its Terrors', *S. & D.N.*, 10 June 1897. When the Dell proposal was first entertained the suggested rail fare was three shillings per month. See J.P.L., J.C.A., Box 221, 'Comparative Statement', April 1896.

44 *Ibid.*

45 J.P.L., J.C.A., Box 225, D. Margolious to A. H. Smithers, 25 August 1897.

46 See, for example, 'The Washing Site Bogy', *Johannesburg Times*, 15 April 1897. Contrast this with the former situation as recounted in 'A Murder Case', *S. & D.N.*, 7 March 1897.

47 For examples of Zarp Botha's activities see brief reports in the following editions of the *S. & D.N.*, 25 October 1895, 2 December 1896, 25 February 1897, and 8 April 1897.

48 For the names and origins of some of these *Dhobis*, who included among their number Naidoos, Pillays, Kistens and Chettys, see *British Parliamentary Papers*, LXVI, *Command Paper Number 5363 of 1910*, pp. 111–112 and 117. Also T.A.D., Gov. Gen., Vol. 706, File 15/7, W. L. Ritch to Under Sec. of State for the Colonies, 7 June 1910, enclosed in Colonial Sec. to Gov. General, 18 June 1910; and File 15/47, W. L. Ritch to Under Sec. of State for the Colonies, 4 August 1910, enclosed in Colonial Sec. to Gov. General, 13 August 1910. I am indebted to Maureen Tayal for providing me with copies of this material.

49 See advertisement in *S. & D.N.* of 13 April 1897, and 'Doings at Darnaway', in *S. & D.N.* of 23 April 1897. For further fragments relating to the Melrose Steam Laundry see advertisements carried in the *S. & D.N.* of 4 August 1897, and 26 July 1898. Also J.P.L., J.C.A., Box 231, Secretary, Melrose Steam Laundry to Secretary, Johannesburg Sanitary Board, 28 March 1899.

50 Interview with Mr S. R. Naidoo, Lenasia, Johannesburg, 19 March 1977. Tape deposited with O.H.P., A.S.I., Univ. of the Witwatersrand. See also, however, T. Naidoo, 'The Temple at Melrose', unpublished typescript, Johannesburg 1978.

51 *S. & D.N.*, 24 August 1897; and *Johannesburg Times*, 24 August 1897.

52 *De Locale Wetten de Zuid Afrikaansche Republiek 1897*, pp. 177–179; and 'Johannesburg's Wash Tub', *The Star*, 20 April 1898.

53 'Vrededorp Laundry', *S. & D.N.*, 18 April 1899; and 'Public Wash House Concession', *The Star*, 17 April 1899. See also Chapter 3 below, 'The Main Reef Road into the Working Class', p. 130.

54 Even before the AmaWasha had moved out to Witbank there had been a small number of women – often Coloured or European widows – who took in laundry in order to make a living. See, for example, 'The Wash Boys' Parade', *S. & D.N.*, 2 July 1895. This trend accelerated, however, once the Zulu males went to Klipspruit and the economy slid into the recession of 1897 – see, for example, *S. & D.N.*, 1 April 1897. More significant still perhaps is the fact that black women started doing laundry at the old sites once the Witbank experiment commenced – see, for example, Smithers' remarks as reported in the *S. & D.N.* of 22 May 1897. After the South African War, and more especially so during the depression of 1906–8, many more European widows took to washing clothes as a means of making a living, sometimes as many as one hundred and fifty in a single suburb. See, for example, 'Poor Women', *The Star*, 22 November 1907.

55 'Crystal Steam Laundry', *Johannesburg Weekly Times*, 19 December 1896; and 'Crystal Steam Laundry Limited', *S. & D.N.*, 30 December 1898.
56 'Auckland Park Steam Laundry', *S. & D.N.*, 1 October 1897.
57 R.C.O., Pretoria, File T. 1501, 'Place Steam Laundry Ltd.'.
58 R.C.O., Pretoria, File T. 1413, 'Transvaal Soap Company Ltd.'.
59 *British Parliamentary Papers*, XXXV, *Command Paper Number 624 of 1901*, evidence of H. Woolf, paras. 1766–1809. For some of the background to the takeover by Lever Bros. see D. K. Fieldhouse, *Unilever Overseas: The Anatomy of a Multinational, 1895–1965* (London 1978), pp. 97–103.
60 For a list of some of these smaller laundries see *Longland's Johannesburg and District Directory 1899*, p. 311. That at least some of these laundries dated back to 1897–8 can be deduced from 'Johannesburg's Wash Tub', *The Star*, 20 April 1898. For mention of the Chinese laundries see G. Aubert, *L'Afrique du Sud* (Paris 1897), p. 237.
61 *Johannesburg Weekly Times*, 16 January 1897.
62 *Johannesburg Weekly Times*, 30 December 1896 and 16 June 1897.
63 For the central events in these proceedings see: *Johannesburg Weekly Times*, 9 January 1897; J.P.L., J.C.A., Box 225, Landdrost voor Crimenele Zaken to Sec., Sanitary Board, 13 March 1897; 'Rate-Payer' to Editor, *Johannesburg Times*, 27 March 1897; *Johannesburg Times*, 15 April 1897; *The Star*, 7 May 1897; *Johannesburg Times*, 19 May 1897; *S. & D.N.*, 22 May 1897; *Johannesburg Times*, 7 June 1897; and *The Star*, 18 November 1898.
64 J.P.L., J.C.A., Box 225, D. Margolious to Sec., Sanitary Board, 25 August 1897; and *S. & D.N.*, 16 September 1897.
65 Para. based on: J. W. Meillon to the Editor, *Volkstem*, 23 December 1896; 'Johannesburg's Wash Tub', *The Star*, 20 April 1898; and J.P.L., J.C.A., Box 232, Report of Health Officer, T. C. Visser, to Mayor and Town Councillors, 13 February 1899.
66 The prices charged by steam laundries appear to have remained more or less constant between 1897 and 1902. Compare G. Aubert, *L'Afrique du Sud* (Paris 1897), p. 237; and 'A Wash Tub Wanted', *The Star*, 29 July 1902. It was also about this time, i.e. 1897–8, that black and Malay women (sometimes in small partnerships with members of the AmaWasha), first started doing ironing at 7/6d per day plus board. See 'Johannesburg's Wash Tub', *The Star*, 20 April 1898.
67 For some examples see the following selection of items drawn from the *S. & D.N.*: 'Sensation at Sans Souci', 29 January 1899; 'Charge of Murder', 9 June 1898; 'Culture and Kaffirs', 24 June 1898; and 'A Washboy's Woman', 18 November 1898. See also 'The Washing Sites', *The Star*, 18 November 1898.
68 See the *S. & D.N.* of 2 December 1897; and *The Star*, 20 April 1898, and 18 November 1898.
69 On the passage of this legislation see: J.P.L., J.C.A., Box 225, H. J. Filmer to Sec., Sanitary Board, 26 September 1897; J.P.L., J.C.A., Box 245, 'Washing Regulations' (1897); and items in *The Star* of 18 November 1898; and *S. & D.N.* of 29 March 1899.
70 See, for example, J.P.L., J.C.A., Box 263, A. H. Smithers, Fortnightly Report No. 30 to Burgomaster, Aldermen and Town Council of Johannesburg, 3 October 1898.
71 Interview with Mr N. H. Buthelezi, Weenen, 25 April 1977. Tape deposited with O.H.P., A.S.I., Univ. of the Witwatersrand.
72 T.A.D., L.A.J., Vol. 9, File 574, A. H. Smithers, Inspector of Natives to Major O'Meara, Acting Burgomaster, Johannesburg, 24 September 1900. I am indebted to Diana MacLaren for drawing this and other reports in this series to my attention. See also, T.A.D., S.N.A., File 941/02, 'Illicit Liquor Traffic – Summary of Cases, November 1901–April 20, 1902'.

73 See especially, T.A.D., S.N.A., N.A. 936/02, D. R. Hunt, Inspector, Native Affairs Dept., to Chief Inspector, 14 April 1902.

74 T.A.D., L.A.J., Vol. 9, File 574, Memo by Major O'Meara, 2 October 1900; and enclosed draft proclamation in Smithers' hand.

75 There were at least three good reasons why this particular site was amongst the first targets of the administration. (i) It had long been a notorious centre of beer selling – see note 73 above. (ii) It was ripe for development as a white residential area. Even before the war the Editor of *The Star*, F. Dormer, had tried to get the site closed down for this reason. See the note on the Richmond location in *S. & D.N.*, 26 January 1899. (iii) The steam laundry owners would have been less than enthusiastic about this source of cheap competition being so close to them.

76 T.A.D., S.N.A., File 392/02, Mahlangu and others to Sir Godfrey Lagden, 12 February 1902.

77 The prospect of a further move by the washermen attracted the attention of yet one more person – Ernest Sheppard, former Field Cornet, Rand Native Labour Association employee, and prominent shareholder in the Crystal Steam Laundry. Sheppard unsuccessfully proposed a further Klip river-type settlement for the washermen to the new administration. See T.A.D., S.N.A., File 446/02, E. Sheppard to Sec. for Native Affairs, 22 February 1902.

78 T.A.D., S.N.A., N.A. 2606/02, D. R. Hunt, Inspector, Native Affairs Dept. to Chief Inspector, 14 April 1902.

79 See the following files in T.A.D., S.N.A. series: N.A. 2606/02, Memo. by Assistant Sec. for Native Affairs, J. S. Marwick, 2 January 1903; N.A. 1486/03, Town Clerk, Johannesburg, to Sec. for Native Affairs, 14 August 1903; N.A. 1486/03, Draft By-Laws approved by the Public Health Committee; and N.A. 2606/02, Sec. of Native Affairs to Commissioner of Police, 14 October 1903.

80 Johannesburg, *Mayor's Minute 1905*, p. 7 and p. 9.

81 See 'Native Mass Meeting' and 'Report of the Proceedings' in *The Star*, 28 March 1904.

82 T.A.D., S.N.A., N.A. 1486/03, *Report B of Medical Officer of Health, Washing Sites in Johannesburg*, p. 2.

83 See, for example, 'A Wash Tub Wanted', *The Star*, 29 July 1902.

84 Johannesburg, *Mayor's Minute 1901–1903*, p. 33.

85 See 'A Wash Tub Wanted', *The Star*, 29 July 1902; or 'W.G.P.' writing to the Editor on 'The Laundry Question' in *The Star*, 13 June 1903.

86 See the following items in *The Star*: 'Laundries', 16 May 1903; 'Palace Steam Laundry', 27 July 1903; and 'Rand Steam Laundries', 26 July 1905.

87 In fact, the seeds of this development were already sown before the war. As early as 1899 the Lorentzville, Bertrams and White Star Laundries were all operating in this part of the town – see *Longland's Johannesburg and District Directory 1899*, p. 311. The most significant part of this development, however, took place after the war – see note 86 above.

88 'Crystal Steam Laundry', *The Star*, 22 July 1902. It seems possible that Nelson first acquired a laundry when the original Rand Steam Laundry went into liquidation during the depression of 1897 – see 'Rand Steam Laundry', *S. & D.N.*, 31 July 1897. Nelson's dominant role in the later consolidated venture can be gathered from the company's full name, 'Rand Steam Laundries, F. O. Nelson & Co.'. See 'Laundries', *The Star*, 16 May 1903.

89 When J. C. Manion visited England later in the same year he left no doubt that the company operated what he called 'a syndicate of mining laundries'. See City of London Polytechnic, Fawcett Library, 'South African Colonisation Collection', Vol. 'Early Transvaal Letters', Alicia M. Cecil to Miss Russell, 23 October 1902. For the continuing importance of the mines' laundry requirements see, for example, 'Rand Steam Laundry', *The Star*, 15 October 1910.

90 'A Wash Tub Wanted', *The Star*, 29 July 1902. Judging from the same source it appears that the Palace Steam Laundry employed a complement of about the same size and sexual composition at this time.
91 T.A.D., S.N.A., Vol. 48, N.A. 2408/04, *Report of the Public Health Committee on the Location Question 1904*. Report B. of Medical Officer of Health, Washing Sites in Johannesburg, pp. 1–3.
92 *Ibid*. See also T.A.D., City of Johannesburg Archive, Vol. 402, File 3/60/12/1294, Report of the Town Engineer to the Town Clerk and Location Sub-Committee, 20 June 1904.
93 See, for example, the Superintendent of Locations' remarks in Johannesburg, *Mayor's Minute 1905*, p. 171.
94 Johannesburg, *Mayor's Minute 1906*, p. IX; and *Mayor's Minute 1907*, pp. 25–26.
95 By 1905, the washermen were still 'losing' substantial quantities of laundry at widely dispersed washing sites – see Johannesburg, *Mayor's Minute 1905*, p. 171. The original estimates for the costs of the Klipspruit site thus also made provision for an annual bill of £500 for 'police and supervision'. See T.A.D., S.N.A., N.A. 2408/04, *Report of the Town Engineer*, 20 June 1904. Between 1938 and 1953 the remaining twenty or so washermen at Klipspruit continued to be supervised by a municipal policeman, Mr Azariah Gumbi. Interview with Mr P. Gumbi, Johannesburg, 16 April 1977. Tape deposited O.H.P., A.S.I., Univ. of the Witwatersrand.
96 See various letters in T.A.D., S.N.A., N.A. 3840/07; and 'Faction Fight – Zulu vs. Baca', *The Star*, 14 November 1907.
97 Table constructed from data in Johannesburg, *Mayor's Minutes* covering period 1905–17.
98 On the changing cost and capacity of the laundry at Klipspruit see the following: 'The Klip Spruit Farm', *The Star*, 5 November 1907; and the following issues of the Johannesburg *Mayor's Minute, 1906*, p. 132; *1907*, pp. 25–26; *1908*, p. XI; and *1918–19*, p. 71.
99 Johannesburg, *Mayor's Minute 1908*, p. XI and p. 27; and *Minutes of the Town Council 1908*, p. 1, p. 197 and p. 1452.
100 On the rising cost of rail transport between Klipspruit and Johannesburg see: Johannesburg, *Mayor's Minute 1906*, p. 132; 'The Klip Spruit Farm', *The Star*, 5 November 1907; and T.A.D., S.N.A., N.A. 3820/10, Complaints Officer, Dept. of Native Affairs to Chief Pass Officer, 10 November 1909.
101 'The Klip Spruit Farm', *The Star*, 5 November 1907. Also, interview with Mr R. Buthelezi, Weenen, 25 April 1977. Tape deposited O.H.P., A.S.I., Univ. of the Witwatersrand.
102 *Ibid*.
103 'The Klip Spruit Farm', *The Star*, 5 November 1907.
104 T.A.D., S.N.A., N.A. 3820/10, Makaza, Mkubalo and other washermen to the Officer in Charge, Pass Office, Johannesburg, 7 November 1909.
105 See correspondence in T.A.D., S.N.A., N.A. 3515/07.
106 Pressure from the White League and the Fordsburg and Newtown Vigilance Association was particularly evident at the height of the depression in 1907. Amongst other things, both of these groups were concerned that 'the number of laundry licences issued to Chinese and Coloured persons are on the increase'. See various documents in T.A.D., City of Johannesburg Archive, File A 518, 'Asiatic Location'.
107 On the earliest Chinese laundries see note 60 above. On the issue of illegal immigrants see, for example, 'The Chinese Invasion', *The Star*, 18 June 1903. It is more than likely that several of these Chinese immigrants had gained experience of the laundry business prior to their move to the Transvaal. See, for example, 'Chinese in the Cape Colony', *The Star*, 30 April 1906.

108 Perhaps the best description of Johannesburg's early Chinese community is to be found in Thomas A. See's letter to the Editor of *The Star*, 5 January 1904 – 'The Chinaman as he is – A Compatriot's Defence'. For a list of Chinese grocers in the city see, for example, *United Transvaal Directory 1911*, pp. 1203–1205.

109 T.A.D., S.N.A., N.A. 2408/04, *Report of the Public Health Committee on Location Question 1904*, Report A of Medical Officer of Health, p. 4; T.A.D., City of Johannesburg Archive, File A 518, 'Asiatic Location', 'Report to Public Health Committee re: Asiatic Trading', 1907; and *United Transvaal Directory 1914*, pp. 1001–1002.

110 See, for example, 'Satisfied' to the Editor, *The Star*, 17 March 1908.

111 Mr Rwanqana Buthelezi remembers his father telling him about at least three such washermen before the First World War – Petrus Zuma, Sikhakane Mchunu and Samuel Dhlamini. Interview with Mr R. Buthelezi, Weenen, 25 April 1977. Tape deposited O.H.P., A.S.I., Univ. of the Witwatersrand. See also T.A.D., G.N.L.B., File 169/647/14/102, Report No. 42 on Washing Site, 25 October 1925.

112 See, for example, some of the following cases which were reported in *The Star*: 'Chinese and European', 15 May 1906; 'A Shocking Charge', 9 October 1908; and 'White Girls in the Employ of Chinamen', 9 February 1910.

113 The moving spirit behind this scheme was apparently Mrs Pauline Lotter of the Undenominational Benevolent Society – see 'Poor Women', *The Star*, 22 November 1907; and P. Hammond to the Editor, *The Star*, 27 November 1907. By March 1908 the scheme seems to have been abandoned for want of funds. See the following items in *The Star*: 'Vrededorp Soup Kitchen', 9 March 1908; 'Another White Woman' to the Editor, 13 March 1908; 'Satisfied' to the Editor, 17 March 1908; P. Hammond to the Editor, 20 March 1908; and 'Satisfied' to the Editor, 24 March 1908.

114 Such as Mr J. R. Naidoo, a former Melrose Steam Laundry employee, who went into business on his own at La Rochelle. Interview with his son, Mr J. Naidoo, Johannesburg, 16 November 1976. Tape deposited with O.H.P., A.S.I., Univ. of the Witwatersrand.

115 See, for example, the *United Transvaal Directory* of 1911 and 1914 on pp. 1277–1279 and pp. 1001–1002 respectively.

116 See especially the item on 'Laundries' in the 'Commercial Notes' of *The Star*, 11 December 1909.

117 'Rand Steam Laundry', *The Star*, 15 October 1910.

118 *United Transvaal Directory 1911*, p. 1277. Also interview with Mr P. Cohen (ex-Advance Laundries), Johannesburg, 16 November 1976.

119 'Advance in Laundry Rates', *The Star*, 1 June 1912.

120 See items reported in *The Star* of 20 August 1902 or 9 April 1903. See also, however, section on 'Laundry Machinery' in B. H. Morgan, *Report on the Engineering Trades of South Africa* (London 1902), p. 157.

121 These changes, and black servants' resistance to the chore of laundry work are discussed in some detail in Chapter 1 above, 'The Witches of Suburbia', p. 26.

122 See, for example, 'The Klip Spruit Farm', *The Star*, 5 November 1907; and Johannesburg, *Town Council Minutes 1908*, p. 1197.

123 T.A.D., S.N.A., N.A. 980/09, unsigned letter to the Protector of Natives, 22 February 1909.

124 T.A.D., S.N.A., N.A. 980/09, Minutes of Meeting held at Klipspruit, Sunday, 20 June 1909.

125 T.A.D., S.N.A., N.A. 3820/10, Makaza, Mkubalo and others to Officer in Charge, Pass Office, Johannesburg, 7 November 1909.

126 T.A.D., S.N.A., N.A. 3820/10, Complaints Officer to Acting Chief Pass Officer, Johannesburg, 10 November 1909.

127 T.A.D., S.N.A., N.A. 3820/10, Chief Pass Officer, Johannesburg, to Director, Government Native Labour Bureau, 11 November 1909. See also, 'Nancefield Location', *Transvaal Leader*, 13 November 1909.
128 T.A.D., S.N.A., N.A. 3820/10, Sec. for Native Affairs to Town Clerk, Johannesburg, 20 November 1909.
129 T.A.D., City of Johannesburg Archive, Vol. 24, File A 676, Minutes of an Informal Meeting held at Klipspruit, 17 January 1910. See also T.A.D., G.N.L.B., File 59/2239/12/20, Superintendent of Location to Director of Native Labour, 9 December 1919.
130 West Rand Administration Board, N.A. 5/15, Manager to Medical Officer of Health, Johannesburg, 12 September 1934. Also, interview with Mr P. Gumbi, Johannesburg, 16 April 1977. Tape deposited O.H.P., A.S.I., Univ. of the Witwatersrand.
131 Bhamu Buthelezi's eldest son – N.H. Buthelezi – became a member of the South African Police at Weenen, while one of his grandchildren (N.H.'s daughter) went on to study at Atlanta University, Georgia, U.S.A., during the course of 1977. Interview with Mr N. H. Buthelezi, Weenen, 25 April 1977.
132 *Ibid.*
133 T.A.D., S.N.A. 980/09, Minutes of a meeting held at Klipspruit on Sunday, 20 June 1909.
134 Union of South Africa, *Minutes of Evidence of the Natal Natives Land Committee 1918* (U.G. 35–18), p. 192. I am indebted to Shula Marks who drew this evidence to my attention.

CHAPTER THREE

The Main Reef Road into the working class

Proletarianisation, unemployment and class consciousness amongst Johannesburg's Afrikaner poor, 1890–1914

> No labour party can be really formidable unless it is based on profound discontent and radical grievances; and the annoyances of the Johannesburg proletariat are, as compared with those of Europe, like crumpled rose-leaves to thorns.
>
> John Buchan, 1903

Historians will be amongst the first to acknowledge that much work remains to be done before our understanding of the industrial revolution which transformed southern Africa in the late nineteenth and twentieth centuries is more rounded. While the development of the country's productive resources, the processes of class formation and the rise of class consciousness have been broadly sketched for the region as a whole, there are many areas in our social and labour history which remain unexplored. For those who are interested in the industrial heartland of the regional economic system – the Witwatersrand – the situation is more promising. The dramatic emergence of large-scale primary industry on the Rand, the struggle of unionised white workers and the mobilisation and control of a pool of cheap black labour have all been relatively well documented. But, even here, where the spotlight of scholarly enquiry has done much to illuminate the drama of capitalist development and class conflict, there are parts of the stage that remain in darkness.

Amongst several of the more important actors still stranded in these shadows are the Rand's urban Afrikaners.[1] In the existing literature, the proletarian origins of this group are invariably traced to the changes which capitalism wrought in the Transvaal countryside in the years around the turn of the century. Thereafter we tend to lose sight of these sons of the soil for a decade or more – until 1907 – when they are portrayed as unhesitatingly entering the mining industry as 'scab' labour during the strike of that year. The implication is thus that most Afrikaners experienced a direct change in status from that of rural *bywoner* to that of urban worker and that in the intervening period, spent largely off stage, members of the group became 'dependent upon the usual means available to such marginalised strata – beggary, whatever doles or charity were available, and perhaps the occasional odd job'. It is further suggested by some that such Afrikaners had a strong aversion to manual labour, and by another that they constituted 'an extremely disorganised stratum with little power on their own to enforce even limited economic demands'.[2]

While this view may have something to commend it, it is so schematic that it immediately prompts a number of questions from those who are in search of more persuasive answers to some of the problems relating to the issues of proletarianisation, unemployment and class consciousness during this period. Clearly, there is no group or class that simply waits patiently in the wings to play its part until such time as it is summoned on to the stage of economic development by a blast on the trumpet of history. How exactly did Afrikaners manage to survive in the decade or more of darkness before 1906–8? Did bywoners really only manage to exchange the grinding poverty of the Transvaal countryside for the debilitation of urban unemployment when they undertook the move to the Witwatersrand at the turn of the century? Were burghers who had significant political access to the state from 1881 to 1899, from 1907 to 1910, and to a lesser extent thereafter, truly as disorganised and powerless as we have been led to believe? In Johannesburg – that cauldron of class conflict where capital and labour were daily pitted against each other – were the Afrikaners of Burgersdorp, Fordsburg, Newlands and Vrededorp only capable of manifesting the fickleness of the lumpenproletariat or the opportunism of the nationalists in their struggle?

In this essay an attempt will be made to advance three sets of related arguments which may go some way towards clarifying our understanding of some of these issues. First, it will be suggested that a significant number of the former bywoners were – by making use of varying combinations of state-aid, craft skill and small capital – capable of establishing themselves in the local community either as the providers of services, or as petty commodity producers. These largely self-employed Afrikaners were thus able to avoid the labour market for several years, and it was only once their enterprises had been eclipsed by larger-scale capitalist developments that they became proletarianised. In the Transvaal therefore, capital had to conquer many Afrikaners not once, but twice, before they succumbed to the position of wage labour – first in the countryside and then in the towns. Secondly, it will be suggested that these unemployed burghers were far from being powerless. Indeed, such was the threat posed by them and other unemployed workers to the developing capitalist system on the Witwatersrand that it called forth a significant response from mine owners and state alike in the form of charity and public relief works. It is thus the Randlords' and their lieutenants' involvement in charitable acts and associations – at least as much as their more formalised policy towards the employment of unskilled white labour – that is in need of analysis when we seek to understand the mining industry's response to the Afrikaner unemployed of the Reef towns. Thirdly, it will be suggested that this Afrikaner corps in the reserve army of labour demonstrated its capacity for organised resistance from an early date, and that in this struggle it manifested an essentially working-class consciousness. Moreover, the nature and extent of this consciousness was at least sufficiently well developed for it to present a local challenge to the dominant ideology of nationalism, and that the Afrikaner ruling class was thus forced into an early attempt to co-opt and defuse it.

The rise of Afrikaner urban enterprise and self-employment, 1886–1906

The discovery of gold and the emergence of Johannesburg must have presented itself, at least initially, as a new and open-ended economic opportunity to many in the Transvaal towns and countryside during the last quarter of the nineteenth century. Amongst the very first arrivals at the mining camps of the Witwatersrand there were therefore several Afrikaners, and of these a small number soon established themselves as claim holders and successful diggers. These aspirant mine owners, however, were soon confronted with two of the many formidable barriers which the infant industry erected – the need for capital and technical know-how. It was largely because of their inability to cope with these problems that most Afrikaner diggers soon sold their claims to established foreign capitalists who did possess the necessary finance and contacts with which to acquire both mining machinery and expert advice. Thus, although some Afrikaners were able to establish a foothold in the industry which was to dominate Kruger's Republic, and that evidence of that pioneering presence lingered for some years thereafter in the form of the names of some of the mines and companies such as the Meyer & Charlton and the Paarl–Pretoria Syndicate, there were no Afrikaner Randlords at the turn of the century.[3]

In Afrikaner eyes, this absence of representation amongst the new urban bourgeoisie of the Rand was hardly compensated for by the existence of a 'Dutch' strand in the middle class comprised largely of attorneys, teachers, civil servants, legal agents, doctors, notaries, clergymen and traders. The majority of these, however, were well-educated professionals drawn from the older and more developed south, and as such their presence hardly offered testimony of any new found mobility amongst native-born Transvaalers. As for the traders, their small number pointed to another set of limitations which confronted many Afrikaners – vigorous competition from other immigrant groups with greater commercial experience, the importance of English as the dominant language of economic discourse and, perhaps more familiarly, a lack of capital, or compensating credit arrangements with the powerful coastal merchant houses.[4]

With most of these avenues to large and smaller-scale capital accumulation long since closed to them, the majority of the Rand's poor and uneducated Afrikaners were forced to seek a niche for themselves somewhat lower down in the economic structure. In this search they received some assistance from the state in the period prior to the outbreak of the South African War. The Kruger government's insistence that only burghers be eligible for service in the police force meant that by 1899 close on 900 young Afrikaner males had secured positions as Zarps – and that despite the fact that a fair percentage of them was illiterate. Others managed to find employment at the most elementary level in the civil service, but even here some of the limitations noted above caught up with them. Thus, of the sixty employees in the Johannesburg Post Office in 1897, only twenty were Afrikaners since, or so it was suggested by a section of the local English press, Afrikaners usually lacked the 'technical' knowledge necessary to make a success of such positions.[5]

Beyond the limited protection afforded by the public sector, the employment prospects facing the jobless Afrikaner were even bleaker. The availability of a larger and cheaper pool of black labour, the dominance and ethnic exclusiveness of immigrant English miners who organised themselves into a trade union, and the lack of industrial skills and discipline which confronts any first generation of proletarians all combined to preclude Afrikaners from successfully seeking work in any numbers with the largest employer of labour on the Witwatersrand – the mining industry. Apart from the couple of hundred burghers taken on as an experiment by the Eckstein group during the worst of the depression years in 1897, there was no significant Afrikaner presence in the mine labour force during the pre-war years.

Yet, despite these limited opportunities, each successive year saw hundreds more Afrikaners undertaking the journey to the Witwatersrand, and this influx was particularly marked in the decade or so that elapsed between 1896–7 and 1906–8. This sustained movement to the urban areas hardly constituted the twitchings of so many Transvaal lemmings making their way to almost certain economic death. Nobody – least of all the former bywoners – needed to be reminded that their expulsion from the countryside had been caused largely by a plague of locusts, intermittent drought, cattle diseases, the upheavals occasioned by the war and the extension of capitalist agriculture. But whatever the immediate cause of their plight, the Afrikaner poor knew – as the poor know everywhere – that when virtually all is lost, the chances of survival are always marginally better in the city than in the countryside. In this case, however, economic instinct was supplemented by the knowledge that a number of their kinsmen had already managed to establish a precarious foothold in certain sectors of the rapidly developing urban economy.

For at least some of these Afrikaners the very means by which they abandoned the countryside proved to be their immediate salvation in the cities. Between the late 1880s and the early 1900s, transport riding offered many rural refugees a living. Before the extension of the railway lines from the coast to the Rand in 1892–5, or the more comprehensive coverage of the Transvaal by a system of branch lines by the First World War, the services of transport riders were in constant demand in order to ensure that the vital flow of machinery to the mines and food to its workers remained uninterrupted. Like the workers, however, the mining machinery also had to be 'fed' and thus the transport of coal from the collieries beyond Boksburg and Brakpan opened up a further set of opportunities within this field. Within the towns themselves yet other Afrikaners were employed in the movement of various commodities by ox-waggon, while the remainder used the smaller but sturdier 'scotch cart' to ferry stone, cinders and other materials to road works, building sites and brickyards.[6]

In several respects these former bywoners were obviously well placed to capture these new business opportunities as they presented themselves. Skills previously acquired with ox and waggon, the limited need for capital and an intimate knowledge of the Transvaal terrain were but some of the factors which allowed for an early Afrikaner dominance of the transport sector. Although it is impossible to be precise about the numbers involved, contemporary sources suggest that in its heyday transport riding afforded 'general' and sometimes even 'lucrative' employment for thousands of impoverished burghers.[7] What is known with greater certainty, is that by the early 1890s the sector was sufficiently prosperous for it to attract considerable attention from the Kruger government. In late 1891, the State President persuaded the *Volksraad* of the need to impose a toll of thirty shillings on each waggon carrying loads of up to 6,000 lbs along the Republic's main roads.[8] This contentious measure, which in various forms remained in operation until at least 1895, proved to be a considerable source of revenue to the state. Over a four-month period during 1894, for example, over £9,000 flowed into the state coffers via the tolls.[9] Given this, it is easier to understand why Kruger and some of his closest colleagues were reluctant to abolish the tolls even though such a move would undoubtedly have earned them a measure of political popularity in the countryside.

But the State President's firmness in the case of the transport riders contrasted sharply with his treatment of a second and less prosperous group of Afrikaners engaged in the transport business – the urban cab drivers. In 1889, the Volksraad granted A. H. Nellmapius the exclusive right to operate an animal-powered tramway within Johannesburg. While this concession was obviously meant to provide the rapidly expanding town with a measure of cheap public transport, it also provided Boer agricultural producers with a ready market for draught animals and fodder, and for this reason Kruger consistently opposed later attempts to electrify the system. It was largely as a result of this latter conflict of interests that Johannesburg for many years had to tolerate an underdeveloped public transport system, and it was only in 1906 that the city eventually acquired an electric tramway. In the intervening decade and a half, the urban economy offered a living to those willing to operate horse-drawn cabs in the city.[10]

Former bywoners with horses, small 'Cape Carts', and the necessary skills were amongst the first to seize the opportunity of becoming owner-drivers of cabs. Poorer kinsmen who could muster the skills but not the other necessary accoutrements of the trade found themselves positions as drivers for the more fortunate. Throughout the 1890s, Johannesburg's cab trade expanded steadily as the city grew and its horse-drawn tramway became increasingly unequal to the task of providing adequate public transport. By the mid-1890s the local authority was issuing over 1,500 licences to cab drivers annually, and of these several hundreds were assigned to the Afrikaners of Fordsburg and Vrededorp. The members of the Sanitary Board were aware, however, that this growing dependence on private transport rendered urban commuters vulnerable to the financial demands of the cab trade, and this problem reached acute proportions during the depression of 1896–7 when the Board, in an attempt to protect the interests of its constituents, sought to halve the fees which cab drivers were entitled to charge within the city limits. The cabbies responded to this threat with an appeal to the government, where Kruger – ever mindful of *his* political constituency – defended the trade against the proposed action by the Board. It was thus longer-term consequences of the tramway concession that allowed many Afrikaners to find a place of economic refuge in the cab trade before the South African War, and then, to a lesser extent, up to 1906.[11]

In addition to transport riding and cab driving, there was one other field of economic enterprise in which newly urbanised Afrikaners managed to establish themselves with some success after the discovery of gold – that of small-scale brick manufacture. From the late 1880s through to the end of the post-war reconstruction period, many former bywoners found that their knowledge of local clays and brickmaking and drying techniques could be put to profitable use in the rapidly expanding towns of the Witwatersrand. While these opportunities opened up to a greater or lesser extent all along the Reef, they were obviously once again most marked in the city with the largest and most spectacular development of all – Johannesburg.

Twenty-four months after the arrival of the first diggers on the Rand in 1886, Afrikaners were already at work making the bricks which helped to transform the mining camp into a more substantial town. In late 1887, the Republican government purchased a portion of the farm Braamfontein with the intention of using the stream which flowed through the property as a source of drinking-water for the growing number of new arrivals. The south-western banks of the *spruit*, however, also had rich deposits of clay and poor burghers soon approached the state with a request that they be allowed to manufacture bricks on the site. The Kruger government, uncertain as to the permanence of the new goldfields, agreed to this request with the proviso that each of the applicants pay the state a monthly fee of five shillings for a 'brickmaker's licence' in lieu of rent.[12]

This site, known simply as the Brickfields at first, and then – from 1897 onwards – more formally as Burgersdorp, was soon converted into a hive of Afrikaner industrial activity as the landscape became dotted with hundreds of 'puddle machines', brick moulds, kilns, horses and carts. The poorest of the former bywoners usually entered the new industry on the lowest possible rung of the economic ladder – as workers employed by their better-established countrymen, earning between eight and ten shillings per 1,000 bricks manufactured. The more fortunate, with access to a limited amount of capital, usually started out by erecting or purchasing an animal-powered puddle or pug machine – the large wood and metal encased cylinder in which the clay was mixed prior to being moulded by hand and then baked into bricks. These machines, which were usually attended by two or three black men, were capable of turning out between 2,000 and 3,000 of the superior type of 'stock' bricks per day, or up to 4,000 of the poorer quality bricks known in the trade as 'slops'.

But since brickmaking was essentially a two-phase production process, the producers of raw bricks frequently had to enter into contracts with adjacent kiln owners in order to get their bricks baked and distributed. It would thus appear that it was this latter group – the kiln owners – who constituted a relatively privileged stratum amongst the brickmakers. In addition to operating their own puddle machines, the kiln owners also had adequate numbers of horses and 'scotch carts' which enabled them to distribute the finished product to local building contractors. Yet despite the potentially dominant economic position which the kiln owners commanded within the industry, the Brickfields community does not appear to have been characterised by marked social differentiation amongst Afrikaners. Restricted access to raw materials, keen competition and the cross-cutting ties of kinship no doubt all helped to ensure that there was, as one observer put it, 'no aristocracy' amongst the brickmakers.[13]

As might be expected, however, the overall prosperity of the Brickfields during the 1890s was largely governed by the booms and slumps which the local building industry experienced; something which in turn simply reflected the more fundamental influence which the changing fortunes of the mines exercised over the local economy. The brickmakers thus benefited from the initial flush of development which Johannesburg experienced in the years immediately after 1887, but by 1890 – along with the mining industry – were suffering a recession. When this recession started to lift in late 1891, however, it heralded the advent of a sustained building boom in the city which lasted into the early months of 1896.[14] The price of 'stock' bricks on the local market moved sympathetically and thus rose from £2 15s 0d per 1,000 in 1888 to £3 3s 0d in 1895, and then to an all time high of £4 10s 0d in early 1896.[15] This peak of prosperity in 1895–6, however, was followed by the post-Jameson Raid depression which ensured that the price of bricks eased considerably between 1897 and the outbreak of the South African War. Some of these economic contours can also be traced in Table 6 below, which lists the number of new buildings erected each year within the Johannesburg Sanitary Board/Municipal area in the decade between 1894 and 1904.[16]

Table 6.   New buildings erected in Johannesburg Sanitary Board/Municipal Area, 1894–1904

Year	Number of new buildings
1894	1,236
1895	2,538
1896	1,491
1897	1,058
1898	444
1899	600*
1900	–
1901	79
1902	1,072
1903	3,000
1904	7,883

* Estimate

By 1892 the Brickfields, originally envisaged simply as a temporary industrial site for impoverished burghers, had acquired a substantial measure of permanence and become the major point of entry into the local economy for the poor, unskilled and unemployed drawn from a wide variety of backgrounds including Europeans, Asians, Chinese, 'Cape Malays' and blacks. Over the next 24 months the area became increasingly congested until it became such a cause for concern to the Sanitary Board's health inspectors that they had to use force to prevent new houses being erected on the marshy ground that was already badly pitted and liberally endowed with pools of stagnant water.[17] Such was the poverty in the countryside and the boom in the city's building industry during the mid-1890s, however, that these efforts proved to be largely in vain. By 1895 not only had the density of population in the Brickfields experienced a further increase, but brickmaking activity had also spread to other sites within greater Johannesburg such as Ophirton, City & Suburban, Booysens and Turffontein.[18] The heart of the industry, though, remained at the original site spread along the Braamfontein spruit, and when the census was conducted in 1896 it revealed that the Brickfields had a population of over 7,000 people of all races and over 1,500 brickmakers who, between them, owned over 1,200 horses and mules and about 450 waggons.[19]

By the mid-1890s the position had thus been reached where brickmaking ranked as the third-largest industry in the Transvaal, being behind only mining and agriculture in terms of the number of people it employed. But despite the industry's remarkable growth, and the prosperity of 1895–6 in particular, these small proprietors faced an increasing number of problems as the decade progressed. With the larger independent operators each requiring the services of between twenty and thirty black workers for their businesses, the brickmakers, along with other employers, felt the impact of rising wages as competition for African labour stiffened before 1895.[20] Other difficulties arose from faltering clay deposits, and from the substantial losses which were incurred during periods of exceptionally wet weather, such as in the summer of 1893.[21] All of these labour and production problems, however, paled into insignificance when compared with the threat that proved to be one of the most menacing of all which the Afrikaner brickmakers of Braamfontein had to face – insecurity of tenure.

When the Kruger government first granted burghers the right to make bricks along the Braamfontein spruit in late 1887, it was the occasion for a minor influx of poor Afrikaners who immediately took the opportunity to erect small cottages on the site. Amongst these and subsequent inhabitants the idea soon took root that their right to squat on the property was secure, provided only that they continued to pay the monthly licence fee to the government. This somewhat comforting train of thought was rudely interrupted in 1889 when local civil servants chose to remind the brickmakers that the land was liable to expropriation without compensation at short notice. The brickmakers, who did not take readily to this idea, appealed to Pretoria with some success. In November 1889 the State President and members of his Executive Committee agreed that a parcel of 200 stands should be surveyed in the Brickfields, and that the poorest burghers should be entitled to the undisturbed occupation of these sites for a period of two years on payment of a monthly licence fee of five shillings.[22]

In June 1892, however, the Executive Committee decided that a portion of the Brickfields should be expropriated and that the land should be put at the disposal of the Netherlands Railway Company for use as a marshalling yard. This move further alarmed the brickmakers who now constituted themselves into the Braamfontein Brickmakers' Association which immediately petitioned the government for the grant of a 99-year lease on the site. Despite this plea the government proceeded with its plans and duly handed over the expropriated land to the railway company in May 1893. This action, however, proved to be most unpopular with the local burghers, and the government soon felt the need to placate some of its more irate constituents. In December 1893 the Executive Committee thus sanctioned the surveying of a further parcel of 160 stands in the Brickfields – sites which were then made available to some of the poorest Afrikaners at a fee of half-a-crown per month.[23]

Having secured this minor concession from the state the brickmakers remained undisturbed at their business for the next thirty months as they took advantage of Johannesburg's mid-nineties' building boom. Then, just as the price of stock bricks reached its peak, the shadow of uncertainty again fell over the Brickfields. In May 1896, it was reported that the Sanitary Board and the Netherlands Railway Company had joined forces in an appeal to the government to put a stop to all brickmaking in Braamfontein; the local authority because it had long complained about overcrowding and its attendant evils in that quarter of the town, and the N.Z.A.S.M. because of its desire to proceed with its plans for a marshalling yard. This plea apparently elicited a sympathetic hearing in Pretoria since, a few weeks later, the railway company erected a fence across its portion of the expropriated property in the Brickfields – a move which effectively denied the brickmakers access to one of the few remaining local sources of clay.[24]

The brickmakers' response to this development was swift, if not entirely successful. Within hours of the fence being erected they persuaded some of the town's building contractors to finance a trip to Pretoria and within days a delegation was briefed to put their case to the State President. When the burghers met Kruger, on 16 June 1896, they impressed upon him the hardship and unemployment that would follow if the site along the Braamfontein spruit were closed down. The State President, however, was reluctant to allow the brickmakers' activities to jeopardise the badly needed expansion of railway facilities in Johannesburg. Kruger therefore informed the burghers that the Brickfields site would soon be closed down; but he also gave them his assurance that his government was aware of its responsibilities, and that it would find them an alternative site for their industry.[25]

When this news was formally relayed to a small meeting in the Brickfields a week later, it met with a chilly reception. The brickmakers felt that it would be economically disastrous for them to vacate their central Braamfontein site for a more distant location which would escalate their transport costs and render them less competitive. They were also of the opinion that as burghers their needs should receive priority over those of a 'foreign' company, and that at very least they should be given ample opportunity to wind down their businesses in the Brickfields.[26]

The government took note of this sullen tone, but did not allow it to deflect it from its purpose. The majority of the brickmakers were given until the end of July to vacate the site, and at the end of this period several of the departing Afrikaners established themselves on the residential stands that were made available to poor burghers in the newly proclaimed township of Vrededorp. One small group of brickmakers, however, was allowed to stay on at the Braamfontein spruit, and in the end it was only some two years later – in December 1898 – that all such industrial activity in the Brickfields finally ceased.[27]

This did not mean that Kruger had forgotten his pledge to the unhappy brickmakers. Indeed, at the very moment that the burghers were being forced to close down their industry in Braamfontein, the government was busy acquiring them an alternative site some way from the city centre. The brickmakers, who had previously voiced their disapproval of any attempt to move them to a more distant location, were by now sufficiently desperate to clutch at any opportunity which presented itself. Thus, in order to secure this gain, and avoid any charge of ingratitude that might emanate from Pretoria, over 200 burghers signed a petition agreeing to the move to the new site provided that it was speedily expedited. By late 1896 many of the Afrikaner brickmakers were again at work, but this time on the Alberts brothers' farm, 'Waterval', some six miles to the north-west of Johannesburg.[28]

Within a matter of weeks of their occupying the new site the brickmakers had the worst of their original suspicions confirmed – namely, that the relocation at Waterval had badly blunted the competitive edge which they had previously enjoyed at Braamfontein by pushing up transport costs. Never slow to react politically, the burghers saw in this the occasion for yet another appeal to Kruger and his colleagues. This time the brickmakers set out to persuade the government that their economic survival depended upon the establishment of a rail link between Waterval and the city centre. After several months of intensive lobbying these agitational efforts eventually bore fruit, and in December 1898 the Executive Committee agreed that tenders be called for the construction of a branch line that would link Waterval to Johannesburg via Fordsburg, the Brickfields and Vrededorp.[29] But, before the scheme could be implemented war broke out and the burghers were thus denied their economic life-line to the city.

After the war the brickmakers quickly regrouped to resume their business. As early as December 1902 it was reported that there were between thirty and forty 'factories' operating in the Waterval area, and that the industry employed 500 white men and many more black workers. Predictably enough, the Afrikaners now proceeded to play a far less prominent part in the lobbying activities of the industry and when the Waterfall Brickmakers' Association was formed in the same month, its executive was dominated by English speakers. The new association immediately took up the old issue of railway facilities for the brickmakers, the unfair trade practice which allowed several companies on mining property to continue manufacturing bricks within the inner-city area, and the need for a more stringent pass system to help control the industry's black labour force.[30]

In general, however, the years after the South African War saw a decline in the activities of Johannesburg's independent brickmakers. At Waterval, some of the small producers got a stay of economic execution as the city's suburbs extended northwards in the period before the First World War, thereby reducing transport costs and partly restoring some of the competitive edge which these brickmakers had once enjoyed in the trade. It was also largely as a result of this expansion that a dozen or more Afrikaner brickmakers and their families – amongst them such local notables as the Grundlinghs, the Andersons and the Steenkamps – were able to survive into the twenties, and in a few exceptional cases well beyond that. W. H. Brummer, the Newlands blacksmith who supplied most of these remaining brickyards with hand-crafted equipment, continued to receive occasional orders for puddle machines right into the 1950s.[31]

Capitalist development and the genesis of Afrikaner urban unemployment, 1890–1908

The dramatic eruption of capitalist gold mining on the Witwatersrand in the late 1880s immediately confronted the government of the small South African Republic with a new and challenging set of demands. Foremost amongst these was the urgent need to provide the land-locked country with adequate links to the coastal cities if the mines were to be allowed to import the supplies of food, fuel and machinery that were vital to the development of the infant industry. Kruger and his colleagues were not slow to respond to these demands, and the decade before the South African War saw a remarkable expansion in railway facilities on and to the goldfields. In March 1890 the so-called 'Rand Tram' which ran from Boksburg along the line of reef was opened and this made for the cheap and efficient distribution of coal supplies to the mining industry. Thirty-six months later, in January 1893, Johannesburg was linked to Cape Town by rail, and within a further thirty-six months there were also lines extending to Delagoa Bay (January 1895) and Durban (October 1895). Thereafter followed a more sedate period of consolidation and by the outbreak of the First World War the greater part of the Transvaal was serviced by a system of branch lines.

This opening of the economic arteries to the new industrial heartland of southern Africa, however, effectively drained the life blood from long-distance transport riding. Then, as if the advent of the railways were somehow not enough to bear, Kruger's toll system and the natural disaster of rinderpest came to add their distinctive burdens to those in the trade. These blows, delivered as they were by the hand of God and the hand of man, combined to make the years between 1890 and 1896 particularly disastrous ones for the Rand's transport riders. But the transport riders, as befitted brave and God-fearing men, did not take all this punishment lightly and on occasion they chose to strike back powerfully at the hand of man.

In 1892 it was reported from Vereeniging that large boulders had been placed across the new railway line from the Cape, and that this was considered to be the work of several angry transport riders who had been forced to vacate the area as a result of the arrival of the iron horse. It was the Transvaal tolls, however, that did most to anger burgher agricultural producers and transport riders, and members of both of these groups spent a considerable amount of time and effort in avoiding or circumventing the toll-houses by taking cross-country routes to their markets. Where these tactics were not possible, the men sometimes took more direct action. At Daspoort, near Pretoria, a group of masked Boers seized the toll-keeper in early April 1894, and after binding and gagging him, handcuffed him to a nearby tree before dynamiting the toll-gate. Almost exactly a year later, the finger of suspicion was again pointed at the transport drivers when the toll office near the Ferreira Battery on the Kimberley Road exit from Johannesburg was burnt down under mysterious circumstances.[32]

But in the end, of course, neither the dynamite of Daspoort nor the fire of Ferreira's could overcome these developments and thousands of transport riders were forced to seek further refuge in the urban economy. In Johannesburg, many sought shelter from the icy economic blast by turning to intra-city transport in the form of 'trolley driving', whilst some of those who were fully proletarianised got work as drivers on the horse-drawn tramway.[33] Even in these nooks and crannies, however, they were soon made to realise that the winds sweeping the country heralded not simply a passing storm of economic competition, but the advent of a full-scale capitalist winter. The introduction of the traction engine, the eclipse of the horse-drawn tramway, and competition from cheaper coloured labour all helped to swamp these struggling survivors and deposit them in the pools of permanent poverty to be found in Burgersdorp, Vrededorp and Newlands. Until well into the first decade of the twentieth century, transport riders continued to form one of the most conspicuous categories amongst the Witwatersrand's Afrikaner unemployed.[34]

Those poor burghers who managed to establish themselves in Johannesburg's cab trade before the South African War fared marginally better than their transport-riding cousins – largely because, as we have noted above, the ruling Afrikaner bourgeoisie sought to protect the City & Suburban Tramway Company as a market for its agricultural producers. But, while this made for a relatively inefficient public transport system, and by so doing gave cab drivers a certain amount of room for economic manoeuvre, it did not indemnify the small-scale operators against all the vicissitudes of capitalism. Thus in 1896 the tramway company, while riding on the crest of the mid-nineties boom, decided to extend the length of its track by 25 per cent. This development, when coupled with the dramatic surge in the prices of draught animals and fodder which came in the wake of the rinderpest epidemic, made 1896 and 1897 economically shattering years for the cabbies. The number of registered cab drivers in the city fell from 1,200 in 1896, to 700 in 1897 as 500 men were thrown out of work in a period of twelve months. This blow fell particularly heavily upon the poorest section of the Afrikaner community where many of the men had long relied on shift work in the cab trade to provide them with a measure of casual employment. Moreover, it came at a moment when broader capitalist transformation was also sealing off other traditional lines of retreat for the burgher poor – transport riding had already passed its zenith, and the Brickfields were in the throes of being closed for the move out of town.[35]

It is true that in the immediate post-war period the cab drivers gained some breathing space as Milner's reconstruction government examined the concession which Kruger and his colleagues had granted to the City & Suburban Company. Poor Afrikaners, however, found it increasingly difficult to maintain their foothold in the trade as they were confronted with the competition provided by an influx of Lithuanian immigrants on the one hand, and the spiralling cost of acquiring and servicing cabs on the other. But Afrikaner and immigrant cabbies alike suffered when the reconstruction authorities opened the new electric tramway system in 1906, and then again in 1909, when the City Council first allowed motorised taxis to cruise the streets of Johannesburg. Over this 36-month period a further 600 cab drivers were thrown out of work, and once again the tide of unemployment unceremoniously dumped most of these men in the suburbs of Fordsburg, Vrededorp, and Newlands.[36]

The city's Afrikaner brickmaking community, as we have already seen, was thrust aside to make way for the needs of an expanding economy when, in 1896, the small producers were forced to abandon their Brickfields site in order to accommodate the marshalling yards of the Netherlands Railway Company. Although it was undoubtedly the subsequent move to Waterval that did most of the short-term damage to these Afrikaner businesses, the eclipse of the 'puddle machine' operators was ultimately assured by what was perhaps a more predictable development – the rise of capitalist brickmaking companies making extensive use of Victorian technology.

In April 1890, a mere 24 months after the first burgher brickmakers had established themselves along the banks of the Braamfontein spruit, Johannesburg's first modern brickmaking factory went into production. The Braamfontein Brick & Potteries Company, employing two specially recruited artisans from Koblenz in Germany, four local whites and 44 Africans proved to be most successful, and it was soon joined by similar concerns as other capitalists sought to benefit from the rapid expansion of the building industry during the early nineties. By 1893 there were at least three other large companies seeking to supply the mining town's seemingly insatiable appetite for bricks – the Rand Brick & Tile Company, Robert Kuranda's Doornfontein Brick Company, and, somewhat further afield, Lewis & Marks's Vereeniging Brick & Tile Company.[37]

The even more spectacular building boom of the mid-nineties saw large amounts of additional capital being invested in the brickmaking industry. Predictably, the ubiquitous Sammy Marks was amongst the first to detect the signs of a heightening demand for bricks and in 1894 the Vereeniging Brick & Tile Company responded to the challenge by importing a larger plant and equipment from the English firm that supplied most of southern Africa's needs for brickmaking machinery – Fawcetts of Leeds. Over the following two years in particular, but right up to the outbreak of war, new firms continued to enter the industry; most notably the Patent Artificial Stone Syndicate (1895), the Johannesburg Brick & Potteries Company (1896), the Ophirton Brick & Tile Works Ltd (1897), and the South African Contracting Association (1899).[38]

In the immediate post-war period these earlier companies were joined by a few more entrants to the industry such as the Eclipse Brick Works (1902), the City & Suburban Brick Company (1903), and Donovan's Brick Works at Newlands (1903). This pattern of measured growth was broken, however, when Johannesburg's building industry once again went through an explosive spurt betwen 1903 and 1905. From an average of ten large concerns supplying the city's need for bricks in 1902–3, the number rose to over twenty during the boom of 1903–5 as several middle-sized producers entered the market, and then slumped back to about ten during the depression of 1906–8. Thereafter, from 1909 to 1914, the figure tended to remain more or less constant as the ten larger firms re-asserted their dominance over the local market for bricks.[39]

This stark cataloguing of the rise in the number of brickmaking companies, however, does not in itself reveal the nature and extent of the damage which these new capitalist enterprises inflicted on their smaller Afrikaner competitors. Firms such as the Patent Artificial Stone Syndicate, the Ophirton Brick & Tile Company and others established their works on mining property. This not only provided them with large customers on their doorsteps, it also accorded them all the benefits that came with protected central sites at precisely the moment that the burgher brickmakers were being forced to move out of town. While this legal manoeuvre was undoubtedly within the letter of the law which did not encompass mining property, it certainly infringed the spirit of a municipal regulation which forbade all brickmaking within a three-mile radius of the city centre.[40]

But the real damage derived not so much from the advantage which capitalist firms enjoyed in terms of transport costs, as from the competitive edge which mechanised production techniques afforded them. The brickmaking machinery with which Fawcetts supplied their clients was capable of both increasing production and reducing the need for manual labour. The plant installed on the Lewis & Marks property in 1896, for example, had the capacity to produce 20,000 bricks a day 'with the minimum of hand manipulation'. Likewise, when the South African Contracting Association opened its new works for public inspection in 1899, it was noted that the 'manual labour required is reduced to a minimum', and that in terms of 'labour saving appliances' the plant was 'a model of ingenuity'.[41]

The full extent and effectiveness of this capitalist onslaught against the small producers is perhaps best reflected in the changing fortunes of the Johannesburg Brick & Potteries Company. Floated with a capital of over £125,000 in the year that the Afrikaner brickmakers were expelled from the city centre – 1896 – this venture was designed to become the local giant of the brickmaking industry. Amongst many other capitalists, this project attracted the interest of Adolf Epler and Samuel Evans, and in subsequent years both of these mining-house notables served as directors of the company.

Although Johannesburg Brick & Potteries along with other companies struggled financially during the recession years of 1897 and 1898, its highly mechanised plant soon enabled it to produce bricks more cheaply than its rivals – a development which drew accusations of unfair trade practice. Whatever the truth of these allegations, the fact remained that from 1897 onwards the company was able to submit the lowest tenders in town, and by so doing won the lion's share of the larger contracts – including, for example, that to supply the Public Works Department of the *Zuid Afrikaansche Republiek*. Thus at the very moment that Kruger's government was attempting to rescue the burgher brickmakers from economic oblivion by providing them with an alternative site at Waterval, it was also forced to award its business to the Afrikaners' capitalist rivals in the city centre.[42]

Immediately after the war the directors reconstructed the company and the additional capital resources generated by this move were used to acquire new clay deposits at Heronmere as well as modernised plant and equipment. By late 1902 Johannesburg Brick & Potteries had the capacity to produce over 60,000 bricks per day at rates even cheaper than those ruling before the war. Samuel Evans – a full partner in H. Eckstein & Co. – used this competitive edge as well as his wide range of powerful contacts to help the company win large contracts from, amongst others, the Royal Engineers, the Johannesburg municipality and the Milner government. In 1903 the company made a profit of £6,000. In the following year, however, the post-war housing boom helped the company to an even more spectacular performance as it recorded a profit of over £10,000 and declared a dividend at 25 per cent – and that despite the fact that it had cut the cost of its bricks by half during the preceding twelve months. This relentless expansion made Johannesburg Brick & Potteries the undisputed leader of the local brickmaking industry between 1897 and 1914.[43]

The shadow of this and other capitalist successes fell over areas which, as we have seen, were already struggling in the gathering gloom of unemployment. Most of the small brickmakers who had somehow managed to survive the move from Burgersdorp, could not withstand this fierce blast of post-war competition. Some battled on in the economic twilight, hoping that the trams would be allowed to convey bricks when the new public transport system was extended to the north-western suburbs in 1906 – the last echo of Kruger's scheme to provide Waterval with a rail link to Johannesburg.[44] Others sought work in the brickyards of the large companies, only to find that imported machinery destroyed jobs almost as swiftly as the building boom created them.[45] The majority, however, joined the ranks of the workless, and when the full darkness of unemployment eventually settled over Fordsburg, Vrededorp and Newlands in 1906–8, there were brickmakers as well as transport riders, cab drivers and former Republican civil servants in the queues at the soup kitchens.[46]

Afrikaner class consciousness and the responses of mining capital and the state, 1895–1914

Throughout the late 1880s and the early 1890s there was always a measure of white unemployment on the Rand in general and in Johannesburg in particular. As was to be expected in a new town based on a single industry, the large majority of the unemployed were miners who were thrown out of work by the periodic slumps in the mining industry as investor confidence rose and fell spectacularly in the period prior to the relatively sustained development of the deep levels. In 1889, for example, it was reported that white miners were experiencing great difficulty in finding jobs, and in the serious recession of 1892–3, E. P. Rathbone – hardly an uncritical observer of the working classes – wrote of how: 'It is heart-breaking to see the number of literally half-starved, competent, sober, intelligent miners that we cannot possibly find work for.' Even in 1894, when the economy had once again experienced an upturn, J. T. Bain of the Witwatersrand Mine Employees' and Mechanics' Union estimated that there were over 2,000 men out of work in Johannesburg alone.[47]

Two related features characterised these early periods of unemployment on the Rand. First, it was noteworthy how, in the years before the Jameson Raid, these immigrant miners had little to turn to by way of large-scale organised assistance or relief. While Rathbone's Rand Labour Bureau which was opened in 1892 undertook to place miners and others in employment in return for five per cent of their first month's wages, such an organisation was – by its very nature – incapable of making serious inroads into what was, after all, a structural problem and not simply a lack of market intelligence on the part of work-seekers. In 1893 J. T. Bain and his colleagues in the labour movement sought a potentially more radical solution when they unsuccessfully appealed to the Kruger government to give consideration to the possibility of opening state mines in an attempt to cope with the problem of white unemployment.[48]

Given these failures, most of the English miners were forced into seeking more personal solutions to their plight, and for the more fortunate some relief came from casual employment gained as barmen, waiters, billiard markers or bookmakers' assistants in the town. Many of the older and less fortunate, however, were reduced to vagrancy, while some of the younger and more daring turned either to petty crime or highway robbery in order to make a living – the latter group in particular constituting the subject of an exciting, but at the moment unwritten chapter in the history of the early Transvaal.[49]

Secondly, it is also noteworthy how relatively few Afrikaners there were amongst the Rand's chronically unemployed in the years before 1895. In part this can be accounted for by pointing to the smaller number of Afrikaners who made their way to the Rand permanently between 1888 and 1894, and the proportionately limited percentage of the overall population of Johannesburg which Afrikaners formed during this period.[50] Probably more important, however, is the fact that these years also coincided with the period during which transport riding, cab driving and brickmaking made their greatest strides within the city. This does not mean that there was an absence of poverty or unemployment within the Afrikaner community – the distress of some of the Brickfields poor on the one hand, and the occasional presence of young highwaymen with names like van Greuning and de Koker on the other, testify to that – but rather that these sectors of the local economy were capable of absorbing and retaining much of Johannesburg's unskilled Afrikaner labour between 1886 and 1895.[51]

For an extremely complex set of social, political and economic reasons, however, both sets of features noted above rapidly gave way between 1895 and 1897. The development of the deep level mines, the 'Kaffir Boom' of 1894–5, and the new rail links to the Reef all helped to draw thousands more British and other miners to the Witwatersrand. While some of this new influx of labour was absorbed during the 'Kaffir Boom', much of it simply served to swell the ranks of the reserve army of labour, and more especially so during the recession of 1896–7.[52] During the same period some of the Randlords, operating at first through the Transvaal National Union and later the South African League, sought to extend their programme of agitation against the Kruger state by developing a popular base. As part of this latter campaign to woo the Rand's English workers – a significant number of whom tended to show pro-Kruger sympathies as part of their struggle against capital – these mine owners lent their support to schemes for the more organised relief of the local unemployed. Amongst the more important of these schemes were the Present Help League, established in 1895 with the generous help of Lionel Phillips, and its extension service – the Rev. Kelly's Relief Stores – which received substantial support from the same Randlords' overtly political organisation, the Reform Committee. Thus from the mid-nineties onwards the struggle for the support and control of Johannesburg's unemployed was becoming increasingly politicised, and the Kruger government showed its prompt appreciation of this fact by temporarily suspending the operation of Kelly's Relief Stores in the days immediately following the Jameson Raid.[53]

At the same time that these intertwining processes were unfolding into their more recognisable forms of organised charity and relief work, an equally complex set of developments was also taking place elsewhere in Johannesburg and in the Witwatersrand's hinterland. The mid-nineties were particularly disastrous years for many Boer agriculturalists and their bywoners, as locusts, drought and particularly rinderpest dealt them successive blows. This acute rural distress occasioned a new and dramatic increase in the flow of poverty-striken Afrikaners to the Rand between 1895 and 1897. But, as we have seen elsewhere, this was precisely the period during which the local economy and particularly the sectors we have focused on – transport riding, cab driving and brickmaking – was experiencing a recession, and thus least capable of absorbing an influx of unskilled labour. Thus these three years saw an unprecedented increase in the number of unemployed Afrikaners in Johannesburg.

By the mid-1890s, therefore, an acute and somewhat contradictory phase had been reached in the development of the city's white unemployment crisis. While such organised charity and relief work as did exist was largely directed towards the 'single', skilled, unemployed English immigrant miner, the greatest poverty and hardship existed amongst the families of unskilled, unemployed Afrikaner workers. This paradox, or at least the full extent of it, was at first not fully appreciated by either the mine owners or the state although the Volksraad did, in May 1897, set up a commission to investigate the need to provide assistance to the burgher poor. This commission made such desultory progress, however, that it was left to a small number of local Afrikaner activists – notably I. D. de Vries and P. C. Duvenhage – to grapple with the problem of destitution in the city's western working-class suburbs.

On the morning of 23 July 1897 a group of 25 unemployed Afrikaners from these suburbs decided to draw a leaf from the pages of English working-class struggle when they set out to march to Pretoria in order to lobby their representative in the Volksraad, A. A. Dieperink, about the problems of local unemployment. But Dieperink, who was much put out by the arrival of the marchers in the capital city, persuaded the men to accompany him on a train journey back to Johannesburg where they would discuss the matter. On the same evening, however, the marchers forced the Volksraad member to address a meeting of over 1,000 needy burghers held in Vrededorp. At this meeting Dieperink agreed to personally examine the extent of poverty in the suburb during the course of the following morning, and to urge upon the state the need for an immediate public works programme – in particular, a scheme to develop more fully the Main Reef Road.[54]

It was also in the immediate wake of this meeting that the Johannesburg Relief Committee was called into being by de Vries, Duvenhage and about a dozen other Afrikaner notables including, amongst others, the lawyers Barent Malraison, S. H. van Diggelen and J. C. Smuts. During the following week the members of this committee debated the virtues of various schemes which could possibly help alleviate burgher unemployment, and on 6 August 1897 a deputation of three was sent to Pretoria to seek the State President's support for the proposed steam laundry for white women workers in Vrededorp, and the Main Reef Road works.[55] Kruger gave de Vries and his colleagues a sympathetic hearing, but urged upon the deputation the need to widen its base and increase its authority by co-opting certain local government officials onto the committee. This the members of the committee readily agreed to, and on 9 August they decided to move further in the same direction by inviting all the editors of the Johannesburg newspapers to serve on the committee.[56]

Then, just at the moment that the Relief Committee had carefully completed laying the foundations of its structure, its efforts were struck by an ideological bombshell which came from the most unexpected quarter. On Saturday morning, 14 August 1897, the most radical and sympathetic of the local pro-government newspapers, the *Standard and Diggers' News*, ran an openly hostile and provocative editorial:

> If we were convinced that local destitution was as terrible as some folks would fain make it out to be, we should be the last to seek to belittle it. But as far as we have yet been able to judge, it appears to us that far too much is being made of a few sporadic cases of genuine penury and want. 'The poor ye have always with you.' In every community – and especially in a town with Johannesburg's characteristics – there is always to be found a considerable residuum of poverty-stricken people – those who, through various causes, fall out of the fighting ranks and join the stragglers at the rear.[57]

Getting into its full Victorian stride, the editorial then proceeded to draw the familiar distinction between the 'deserving' and 'undeserving' poor, and to argue that the degree of local unemployment was simply the 'normal' and to be expected in any modernising and mechanising economy.[58] 'It is simply hysterical folly', the leader writer concluded, 'to declaim under an illusory supposition that abnormal destitution exists.'

These claims incensed de Vries, Duvenhage and some of the other more militant members of the Johannesburg Relief Committee, and within hours of the newspaper appearing on the streets these men had arranged for a meeting of the burgher unemployed on Market square. By mid-morning, between 500 and 600 Afrikaners drawn from Burgersdorp, Fordsburg and Vrededorp were in attendance when de Vries and Duvenhage led a relatively orderly procession down Loveday street towards the city offices of the Relief Committee amidst shouts of 'Berlin! Berlin!' Once the crowd reached this destination it paused and 'demonstrated' outside the offices for several minutes.[59]

From there, however, the men turned towards the Harrison street works of the *Standard and Diggers' News*, and it was at this stage that the procession was joined by more of the local unemployed, curious bystanders, and by others whom the newspaper later chose to describe as some of the European 'flotsam and jetsam' of the city. By the time that the leaders of the procession were met by the acting editor of the newspaper, Joseph van Gelder, the crowd had swollen to between two and three thousand people, and its conduct was becoming less orderly. De Vries and Duvenhage then 'invited' the editor to address the marchers on his views about unemployment.[60]

Van Gelder spoke to the crowd and offered to insert the names, addresses and 'handicrafts' of all the unemployed in the columns of his newspaper – not a particularly helpful suggestion to indigent burghers who wanted his editorial support for a state public works programme. He then proceeded to tell the gathering of more than 2,000 that Mr Blane, a mining engineer, 'was ready to engage ten good men at once at five shillings a day, sleeping accommodation included'. But since the majority of the unemployed were unskilled Afrikaner males with their own homes, it was perhaps understandable that, 'The offer met with considerable disfavour'. By this time there were already sporadic shouts of 'maak hom dood' – 'kill him', and some scuffling within the ranks of an increasingly impatient procession. Hearing this, van Gelder again addressed himself to de Vries and Duvenhage, who promptly extracted from him the same pledge that they had earlier forced from Dieperink under slightly different circumstances – the promise that he would undertake a personal tour of inspection of the western suburbs in order to assess the nature and extent of Afrikaner poverty. When this 'agreement' was announced to the assembled ranks of the unemployed, however, it did little to appease them. Some members of the procession grabbed van Gelder and dragged him across the road, and when a fight flared up in a nearby section of the crowd the police swiftly intervened to form a bodyguard for the editor whom they eventually hustled into the safety of the back yard of the Palace Hotel. With the immediate object of their displeasure removed from their focus, the temper of the marchers abated somewhat, but even so it was several hours before the crowd finally dispersed.[61]

Both the composition of this crowd, and the militancy of its leadership took the editorial staff of the Standard and Diggers' News by complete surprise. 'We had expected the English-speaking variety', van Gelder admitted in the columns of the following Monday morning's edition. The acting-editor also acknowledged that after his trip to Fordsburg and Vrededorp he was convinced that there were cases of 'real distress', and that a significant part of this could be attributed to the collapse of employment opportunities in the Brickfields. Still smarting from the trouncing which he had experienced at the hands of de Vries and Duvenhage, however, he also went on to note that 'professional agitation will never alleviate suffering', and was further of the opinion that 'nothing of a practical nature was attained' by the 'demonstration'.[62]

Van Gelder was wrong. For several months before this 'demonstration' sensitive observers of the local scene had been noting with increasing concern the rapid growth of white unemployment in the city and the potential which this held for radical action. By the end of the first quarter of 1897, the 'plague of vagrancy' and 'rampant street begging' of late 1896 was giving way to a more aggressive posture on the part of the unemployed. On 2 April 1897, for example, The Comet pointed out how the level of local unemployment was becoming dangerously high and that, 'unless remedial steps of some kind are very quickly taken the police will be face to face with an uncommonly nasty problem'. Within two weeks of this observation having been made the point was underscored when a fire broke out in a Market street shop and a large crowd of whites promptly smashed the windows of an adjacent outfitter and looted the premises. The march of the unemployed to Pretoria and the fracas outside the *Standard and Diggers'* offices in which a pro-Kruger and alleged supporter of the working classes escaped with his life, thus contributed to a developing pattern of mass action. As such it left the Transvaal ruling classes with a clear message, and this in turn meant – contrary to van Gelder's opinion – that a good deal of 'a practical nature was attained' in the wake of the 'demonstration'.[63]

Within four days of the 'demonstration', J. P. FitzPatrick – acting on behalf of H. Eckstein & Co. – had agreed to employ 200 unskilled Afrikaners on surface work at the Crown Deep mine. In addition, Eckstein's also approached the Kruger government with the offer to take on a number of younger Afrikaner males between the ages of sixteen and twenty, in order that they might be given the necessary training which would enable them to cope with underground work. Eckstein & Co. were soon joined by the Robinson and Consolidated Gold Fields groups, and by early September 1897 Johan Spaan of the Johannesburg Relief Committee could proudly point to the fact that over 500 unskilled burghers had been found positions on the mines.[64] Although Afrikaners did not look upon this opportunity as providing them with long-term employment – indeed the majority of those engaged on underground work soon left the mines – their militancy had at least forced the Randlords to acknowledge and respond to the claims of this new generation of Transvaal proletarians to employment within the premier industry of the Boer state.

The Kruger government, too, moved 'with commendable promptitude in regard to the question of relief to the indigent', and within days of the 'demonstration' the state gave its approval, in principle, to the proposed steam laundry for workless women in Vrededorp, a scheme for an 'industrial school' which would train some of Johannesburg's Afrikaner youth, and the Main Reef Road project which would provide work for the Rand's unemployed burghers.[65] Of these various schemes, however, it was only really the last one which provided substantial relief to the poor of the city's western suburbs in the period before the war. Between early 1898 and late 1899 the Kruger government allocated over £30,000 for the Main Reef Road works and this in turn provided short-term employment for hundreds of Afrikaners.[66]

But if the events leading up to the affray outside the *Standard and Diggers' News* in August 1897 had instantly commanded the attention of Randlords and the Kruger government, then it also managed to concentrate the minds of the local shopkeepers wonderfully. In the wake of the march by the unemployed through the city's streets and past their shops, W. Hosken of the Chamber of Commerce, Sam Foote of the Witwatersrand Licensed Victuallers' Association, and J. W. Quinn – the city's foremost baker and a member of the local Sanitary Board – all became closely involved in the activities of yet another newly formed charitable association, the Rand Relief Committee, and supported its efforts in the western suburbs with donations in cash or in kind. It was also these men who persuaded Eckstein & Co., Consolidated Gold Fields, Robinson, A. Goerz & Co., Farrar, S. Neumann & Co. and Lewis & Marks to extend their existing support to the relief programme by making further substantial cash donations to the Rand Relief Committee. Thus by taking their struggle on to the streets of Johannesburg, the Afrikaner and other unemployed in the town managed to extract significant concessions from the state, the mine owners and the local petty bourgeoisie between 1897 and 1898.[67]

When confidence in the Rand was partially restored during the last quarter of 1898 and the early months of 1899, the local economy revived somewhat and employment prospects for skilled workers in the mining industry brightened considerably. This, and the state's continuing public works programme for unskilled burgher labourers, did much to help alleviate the crisis of white unemployment, and by mid-1898 class tension within the city had eased significantly. The mine owners and shopkeepers, who earlier had willingly shared the burden of providing relief to the Afrikaner and other poor, now made repeated efforts to pass the full responsibility for providing aid to the local indigent to the Kruger government. When these efforts failed, the affairs of the Rand Relief Committee were wound up in September 1898. Thereafter, much of the charity and relief work in the western suburbs fell to the churches and other voluntary associations. By early 1899 the editorial nerve at the *Standard and Diggers' News* had been sufficiently restored for the newspaper to run a cautiously worded leader on another well-worn Victorian theme – the problem of 'Indiscriminate Alms Giving'.[68]

This situation, however, changed again when war was declared in October 1899 as most of the immigrant miners left for the coastal cities, and the Afrikaner men left to join their commandos for the coming struggle in the countryside. This exodus significantly altered the class composition of the city, or in the more genteel words of L. S. Amery, it meant that for the war years 'a large percentage of the normal inhabitants of Johannesburg were either very poor or very rascally'.[69]

Amongst the 'very poor' whom Amery had noted, there were many of the wives and children of burghers who were congregated in the Brickfields, Vrededorp, and to a lesser extent, Fordsburg. It was these families who, in the period immediately prior to the war, had been amongst the principal beneficiaries of the state's Main Reef Road scheme, and they were thus amongst the first to suffer when all organised relief operations were suspended. Within a month of the outbreak of hostilities the plight of these families was such that Afrikaner women in the Brickfields were forced into the sporadic looting of unoccupied homes and business premises in the city. In order to contain this assault on private property, the Republican officials who had been left in charge of the city were forced into setting up a new fund for the relief of the local poor. Thus in the months leading up to the British occupation of Johannesburg, the city's remaining merchants and shopkeepers were again called upon to channel donations in cash or in kind down increasingly familiar avenues. This they did – some no doubt simply out of compassion, others out of the desire to help defuse the possibility of further militant independent action by Afrikaner women.[70]

When this source of relief was cut off through the arrival of Lord Roberts and his troops in June 1900 the response of the Afrikaner destitute and the 'rascally' was once again swift and unambiguous. Within days of the city being handed over to the British army, the Imperial troops were called upon to suppress a new – and far more serious – outbreak of looting by 'some of the poor Dutch' and 'the riff-raff of the foreign population' in the western suburbs.[71] After this, there were no further serious wartime incidents of this kind in the city – partly because there was an occupying army to draw on to help protect private property, and partly because the British authorities took urgent and energetic action under the provisions of martial law to rid the town of nearly 2,000 'undesirables' whom it either imprisoned or deported.[72]

These events of 1899–1900, like the earlier ones in 1897, did not escape the notice of Johannesburg's ruling classes who now saw in the Imperial intervention the opportunity to engage in a round of radical social engineering which could do much to rid the inner city of its concentration of Afrikaner unemployed, and its even more volatile lumpenproletarian element of all colours. As early as February 1902, J. W. Quinn, a member of Milner's nominated Town Council and Chairman of its Public Health Committee, advocated that the Brickfields, Burgersdorp and a portion of lower Fordsburg be declared an 'Insanitary Area', expropriated, demolished and redeveloped. Quinn was also quick to point out to his fellow councillors that it was particularly opportune to move in this direction while the burghers were still away on commando, or else detained in the camps as prisoners of war.[73]

It was not simply the city baker's thoughts that were running in this direction, however. In the boardrooms of the mining companies some of the more influential Randlords were also thinking about the need to plan for the arrival of the army of unemployed which would make its way to Johannesburg when the war ended. 'The argument which I could not press in public but which we use in private and in council', FitzPatrick confided to his partner Wernher in July 1902, 'is that many thousand men who will be disbanded here within a few weeks and who may be without means of subsistence, must be regarded as an extremely serious possible danger.' 'If they become a starving and disorderly rabble', he warned, 'it will cost us money, exertions, repute and stability ten times what it may cost to tide them through the period until they can be absorbed into the working community.'[74] These strictures echoed loudly in the ears of Milner and his young officials, and the reconstruction administration responded swiftly to these suggestions.

In September 1902, a mere six months after Quinn had first publicly announced the possibility of an enquiry into the Brickfields–Burgersdorp–Fordsburg area with a view to eventually expropriating it, the Governor of the Transvaal appointed a commission to examine the problem. The Town Council's case – in essence also the reconstruction government's case since the former was still a nominated rather than an elected body – was lead by Quinn as Chairman of the Public Health Committee, and by Milner's choice as Johannesburg Town Clerk, Lionel Curtis. It was Curtis, however, drawing on his experience at the London County Council and his knowledge gained as Honorary Secretary to the Mansion House Committee on the Dwellings of the Poor, who really master-minded the authorities' case. Modelling his approach along the lines of the Westminster Housing of the Working Classes Act of 1890, Curtis and his colleagues carefully steered the Johannesburg Insanitary Area Improvement Scheme Commission to the conclusion that – largely on grounds of public health – the buildings under consideration should be demolished. Shortly after the commission reported in 1903, the city's oldest Afrikaner industrial site, already eclipsed by larger capitalist developments and reduced to a residential area for the 'labouring classes and the dangerous classes', was forced to give way to the redeveloped industrial and business sites of Newtown. This, together with the rapid escalation of rents during the post-war housing crisis, did much to push some of Johannesburg's Afrikaner unemployed into the outlying suburbs such as Newlands during the reconstruction era.[75]

But if it was largely Lionel Curtis who responded to Quinn's suggestions in respect of the 'Insanitary Area', then it was Milner himself who paid most attention to FitzPatrick and the other mine owners' warnings about the need to exercise careful control over the unemployed in the immediate post-war period. As Governor of the newest British colony he therefore established the Rand Refugee Department and it was largely this arm of the state, operating with a government grant and mining-house money, together with the older Present Help League which continued to be privately funded, that did most to provide charity, relief and temporary shelter for hundreds of semi-skilled English workers during the earliest months of demobilisation.[76]

By late 1902, however, Milner – already hard-pressed by Whitehall about the cost of the war and reconstruction – was of the opinion that the full burden of meeting these costs could legitimately be passed on to FitzPatrick and his friends. Moreover, he, and Lionel Curtis, who was even more familiar with the role and function of the Charity Organisation Society in London, felt the need to centralise all relief operations on the Rand in order to avoid duplication of effort and to minimise the problem of 'indiscriminate alms giving'.[77] Thus in January 1903 the Refugee Department and the Present Help League were moulded into a single organisation – the Rand Aid Society – with Milner as its patron and R. W. Schumacher, Carl Hanau and J. W. Quinn, amongst others, serving on its board of trustees.[78] For at least the next two decades the Rand Aid Association, with the active financial support and guidance of the more far-sighted mine owners, virtually dominated Johannesburg's organised relief programmes.[79]

The reconstruction government and the Randlords thus entered the first months of the post-war period with some equanimity – soothed in the knowledge that the problem of the Afrikaner proletariat in the 'Insanitary Area' on the one hand, and the threat posed by the unemployed English miners on the other, were both well under control. Indeed, there was at least one of Milner's young officials who was so confident that there was sufficient social grease on the squeakier wheels of Rand capitalism, that he could foresee no future for white working-class radicalism. 'No labour party can be really formidable unless it is based on profound discontents and radical grievances', wrote John Buchan in 1903, 'and the annoyances of the Johannesburg proletariat are, as compared with those of Europe, like crumpled rose-leaves to thorns.' 'There is', he concluded, 'too strong a force of social persistence in the city to suffer it ever to become the prey of a well-organised gang of revolutionaries.'[80]

If this somewhat hasty judgement served subsequently to embarrass an older and much wiser Buchan in 1907, 1913 and 1922, then there was admittedly little to suggest that he was wide of the mark between 1903 and 1905. As FitzPatrick and his colleagues had hoped, many of the skilled and semi-skilled workers were gradually re-absorbed into the working community during this period, with the Rand Aid Association successfully taking the sting out of much of the class antagonism during the intervening spell of unemployment. The unskilled Afrikaner workers, for their part, used the delay in the introduction of the electric tramway and the post-war building boom to re-establish themselves – albeit on a diminished scale – in their old jobs as cab drivers, brickmakers and casual labourers. The effect of this latter development was to remove temporarily the plight of the urban Afrikaner worker from the view of not only the British administration, but also from the former Afrikaner ruling class which at that moment was engaged in the task of politically reconstituting itself. Thus, when Louis Botha addressed the 'Boer Congress' held in Pretoria in May 1904, he was of the opinion that – as far as the Afrikaner poor were concerned – there were only two categories of importance that had to be catered for, the former Republican civil servants in the towns, and the ex-bywoners in the countryside.[81]

This brief interlude in the struggle came to an end when, from late 1905 onwards, the Rand economy rapidly slid into a full-scale depression. Early in 1906 the electric tram made its first appearance in the streets of Johannesburg, and over the next twelve months hundreds of Vrededorp cab drivers as well as scores of others in associated trades such as coach-builders, blacksmiths, farriers and harness-makers were thrown out of work. More serious by far, however, was the dramatic collapse of the building industry as the post-war housing boom came to an end. While this took a predictable toll on hundreds of small brickmakers and their workers in Albertskroon and Newlands, it also rendered thousands of bricklayers, stonemasons, carpenters, electricians, plasterers, painters and handymen in other working-class suburbs unemployed. Redundancies on this scale were inevitably reflected in reduced consumer demand, and this in turn cost scores of clerks and shop assistants their jobs. Within a matter of months the streets of the city assumed an aspect which had last been seen a decade earlier in 1896.[82]

On this occasion, however, Johannesburg's ruling classes had the benefit of an institutionalised monitoring agency which could provide them with an early warning of any unusual build-up in the size of the Rand's reserve army of labour. In March 1906 the Rand Aid Association addressed a letter to Lionel Phillips in which it alerted him to the fact that the new situation would demand resources well in excess of its current government and municipal grants, and appealing to him to enlist the support of his company. But even Wernher, Beit & Co.'s substantial grants – then and later – as well as those of other Randlords, were not sufficient to the task of social control during a period of deep depression.[83] The Rand Aid Association thus also urged another of its influential members, the Mayor of Johannesburg and the man immediately responsible for the city's welfare, W. K. Tucker, to approach the state for further assistance.[84]

In May 1906 Tucker warned Milner's successor in Pretoria, Selborne, that the problem of unemployment in the city was sufficiently serious to merit the urgent attention of the government. The new governor, who was at least partly convinced by the Mayor's arguments, duly appointed a seven-man commission of enquiry to examine the problems of poverty and unemployment in the colony. When the Transvaal Indigency Commission met for the first time in November 1906, however, it was led by a familiar team of social engineers which revealed that it was Johannesburg rather than the colony as a whole which was of concern to the state. In addition to having J. W. Quinn as its chairman, the commission was also served by Lionel Curtis, his successor as the city's Town Clerk, Richard Feetham, and yet another of Milner's choices for the task of reconstruction, Phillip Kerr.[85]

This political response to the plea of Johannesburg's ruling classes, however, did little to improve the economic lot of those most immediately affected – the unemployed – who became increasingly anxious as the year drew to a close. Early in December 1906 hundreds of skilled and semi-skilled workers without jobs gathered on the Market square to discuss their dilemma, and at the conclusion of the meeting formed themselves into the 'Unemployed Organisation' under the leadership of Joseph Hale. This body, which was largely composed of the unemployed drawn from the building and allied trades, met at irregular intervals throughout the month in an attempt to solve the problems of its members. The Unemployed Organisation regularly called on the municipality or the government to initiate a public works programme, or in more reactionary vein, appealed to these employers to discharge black workers and take on white men in their place. At a mass meeting held on Boxing Day, for example, it passed a resolution calling on the government 'to remove all coloured men from pumping stations, lamp-cleaning, light porterage and stores tending, and such other work as may fitly be done by white men, and fill the vacancies thus created with Europeans'.[86]

Tucker and his fellow councillors, who were closer to these meetings of hundreds of the unemployed in the city centre than the outgoing British administration in Pretoria, read these signs with growing concern and in mid-December 1906 the Johannesburg Town Council did indeed take on several hundred unskilled labourers – including a few score Afrikaners – into a local public works programme. In addition to this, the Mayor unsuccessfully approached the Chamber of Mines with a formal request that it consider the possibility of taking on some of the local citizens who were jobless.[87]

Within three weeks of these developments, however, on 4 January 1907, Tucker was again approached by a delegation from the Unemployed Organisation and this time with a far more disturbing request. Hale and his colleagues now wanted the Town Council to make available to them a central camp site in order that the members of their organisation might enjoy rent-free accommodation whilst they searched for work. But the Mayor, who was already concerned about the security of the city, refused to entertain a proposition which would – for the foreseeable future – concentrate a large number of the unemployed on a single site. Instead, Tucker put new pressure on the authorities in Pretoria to consider a state public works programme which would draw off some of the unemployed from Johannesburg.[88]

In the weeks that followed, Hale and his colleagues developed a two-pronged strategy to increase their pressure on the ruling classes. On the one hand, they deliberately escalated the demands which they made of the Rand Aid Association in order to embarrass the authorities and hasten the announcement of a state public works programme. On the other, they exploited one of the few major divisions amongst the Randlords by approaching J. B. Robinson with the request that *he* came to the financial assistance of their members. The latter move reaped an immediate dividend. Robinson – ever anxious to extend his feud with the Chamber of Mines – promptly made £5,000 available to the members of the Unemployed Organisation. As part of their efforts to provide the unemployed with accommodation, Hale and his committee used some of this grant to acquire eighteen large tents – this despite the fact that they were still without the use of a camp site.[89]

On 14 February 1907 the government finally made its long-awaited announcement about relief works for the Rand's unemployed. This work, which had to be applied for through the offices of the Rand Aid Association, would take the form of road building in the Rustenburg district where the unemployed would also be provided with food and tents. In addition to this, those who enlisted would be paid a small cash wage for their services but, in an attempt to prevent an influx of unemployed from other parts of South Africa, this would be restricted to the sum of two shillings per day.[90]

The prospect of earning two shillings a day on road works at Rustenburg did not elicit much enthusiasm amongst Johannesburg's unemployed. When asked about their opinions, however, the members of the Unemployed Organisation at first simply said that the offer was unsuitable for married men who were unwilling to desert their families during such hard times, while some of the younger men were of the opinion that they would only be in a position to leave the city after they had voted in the election. Hale, disappointed with the government's response, then appealed to Selborne to provide his members with the camp site which the Town Council had earlier refused them. On 15 February the Governor replied, pointing out that all public property in Johannesburg was under the control of the Town Council, and that in any event all such requests should – in the first instance – be directed through the Rand Aid Association.[91]

By this time the members of the Unemployed Organisation were both tired and angry – tired of making unproductive appeals through official channels, and angered by the miserly response of the state to their insistent pleas for help. Despite this, the committee directed one final appeal for a camp site to Selborne. On Friday morning, 16 February, Hale summoned the unemployed to a meeting on the Union Ground and in the address that followed he lost no time at all in making what he considered to be the central points. 'It was a disgrace', he said, 'that the Government should ask white men to work for less pay than they would offer a Kaffir.' Because of this insulting offer, it was now vital for them to acquire a camp site and 'whether consent came or not they would have the ground, and have it that day'. Hale assured his audience that he already had a site in mind, and that it was 'Parktown way'. Amidst growing applause he told the unemployed that 'It might be that it was Sunnyside – the Governor was away and his house was unoccupied.' Finally, Hale warned the 'big people' in the Transvaal that they should not be surprised to see, 'before the month was out, such an upheaval in the country as they had never anticipated'. The meeting closed on this militant note with the crowd dispersing to await a reply from Selborne. When no reply had been received by late afternoon the unemployed regrouped and over 700 men and eight families marched into the city centre where they seized and occupied – not the Governor's official residence – but the Braamfontein Show Ground which was under municipal control.[92]

These developments – the formation of the Unemployed Organisation, the soliciting of the J. B. Robinson gift, the organised attempts to embarrass the Rand Aid Association, the plea for a public works programme and the seizure of the Show Ground were all followed with great interest by the unemployed of Vrededorp. Indeed, several Afrikaners had been party to at least one of these events when, on 14 February, 400 men had simultaneously invaded the offices of the Rand Aid Association to demand food before being persuaded to disperse by their leaders.[93] The seizure of the Show Ground, however, held little appeal for the Afrikaner unemployed – in fact, it left them in somewhat of a quandary since as home-owners in Vrededorp they had no immediate need for shelter, while the creation of an exclusive camp for the workless in effect denied them access the the Robinson relief funds.

On the morning following the seizure of the Show Ground, therefore, about eighty of the Afrikaner unemployed under the leadership of a former lieutenant in Kruger's State Artillery, N. P. Oelofse, met on the Union Ground to discuss their predicament. Oelofse opened the meeting with more disturbing news for the Vrededorp unemployed. The local committee of Het Volk – deeply suspicious that the Rand Aid Association was an instrument of their political opponents, the Progressives – was of the opinion that no loyal Afrikaner should accept relief from that agency until after the election. He thus urged all those present who had previously received assistance from the Rand Aid Association to return such goods or food to that body, or face the possibility of being disenfranchised when Het Volk assumed office in a few days' time.[94] The meeting agreed to this suggestion, which left the Afrikaners with no alternative but to extract aid from the remaining non-Progressive source of relief in the city – the Robinson fund. Four days later, on 22 February 1907, some of the Afrikaner unemployed of Vrededorp – drawing on the lessons which they had learned earlier in the month from the Unemployed Organisation – invaded the nearby Braamfontein camp, where 'they demanded from the Committee their share of the provisions, and a just share of money out of Mr J. B. Robinson's gift'. After a heated argument Hale and his committee agreed to 'register' these men, and once the Vrededorpers had been issued with provisions they 'departed without coming to blows, being content with a battle of words'. Thereafter, the Unemployed Organisation continued to provide relief not only to its immediate camp followers composed largely of English artisans, but to such 'registered' outsiders who consisted mainly of unskilled Afrikaner workers.[95]

A week later the Johannesburg Town Council, which had succeeded in keeping a remarkably low profile throughout these events, met for the first time to consider the seizure of the Show Ground. Tucker and his colleagues, however, like a reporter from the *Transvaal Leader*, did not fail to notice that 'there were many ex-soldiers in the camp, well used to discipline'. The Mayor and town councillors therefore settled on the prudent policy of non-confrontation with the members of the Unemployed Organisation, and decided instead to redouble their efforts to absorb the local unemployed into a municipal or state public works programme. Accordingly, throughout late February, March and April 1907, the council steadily retrenched hundreds of black labourers earning two shillings a day and systematically replaced them with unemployed whites who were paid between five and six shillings per day for the same tasks. Much to Tucker's and the ratepayers' relief, the additional expenditure incurred through this racist manoeuvre was partly, although not wholly, subsidised by the new Het Volk government. It thus cost hundreds of blacks their jobs and thousands of pounds in hard cash in an attempt to reduce the level of white unemployment and its attendant threats in Johannesburg during the first quarter of 1907.[96]

But if this muncipal–state strategy blunted the initiative of the reserve army of labour as a whole, then it certainly did not succeed in removing the cutting edge of class consciousness from the Braamfontein camp. Here, skilled workers steeped in a trade union tradition proved more difficult to absorb into the cheap unskilled labour of a public works programme than their unskilled counterparts in Vrededorp, and the numbers in the camp only diminished slowly from 700 in February to 460 in April. It was thus this more concentrated and self-conscious core of the workless that presented itself as a natural constituency for the socialists of the newly formed Independent Labour Party (I.L.P.) to cultivate. From mid-March onwards Joseph Hale, in the face of more radical and persuasive arguments by J. T. Bain, Archie Crawford and W. C. Salter, found it difficult to retain control over his increasingly militant followers. On 8 April Hale appeared before the Transvaal Indigency Commission and gave evidence which the majority of his members considered to be insulting or prejudicial to their interests. He and his committee were swiftly deposed from the leadership of the Unemployed Organisation, and replaced by what the camp inhabitants, after the style of the 1906 Russian election, termed the 'New Duma'.[97]

On 1 May 1907 a column of several hundred of the unemployed under the leadership of Archie Crawford marched into Pretoria to seek an audience with the Colonial Secretary, J. C. Smuts, in the hope that they would be able to persuade the government 'to employ white labour at fair wages', at a place closer to their 'natural field of employment'. But, as I. D. de Vries and P. C. Duvenhage had discovered a decade earlier, Smuts was never very enthusiastic about the idea of Johannesburg's unemployed marching into the Transvaal capital. When Crawford and the members of his deputation met the Colonial Secretary, a day later, they found Smuts as firm as ever. The government was reluctant to pay more than two shillings a day as a basic wage to the unemployed, but it would – if the men were willing to find their own food – consider raising this to three shillings and sixpence. The Colonial Secretary 'was sorry to have to send them as far as the Zoutpansberg district, but it was being done only after the fullest enquiries'. He felt that they should consider this new offer, and he concluded the meeting with a warning to the men that they should not become a public 'nuisance' and that if they did there would be 'law for all'.[98] Crawford's deputation then withdrew. At a meeting held on the racecourse later in the afternoon a full gathering of the unemployed unanimously rejected Smuts's latest proposal, and then set out on the long march back to the Rand. But by the time that they had reached Johannesburg, the spotlight of public attention had already swung away from them to focus on a new and more serious manifestation of class conflict.[99]

On the same day that some of Johannesburg's unemployed marched into

Pretoria, 1 May 1907, the white miners at Knights Deep on the East Rand went on strike when the management insisted that they undertake the supervision of three rather than two drills during the course of their duties underground. This demand from the mine owners' middlemen held obvious long-term structural consequences for white labour in the industry, and within a little more than a week the strike had spread, with the active encouragement of the Transvaal Miners' Association (T.M.A.), to several of the largest mines on the central Rand. On 22 May, the T.M.A. deemed the strike to be 'general' and it was thus extended to include all those mines along the length of the Witwatersrand that were affiliated to the Chamber of Mines.[100]

These moves by organised labour meant that all mines – with the exception of those controlled by the still recalcitrant J. B. Robinson – were nominally affected by the strike. Thus, while Robinson donated £2,000 to the strikers' fund for the support of their dependents, many of the mine owners were forced to look around for an alternative supply of white labour which would enable them to defeat their working-class challengers. The Randlords were encouraged in this search by the knowledge that they would not have to look very far. Since at least 1897 the mine owners had been aware of the growing Afrikaner corps within the Rand's reserve army of labour – not least of all because they had periodically been called upon to help defuse its militancy through their involvement in organised charity. Now, with a Het Volk government in power, the Randlords sensed the exciting prospect of being able to combine political expediency and economic self-interest by employing Afrikaners as strike-breakers. And when the mine owners sniffed nationalism, their journalistic mouthpiece sneezed patriotism. 'No patriotic South African', *The Star* announced to its readers on 22 May, 'is likely to complain that the burden of indigency is being shifted from the men of the country to the sojourners from overseas.'[101]

The Chamber of Mines started its campaign to shift the burden of indigency to the 'sojourners from overseas' by recruiting the modest amount of Afrikaner scab labour that was needed during the early days of the strike from areas well beyond the Witwatersrand – in the Pretoria, Potchefstroom and Kimberley districts.[102] This, according to *The Star*, had the virtue – amongst many others – of helping to break down the barriers that existed between 'town and country, race and race'.[103] But as the strike spread and enveloped some of the central Rand mines during mid-May, so the mine owners' agents cast increasingly envious eyes in the direction of the larger and more proximate pools of untapped proletarian labour that lay in the urban areas of Vrededorp and Newlands.

The Transvaal Miners' Association and its closest political ally, the Independent Labour Party (I.L.P.), opposed the introduction of scab labour by the Chamber of Mines with a two-pronged counter-attack. On the one hand, senior officials from these organisations donned their velvet gloves and toured the rural centres explaining the origin of the strike to Afrikaners, appealing to them to support the miners' cause by refusing to accept the job offers that were now being made to them by the Rand capitalists.[104] On the other, rank and file members back on the Witwatersrand used the more familiar iron fist to intimidate and assault those Afrikaners who had been foolish enough to reject advice that had been offered to them in good faith.[105] It was this same combination of tactics, which was used with indifferent success throughout the strike, that was quickly brought into play when the T.M.A. and I.L.P. first sensed that the Chamber's agents were turning their attention to Johannesburg's western suburbs as a possible alternative source of white labour for the mines.

On 11 May 1907 *De Volkstem* carried, in Dutch, an 'Important Notice to all Afrikaners' on the Rand. This notice, inserted into the newspaper at the request of the T.M.A., outlined the cause of the current industrial dispute and appealed to all Afrikaners – as 'fellow South Africans' – not to harm the miners' cause. Over the next three or four days the T.M.A. followed up this initiative by holding a series of meetings in the western suburbs of the town. At Vrededorp, on 14 May, N. Mathey and M. Trewick of the Miners' Association addressed a well-attended meeting held in the government school. Here, the audience listened attentively to the miners' case but, significantly, the meeting ended without any clear statement of support from the audience. The meeting held at Newlands on the following afternoon, however, was far more satisfactory from the miners' point of view – perhaps not least of all because the T.M.A. had taken the precaution of having the meeting addressed and run by an Afrikaner striker from the Langlaagte Deep mine. Here, the audience agreed that no Afrikaners should become 'blacklegs'.[106]

The silence that followed the Mathey–Trewick meeting in Vrededorp, however, was followed by two weeks of intense political ferment within that community. Immediately after the address by the two T.M.A. officials, the Vrededorp Vigilance Association called a meeting of its own under the chairmanship of S. A. Smit to discuss the issues raised by the strike. This meeting revealed the deeply ambiguous feelings that the oldest urban Afrikaner proletariat in the Transvaal entertained about the new conflict. Many, possibly most of those present, felt that the strike afforded them a desperately needed chance to secure employment, but at the same time they feared the strikers' capacity to protect their jobs – the T.M.A.'s iron fist. The leader writer at *The Star* probably assessed this strand in the Afrikaners' thinking correctly when he noted that 'Vrededorp is rather too near the scene of action to proceed without circumspection'.[107] Others at the meeting, however, were of the opinion that as members of the working class they should show solidarity and support the miners in their struggle against the capitalists. Faced with these diverging viewpoints, Smit and his closest advisers drafted a skilful compromise. The members of the Vrededorp Vigilance Association would agree not to act as 'scab' labour provided that the T.M.A. first provided them with an assurance that 'when the strike was over the union would assist Afrikaners to get work on the same terms as British miners, the former agreeing not to work more than two machines or work for a lower rate of wages'.[108] This offer was duly conveyed to the Transvaal Miners' Association shortly after 15 May.

Five days later, when the Vrededorp Vigilance Association had still not received a reply from the T.M.A., Smit and the unemployed again met to discuss what the correct course of action should be. This time Smit suggested that they should seek the advice of their Het Volk Member of the Legislative Assembly, Johannesburg's former principal public prosecutor under the Kruger government, Dr F. E. T. Krause. Krause's response to the predicament of the unemployed came in the form of an open letter addressed to his constituents:

> Gentlemen,
> It has come to my notice that in consequence of the strike on certain mines certain persons have advised you to support the strikers by not going to look for work on these mines. As I consider it my duty as your representative to inform you what my attitude is under the circumstances, I wish to say that, although I have great sympathy with the strikers, I believe that you will not be justified not to go out and look for work. My earnest advice therefore is, do not allow yourselves to be persuaded, but go and look for work wherever you can get it. Take care, however, that you obtain a guarantee from the employer that you will not be discharged after a short time, and do nothing to lower the amount of wages.
> I understand that a resolution to this effect has already been taken. I have the honour to be,
>
> Yours faithfully,
F. E. T. Krause[109]

This letter did much to nudge the hesitant Afrikaners towards accepting positions on the mines as scab labour.

Following the receipt of this letter, on 21 May 1907, between 150 and 200 of the Vrededorp unemployed once again assembled under the leadership of S. A. Smit. This time the Afrikaners formed themselves into a single body of men and marched to the offices of Consolidated Gold Fields in the centre of the city where their delegates attempted to negotiate for employment under conditions similar to those that prevailed before the strike. Before these discussions could be finalised, however, this formidable contingent of Afrikaners was spotted – not by the members of the T.M.A. who were away at picket duty on the mines, but by R. L. Outhwaite, W. Lorimer and J. F. Back of the Independent Labour Party. These three I.L.P. stalwarts persuaded Smit and his followers not to make any final decision about accepting employment on the mines until such time as they had all had a chance to have a further discussion with Krause. The phalanx of unemployed thereupon withdrew, and marched back to Vrededorp for a meeting with Krause, accompanied by the three socialist watch-dogs.[110]

At their meeting with the Het Volk M.L.A., the I.L.P. contingent attempted to persuade Krause that his advice to his constituents had been primarily motivated by political considerations, and that as such it was likely to jeopardise future cooperation between English and Afrikaner workers. Krause responded by saying that he had acted simply to ensure the economic well-being of his constituents, and by pointing out that in any case 'complaints had been made to him by Afrikaners that they had not been able to get work *before* the strike because the British miners objected to their presence on the mines'. In short, the attitudes of the immigrant miners before the strike, as well as the T.M.A.'s refusal to respond to the proposal put to it by the Vrededorp Vigilance Association during the strike, both suggested that the

English miner was no particular friend of the Afrikaner unemployed. This information may or may not have come as news to Outhwaite and his colleagues but, in either event, it left them with little effective reply. Making the best of what was rapidly becoming a most unpromising situation, the I.L.P. members again pleaded with the unemployed to 'defer action' – this time so that they could make further representations to the T.M.A. with the request that it 'define' its attitude towards accepting Afrikaners as fellow mineworkers after the strike. Once more, the men of Vrededorp agreed to wait.[111]

The following morning the strike was declared to be 'general' and Prime Minister Botha responded by dispatching Imperial troops to the Witwatersrand. Over a week later, Johannesburg's Afrikaner unemployed were still awaiting a reply from either the T.M.A. or its I.L.P. intermediaries. The reply never came. On 25 May *De Volkstem* lent its editorial support to the advice which F.E.T. Krause had been offering his constituents. The newspaper – like the Het Volk M.L.A. before it – pointed out that it was not only the Randlords, but the muscle of the immigrant miners that had hitherto blocked the Afrikaner's entry into the mining industry:

> . . . up to the present, there has not been the slightest consideration given to the Afrikaner's claim to the better positions on the mines. Most of the companies have given in to the English miners' wish that their countrymen be given exclusive access to such bread-winning opportunities.[112]

De Volkstem was of the opinion that, under the circumstances, the local unemployed owed the Transvaal Miners' Association no favours and that Afrikaners should go out and seek work – making sure that they were not being used only as strike-breakers by demanding a two-year contract from the mining companies.

It was only after this point had been reached that urban Afrikaners in any numbers decided to take up employment in the mining industry. While their country cousins had readily grasped at the job opportunities that had been presented to them from the earliest days of the strike, Johannesburg's Afrikaner unemployed had – through a mixture of fear and class consciousness – hesitated before accepting work as 'scab' labour. From 25 May onwards, however, a growing number of men from Vrededorp took up work at nearby mines such as the Crown Deep and the Crown Reef. The T.M.A. responded by publicly posting the names of 'blacklegs' on the Market square of adjacent Fordsburg, but when – on 1 June – the all important S.A. Engine Drivers' Association also refused to come out in support of the union, the miners lost their battle and the strike gradually disintegrated.[113]

It is estimated that between May and June 1907 some 2,000 to 3,000 Afrikaners gained employment in the Transvaal's premier industry for the first time, and of those a couple of hundred were undoubtedly drawn from Vrededorp and Newlands.[114] As the strike slowly drew to a close, however, scores – if not hundreds – of Afrikaners also *left* the mining industry. Some were cynically dismissed by mine managers once the strike was over, while others left of their own accord because of their distaste for the hard, unfamiliar and dangerous work underground. Many others – as has often been suggested – lost their jobs 'because of their inefficiency'.[115] But amongst the many who left there were also several who were forced out by a campaign of organised terror mounted by a group of immigrant miners.

In early June several Afrikaners received anonymous letters typed in red ink which threatened them with dire consequences if they did not immediately relinquish their newly gained posts on the mines. The style, frequency and distribution of these letters left some observers – including one who had been sympathetic to the T.M.A.'s struggle – with 'the opinion that there is existing some kind of society whose efforts are directed towards intimidating employees in this nefarious way'.[116] What is significant about those cases that were reported in the press, however, is that virtually all of them relate to those Afrikaners who were permanently resident on the Witwatersrand rather than those who had been recruited in the rural districts during the course of the strike. In large part this can be accounted for by the fact that such Afrikaners tended to live with their families in the suburbs, and that because of this they could be more readily isolated and got at than their 'single' country cousins who lived in the massed shelter of the boarding-houses on the mining properties.[117] What it also suggests, however, is that the fully proletarianised urban Afrikaners were more likely to cling to their jobs, and that they therefore presented the immigrant miners with a greater challenge than that posed by the less committed newcomers from the countryside. This hypothesis is perhaps further strengthened when we consider how, in the case of the resident Afrikaners, the 'red ink' warnings sometimes evolved beyond mere 'intimidation' into fully-fledged attempts at murder.

At dusk on 12 June a miner named Redlinghuis was cycling towards his home at Klipriversberg in southern Johannesburg when, near Regent's Park, three men armed with revolvers opened fire at him, discharging nine shots. Redlinghuis escaped with a leg wound and minor injuries. Two days later, as the early morning shift was changing at the Simmer East shaft on the East Rand, a crowd of men wielding revolvers forced miners Oosthuizen and van der Merwe to jump on their cycles, and flee at great pace down a deserted footpath. On rounding a corner, the cyclists 'were brought heavily to ground by coming into contact with a rope, which had been placed across the road'. Here again, the men were lucky enough to escape with minor injuries.[118]

Others – although admittedly not Afrikaners – were less fortunate. Twelve hours after the attack on Oosthuizen and van der Merwe at Boksburg North, on 14 June, a house occupied by three English miners who refused to support the strike was demolished by a dynamite explosion. Although the owners of the house – a shift boss and his family – were unharmed, one of their lodgers, a miner from the New Comet named Webb Richard, was killed by the blast.[119] It is possible that this attack on the East Rand, where the strike originated and was always most strongly supported, also served as the 'model' for an attempt on the lives of a family of Afrikaner miners in Johannesburg two weeks later.

On 25 June 1907 the Goosen family of the corner Third and Locatie Streets, Vrededorp, received an anonymous typewritten letter containing the familiar 'red ink' threats. Sam Goosen and his two adult sons – all miners –

ignored these warnings to give up their newly acquired positions on the nearby Crown Reef. When the father and his two boys woke up to go on shift early on the morning of 2 July, they discovered an unexploded charge of one and a half pounds of gelignite, a faulty detonator and 70 inches of fuse attached to the window sill of their home.[120] In this case, thanks to the defective detonator, the family escaped injury.

All of these incidents, however, were well publicised and it is certain that they, as well as many of those cases that remained unreported, must have left the desired impression on those who had been employed as 'scab' labour during the strike.[121] But, whatever the cause, the fact remains that by the last quarter of the year many, if not most of those urban Afrikaners who had gained employment during the course of the strike, were again jobless. This meant that by late 1907, unemployment and discontent amongst the inhabitants of Vrededorp – and to a lesser extent amongst other groups within the city – had again reached a level that was considered by some to be dangerously high. This time the ruling classes attempted to cope with the rumblings from below with a more broadly based response.

Between August and December of 1907, Vrededorp was invaded by the agents of largely middle-class organisations seeking to cast the women and children of the suburb into a more proletarian mould which, they believed, could open gateways to a new and more industrious life for the poor whites of the city. The South African Women's Federation, for example, besides running a much-appreciated soup kitchen, attempted – with less success – to establish 'cottage industries' in the hope that this would help produce 'a contented and self-supporting population' in Vrededorp.[122] The newly formed Undenominational Benevolent Society, under the patronage of Mrs Louis Botha tried – also unsuccessfully – to build on an idea that had first been put to President Kruger by the members of the Rand Relief Committee a decade earlier: namely, that a public laundry be erected in the suburb which would not only provide work for unemployed Afrikaner women, but also draw off some of those already working, 'with a danger to their morals', in the small hand-laundries of Indian and Chinese employers.[123] The Salvation Army, for its part, concentrated on a 'practical scheme of industrial training' for the older children of Vrededorp, teaching them printing, needle-work, drawing and woodwork.[124]

These schemes, however, produced neither an immediate nor an adequate flow of funds to the starving families of the western working-class suburbs, and nobody was more aware of this than the still hard-pressed Mayor of Johannesburg, W. K. Tucker. It was largely because of this reason that Tucker and his fellow councillors agreed to extend the municipal relief works by taking on additional white men to work on the development of the city's water-borne sewerage system. Thus during the closing months of 1907 some 240 whites – including many from Vrededorp – were engaged as pipe-makers in lower Fordsburg or as trench-diggers in Braamfontein, at piece-work rates which averaged out at about five shillings per day.[125]

When this round of temporary and restricted municipal employment came to an end it heralded the advent of a new and even more serious crisis for the Afrikaner unemployed of the city. Early in 1908 the government attempted to partly alleviate the deepening distress in the western suburbs when it appointed R. Shanks and S. A. Smit as Inspectors of White Labour in Johannesburg. Amongst others, it was the duty of these officials to assess the extent of local destitution and, where possible, to place the most needy in government employment. Unfortunately for the two Inspectors, however, such opportunities as were offered by the state were both limited and financially unrewarding when compared with the municipal relief schemes – something which in turn reflected the fact that while the government had to cater largely for the landed Afrikaners of Het Volk, the Johannesburg municipality had to live with the working classes and the Independent Labour Party. In particular, the offer of work on the construction of the Pietersburg railway line at three shillings and fourpence per day 'plus mealie meal' proved to be most unpopular with the Rand's reserve army of labour. Thus, while the appointment of Smit might have swept one Afrikaner from the more radical ranks of the Vrededorp unemployed into the arms of officialdom, it apparently did very little for the remainder of the unemployed in the suburb.[126]

Throughout the first two months of 1908 the poor of Vrededorp vainly awaited the announcement of some new relief scheme, their awful plight made bearable only by the continued issue of rations by the Rand Aid Association. Then, in mid-February, disaster struck. The Rand Aid Association, which since October 1907 had been operating on an expanded scale with a special grant made to it by Wernher, Beit & Co. and the Witwatersrand Native Labour Association, came to the end of these emergency funds. This forced the Association to retract its efforts to within the 'normal' limits set by its more modest municipal and government grants. In the last week of February the Rand Aid Association 'had to strike off the list of recipients the names of the representatives of about one thousand people'. Within days this drastic action reflected itself in the starvation and despair of the Afrikaner unemployed.[127]

On Saturday afternoon, 1 March 1908, the Vrededorp unemployed met under the leadership of three men – Paul Das, Editor of *De Transvaler*, ex-Fieldcornet M. J. Bekker and L. Minaar – to discuss the latest crisis confronting their families. At this meeting it was decided that the Colonial Secretary should be petitioned in order to determine what possible assistance the government could offer the Afrikaner poor of the city. Before this could be formally organised, however, Das took it upon himself to visit Smuts and point out to him the gravity of the situation in Johannesburg, and on the following Monday evening the editor of *De Transvaler* reported back on his informal discussions with the Colonial Secretary to a meeting of some 200 of the unemployed.[128]

Das knew that he would be addressing an aggressive white working-class audience and his speech reflected this. He told the meeting that 'General Smuts appeared to have no idea that the distress in Johannesburg was so acute or widespread as it was'. He related how, when the Colonial Secretary attempted to fend off criticisms of neglect by pointing to the Inspectors of White Labour, he countered by telling Smuts that 'Mr Smit was one of those who drove around in cabs and looked down on the Afrikanders working in the streets in the town' – i.e. on those employed as trench-diggers in the municipal sewerage extension scheme. If Het Volk could not accommodate their immediate needs, he suggested, then 'the Ministers of the Government should drop £1,000 each from their salaries for the benefit of the poor people'.[129]

Afrikaners at work on municipal pipe-laying scheme, 1907

Then, getting into his stride, Das extended his speech along popular I.L.P. 'white labour' lines when he pointed out to the meeting that he had asked General Smuts 'whether an Act should not be passed prohibiting the employment of Kaffirs by the Johannesburg Municipality'. When Smuts drew attention to the employment possibilities that existed on the construction site of the Pietersburg railway line, Das responded with a deft nationalist ideological deflection which avoided the more fundamental issues of locality and wage rates. 'Such an offer', Das told his Vrededorp audience, 'was most insulting to the Afrikander nation. A man who called himself an Afrikander should not go and work for 3s. 4d. per day and a bag of mealie meal per month. The sting of the whole thing lay in the offer of mealie meal. It was placing them on a level with Kaffirs.'[130]

But the Editor of *De Transvaler* had not made his way to Pretoria simply to criticise a Het Volk leader, he had also gone to offer some constructive advice. He had put it to Smuts that the government should consider the 'establishment of labour colonies on lines similar to that on which Kakamas Colony' in the Cape was run, but the Colonial Secretary was not particularly enthusiastic about that suggestion because of the government's indifferent success with its own Middelburg scheme. Smuts did, however, agree to think about other ways in which some of the urban Afrikaner unemployed could be placed back on the land. Das rounded off his speech by relating some of the other ideas which he had put to the Colonial Secretary, and the meeting closed with the election of a deputation composed of Messrs Das, Minaar and Bekker, who would attempt to meet Smuts formally as soon as was possible.[131]

These new stirrings amongst the unemployed in the western suburbs rang all the old alarm bells for the ruling classes in the town hall. Johannesburg's new Mayor, James Thompson, was as aware as his predecessor that a high level of unemployment and the simultaneous collapse of organised charity in the city constituted a particularly explosive social mixture. Within 48 hours of Das's meeting with the Afrikaner unemployed therefore, Thompson made two moves in an attempt to help defuse the rapidly developing crisis. First, the Town Council again extended its relief works programme by agreeing to immediately include the Ferreirastown and Marhshalltown districts into the municipal sewerage scheme. In three days, between 5 and 7 March 1908, 240 married men earning five shillings a day were taken on as trench-diggers while hundreds of other disappointed applicants had to be turned away. It was noted that, of those employed, 'a very large proportion were Dutch-speaking citizens, and a little enquiry showed that some had come in from as far out as Maraisburg and Sophiatown, though undoubtedly the majority were from Vrededorp'. Secondly, the Mayor called a meeting of 'representatives of public bodies and benevolent institutions, members of Parliament and prominent citizens' to discuss the crisis.[132]

The swift responses by the editor of *De Transvaler* and the Mayor of Johannesburg to the new situation, however, left at least one set of local leaders somewhat flat-footed and embarrassed – the Het Volk M.L.A. for Vrededorp, Dr F. E. T. Krause, and the hapless Inspector of White Labour, S. A. Smit. Krause, both by training and temperament, found it hard to relate to the majority of his working-class constituents and to empathise with their problems. As a lawyer, he was much more at home in the House of Assembly where, between 1907 and 1908, he and Smuts did much to steer through the Vrededorp Stands Ordinance and its subsequent amendments which enabled his constituents to acquire the freehold rights to their properties from the Johannesburg Town Council.[133] Smit, by contrast, was usually much more closely involved with the local community and had come to earn for himself the unofficial title of 'Mayor of Vrededorp'. His recent elevation to the position of Inspector of White Labour, however, not only placed him on the Het Volk payroll but also succeeded in temporarily alienating him from many of his more radical supporters. Both he and Krause therefore felt the need – although for somewhat different reasons – to show that they too were aware of and concerned about the plight of the Afrikaner unemployed. To this end, they too called a meeting to discuss the situation.

This meeting, which reflected some of the embryonic class tensions within Vrededorp society as well as the problems which Het Volk experienced in dealing with this relatively radical Afrikaner proletarian constituency, took place on the evening of 6 March 1908. Krause, who opened the meeting, made a lengthy appeal to the government to come to the aid of those former Republican civil servants such as the Zarps who were now unemployed, by providing them with a pension – an old Het Volk plea which possibly contributed, some six months later, to the appointment of the South African Republican Officials' Pensions Commission.[134] As a former principal public prosecutor in Johannesburg, Krause was particularly well known to the one-time members of Kruger's police force, several of whom resided in Vrededorp.

The Inspector of White Labour, however, knew that Vrededorp's most urgent problem centred around the need to find employment for the vast majority of its unskilled workers, rather than the need to secure the longer-term security of a score or more former civil servants. In his address, therefore, Smit made a conscious effort to recover some of the ground which had been lost to Paul Das and his colleagues by advocating more radical solutions along the lines pioneered by the Independent Labour Party. The Inspector of White Labour – possibly in an attempt to distance himself from his new Het Volk masters – opened his speech with the populist suggestion that the government ministers accept a reduction in salary in order to benefit the poor. Smit then went on to suggest an improved and expanded public works programme, the need for land settlement schemes to help absorb the urban unemployed, and he closed his address with a plea for state-owned gold mines which would give Afrikaners the more permanent local employment which they had so long hankered after.[135]

But despite this valiant attempt by Smit, both he and Krause knew by the end of the evening that they had failed to seize the initial political moment in the new crisis, and that they had therefore lost the majority of Vrededorp's support to the Editor of *De Transvaler*, Minaar and Bekker. Krause thus closed the meeting with a somewhat sour warning to his constituents about the activities of Das and his colleagues. As a rather bemused observer from the English press noted in his report: 'There appears to be a regrettable difference amongst the poor Dutch of Vrededorp as to the rival claims of two gentlemen who are anxious to be spokesmen.'[136]

The following morning's news did not bring the beleaguered M.L.A.

for Vrededorp or the Inspector of White Labour much joy either as they discovered that, hours before they had held their meeting, the Colonial Secretary had formally received their rivals Minaar and Bekker – Das, unfortunately, being unable to attend. Smuts, who remembered all too clearly his previous meeting with a deputation from the Rand's indigent under the leadership of Archie Crawford, had long been worried by the inroads which I.L.P. socialists had been making amongst the urban Afrikaner unemployed and he thus welcomed the two men from Vrededorp 'and urged them not to be led away by interfering agitators, but to look after their interests themselves'. This Minaar and Bekker proceeded to do with some skill, and in a remarkably conciliatory meeting the Colonial Secretary went out of his way to accommodate most of the points they raised – a development which tended to leave Krause even more stranded than before.[137]

The men from Vrededorp raised four major issues in their discussions with Smuts, starting with those closest to home. First, both Minaar and Bekker contended that the appointment of S. A. Smit as a 'Government Inspector' had been 'unnecessary, and that in any case he was not the most satisfactory man for the post'. The Colonial Secretary agreed to investigate the matter. Secondly, 'the question of the minimum wage that should be paid for white unskilled labour was then discussed at considerable length'. Here, there appeared to be a difference of opinion amongst the members of the deputation. While Minaar favoured a minimum wage of fifteen shillings per day, 'Bekker disassociated himself from his confrère's suggestion, and thought seven shillings and sixpence to ten shillings a day would give satisfaction'. Both of these figures must undoubtedly have come as a shock to Smuts, but he did indicate that the government was rethinking its position on this very important question and that the figure of seven shillings and sixpence was probably a reasonable one. Thirdly, Minaar and Bekker pointed out to their Het Volk leader that while the position had improved somewhat since the strike of the previous year, Afrikaners were still not getting their fair share of jobs in the mining industry. The Colonial Secretary said that he would shortly 'visit the Rand and interview the mining people on their behalf'. Fourthly, the question of land settlement schemes was discussed and Smuts indicated that while this possibility had been receiving the government's attention for some time, it now intended to implement such plans with all possible haste. 'In conclusion, General Smuts said he was very glad indeed that they had come to him with their grievances. He would always assist impoverished Afrikaners as far as possible, and also the working-class people as a whole.'[138]

Minaar and Bekker left the meeting delighted with the progress that they had made with the new friend of the working class and returned to Johannesburg where, at five o'clock on the afternoon of 7 March 1908, on the vacant stands adjoining Bekker's home, the two men related to the assembled unemployed of Vrededorp what had transpired at their meeting with the Colonial Secretary. The Afrikaner unemployed, many of whom in the first instance simply wanted bread, were greatly relieved to hear that Smuts had promised that he 'would certainly look after those who had no food'. They were further cheered by the news of the other schemes that had been discussed with the Colonial Secretary and in general there was a feeling 'that the fog of depression and misery was lifting, and that the people were anticipating work for all those at present idle'.[139]

Smuts, who must have been pleased to hear that reports of his meeting with Minaar and Bekker had done much to 'restore confidence in the Government's promise of assistance' amongst the Afrikaner unemployed, now sought to consolidate Het Volk's position by indicating that he would also travel to Johannesburg in order to attend the Mayor's emergency meeting on 9 March. This meeting attracted not only Smuts and H. C. Hull from the government's front bench, but more than a half-dozen Members of the Legislative Assembly, George Goch, L. S. Reyersbach and Lionel Phillips for the mining industry, representatives from various charitable organisations, virtually all of the town's ministers of religion, various other prominent citizens and the government's two Inspectors of White Labour. Perhaps the only prominent local person conspicuously absent from this important gathering was the unhappy and politically isolated Member of the Legislative Assembly for Vrededorp – F. E. T. Krause.[140]

The meeting was opened with an address from the Chairman of the Transvaal Indigency Commission, J. W. Quinn, who dwelt on the familiar distinction between the deserving and undeserving poor and then proposed the appointment of a broadly based committee to deal with the problems of unemployment in Johannesburg. The tone and direction of the debate that followed, however, was set by three speakers affiliated to the Independent Labour Party who pointed out that 'charity was a safety valve for capitalism', and that more radical solutions ought therefore to be sought. Councillor Wilfred Walker, who had been closely involved with the municipality's relief works programme, was of the opinion that most of their difficulties stemmed from the fact that they 'were attempting to build up the country on the foundation of the niggers'. Harry Sampson, M.L.A., and yet another councillor, J. J. Ware, took this as their cue to propose an unsuccessful amendment to Quinn's motion which urged the government to open a state mine worked exclusively by white labour, and to offer those of the European unemployed who were 'stranded' on the Reef a free rail passage out of the country.[141]

In his reply to these speeches and one in between by Lionel Phillips, the Colonial Secretary sought to steer a course which avoided a head-on collision with the representatives of either capital or labour. Smuts acknowledged that, as far as the economy was concerned, it was possible that 'the foundation might be rotten' – an admission which accommodated the many I.L.P. members present. He continued to warn the advocates of a 'white labour' policy that the government's experiments on the railways had hardly been an unqualified success, however, and that 'it was one thing gradually to introduce a principle the value of which they understood and believed in, and it was quite another to upset the whole economic condition of society'.[142] It was precisely because he did not want to upset the whole economic condition of society that the Colonial Secretary then appealed to the mine owners – not 'in a spirit of criticism, but in a spirit of genuine goodwill and fellow-feeling' – to do their duty and take on more unskilled workers. Then, in a glance over his shoulder at his own and more immediate political constituency, Smuts offered a lengthy outline of Het Volk's plans for a land settlement scheme. The Colonial Secretary rounded off his address by strongly supporting J. W. Quinn's plea for the appointment of a broadly based committee to tackle the problem of local unemployment.

The Rand Unemployed Investigation Committee (R.U.I.C.) which came into being as a result of this meeting temporarily ousted the Rand Aid Association, and for the next eighteen months – until the economy again improved in mid-1909 – it became the controlling relief agency in Johannesburg. The creation of R.U.I.C. marked a shift from a relatively narrowly focused charity drive mounted by the mine owners and the state, to a more broadly based effort by the ruling classes in which they were forced to acknowledge the need to provide both relief *and* jobs for the unskilled whites of the city's western suburbs. While at one level this might simply be interpreted as a pragmatic change from above in the ruling classes' strategy for dealing with the reserve army of labour during a depression, at another – and deeper level – it also demonstrates just how serious and vibrant the challenge from below was during this period of marked class struggle. From being solely the objects of charity under the Rand Aid Association, organised elements of the white working class became partners – albeit very minor partners – in the planning of relief and job-creating possibilities under R.U.I.C. At least some of these realities were reflected in the composition of the new committee which was constituted from: The Mayor of Johannesburg – James Thompson (Chairman), the President of the Chamber of Mines – Lionel Phillips, the Chairman of the Mine Managers' Association, the Mayors of the different municipalities along the Reef, the Chairman of the Indigency Commission, a Government Inspector of White Labour – R. Shanks, two delegates from the Rand Aid Association, the Chairman of the Trades and Labour Council, and two representatives of the Unemployed Organisation (by now a full affiliate of the I.L.P.) – Harry Sampson and Wilfred Walker.[143]

Three days after its formation, on 11 March 1908, the members of this formidable committee met for the first time in an attempt to ease the problem of unemployment in Johannesburg and some of the smaller Reef towns. As representatives of the potentially largest employers – the mines and the municipality – Lionel Phillips and James Thompson played the dominant roles in the deliberations, and the two men soon agreed on the central elements of what was to become R.U.I.C.'s major plan for job creation. The municipality, which already had some 400 men at work as trench-diggers on its sewerage system would, through the good offices of the Chamber of Mines, offer all of these men who had demonstrated their willingness and capacity to undertake hard manual labour permanent positions as unskilled workers on the mines. This manoeuvre would enable the municipality to take on and test a further 400 unskilled workers who would, in their turn, make their way to the mines where they would eventually be absorbed into the permanent labour force. In addition to this, R.U.I.C. would, through the relevant government departments, place smaller numbers of unskilled workers on the Main Reef Road works at Krugersdorp, and on railway construction sites in the Transvaal countryside.[144]

In the last week of March 1908 the Johannesburg municipality started to implement the R.U.I.C. plan when it paid off all 400 of the men who had hitherto been employed as trench-diggers on the sewerage system. The members of this group, some of whom had been earning the minimum of five shillings a day but many of whom had managed to make between ten and fifteen shillings per day on piece-work, were then offered permanent positions as unskilled workers on those mines that were most accessible from the city's western suburbs.[145] Of these 400 men, 70 were unwilling to work on the mines under any circumstances and thus only 330 indicated their readiness – in principle – to give the offer further consideration. Of these 330 who reported to the mines on the first day, however, a further 198 refused to proceed when it became apparent that the positions they were being offered entailed working underground.[146] This meant that in the end – for one reason or another – only 132 of the original trench-diggers made the transition to the mines. The municipality, which in the interim had re-opened its books to accommodate 400 new trench-diggers, was swamped with applications from over 1,500 unskilled workers – as before, the large majority of these being Afrikaners.[147]

Meanwhile, the 132 erstwhile trench-diggers who had been allocated to hand-drilling operations on the mines at piece-work rates were rapidly becoming disillusioned. Within 48 hours of their new jobs commencing, it became clear to these men that they had been forced to exchange unskilled manual labour in the open air at ten shillings a day, for dangerous semi-skilled work underground at rates which – at best – would allow them to earn two to three shillings a day.[148] This supposedly new deal for the unemployed during the darkest days of the depression aroused intense anger amongst a section of the working class which now believed that it was being cynically used in an experiment by the Chamber of Mines to undercut 'kaffir labour'.[149]

Early on the morning of 3 April, instead of reporting for work, the 132 former trench-diggers – most of whom were from Vrededorp – together with 150 or more of the city's unemployed, met on the Market square to discuss these grievances. At the end of the open-air discussions, a deputation of four under the leadership of G. Murray of the Unemployed Organisation was elected to put their views to the Chairman of R.U.I.C. While this four-man delegation set out to interview James Thompson, however, the column of 200–300 unemployed set out on a noisy demonstration of their own through the city centre. Marching and shouting their way through the financial quarter, the former trench-diggers and their followers paused only to vent their spleen at 'the bloodsuckers of Corner House', before turning towards Braamfontein where the municipal works on the sewerage system were still in progress with the aid of a new set of largely Afrikaner workers. Here the demonstrators successfully used a combination of persuasion and intimidation to convince the replacement trench-diggers to down tools 'until the dispute was settled'. The demonstrators then made their way back to the Market square to await the report of the delegation which they had sent to the Chairman of the Rand Unemployed Investigation Committee.[150]

Murray and his team, in militant mood, met James Thompson and three of his fellow R.U.I.C. members – Shanks, Walker and Sutherland – in the library of the municipal offices. Murray pointed out to the Mayor that the 400 former trench-diggers considered that they had been 'deluded out of their sewerage jobs' into a cheap labour experiment by the 'bloodsuckers of Corner House' and his friends in the Chamber of Mines. All the men demanded to be reinstated in their former jobs which, as ratepayers, they in any case considered to be 'their own work'. Furthermore, Murray pointed out, 'certain unemployed who left their trenches to go to the mines had said that if anyone

Unsuccessful applicants for municipal trench-digging jobs. Johannesburg, 1908

attempted to finish their trenches they still had a pick shank to clear them out of it'.[151]

The Chairman of R.U.I.C. and his colleagues were both dismayed and alarmed by these allegations and the fighting talk with which they were accompanied. Wilfred Walker, in particular, was concerned that the I.L.P. would lose its credibility with the unemployed and strongly defended the Town Council against the charge that it had knowingly sent the former trench-diggers into a Chamber of Mines cheap labour experiment. Thompson assured Murray and his men that R.U.I.C. would reconsider the position as speedily as possible but, he concluded, 'violence was not going to help them, and if there was anything of the sort the responsibility was with them'. The deputation then withdrew.[152]

Back on the Market square Murray related these proceedings to the assembled unemployed who, after further discussion, passed two resolutions. The first, of a more general nature, called on the government to examine 'the ignominious way in which the white workers of Johannesburg had been treated after they had shown their willingness to do servile labour'. The second, which more specifically reflected the sentiments of the men drawn from Vrededorp, called on the Prime Minister and the Colonial Secretary to present themselves in the city 'to meet the masses in order that they could show cause why land was not opened up for the purposes of agriculture, and why work should not be immediately supplied to starving white workers'. Then, still angry, the men abandoned the city centre and made their way to the Braamfontein trenches to make sure that nobody worked until such time as 'a settlement' was arrived at.[153]

The outline of a settlement was reached within 24 hours. On the afternoon following their demonstration the unemployed were informed by James Thompson that Shanks, the Inspector of White Labour, had – on behalf of R.U.I.C. – negotiated the basis of a new arrangement with the mine owners. In terms of the new scheme the former trench-diggers would no longer be called upon to work underground at rates that competed with black labour, but would instead be allocated to surface jobs which would enable them to earn between three and five shillings per day. This suggestion apparently proved acceptable to the unemployed who, after the proposal had been formally approved by R.U.I.C. a few days later, returned to work.[154]

Over the next eighteen months, as the economy gradually improved from April 1908 to October 1909, R.U.I.C. retained control over Johannesburg's reserve army of labour without further major conflict. Besides co-ordinating the city's relief operations so as to avoid the problem of 'indiscriminate charity', R.U.I.C. during the same period succeeded in placing 550 men on government public works, 652 on the municipality's relief works and over 3,000 men in positions as unskilled workers on the mines. The latter exercise, however, no longer held much appeal for the mine owners and R.U.I.C. officially described the results as being 'disappointing' while the work was seen as simply constituting 'another form of charity'. In addition to this, a couple of hundred urban Afrikaners were placed on various land settlements in the Transvaal countryside after the Indigency Commission had presented its report in July 1908.[155]

All of these jobs, however, as well as the conditions attached to them, had been won from the ruling classes during the course of the struggle that had been waged by the unemployed and the workers from late 1906 onwards, and nowhere had that struggle been more intensely fought than in Vrededorp. Between 1906 and 1908, a substantial part of the Afrikaner proletariat that had been developing in the city's western suburbs since 1896 came – for the first time – to view self-consciously itself as part of the working class. To the distress of certain Het Volk notables in general, and the hapless F.E.T. Krause in particular, these ideas continued to flow through a large part of Vrededorp's political channels for some time after the storms of the depression had passed.

Amongst the first to detect this development in the political thought of the Afrikaner workers was the Chairman of the Vrededorp Vigilance Association, S. A. Smit. From at least the time of the miners' strike Smit had shown considerable interest in the labour movement and when he and Krause had been left politically up-staged by Das and his colleagues in early 1908 this interest increased. Although he never came out openly in support of the Labour Party between 1907 and 1910, Smit consistently encouraged its activities while, at the same time, he sought to avoid a head-on confrontation with Afrikaner nationalists. In July 1908, for example, it was Smit who presided at the meeting when the Labour Party first sought to establish a branch in Vrededorp. On this occasion he 'criticised the attitude of the Nationalist Party towards the working class interests on the Rand'.[156]

It was also during the same year, 1908, that S. A. Smit was returned as a town councillor for Vrededorp. This election not only reflected the grass-roots support which Smit enjoyed in the constituency, it also succeeded in thrusting him into even more direct contact with the numerous Labour Party activists on the council. From Het Volk's point of view, however, this growing tendency for urban Afrikaners to sympathise with the labour movement was unfortunately not confined to the Rand; it also manifested itself to a considerable degree in the only other sizeable pool of Afrikaner workers in the Transvaal at Pretoria. By mid-1909, when the economy had improved somewhat and the leadership had more time to reflect on such matters, Het Volk was giving serious consideration to the problem of Afrikaner working-class consciousness.

Early in October 1909, at the Empire Hall in Pretoria, Het Volk launched an 'independent' Dutch Labour Society named *Arbeid Adelt* – 'Labour Ennobles'. In his opening address to a meeting attended by over 300 workers, the Chairman, J. J. Naude, pointed out that the need for 'a Labour Society for Dutch-speaking people had been felt for a long time'. The essential difference between the new organisation 'and the English Labour Party was that in Arbeid Adelt most of the members were unskilled'. While the existing labour movement would continue to look after the interests of the skilled workers, such as the English craftsmen, Arbeid Adelt would protect most of those who were unskilled or unemployed – the Afrikaners. Naude, a long-time activist amongst the Pretoria unemployed, then went out of his way to deny allegations that the new organisation was simply 'a daughter of Het Volk' by saying that Arbeid Adelt had 'nothing to do with politics' – a claim that was promptly denied by one of the next speakers, Advocate Gregorowski M.L.A., who bluntly stated that as far as he could see all those present were 'good members of Het Volk'.[157]

Back on the Rand, F. E. T. Krause – and to a lesser extent S. A. Smit – were quick to spot the possibilities which the new organisation could offer them in Vrededorp. A Dutch labour society under the control of Het Volk, which could help arrest the drift in sympathy towards the Labour Party, held obvious appeal for Krause who was always somewhat at a loss as how to best deal with his volatile working-class constituency. For Smit, on the other hand, an involvement in Arbeid Adelt would help to maintain his balance on the tightrope that he had been walking between the labour movement and Het Volk. Both men thus readily agreed to support the new organisation when it sought to expand to Johannesburg.

On Saturday night, 16 January 1910, Krause presided over the inaugural meeting of Arbeid Adelt held in the government school at Vrededorp. This well-attended gathering followed a familiar pattern. After the chairman had indicated the desire of the new organisation to protect the interests of unskilled and unemployed workers, J. J. Naude outlined the remaining objectives of the association which already had 700 members – laying particular stress on Arbeid Adelt's efforts to get the children of the poor trade apprenticeships. E. Rooth M.L.A. and J. Alleman, Government Inspector of White Labour on the Railways, then rounded off the addresses for the evening – the former emphasising that the society was 'a non-political body', and the latter pointing out that the 'heads of the administration' were 'very sympathetic' to the movement and that they could therefore look forward to the cooperation of the government.[158]

Vrededorp gave the promoters of the new labour society an enthusiastic reception. Both as unskilled workers and as members of the unemployed these men knew, from bitter first-hand experience, the strengths and weaknesses of a labour movement that was narrowly constructed around craft unionism. In Arbeid Adelt then, these Afrikaners saw the possibility of becoming involved in a wider working-class movement on a sustained basis – an opportunity which had previously always been denied to them as they staggered through one capitalist crisis after another. At the end of the meeting, therefore, they decided to appoint seven members to the local committee of Arbeid Adelt, and to open an office for the organisation in Tol street. Within two weeks the Vrededorp branch of Arbeid Adelt boasted a membership of 100, while – back in Pretoria – the promoters spoke enthusiastically about expanding the movement to Boksburg, Germiston and Krugersdorp.[159]

But if in 1910 the Afrikaners of the Rand already knew about the limitations of craft unionism, they were only beginning to experience what the nationalist embrace of a working-class movement entailed. Within days of the opening of the Tol street office it became clear to the workers, and particularly the unemployed of Vrededorp, that their hopes and ambitions were being channelled down all too familiar government avenues – the Inspector of White Labour, relief works on the railways or the land settlement schemes. The sense of disillusionment which this caused spread rapidly through the community and by mid-March the majority of members of the 'labour society' had come to the conclusion that it was simply a 'propaganda arm' for Het Volk, and taken the active step of resigning from the organisation. In Vrededorp, Arbeid Adelt was all of a six-week wonder.[160]

The collapse of Arbeid Adelt, followed shortly thereafter by the absorption of Het Volk into the South African Party as the Union came into being, once again left the Afrikaner workers of Vrededorp without any obvious party-political brokers. In a community where poverty and unemployment continued to remain at a high level, however, the need for relief and jobs did not wait on national political developments and nobody appreciated this more than the indefatigable S. A. Smit. Throughout the period 1908–11, and indeed for some years thereafter, Smit made skilful use of his position on the Town Council to place many of his poorest constituents on the municipal relief works – trench-digging on the sewerage system by now having become an almost permanent feature of Johannesburg's unskilled labour market for whites.[161]

Whether it was his growing indebtedness to his colleagues on the Town Council, or the space created by the departure of the Transvaal nationalists for the debating chambers of Cape Town – or, more likely, a combination of both – S. A. Smit during this period came, to an ever increasing degree, to see his political future as resting with labour. On 1 July 1911, at a large meeting in Vrededorp, 'the only Africander who had ever been behind the scenes at Trades Hall', finally took the plunge and publicly joined the Labour Party. Given Smit's considerable personal popularity amongst Afrikaner workers, the Labour Party looked upon this formal act of allegiance by the 'Mayor of Vrededorp' as an event of considerable political importance.[162]

In the rowdy municipal election meetings that followed, however, Smit soon discovered that while most of his supporters had turned left with him, there were still a significant number of stragglers on the right who hankered after nationalism. In an attempt to cope with this problem Smit was forced to call in an old political debt, and ask F. E. T. Krause to campaign on his behalf. In an ironic reversal of roles, Vrededorp audiences now heard an unlikely Krause singing the praises of Smit, and in a distinctly lower key, those of the Labour Party. As the political reporter of *The Star* noted with wry amusement: 'Mr S. A. Smit is performing a gymnastic turn which involves hanging to the Nationalists with his feet and gripping the Labour Party with his hands.'[163]

But the purists of the Labour Party had no taste for such political gymnastics, and in May 1912 Smit was forced to resign from the party. This time several of Smit's supporters stayed on and did not immediately follow their spokesman back into the arms of the South African Party, and thus right up to the outbreak of the war the Labour Party continued to enjoy a significant following in Vrededorp. Smit in the meantime continued his drift to the right when, in July 1914, he and a number of his supporters abandoned the South African Party in order to establish a new branch of the Nationalist Party.[164]

As always, however, this pronounced fluctuation in Vrededorp's political weather was ultimately determined by the underlying realities of an economic climate which – although to a lesser degree than in 1896–7, or 1906–8 – continued to be dominated by poverty and unemployment. Neither this ongoing political ferment, nor its economic causes were lost on Johannesburg's ruling classes who continued to view this volatile white working-class community with a mixture of fear and genuine concern. Thus when the Town Council was forced, through financial constraints, to curtail its expenditure on the maintenance of this reserve army of labour by 1914 – by abandoning its expensive municipal relief works which had been running continuously since

1906, and by ceasing to contribute to local charitable bodies such as the Rand Aid Association – it was particularly anxious that the state should assume the burden of poor relief.[165]

In its submissions to the Relief and Grants-in-Aid Commission in May 1914, the Johannesburg Town Council contended that the unskilled workers of the western suburbs, 'Instead of getting into other spheres of employment became a powerful influence in municipal elections to secure an increase in their wages, the standard of which was now six and sixpence.' More specifically, it was suggested that in Vrededorp:

> . . . there was growing up a population poverty stricken, ignorant, and a danger to the community. This population was the bane of all political effort. Every political party truckled to this mass of voters and endeavoured to find employment for them. The mass had overturned every political party, and would overturn any political party which might be in power unless a remedy was provided to remove their appalling poverty and degradation.[166]

More eloquent testimony to the strength and vitality of this section of the Afrikaner working-class struggle could hardly be constructed. If it had been necessary, however, members of Kruger's government, the Milner administration, Het Volk, Arbeid Adelt, the Labour Party and the South African Party could all have offered additional evidence of Vrededorp's restless search for political shelter. But then perhaps it is inevitable that, under capitalism, the poor and the unemployed should be politically homeless.

Conclusion

For some Afrikaners, the discovery of gold on the Witwatersrand during the mid-1880s opened up a limited range of economic opportunities which allowed them to become directly involved in the subsequent development of the mining industry. Of these, several were farmers who used the sale of their land as the economic device with which to secure a share in the new mining ventures. Others, more numerous and with notably less success, attempted to negotiate the more difficult terrain that lay between the status of 'digger' on the one hand, and that of mining company shareholder on the other.

But for the vast majority of Afrikaners – who in the earliest years could become neither mine owners nor unskilled workers in the industry – the discovery of gold brought, at best, rather more indirect opportunities. The growth of the Witwatersrand as a produce market, for example, hastened the arrival of capitalist agriculture in the countryside and while this certainly strengthened the position of many Afrikaner farmers it simultaneously impoverished hundreds of their bywoner tenants. Even for the distressed members of this latter category, however, the emergence of the Rand offered some economic consolation during the closing years of the nineteenth century.

In the decade between 1886 and 1896 in particular, and to a lesser extent in the years thereafter until 1906, the growth of Johannesburg allowed thousands of poor bywoners to establish a precarious economic presence in the city in the fields of transport riding, cab driving and brickmaking. Despite the vulnerable economic position which they occupied within the local economy, the members of these groups were sufficiently successful in their sale of goods and services for Afrikaner unemployment to remain at a relatively low level throughout the first decade of the city's development. It was only after the transport riders had been defeated by the railways, the cab drivers by the electric tramway, and the small brickmakers by the capitalist companies that chronic and extensive Afrikaner unemployment became a notable feature of the urban areas. The significance of 1896–7 as a date in the history of Afrikaner proletarianisation lies not only in the increased flow of bywoners to the towns occasioned by a new series of rural disasters, but in the fact that it also marks the point where these sectors of the urban economy started to collapse in the face of broader capitalist development. On the Witwatersrand there was thus an urban as well as a rural road into the Afrikaner working class and it is therefore insufficient to simply note 'the increasing number of "poor whites" drifting into the towns',[167] or to chart 'rural failures'[168] when attempting to account for its growth.

As might be expected, those Afrikaners who found themselves being pushed down the urban road into the working class vigorously resisted the process of proletarianisation – the transport riders in several instances resorting to sabotage. The cab drivers and the brickmakers instead made use of their political access to the Kruger government in various attempts either to deflect or delay the capitalist onslaught to which they were being subjected. In these efforts they were not always entirely unsuccessful. The cab drivers undoubtedly helped to delay the introduction of the electric tramway system into Johannesburg, while the brickmakers obtained both an alternative site for their businesses as well as the promise of a rail connection from the Kruger government. But, in the end, the demands of an expanding capitalist economy assured the economic demise of transport riders, cab drivers and brickmakers alike.

Once they had been forced into the reserve army of labour as unskilled workers, however, these Afrikaners showed – both before and after the South African War – that they had lost little of their capacity to resist. During periods of crisis, such as 1896–7 and 1906–8, angry unemployed Afrikaner workers took to the streets – sometimes with, but usually without the support of their more skilled European counterparts – to bring home the extent of their plight to the ruling classes. It was largely through these militant demonstrations that the poor of Vrededorp extracted concessions in the form of charity, relief works or white labour experiments from the mine owners, the municipality and the state.

Organised charity's origins in Johannesburg lay, in the first instance, in an attempt by a section of the mine owners to exert political influence and control over unemployed English miners via the Present Help League in the period leading up to the South African War. After the war this programme was slightly modified and placed on a more established basis when Milner and the mine owners – drawing on the model of the Charity Organisation Society in London – established the Rand Aid Association to help cushion the blow of unemployment in the years after demobilisation. But, although the Present

Help League and the Rand Aid Association had both been created with the 'single' skilled English craftsman in mind, both organisations found that with the passage of time the bulk of their resources had to be devoted to married unskilled Afrikaner workers. After reconstruction and the assumption of power by Het Volk, the mine owners and the government – for different reasons – lost some of their enthusiasm for the work of the Rand Aid Association. It was partly as a result of this, and largely because of a new and vigorous thrust by the Afrikaner unemployed, that the Rand Unemployed Investigation Committee came into being in March 1908. The latter organisation, which was constituted from a more broadly based coalition of class interests, reflected a stark political reality – namely, that after 1906 it was the unskilled workers of Vrededorp who did most to determine the nature and pattern of charity in the city. In Johannesburg, as elsewhere, 'charity' was *won* from the ruling classes – it derived from class struggle in the streets rather than from benevolence in the boardroom.

But perhaps even more significant than these gains made in the realms of charity were the achievements of the Afrikaner unemployed in obtaining 'relief work'. In the 28-year period under review here, the state and the Johannesburg municipality were, between them, forced to maintain relief works for at least ten of those years. Large sections of the Main Reef Road (1898–9), most of the trenches for Johannesburg's water-borne sewerage system (1906–14), and portions of the rail network in the Transvaal countryside (1906–14) were all constructed with white labour drawn from Fordsburg, Vrededorp and Newlands. Unemployed Afrikaners, however, did more than merely secure work as unskilled manual labourers: through exercising their political muscle they also did much to determine the wage rates attached to these jobs. This action not only increased wages for such unskilled labour between 1906 and 1914, indirectly it also materially influenced the mining industry's experiments with cheap white labour in 1897 and 1908. The 'failure' of Afrikaners to accept positions as unskilled mineworkers at 'economic rates' during periods of recession, can only be understood within the context of their success in achieving alternative employment at higher wages on relief works. It is only by neglecting to examine these important dimensions of the class struggle that one could come to the conclusion that during this period poor whites were 'an extremely disorganised stratum with little power on their own to enforce even limited economic demands'.[169]

It was during the course of this struggle – first while resisting the ravages of proletarianisation, and then while attempting to win employment at a living wage – that urban Afrikaners came to perceive themselves in class terms. Given the pace of capitalist development on the Witwatersrand at the turn of the century, this consciousness did not take long to emerge. In 1893 the Braamfontein brickmakers pointed out in a petition to Kruger that they were 'poor people whose sole income derived from brickmaking', and that if they were not afforded a measure of state protection the entire industry would rapidly fall into the hands of the 'rich speculators'.[170] In 1896 the cab drivers appealed to the State President and the Members of the Executive Committee as the 'protectors of the working classes'[171] in an attempt to maintain the tariff structure in their trade; while eight months later, in August 1897, the police had to come to the rescue of the Editor of the *Standard and Diggers' News*, who had incurred the wrath of angry unemployed Afrikaner workers demonstrating in the city centre.

Immediately after the South African War there was further recognition of the threat which Johannesburg's Afrikaner unemployed posed to the ruling classes. Acting in accordance with Milner's political maxim that, 'Among civilised peoples of more or less equal size that one will be, as it will deserve to be, the strongest, which is most successful in removing the causes of class antagonism in its midst', the incoming British administration embarked on a programme of social engineering to disperse the city's working classes.[172] It was partly as a consequence of this that the racially integrated inner-city ghetto of Burgersdorp gave way to Newtown, and that most of the Afrikaner unemployed found themselves concentrated in Vrededorp.

But, for all this, Vrededorp remained one of the principal sources of class antagonism in Johannesburg and, as half-a-dozen political movements discovered to their cost between 1906 and 1914, one that was notoriously difficult to win and control. In their restless search for political direction the unskilled Afrikaner workers of Vrededorp demonstrated not only an aggressive working-class consciousness, but also a considerable degree of acumen – as when in 1910 it took them six weeks to try on and reject the yoke of a nationalist-dominated labour movement. That in the succeeding decades the same workers should have fallen prey to the nets of a narrow nationalism is one of the many tragedies of modern South Africa.

Notes

1 The first step to rectify this position was taken by J. J. Fourie. See his invaluable contribution to E. L. P. Stals (ed.), *Afrikaners in die Goudstad*, Deel 1, 1886–1923 (Pretoria 1978).

2 The quotations in this para. are taken from a work which specifically seeks to address itself to a historical analysis of 'class formation and class relations' – R. H. Davies, *Capital, State and White Labour in South Africa, 1900–1960* (Brighton 1979), pp. 77 and 101. Davies, however, also subscribes to some – but not all – of the other interpretations offered in this para. See the relevant passages in his work on pp. 57, 76, 102–3.

3 This question is explored in greater detail in J. J. Fourie, *op. cit.*, pp. 19–28.

4 *Ibid.*, pp. 58–70.

5 This para. is reconstructed from fragments collected from several sources. It was noted in the *Standard & Diggers' News* (hereafter, *S. & D.N.*) of 10 February 1894 that, 'The class from which the police is now recruited are the unemployed young Boers to be found in the town and elsewhere . . . many can neither read nor write.' See also Commandant D. E. Schutte to the Editor, *S. & D.N.*, 11 October 1894. On Post Office officials, see Transvaal Archives Depot (T.A.D.), Pretoria, S.S. Vol. 5533, R9152/96, 'Opgawe', pp. 111–12. Also, 'Nationality of Telegraphists', *The Star*, 15 May 1897.

6 For a glimpse into the life of a Transvaal transport rider prior to the advent of the branch-line system, see University of the Witwatersrand, African Studies Institute, Oral History Project, Tape Nos 35 and 36, M. S. S. Ntoane's interview with G. K. Skhosana at Lydenburg on 7 and 8 September 1979.

7 See, for example, 'The Problem of the "Arme" Burgher', *The Star*, 30 August

1897, or D. Hobart Houghton, 'Economic Development, 1865–1965, *in* M. Wilson and L. M. Thompson (eds.), *The Oxford History of South Africa* (Oxford 1971), Vol. 2, p. 20.

8 C. T. Gordon, *The Growth of Boer Opposition to Kruger, 1890–1895* (London 1970), p. 30.

9 Gordon is therefore mistaken in his suggestion that the tolls were abandoned in 1892 – C. T. Gordon, *The Growth of Boer Opposition*, p. 30. By way of contrast see, for example, reports on the tolls in the *S. & D.N.* of 16 June 1894 and 2 May 1895.

10 Para. based on Vol. 1, Chapter 4, 'Johannesburg's Jehus, 1890–1914'.

11 *Ibid.*

12 J. J. Fourie, *op. cit.*, pp. 51–2. Between 1886 and 1891 these sites were rent free. From the latter date, however, the brickmakers were required to pay two sets of small licence fees. See also J. Finch, *To South Africa and Back* (London 1890), p. 136.

13 The two preceding paras are based on 'The Brickmakers', *The Star*, 9 September 1896, and an extended interview with W. H. Brummer in Johannesburg on 31 March 1980. From shortly after the First World War until his retirement in the late 1950s 'Oom Willie' Brummer was the blacksmith in Newlands, Johannesburg, who regularly manufactured 'puddle machines' – the so-called 'pokmeule' – and brick moulds for the remaining Afrikaner brickmakers in the city. Of course, even England during the course of the industrial revolution still relied on such 'primitive' machinery. See, for example, R. Samuel's, 'The Workshop of the World', *History Workshop*, 3, 1977, pp. 30–1.

14 Some idea of these developments can be obtained from a scrutiny of the following reports in the *S. & D.N.*: 'Building Contractors', 23 May 1892; 'The Building Boom', 18 June 1892'; 'Kuranda & Marais', 27 December 1892; the leading articles of 15 September 1893 and 3 January 1894; and 'Coloured Labour', 30 August 1897. See also, however, the following items in *The Star*: 'The Cry of the Contractors', 20 September 1895; 'The Building Boom', 20 May 1895; and 'The Building Trade', 5 June 1895.

15 These prices for 'stock bricks' were compiled from the following fragments: Johannesburg Public Library (J.P.L.), Johannesburg City Archives (J.C.A.), Box 208, Quotation to build a house supplied by contractors H. Smith and D. Wood; 'East Rand Notes', *S. & D.N.*, 19 June 1895; 'City & Suburban Notes', *S. & D.N.*, 23 September 1895; 'The Brickmakers', *The Star*, 9 September 1895; 'The Brickmakers', *The Star*, 9 September 1896; and 'Company Meetings', *S. & D.N.*, 29 March 1898.

16 Table compiled from: *Transvaal Leader*, Christmas Number, 1904; and R. Krut, ' "A Quart into a Pint Pot": The White Working Class and the "Housing Shortage" in Johannesburg, 1896–1906', B.A. (Hons) dissertation, University of the Witwatersrand, 1979, p. 3.

17 See, for example, J.P.L., J.C.A., Box 218, Health Inspector's Report to the Chairman and Members of the Sanitary Board, 20 November 1894.

18 See especially 'City & Suburban Notes', *S. & D.N.*, 23 September 1895.

19 *Johannesburg Census 1896*, Part XII, 'Occupations', and Part IX, 'Dwellings, Buildings, Live Stock, etc.'.

20 For an idea of the size of the African complement at brickyards during the mid-1890s see, for example, J.P.L., J.C.A., Box 263, Folder 113, Applications to allow Natives to sleep on premises, 1895. For the conditions under which such workers lived see, for example, J.P.L., J.C.A., Box 216, Medical Officer of Health, A. van Niekerk to Chairman and Members of the Sanitary Board, 24 May 1893; or Report of Inspection carried out at the Brick & Tile Co., 31 May 1893.

21 T.A.D., S.S. Vol. 4677, Petition by M. de Beer and 93 other Brickmakers addressed to His Honour, The State President, and Members of the Executive

Committee, 4 April 1893.
22 J. J. Fourie, *op. cit.*, p. 52.
23 *Ibid.* p. 53. For additional detail, however, see also T.A.D., S.S. Vol. 4677, Petition by M. de Beer and 93 other Brickmakers addressed to His Honour, The State President, and Members of the Executive Committee, 4 April 1893; and letter to the editor from the Joint Secretaries, The Braamfontein Brickmakers' Association, *S. & D.N.*, 10 February 1894.
24 This para. based on: 'Sanitary Board Meeting', *S. & D.N.*, 11 April 1895; *S. & D.N.*, 14 May 1896; 'The Brickfields', *The Star*, 9 June 1896; and 'Poverty Point', *The Star*, 3 September 1896.
25 Para. based on: 'The Brickfields', *S. & D.N.*, 15 May 1896; 'The Brickfields Difficulty', *The Star*, 17 June 1896; and 'The Brickmakers', *Johannesburg Times*, 24 June 1896.
26 *Johannesburg Times*, 24 June 1896.
27 See also *The Star* for 11 and 31 July 1896; and *Staatscourant de Zuid Afrikaansche Republiek*, 16 November 1898, p. 1609.
28 J.P.L., J.C.A., Box 224, V. F. Schutte (Chairman), M. P. Koen (Secretary) and other brickmakers to Chairman and Members of the Sanitary Board, 19 August 1896. Also T.A.D., S.S. Vol. 5735, R12210/96, A. J. Alberts to Mining Commissioner, 25 August 1896; and L. J. Alberts to Mining Commissioner, 26 August 1896.
29 T.A.D., S.S. Vol. 5735, R2553/96, H. C. Swanepoel and others to Executive Committee, 31 January 1897. See also, *Z.A.R. Executive Committee*, Resolution 16, Article 462, April 1898; and Resolution 17, Article 1251, 14 December 1898.
30 'Albertskroon Brickmakers', *The Star*, 8 and 11 December 1902.
31 Interview with W. H. Brummer, Johannesburg, 31 March 1980.
32 Para. based on items reported in the *S. & D.N.* of 24 September 1892, 16 April 1894, and 2 May 1895.
33 Here it is significant to note that while the City & Suburban Tramway Co. nominally held the right to convey goods on their trams, the Kruger government never allowed them to exercise this right. This appears to have been one of the few concessions which the Republican government made to the Afrikaner transport riders. See T.A.D., Gov. Vol. 463, 'Johannesburg City & Suburban Tramway Concession', 22 October 1901. On Afrikaner employment in related fields see, for example, *Evidence to the Transvaal Indigency Commission 1906–1908* (Pretoria – T.G. 11, 1908), testimony of Lieut Col O'Brien (Acting Commissioner of Police), para. 1445, p. 63; and Dr T. B. Gilchrist, p. 24. (Hereafter cited as *Transvaal Indigency Commission 1906–1908.*)
34 See, amongst others: 'The Problem of the "Arme" Burgher', *The Star*, 20 August 1897; 'Brick & Potteries Co.', *The Star*, 18 March 1902 (introduction of traction engine); *Transvaal Indigency Commission 1906–1908*, evidence of S. J. Halford, p. 9 and Dr T. B. Gilchrist, p. 240; and *Report of the Relief and Grants-in-Aid Commission 1916* (T.P. No. 5 – 1916), para. 35, p. 17. (Hereafter, *Relief and Grants-in-Aid Commission 1916.*)
35 Para. based on Vol. 1, Chapter 4, 'Johannesburg's Jehus', p. 175.
36 *Ibid.*, p. 195. More specifically, see Dr T. B. Gilchrist's evidence pertaining to Fordsburg in *Transvaal Indigency Commission 1906–8*, para. 5639, p. 241. Out of comparative interest, see also *Report of the Commission on Pretoria Indigents 1905*, paras 10 and 12.
37 It would appear that one of the first and most important of these brickworks – the Rand Brick & Tile Co. – was started by T. M. Cullinan, who later developed close connections with H. Eckstein & Co., and who obtained a 'concession' to import brickmaking machinery from the Kruger government. See N. Helme, *Thomas Major Cullinan* (Johannesburg 1974), pp. 18–20, and note 42 below. The

remainder of this paragraph is based on items drawn from the following editions of the *Standard & Diggers' News*: 9 May 1890, 23 April 1892, 23 May 1892 and 21 September 1892.

38 Para. based on the following items drawn from the *S. & D.N.*: 'Cornelia Coal Mine', 12 March 1894; 'A Local Industry', 16 March 1895; 'The Vaal River Colliery', 13 January 1896; 'Company Meetings – Ophirton Brick Co.', 29 March 1898; 'Company Meetings – Brick & Potteries Co. Ltd', 4 October 1898; and 'A New Brick Factory' in *The Star*, 3 March 1899.

39 Para. based on several fragmentary sources. A schematic idea of the rise of the capitalist brickmaking industry during this period, however, can be gained from a close examination of *Longland's Johannesburg & District Directory*, 1897–9; *Longland's Transvaal Directory*, 1903–7; and the *United Transvaal Directory*, 1908–14.

40 See the complaints of the small brickmakers on this score in 'Albertskroon Brickmakers' in *The Star* of 8 and 11 December 1902.

41 See 'The Vaal River Colliery', *S. & D.N.*, 13 January 1896; and 'A New Brick Factory', *The Star*, 3 March 1899.

42 Two preceding paras based on: 'Company Meetings – Brick & Potteries Co. Ltd', *S. & D.N.*, 4 October 1898; and 'Brick & Potteries Company', *The Star*, 18 March 1902. It seems possible that, before the war, the Brick & Potteries Co. operated with a monopoly right to manufacture machine-made bricks in Johannesburg. In 1900, Violet Markham noted: 'The brick and cement monopolies affect this question [housing] to a large degree. Machine-made bricks cost no less than £4 10s 0d per 1,000 or about five times the cost of bricks in this country'. V. R. Markham, *South Africa Past and Present* (London 1900), p. 376. This contention about monopolistic trade practice was also made in 'Alpha's' letter to the editor, *The Star*, 19 June 1896.

43 See the following important reports in *The Star*: 'Brick & Potteries Company', 18 March 1902; 'Company Meetings – Brick & Potteries Co. Ltd', 20 September 1903; 'Brick & Potteries Co. Ltd', 23 September 1905; and 'Brick & Potteries Co. – A Successful Industry', 27 September 1909.

44 'Vrededorp Vigilants', *The Star*, 21 February 1906.

45 See, for example, the evidence of Dr T. B. Gilchrist to the *Transvaal Indigency Commission 1906–8*, p. 240.

46 Unfortunately we do not have a detailed breakdown of the Afrikaner unemployed in Johannesburg during the immediate post-war period. There is, however, such a breakdown for Pretoria – an area where capitalist brickmaking companies also made noteworthy strides during the post-war period – and here the evidence points to a substantial number of former brickmakers amongst the unemployed. See *Report of the Commission on Pretoria Indigents 1905*, p. 3, para. 10.

47 Para. based on items drawn from the following editions of the *S. & D.N.*: 17 December 1889, 17 July 1893 and 22 January 1894.

48 On these two schemes see items in the *S. & D.N.* of 12 July 1893, and 16 November 1893.

49 For casual employment see, for example, 'Johannesburg by Night' by 'Vagabond' in *S. & D.N.*, 19 January 1895. Many of the Transvaal's highway robbers during the period 1890–3 were unemployed miners waylaying black migrant workers making their way home to the rural areas with their cash wages. See, for example, the case of J. R. Lee as reported in the *S. & D.N.* of 18 July 1893. By the mid-1890s this problem was sufficiently serious for the Chamber of Mines to employ its own police force to combat the negative influence which this had on the flow of migrant labour. See Transvaal, *Report of the Chamber of Mines 1895*, pp. 69–70; *Report of the Chamber of Mines 1896*, pp. 170–1; and D. M. Wilson, *Behind the Scenes in the Transvaal* (London 1901), pp. 196–7.

50 See J. J. Fourie's useful table, 'Die Trek van die Afrikaner na Johannesburg, 1886–1899 (Mans bo 16 Jaar)' in *Afrikaners in die Goudstad*, p. 39.

51 For the van Greuning and De Koker case see *S. & D.N.*, 31 May 1892.

52 The role of cheaper passages from Europe and the rail link to the Transvaal during this period was widely recognised as a contributing factor to the growing number of unemployed on the Rand. See in the *S. & D.N.*, for example, 'Our Unemployed', 7 August 1895; and 'The Distress', 14 August 1897.

53 See, in the *S. & D.N.*, 'Present Help League', 29 November 1895; and 'Kelly's Relief Stores – Still Closed', 27 January 1896.

54 See 'Poverty on the Rand', *Johannesburg Times*, 24 July 1897; and 'Needy Burghers' and 'The Starving Poor' in *The Star* of 24 July 1897. For an excellent account of Dieperink's visit to the western suburbs see, 'Darkest Johannesburg', *Johannesburg Times*, 26 July 1897.

55 The proposed steam laundry eventually gave rise to the establishment of *De Maatschappy tot nut van het Algemeen* and is discussed, in a different context, in Chapter 2 above, 'AmaWasha – the Zulu washermen's guild of the Witwatersrand', pp. 86–7.

56 See, 'Distress in Johannesburg' and 'Rand Relief Committee' in *The Star*, 7 and 10 August 1897. Somewhat misleadingly, this Johannesburg Relief Committee was known locally as the 'Rand Relief Committee', and it should not be confused with a later 'Rand Relief Committee' formed to work primarily in the uitlander community in 1898 (see p. 130). I am indebted to Diana McClaren for first drawing this important distinction to my attention.

57 'The Distress', *S. & D.N.*, 14 August 1897.

58 For the Victorian basis to these various ideological strands – including that of the residuum – see G. Stedman Jones, *Outcast London* (Oxford 1971).

59 'The Indigent', *S. & D.N.*, 16 August 1897. The reference to 'Berlin' in this context is unclear. It is possible, however, that it refers to the demonstrations held at the International Congress for the Protection of Workers held in Berlin in March 1890 – an event that also coincided with Bismarck's fall from power.

60 See 'The Unemployed', *The Star*, 14 August 1897; and 'The Indigent', *S. & D.N.*, 14 August 1897.

61 *Ibid.*

62 'The Indigent', *S. & D.N.*, 14 August 1897.

63 Para. based on: 'Street Begging Rampant', *Johannesburg Weekly Times*, 14 November 1896; 'The Vagrancy Plague', *S. & D.N.*, 20 January 1897; 'The Unemployed', *The Comet*, 3 April 1897; and item in *S. & D.N.* dated 12 April 1897.

64 J. J. Fourie, *op. cit.*, pp. 82–3.

65 See the following items in the *S. & D.N.*: 'To the Relief', 19 August 1897; and 'Relief for the Poor', 10 September 1897.

66 See J. J. Fourie, 'Die Geskiedenis van die Afrikaners in Johannesburg, 1886–1900', D.Phil., 1976, Randse Afrikaanse Universiteit, pp. 135–7. See also, 'Main Reef Road', *S. & D.N.*, 23 March 1899.

67 Para. based on 'The Destitution', *S. & D.N.*, 16 July 1898; 'The Destitution', *S. & D.N.*, 20 August 1898; 'The Destitution', *The Star*, 23 August 1898; and 'Rand Relief Fund', *S. & D.N.*, 6 September 1898.

68 *Ibid.* See also 'Indiscriminate Alms Giving', *S. & D.N.*, 27 February 1899. On the alleged 'innate desire' of the Boer population as a whole 'to live on charity' see 'The Boer Population – A Depraved People', *The Star*, 27 January 1899.

69 L. S. Amery, *The Times History of the War in South Africa 1899–1902* (London 1909), Vol. IV, pp. 149–50.

70 See, amongst others, the following items drawn from the *S. & D.N.*, 'Wives of Fighting Burghers', 10 November 1899; 'Rand Day by Day', 24 November 1899;

and 'Rand Day by Day', 1 December 1899.
71 L. S. Amery, *Times History of the War*, Vol. VI, p. 590.
72 *Ibid.*, p. 594.
73 'Johannesburg Slums', *The Star*, 20 February 1902. See also, however, Quinn's evidence to the *Johannesburg Insanitary Area Improvement Scheme Commission 1902–1903*, para. 2839, p. 140.
74 A. H. Duminy and W. R. Guest (eds.), *FitzPatrick* (Johannesburg 1976), FitzPatrick to J. Wernher, 5 July 1902, p. 333.
75 *Report of Johannesburg Insanitary Area Improvement Scheme Commission 1902–1903*, especially pp. 38, 154–5 and 222–3, paras 138–51, 3208–24 and 5220–74 respectively. On the question of inner city rents and the movement of the Afrikaner poor see *Transvaal Indigency Commission 1906–1908*, evidence of Dr T. B. Gilchrist, p. 240 and especially p. 242, paras 5666–70; and evidence of Sister Evelyn, p. 73, paras 1719–26.
76 See reports on 'The Rand Aid Association' in *The Star* of 9 April 1903 and 5 January 1904.
77 On the Charity Organisation Society (C.O.S.) role and function in London see, G. Stedman Jones, *Outcast London*, pp. 256–9. That the C.O.S. formed the model for the Rand Aid Association seems clear from the editorial on 'The Rand Aid Association' in *The Star*, 9 April 1903. Lionel Curtis was certainly well aware of the role of the C.O.S. and the need for such a body on the Rand – see, *Transvaal Indigency Commission 1906–8*, p. 64, paras. 1481–5.
78 'Rand Aid Association – A Year's Work', *The Star*, 29 February 1904.
79 At least one eminent observer was thus off the mark when he suggested that: 'I had that uncomfortable feeling in Johannesburg which one has in so many American cities, that it lacks genuine public sprit. It owes nothing to its millionaires, not even to their charity.' J. Ramsay Macdonald, *What I Saw in South Africa* (London 1902), p. 102.
80 J. Buchan, *The African Colony: Studies in the Reconstruction* (London 1903), p. 321.
81 Extract from Louis Botha's speech as reported in *The Star*, 23 May 1904. See also – a few weeks earlier – Sammy Marks's offer to take on the Afrikaner poor as share-croppers on some of his estates; 'Mr S. Marks' Offer', *The Star*, 29 March 1904. The reconstruction government, and especially the more conciliatory Selborne, took the point about rural unemployment seriously and attempted to accommodate it. See S. Marks and S. Trapido, 'Lord Milner and the South African State', *History Workshop*, 8, 1979, p. 70.
82 This para. is based on several sources, only the principal of which are cited here. On cab drivers, see Vol. 1, Chapter 4, 'Johannesburg's Jehus'. On the building industry and its collapse see: 'How the Poor Live', *Rand Daily Mail*, 29 June 1906; 'Influx of Unemployed', *The Star*, 26 October 1906; statistics as supplied to the *Transvaal Indigency Commission 1906–8* by Joseph Hale (President of the Unemployed Organisation), p. 243; and *ibid.*, evidence of W. R. Boustred (Johannesburg Chamber of Commerce), p. 293. On shop assistants, see 'Influx of Unemployed', *The Star*, 26 October 1906; 'The Unemployed', *Transvaal Leader*, 23 February 1907; and 'Poor Whites', *Transvaal Leader*, 27 February 1907.
83 For Rand Aid's approach to Phillips, see M. Fraser and A. Jeeves (eds.), *All That Glittered* (Cape Town 1977), pp. 153–5, L. Phillips to F. Eckstein, 12 March 1906. On subsequent grants from Wernher, Beit & Co. and W.N.L.A. to the Rand Aid Association see 'Notes and comments – The Problem of the Destitute' and 'The Present Distress' in *The Star* of 3 and 5 March 1908.
84 'The Unemployed', *Transvaaal Leader*, 17 May 1906.
85 The remaining members of the commission were: L. S. Ferreira, H. Crawford, J. Reid, J. Rissik and F. B. Smith. See *Transvaal Indigency Commission 1906–8*.

86 'The Unemployed', *Transvaal Leader*, 17 May 1906.
87 Johannesburg,*Minutes of the Public Health Committee*, 19 December 1906, p. 140. See also 'With the Workless', *Rand Daily Mail*, 5 February 1907. The Johannesburg Town Council had also apparently taken on a few hundred unskilled workers during the earlier post-war recession of 1903–4 – see J. J. Fourie,*op. cit.*, p. 77.
88 These proposals – as well as others made later during the depression – included the suggestion that the unemployed be transported to more promising labour markets elsewhere. See especially 'With the Workless',*Rand Daily Mail*, 5 February 1907.
89 Para. based on 'Relief Work' and 'The Unemployed',*The Star*, 14 February 1907. This response by Robinson angered many amongst the ruling class, including J. W. Quinn. See, for example, Quinn's comments in 'Indigency and Politics', *Transvaal Leader*, 16 March 1907; and his questioning of Joseph Hale in *Transvaal Indigency Commission 1906–8*, p. 243, paras. 5709–19.
90 'Relief Work – The Government's Offer', *The Star*, 14 February 1907.
91 Para. based on items drawn from the *Rand Daily Mail*, 16 February 1907.
92 Para. based on: 'On the Union Ground – A Fiery Speech', *Rand Daily Mail*, 16 February 1907; 'The Unemployed – Seizing the Show Ground',*Transvaal Leader*, 18 February 1907.
93 'The Unemployed', *Transvaal Leader*, 18 February 1907.
94 *Ibid.*
95 'The Unemployed', *Transvaal Leader*, 23 February 1907. See also 'Feeding the Hungry', *Transvaal Leader*, 2 March 1907.
96 See 'Poor Whites' and 'Government Contribution' in *Transvaal Leader*, 27 February 1907; 'Feeding the Hungry',*Transvaal Leader*, 2 March 1907; and 'The Unemployed', *Rand Daily Mail*, 19 March 1907.
97 Para. based on: 'The Unemployed', *Rand Daily Mail*, 19 March 1907; 'The Unemployed – I.L.P. Agitators',*Transvaal Leader*, 24 March 1907; 'Unemployed "Stiffs" ',*Rand Daily Mail*, 10 April 1907; and 'March on Pretoria',*Rand Daily Mail*, 22 April 1907. For Hale's evidence to the commission see, *Transvaal Indigency Commission 1906–8*, p. 243.
98 See 'March on Pretoria',*Rand Daily Mail*, 22 April 1907; and 'The Unemployed – The Workless Army', *Rand Daily Mail*, 3 May 1907.
99 See the following items in the *Rand Daily Mail*: 'March on Pretoria', 22 April 1907; 'The Unemployed – The Workless Army', 3 May 1907; and 'Government Offer Rejected', 3 May 1907.
100 E. N. Katz, *A Trade Union Aristocracy* (Johannesburg 1976), p. 131. On the T.M.A.'s interpretation of the cause and consequences of the strike see J. Mathey's address at 'Another Pretoria Meeting', *The Star*, 17 May 1907.
101 'The "General Strike" ', *The Star*, 22 May 1907. As Alan Jeeves has shown in his 'Het Volk and the Gold Mines – The Debate on Labour Policy 1905–1910' (Seminar Paper, African Studies Institute, University of the Witwatersrand, June 1980), pp. 12 and 18, even before the election, Het Volk had approached the Chamber of Mines with a request that it take on Afrikaner miners in the hope that this would help relieve indigency. The Randlords' policy was therefore always likely to meet with the tacit approval of the Het Volk government.
102 For examples of such Afrikaner labour recruited from 'outside districts' during the course of the strike see, amongst others, the following items drawn from *The Star*: 'Dutchmen Repent', 10 May 1907; 'Riot at Langlaagte Deep', 16 May 1907; 'Recruiting at Pretoria', 16 May 1907; 'Wages of Recruits', 17 May 1907; 'Potchefstroom Recruiting', 20 May 1907; and 'Country Recruiting', 24 May 1907.
103 'The "General Strike" ', *The Star*, 22 May 1907.
104 See, for example, 'Feeling at Pretoria – Dutch Labour Available', and 'Another

Pretoria Meeting', *The Star*, 17 May 1907.

105 See, amongst others, the following items culled from *The Star*: 'Dutchmen Repent', 10 May 1907; 'The Miners' Strike – Riotous Proceedings', 16 May 1907; 'Riot at Langlaagte Deep', 16 May 1907; 'Situation To-day', 17 May 1907; and 'On the West Rand', 7 June 1907.

106 Para. based on: 'Belangryke Kennisgewing aan alle Afrikaners', *De Volkstem*, 11 May 1907; 'A Dutch Meeting', *The Star*, 15 May 1907; and 'Meeting at Newlands', *Rand Daily Mail*, 16 May 1907.

107 'The "General Strike" ', *The Star*, 22 May 1907.

108 'The Miners' Strike', *The Star*, 21 May 1907.

109 *Ibid*.

110 *Ibid*.

111 *Ibid*. (My emphasis.)

112 'De Werkstaking', *De Volkstem*, 25 May 1907.

113 Para. based on the following items drawn from *The Star*: 'Strike Items', 17 May 1907; 'The "General Strike" ', 22 May 1907; 'The Fordsburg District', 28 May 1907; and 'The End of the Strike', 1 June 1907. See also, E. N. Katz, *A Trade Union Aristocracy*, p. 131.

114 Estimate drawn from A. Jeeves, '*Het Volk* and the Gold Mines', p. 18.

115 E. N. Katz, *A Trade Union Aristocracy*, p. 132.

116 See especially, 'Notes and Comments – Strike Echoes', *The Star*, 13 June 1907.

117 For the accommodation arrangements made for some of these 'single' Afrikaners brought in from the countryside during the strike see, for example, 'Riot at Langlaagte Deep', *The Star*, 16 May 1907.

118 See the following items drawn from *The Star*: 'Miner Fired At', 13 June 1907; 'Lurking Dangers', 14 June 1907; and 'Further Particulars', 15 June 1907.

119 'Dastardly Outrage', *The Star*, 15 June 1907.

120 'Diabolical Attempt', *The Star*, 3 July 1907.

121 ' "Numerous cases of employees receiving intimidating letters are being daily reported" '. 'Notes and Comments – Strike Echoes', *The Star*, 13 June 1907.

122 See 'Charity at Vrededorp – Soup Kitchens and Spinning', *The Star*, 29 August 1907; and 'Work for the Needy – Cottage Industries', *Transvaal Leader*, 16 September 1907.

123 'Helping the Poor', *Transvaal Leader*, 13 November 1907.

124 'Salvation – New Vrededorp Scheme', *Transvaal Leader*, 4 October 1907. This scheme by the Salvation Army was presumably also designed to supplement a drive by employers to give white working-class lads in the city jobs in place of 'Kaffirs'. See, for example, 'All White – Lads Replacing Kaffirs', *Rand Daily Mail*, 26 August 1907. Of especial interest, however, is the experiment which J. W. Quinn attempted in his bakery during the depression. See evidence of J. W. Quinn to *Select Committee on European Employment and Labour Conditions 1913* (Cape Town, S.C. No. 9 of 1913), pp. 457–9, paras. 3335–8.

125 'The Unemployed', *Transvaal Leader*, 10 September 1907; 'Work for Whites', *Transvaal Leader*, 12 September 1907; and 'Notes and Comments – The Sewerage Scheme', *The Star*, 30 September 1907. See also the written statement submitted by the Johannesburg municipality to the *Transvaal Indigency Commission 1906–8*, pp. 378–9.

126 Para. based on 'We Want Work', *Rand Daily Mail*, 4 March 1908.

127 Para. based on: 'Unemployed – Starving and Destitute', *Transvaal Leader*, 2 March 1908; and 'Notes and Comments – The Problem of the Destitute', *The Star*, 3 March 1908.

128 Para. based on: 'Unemployed – Starving and Destitute', *Transvaal Leader*, 2 March 1908; and 'We Want Work', *Rand Daily Mail*, 4 March 1908. See also, J. J. Fourie, *op. cit.*, p. 77.

129 'We Want Work', *Rand Daily Mail*, 4 March 1908.
130 *Ibid*. The irony of this rhetoric lay in the fact that at the very moment that Das was making this speech, some of Vrededorp's Afrikaners were reported as living on 'mealie-pap and water, the mealie meal often begged from Kaffirs'. See 'Unemployed', *Transvaal Leader*, 2 March 1908.
131 'We Want Work', *Rand Daily Mail*, 4 March 1908.
132 Para. based on: 'The Starving Poor', *The Star*, 5 March 1908 and 'Problem of the Poor', *Transvaal Leader*, 7 March 1908.
133 Even here, however, Krause found it hard to identify fully with the Vrededorp poor. On being asked whether he considered £15 to be a suitable transfer fee, he replied that he did 'but whether his constituents would be satisfied was for them to decide', *Transvaal Legislative Assembly Debates*, 10 August 1908, cols 1482–3. For a summary of legislation as it affected Vrededorp between 1893 and 1912, see *Report of the Transvaal Leasehold Townships Commission 1912* (U.G. 34 – 1912), pp. 95–7.
134 See *First Report of the South African Republic Officials' Pension Commission*, January 1908, (T.G. 10 – 1909). As has been noted above, the need for pensions was mooted well before the unemployment crisis of 1906–8. Neither Krause nor Smuts, however, would have failed to notice how some of the ex-Republican civil servants such as N. P. Oelofse and M. J. Bekker took up prominent roles amongst the more radical unemployed Afrikaners. Thus, both the Vrededorp Stands Ordinance 1906 (as amended 1907 and 1908), and the South African Republic Officials' Pension Commission would have helped to divide this volatile community along class lines during the depression. For Krause's speech see 'The Unemployed Dutch', *The Star*, 7 March 1908.
135 'The Unemployed Dutch', *The Star*, 7 March 1908.
136 *Ibid*.
137 'Problem of the Poor – Government Active', *Transvaal Leader*, 7 March 1908.
138 *Ibid*.
139 *Ibid*.
140 'Indigency Problem', *The Star*, 10 March 1908.
141 *Ibid*.
142 *Ibid*.
143 R. H. Davies thus gets a good bit more than his dates wrong when he suggests that: 'Indeed, at first (1907–1909) even the co-ordination of "relief work" programmes had been undertaken by a committee of "private" capitalists (the Rand Unemployed Investigation Committee) rather than by a Department of State.' R. H. Davies, *Capital, State and White Labour*, p. 103. For the composition of the Rand Unemployed Investigation Committee see *The Star*, 10 March 1908.
144 Para. based on: 'The Unemployed', *The Star*, 12 March 1908; 'The Unemployed', *The Star*, 31 March 1908; 'Unemployed', *Rand Daily Mail*, 1 April 1908; and the evidence of the Secretary to R.U.I.C., H. E. Sutherland, to the *Select Committee on European Employment and Labour Conditions 1913*, pp. 385–9, paras. 2721–65.
145 Evidence of H. E. Sutherland (Sec., R.U.I.C.) to *Select Committee on European Employment and Labour Conditions 1913*, pp. 388–9, paras. 2764–5.
146 Besides their misgivings about an enormous drop in wages which such a move would entail (see below), the fear of contracting miners' phthisis was particularly widespread amongst the Afrikaner poor of Vrededorp at the time. See especially the evidence of R. Shanks to the *Select Committee on European Employment and Labour Conditions 1913*, p. 393, para. 2861. On the numbers involved at the various stages of this operation see 'The Mines and the Unemployed', *The Star*, 7 April 1908.
147 See, 'Unemployed', *Rand Daily Mail*, 1 April 1908; and 'The Unemployed', *The Star*, 3 April 1908.

148 See evidence of H. E. Sutherland to the *Select Committee on European Employment and Labour Conditions 1913*, p. 388, para. 2763. See also 'Poor Whites and the Mines', *The Star*, 6 April 1908.

149 'The Unemployed', *The Star*, 3 April 1908. For a selection of Afrikaner responses to this situation, see the extracts reprinted from the 'Dutch Press' in *The Star*, 6 April 1908. Of particular interest is the extract from an editorial in *De Transvaler* in this selection.

150 'The Unemployed – Deputations and Demonstrations', *The Star*, 3 April 1908.

151 *Ibid.* Since it was the braver souls who had made the transition to underground work in the mines, the Mayor presumably did not take this threat lightly.

152 *Ibid.*

153 Para. based on the following items drawn from *The Star*: 'The Unemployed – A New Scheme', 4 April 1908; 'The Mines and the Unemployed', 7 April 1908; and 'Notes and Comments', 17 April 1908.

154 See the following items drawn from *The Star*: 'The Unemployed – A New Scheme', 4 April 1908; 'The Unemployed', 7 April 1908; and 'Notes and Comments', 17 April 1908. For the first full-length reports on the activities of R.U.I.C., however, see 'The Unemployed', *Transvaal Leader*, 7 August 1908; and 'Rand Unemployed', *The Star*, 16 October 1909.

155 Para. based on: 'The Unemployed', *Transvaal Leader*, 7 August 1908; 'The Rand Poor Whites', *Transvaal Leader*, 8 May 1909; 'Rand Unemployed', *The Star*, 16 October 1909; and 'The Dole System', *The Star*, 8 November 1909. See also, the evidence of F. C. Steinmetz (Sec., Rand Aid Association), H. E. Sutherland (Sec., R.U.I.C.) and D.P. Liebenberg (Inspector of Land Settlements) to the *Select Committee on European Employment and Labour Conditions 1913*.

156 'Labour Propaganda – Missioners in Vrededorp', *The Star*, 1 July 1908.

157 'White Labour – A New Party Formed', *Rand Daily Mail*, 14 October 1909.

158 'White Labourers', *The Star*, 18 January 1910.

159 Para. based on the following items drawn from *The Star*: 'White Labourers', 18 January 1910; 'Arbeid Adelt', 1 February 1910; and 'Arbeid Adelt – Constitution and Rules', 31 March 1910.

160 The collapse of the labour society is noted in J. J. Fourie, *op. cit.*, p. 80.

161 See, for example, the evidence of H. O. Buckle, Johannesburg's Resident Magistrate, to the *Select Committee on European Employment and Labour Conditions 1913*, pp. 378–9, para. 2671.

162 See the quotation from the *Transvaal Leader* of 23 September 1913 and cited in J. J. Fourie, *op. cit.*, p. 104.

163 'Town and Reef', *The Star*, 27 September 1911.

164 J. J. Fourie, *op. cit.*, pp. 103–8.

165 See, 'Problem of Poverty – Inequitable Municipal Doles', *Rand Daily Mail*, 25 May 1914.

166 *Ibid.*

167 R. H. Davies, 'The 1922 Strike on the Rand: White Labour and the Political Economy of South Africa', *in* P. Gutkind, R. Cohen and J. Copans (eds.), *African Labour History* (London 1978), p. 83.

168 E. Jensen, 'Poor Relief in Johannesburg', *The Journal of the Economic Society of South Africa*, February 1928, 2, 1.

169 Davies, *Capital, State and White Labour in South Africa*, p. 101.

170 T.A.D., S.S. Vol. 4677, M. de Beer and 93 others to His Honour The State President and the Executive Committee, 4 April 1893.

171 T.A.D., S.S. Vol. 4934, Petition to His Honour The State President and the Executive Committee, 8 December 1896.

172 B. Semmell, *Imperialism and Social Reform: English Social Imperial Thought 1895–1914* (London 1960), p. 181.

CHAPTER FOUR

The Regiment of the Hills – Umkosi Wezintaba

The Witwatersrand's lumpenproletarian army, 1890–1920*

Since the mid-1960s, and particularly since the publication of Fanon's *Wretched of the Earth*, sociologists and political scientists with an interest in the Third World have been debating the revolutionary potential of those heterogenous groups that are marginal to society and which are collectively termed the 'lumpenproletariat'.[1] In an adjacent discipline but with a predominantly different geographical focus, scholars like Gareth Stedman Jones, George Rudé and Eric Hobsbawm have been skilfully exploring aspects of marginality in European history.[2] Despite the fact that several of these scholars share a common intellectual tradition and interest, there has been little cross-fertilisation between these distinct fields of research. This is hardly surprising since Third World social structures and European historical case studies cannot be expected to articulate particuarly well. What is and what was required, were Third World case studies.[3]

Within the context of this broadly defined problem, the social historian of South Africa seems to have a special responsibility, and the opportunity for particularly stimulating research. South Africa was the first country in Africa – and the only one with nineteenth-century roots – to undergo a fully-fledged industrial revolution. Within 75 years of gold being discovered on the Witwatersrand in 1886, capital transformed the face of the subcontinent and generated successive social formations which left an increasingly well-entrenched white ruling class. Those same transforming processes prised black South Africans off their land, separated them from their families, reduced them to the status of workers, and then ruthlessly reallocated them to the towns. There, on the bureaucratic leash of the pass laws, they were soon exposed to two sociologically similar institutions which served the rapidly industrialising economic system particularly well – the prisons and the mine compounds.[4] In a matter of decades, and sometimes perhaps within the space

*World Copyright: The Past and Present Society, Corpus Christi College, Oxford, England. An earlier version of this chapter first appeared in *Past and Present: a journal of historical studies*, no. 80 (August 1978), pp. 91–121. The present essay has been slightly modified so as to incorporate new evidence that has been uncovered in subsequent research. This essay would not have been possible in either form, however, had it not been for the generous assistance of Tim Couzens. I would also like to thank another colleague, Vusi Nkumane, for elaborating on the Zulu terms used in this essay.

of even a single generation, Africans could successively be pastoralists, peasants, proletarians or prisoners. No blacks could have found this downward socio-economic spiral comfortable, and in those cases where the time-span was telescoped the experience must have been singularly traumatic. If ever there was scope for the study of 'marginality' then surely it is here.

This study, then, will be generally concerned with those marginalised black groups who at the turn of the century made their way to the heart of industrialised South Africa – the Witwatersrand. More specifically, it will focus on an association of men who, at different times between 1890 and 1920, called themselves 'The Regiment of the Hills' (*Umkosi Wezintaba*), 'The Regiment of Gaolbirds' (*Umkosi we Seneneem*), 'The People of the Stone' (*Abas'etsheni*), '*Nongoloza*', or 'Ninevites'. Through this study it is hoped to gain greater insight into the emergence of the black lumpenproletariat, understand one of its more identifiable formations, assess its potentialities and limitations, and to speculate on a form of African resistance hitherto neglected in South African historiography.

The Regiment of the Hills, 1890–1899

In 1867, a Zulu woman named Nompopo presented her husband with a new son. The boy, one of six children born to the couple, evidently caused something of a stir on his arrival, since his parents christened him Mzoozepi – meaning 'where did you find him?'. Shortly after this event, the father, Numisimani Mathebula, must have considered that his grazing lands in Zululand had become inadequate since he moved his wife and children onto land owned by a Mr Tom Porter, 'near to where the River Tugela takes its course from the Drakensberg'. Numisimani, however, continued to spend most of his time at a kraal near Mzimkulu where he was an *induna* or headman whilst his dispersed family worked on the Porter farm in return for the use of land.

In 1883 the sixteen year old Mzoozepi Mathebula undertook his first six-month spell as a migrant labourer when he entered employment as a 'garden boy' with Mr Tom J. of Harrismith. During the following three years he again undertook a spell of labour in Harrismith; this time acquiring new skills as a groom in the employ of a certain 'Mr M.'. It was thus in about 1886, when he was nineteen years old, that Mzoozepi once more entered service with Mr Tom J. as a groom. It was also at this juncture that events occurred which helped to shape the future course of Mzoozepi's life, and the story is best told in his own words:

> Before I had finished the first month of this employment one of the horses got lost. On informing my master of this he accused me of being negligent and blamed me for it and told me to go and look for it. I told him that as I was working in the garden on that day he could not hold me responsible for the loss, as all the horses were out grazing alone. He then threatened to place me in gaol if I did not go out and look for the horse that was missing, so I searched but did not find it. He then told me to go

back to my kraal and work for Mr Tom P. again, and added that Tom Porter would then bring to him the value of the horse that was lost. This amount would represent my wages for about two years . . . On return I asked my brother whether it was the law, and whether he thought it fair that I should work and have my wages kept back to pay for the horse which I did not lose. He told me that I must work or they would put me in gaol and added that he did not want to see me there. I told him that I could not work for what I did not lose . . .[5]

Unimpressed with his brother's suggestion and aggrieved by what he felt to be an obvious injustice,[6] the young Mathebula decided to escape from his 'employer'. When Tom Porter sent him and another black servant to the new Witwatersrand goldfields later in the same year, he took the opportunity to desert and to give himself a new name – Jan Note.

The transformation of Mzoozepi Mathebula to Jan Note was neither instant nor painless. For twelve months the young man was employed as a 'houseboy' in the Johannesburg suburb of Jeppe, and throughout this period he continued to fulfil his familial obligations by sending cash remittances to his mother via the many migrant friends who were making the journey back to Natal. The problem of Tom J.'s missing horse, however, pursued him relentlessly and more especially so when his elder brother came to work in the same town in about 1887. In yet another attempt to rid himself of his persecutors, Mzoozepi handed his brother £3 which was to be paid to Tom J. in final settlement of the latter's loss. The brother willingly accepted this money, but he also insisted that Mzoozepi accompany him home so that he could be present when the cash was handed over to the white man. This the younger brother refused to do. Increasingly cynical about the European's sense of justice, Mzoozepi decided instead to once more make use of the cover provided by the sprawling mining town and search for new employment in a different suburb.[7]

The independent-minded young Note, of course, was not the only one to perceive Johannesburg as a centre of comparative freedom and opportunity in the late 1880s. Black and white migrants drawn from throughout southern Africa and Europe had come to the Witwatersrand in their thousands in the belief that, if they could not make their fortunes, then they would at least gain steady employment in the mushrooming town. For many the latter – and more modest – objective was easily achieved. For others, however, the problem was that the early mining economy not only boomed – periodically it slumped. As one of the Johannesburg newspapers editorialised in 1895: 'In South Africa it is invariably a case of feast or famine, of boom or bankruptcy. The happy medium is seldom hit.'[8] The effect of this constant influx of immigrant labour, when compounded by marked economic slumps, was to constantly 'marginalise' the most vulnerable lower echelons of the working class.[9] Yesterday's immigrant and today's worker were tomorrow's unemployed. It was at least partly for these reasons that redundant miners, unemployed clerks, failed businessmen, ex-colonial troopers, and a large number of deserters from the British armed services[10] transformed themselves into pimps, card-sharps, canteen pianists, bottle collectors, billiard markers, fences, skittle-alley attendants, petty thieves, burglars, safe robbers, illicit liquor sellers or highway robbers.[11] When Jan Note moved from Jeppe to Turffontein and 'got a job as a kitchen boy and groom to four single men who were living in a house at the foot of a hill near a small railway station'[12] he unconsciously stumbled across one of the many entrances to the 'white' underworld.[13]

Two of his new employers at Turffontein, Tyson and McDonald, gave the black servant some rather curious instructions and in return offered to remunerate him comparatively generously. He was not to allow any of his black friends near the house, he was to attend to the horses most carefully and just in case the groom failed to understand the message they showed him a revolver and threatened to shoot him should he disobey. Jan Note did not disobey, but he did observe that his new employers kept rather strange hours:

> After breakfast the four men would go out at about 8 or 9 a.m. on their horses and would return at midday for dinner and remain at home until it was dusk. They would then go out again and not return until about midnight. They always seemed to bring back some money with them and I used to see them counting it at night.[14]

It presumably took the young man very little time to realise that he was in fact being employed by a gang of European criminals but, at a wage of £6 per month, he would have been equally quick to appreciate the virtue of silence.[15]

It was probably during 1888, after a few months of 'loyal' service, that Tyson first invited Note on an expedition. In the succeeding months, still cast in the role of black servant, Note joined the gang on several expeditions, serving a criminal apprenticeship by observation. He saw how Tyson and his men held up passenger coaches and robbed white travellers, ambushed the company carts that conveyed the workers' wages to the more isolated gold mines,[16] and how the *abathelisi* or 'tax collector' trick could extract small but constant sums of cash from black workers. Here the gang would approach a party of African travellers pretending to be policemen, demand to see a document such as a pass or vaccination certificate, handcuff the victims while 'inspecting' them, and then remove their money before releasing them. In this case the gang simply did what countless official state robbers – border guards, police, customs officials and railway conductors – did to migrants throughout southern Africa.[17]

Whilst learning these basics of the criminal craft Note was presumably willing to tolerate his role as 'servant'. Crime and the colour bar, however, were not readily compatible. Given the size of the gang's takings and his modest wage, as well as his pride and well-developed sense of justice, it did not take Note long to become discontented with his lot as white man's 'boy'. In the belief that there were probably greater earnings to be made if he worked with criminals of his own colour, Note decided to break with Tyson's gang and to seek out the members of the Witwatersrand's black underworld.

Working his way along the particular ethnic cleavages of black society with which he was most familiar, Note soon discovered that most of the Reef's Zulu-speaking petty thieves and minor criminals – the *izigebengu* – did not live within the more densely populated urban areas. Hounded and harassed in the towns by the police and pass laws, most of the izigebengu had taken refuge in the nearby Klipriversberg hills immediately to the south of Johannesburg.[18]

There, living in the kloofs and caves of a place they called *Shabalawawa* some two hundred men, women and children had placed themselves under the leadership of a man named Nohlopa who hailed from Kwabe in Zululand.[19] At the heart of this loosely knit community, however, there was also a more hardened core of brigands and it did not take long for a man with Note's talent and spirit to bring himself to the notice of these izigelekeqe. Within a short period of time Note attained the position of induna within the community, acting as Nohlopa's closest adviser and assistant.

It was probably at some time during 1889 that the community at Shabalawawa first started to experience a series of organisational and ideological tremors in their mountain stronghold. First, the inhabitants were startled to learn that their leader, Nohlopa, had been arrested and convicted for breaking into a tailor's shop in Kerk street, Johannesburg. A second surprise also lay in store for them. While serving his sentence Nohlopa learned to read and write, and spent a considerable amount of his time studying the Bible. On his release he returned to the Klipriversberg and, after discussions with Note, announced to the assembled ranks that he no longer wished to be associated with the underworld and that in future he would spend his time preaching to his black brothers on the Rand. This decision left the izigelekeqe under the undisputed leadership of Jan Note for the first time.

Shortly after these events the new leader started to do a little reading of his own. Using that same splendidly ambiguous text that had so influenced Nohlopa – the Bible – he derived inspiration which drove him in a radically different direction.[20] It was the Old Testament book of *Nahum* which particularly impressed Note, and in it he read 'about the great state Nineveh which rebelled against the Lord and I selected that name for my gang as rebels against the Government's law'.[21] To this generalised ideological vision Note added vital para-military conceptions, sending the really powerful shock waves through Shabalawawa which transformed it from a loosely organised underworld community into the more tightly knit Umkosi Wezintaba – the Regiment of the Hills. As Note himself put it later:

> The system I introduced was as follows: I myself was the Inkoos Nkulu or king. Then I had an Induna Inkulu styled lord and corresponding to the Governor-General. Then I had another lord who was looked upon as father of us all and styled Nonsala. Then I had my government who were known by numbers, number one to four. I also had my fighting general on the model of the Boer vecht generaal. The administration of justice was confided to a judge for serious cases and a landdrost for petty cases. The medical side was entrusted to a chief doctor or Inyanga. Further I had colonels, captains, sergeant-majors and sergeants in charge of the rank and file the Amasoja or Shosi – soldiers.[22]

'This reorganisation', the 'king' pertinently pointed out, 'took place in the hills of Johannesburg several years before the 1899 war was dreamed of.'

Just how extensive, active, or successful Note's reorganised izigelekeqe were, however, is extremely difficult to assess. What is generally known is that the decade leading up to the Anglo-Boer War was a particularly successful one for highway robbers in the South African Republic.[23] This is more especially true of the early 1890s, prior to the arrival of the railways on the Witwatersrand, when there were large African labour flows which brigands could capitalise on. In 1890, for example, it was estimated that about 3,000 black workers made their way on foot to the goldfields each month,[24] and in 1892 the mining magnate Hermann Eckstein estimated that there were about 1,000 Africans on the move between Johannesburg and Kimberley at any one time.[25] Migrant labour on this scale, much of it funnelling through the Klipriversberg, must have made the environs of Shabalawawa a particularly happy hunting ground for highway robbers.[26] It is unlikely that the Regiment of the Hills failed to claim its share of the workers' wages that passed through the countryside.

Within Johannesburg itself there are also some tell-tale signs which point roughly in the direction of Shabalawawa. Early in 1890, for example, the *Standard and Diggers' News* complained about the activities of a well-organised gang of 'Zulu' burglars in the town.[27] Court cases arising from the abathelisi trick – especially those involving 'policemen' with their own 'ranks' – are even more suggestive.[28] More concrete still is Jan Note's own testimony that the gang penetrated the prisons of the South African Republic where it gained recruits and taught prisoners – including black miners and 'houseboys' – the organisation structure of Umkosi Wezintaba.

Although much of this early activity of the organisation was essentially of an anti-social nature, it was not exclusively so – a fact which testified to Note's influence and the more broadly based notions of justice which concerned the Regiment of the Hills during its formative years. In June 1896, for example, a country correspondent of the *Natal Witness* recounted how certain Zulu speakers who had worked in Johannesburg had reported to him how Africans there had formed themselves into a 'secret society' in order to protect themselves against injustices. His informants told him:

> When a man has a wrong to redress as, for instance, when his master has 'done him' out of his wages, he makes his grievance known to the Izigebengu, some of the members of which are thereupon told off to knock the offending master on the head. These watch their opportunity, and in due course carry out their orders. Reports say that the favourite method is to knock at the door of the former master at night, and if he opens it himself, he is there and then 'settled'. Should someone else open the door, an excuse is made . . . and another occasion is awaited . . . '*Ba gwenza*', a man of some standing said, '*ngoba ngu muzi onge na 'meteto*' – They do it because it is a town without law.[29]

Unfortunately, this illustration which resonates so strongly with the experience of the young Mzoozepi Mathebula, is the only example we have of this aspect of Note's organisation in the period before the South African War.

Much of the evidence relating to this early period, however, is scattered, fragmentary and circumstantial; and on balance it is probably best to see the years 1890–9 as simply constituting a broadly formative period for the Ninevite organisation. Up to the outbreak of the war, the Regiment developed in one of those 'types of human society which lie between the evolutionary phase of tribal and kinship organisation, and modern capitalist and industrial society',[30] and probably consisted largely of migrants and landless labourers.[31] Like the Mafia its origins lay in the countryside,[32] and the early community of men, women and children at Shabalawawa operated in a rural milieu on the margins of the Witwatersrand where a state, with as yet limited coercive capacity, could not readily control its members. But under the new leadership of Note, the Umkosi Wezintaba had already begun its transformation into an essentially urban and exclusively male organisation based within the prisons and urban areas.[33]

Both the pace and trajectory of that transformation, however, were greatly enhanced by subsequent events and processes, and of these, three were of particular importance. First, the war itself and the social upheaval which it occasioned left its imprint on the Ninevite membership. Secondly, the development of the post-war organisation was largely fashioned within the context of an economic system that was industrialising more rapidly than ever before. Thirdly, and most importantly, this accelerated economic development was accompanied – and in part made possible – by a marked increase in the coercive capacity of the state and the mining industry. It was because of this heightened coercive capacity that the Ninevites in the post-war period, to an ever increasing extent, found themselves thrust into those exclusively male institutions which served the industrialising system to well – the prisons and the mine compounds. The influence of all of these factors could be detected as, after 1902, the Regiment of the Hills gave way to 'The People of the Stone' and 'Nongoloza'.

People of the Stone and Nongoloza, 1902–1906

One of the initial effects of the war of 1899–1902 was to disperse a large part of the labouring population of the Witwatersrand throughout southern Africa. In the earliest months of the conflict thousands of migrant workers poured into the towns seeking travelling passes and some means of organised transport to their rural homes. It seems reasonable to assume, therefore, that the general air of tension and anxiety also permeated into the ranks of the izigelekeqe in the Klipriversberg. Most of Note's men led a parasitic existence which relied on the regular robbery of small bands of migrant workers making their way through the countryside. The long-term viability of this mode of operation, however, was threatened by rapid large-scale movements and by a war which would probably terminate the flow of migrant labour altogether. For these, and other reasons, the inhabitants of Shabalawawa joined the black throng making its way into Johannesburg.

This sudden influx of impoverished black workers, infused with a strand of professional criminals at a time when the resources of the state were even more strained than usual, helped in the proliferation of crime in the town. The Kruger government thus had at least a partial interest in ensuring that most of the 'surplus' black population was evacuated to its rural hinterland as soon as possible. On a single day in October 1899 over 3,000 workers boarded the train for Mozambique whilst hundreds of others walked to the borders of the Republic. The workers from Natal and Zululand, however, found themselves in a slightly different situation, and as one author has noted:

> The office of J. S. Marwick, the Natal Native Agent in Johannesburg, was surrounded by thousands of African workers, aware that no arrangements had been made for their return home, and anxious lest their earnings be confiscated before they left the Republic.[34]

The predominantly Zulu-speaking crowd that congregated outside Marwick's office constituted the most natural meeting place for Note's troops and it seems that when the Agent got permission to march these migrants to the Transvaal–Natal border several of the izigelekege inserted themselves in the refugee column. Immediately after the war, the Natal African newspaper, *Ipepa lo Hlanga*, claimed that Marwick's party contained 'many persons of disrepute', including a 'self-organised gang of native desperadoes'.[35] It appears, therefore, that some of the most important of the criminal elements on the Witwatersrand complex were spread to other parts of southern Africa during the early months of the war.[36]

But if the beginning of the war saw the dispersal of Africans, there was ample opportunity for them to regroup as the conflict unfolded. Much of this regrouping was involuntary as the war threw together existing criminal elements and more law-abiding peasants experiencing the trauma of large-scale social upheaval. Several thousand rural people thus found themselves herded into the concentration camps set up by the invading British authorities. Many of those in need of a livelihood, including petty criminals, were employed in a variety of occupations by the British army – significantly, of those who subsequently joined the ranks of the Ninevites many gained their first experiences of both crime and urban conditions while serving with the British troops.[37] Those who found their way to prison stood the risk of being conscripted for service with military units in Natal, while on the Witwatersrand itself the most important meeting place was at the Ferreira Deep Mine compound, where the army established a reception centre for 'vagrants' who were compelled to earn the five shillings necessary for a pass by stone-breaking.

By their very nature the concentration camps, prisons and compounds exercised a high degree of control over their black inmates. This was not solely a wartime exigency, for in several important respects these institutions served as models for those labour-repressive instruments that continued to function under the post-war administration. As has been noted in one study of the war and its subsequent effects on blacks:

> The Milner regime extended the pass department, created a system of courts to deal with breaches of masters and servants legislation, introduced a scheme to register the fingerprints of all mining employees to help identify workers who deserted, and established regulations to prohibit mining companies recruiting workers in labour districts. The possibility of African workers exchanging employers to find the most congenial working conditions was therefore considerably reduced.[38]

In 1903 the mining companies contributed to this coercion when they tightened up the functioning of their compounds, and in 1905 the new British administration opened the Cinderella Prison on the East Rand which – amongst other things – supplied local mines with convict labour.[39]

The web of coercive legislation and its supporting institutions of compounds, courts and prisons, besides reducing the mobility of black workers, also had some unintended consequences. Constant infractions of the pass laws in an industrial system with an increased law enforcement capacity produced a labouring population characterised by its high degree of nominal 'criminal' experience, ensuring that the working class had great familiarity with the two similar institutions of prison and compound. Labourers and lumpenproletarians were forced to rub shoulders to a greater extent than they might otherwise have done. The pass laws and the newly efficient police system drew *all* Africans, law-abiding and law-evading alike, into the Witwatersrand complex and kept them there. It was perhaps predictable, therefore, that when Note's organisation re-emerged after the war it was more urban-based than before and that its natural home would be the prison–compound complex.

It is possible that the post-war Ninevite organisation first re-emerged amongst the 'stone-breakers' at the Ferreira Deep Mine compound. What is known with greater certainty, however, is the fact that the organisation existed in unmistakable form in other prisons immediately after the war. In 1904, J. S. Marwick – by then Assistant Secretary for Native Affairs in the Transvaal – had noted its presence in the prisons where its members referred to themselves as the 'People of the Stone'.[40] But from at least the same date, and more especially during the depression years of 1906–8, 'loafers', 'vagrants', the unemployed, petty criminals and those without passes also joined the society under yet another name for Jan Note – 'Nongoloza', the man with the piercing eyes. Whereas the People of the Stone met in prison, it would appear that those who joined Nongoloza did so in abandoned prospect holes, disused mine shafts, derelict buildings or old quarries.[41] By 1906 the Ninevite organisation was thus already operating on two fronts – one based inside, and the other outside of the Witwatersrand prisons.

Despite the different conditions under which they operated, the People of the Stone and the Nongoloza shared important features which betrayed their common origin. Both associations were clearly based on the model devised by Note, and the *Abas'ethsheni* and the members of Nongoloza alike pledged their allegiance to him as 'king'. Moreover, both arms of the Ninevite organisation manifested a high incidence of homosexuality, particularly so after the post-war Chinese indentured labourers began to leave the compounds and be replaced in larger numbers by black migrant workers.[42] The mines as well as the prisons successfully excluded women from urban life, and by 1906, when, under pressure from the missionaries the Chamber of Mines conducted an enquiry into 'unnatural native vice', it was:

> ... common legend throughout the mines that a Shangaan named 'Sokisi' [possibly George Schoko, a noted Ninevite leader] had, while in prison [Cinderella?], practised unnatural vice, and that he had introduced the custom of keeping *'izinkotshane'* [boy wives] at the Brakpan Mines, from whence it spread until at the present day there is no doubt it is commonly practised throughout all the mines on the Witwatersrand.[43]

But for all the similarities between these two arms of the movement, the Ninevites did not achieve the same degree of organisation, unity and discipline before 1904 as they were to in the succeeding years. While this early stage of relative fluidity in the structure of the organisation can to some extent be explained by the dislocations caused by the war, it can perhaps also be partly accounted for by the absence of the man who the authorities claimed was 'held in superstitious veneration by the rank and file',[44] and who was greeted in a hushed voice with the salute usually reserved for Zulu royalty – 'Bayete'.[45] That 'short thick-set Zulu', about 30 years of age and apparently 'with no appearance to command respect'[46] was, of course, Jan Note.

The Ninevites in the ascendant, 1906–1912

Regrettably, very little is known with any certainty about Jan Note's movements during the war or in the years immediately thereafter. It is just possible that the leader of the underworld for some time became a member of a gang of bandits – the 'Brigands of De Jager's Drift' – who terrorised a large part of northern Natal with a series of spectacular armed robberies during mid-1903.[47] Certainly the half-dozen bandits included amongst their number one 'Nkulu Zulu', who, along with other members of the gang, was sentenced to a long term of imprisonment at Dundee in the same year.[48] If 'Nkulu' was Note, however, he must have escaped from his Natal prison shortly thereafter since there is no doubt whatsoever that the chief Ninevite was back on the Witwatersrand twelve months later. In November 1904, a short-term prisoner appearing before the Johannesburg Prison Enquiry Commission gave a vivid account of how Note personally exercised control and discipline over fellow black inmates.[49]

On his release from prison in Johannesburg, Note and eight of his recruits formed a new gang which for several months during 1906 operated with considerable success as store and house-breakers in the Standerton district. But by early 1907 the police were getting sufficiently close to these izigelekeqe for the members of the gang to decide to disperse into northern Natal and Zululand. A few months after this Note was arrested, and sentenced to another term of imprisonment in the Volksrust prison on the Natal–Transvaal border.

This small prison, however, held few terrors for Nongoloza and in mid-1908 he and two of his fellow inmates – William Masaku and 'Ben Cronje' – broke out of the Volksrust prison and into the local magistrate's court where they stole two revolvers and 75 rounds of ammunition before making their escape from the town. Further north-east, at the village of Wakkerstroom, the three men entered a home and fired at its elderly white occupant who resisted their demands for cash. The noise of the shooting soon attracted the attention of neighbours and when the local police sergeant and a European volunteer attempted to corner and arrest the invaders, the Ninevites again opened fire before staging a successful retreat. From there the three made their way north along the Swaziland border before turning towards the eastern Transvaal mining town of Barberton.

The unheralded arrival of the Ninevites in Barberton coincided with the more boldly proclaimed preparations for a civil reception to be held in a local hotel. At nightfall Note and his two black accomplices let themselves into the hotel dining-room where, after their long journey, they proceeded to make merry on the food and drink set aside for the white dignitaries of the following day. On leaving the premises, however, they were spotted by an African policeman who in a heady moment chose to pursue the Volksrust fugitives – a foolish decision since Nongoloza promptly rewarded him with a bullet through the leg. But, as in Wakkerstroom, the noise of the shooting attracted further attention and this time a slighly inebriated Note and Ben Cronje were captured – William Masaku successfully eluding the police for a further six months. Soon thereafter Note appeared in court charged with escape from lawful custody and several counts of attempted murder, and was sentenced to life imprisonment. From Barberton the authorities transported Note to Pretoria where they not only consciously placed him in the local prison, but also unconsciously dumped him within convenient distance of the very heartland of Ninevite country – the Witwatersrand's urban prison–compound complex.[50]

Within Pretoria Central Prison and more particularly within that section set aside for long-term black offenders – the so-called 'Reserve Camp' – Note at once set about the task of forging for himself a new and highly disciplined Ninevite corps. With the loyal and ruthless support of fellow black notables such as Meshine ('Government'), Jinoyi ('Fighting General'), Charlie ('Doctor') and Jim Dunde ('Judge'), Nongoloza and his followers ensured that the period 1908–10 was one of the most troubled and turbulent in the history of the prison.[51] Once he had re-asserted his right to the title of *Nkosi Nkulu* or Great King within the prison, however, Note proceeded to extend his criminal empire to embrace the larger part of the Transvaal – from Pretoria in the north to Klipriver in the south, from Heidelberg in the east to Potchefstroom in the west. This he achieved over the next 48 months by uniting under his leadership various criminal gangs entrenched in regional strongholds, and more especially those of the adjacent Witwatersrand.

To the immediate west of Johannesburg, Note succeeded in gaining the allegiance of 'Chief' George Schoko (alias 'Kleintje') and his gang which, centred on the abandoned prospect holes in the vicinity of Canada Junction, specialised in abathelisi robberies of workers making their way to and from the West Rand. Not far from this Nongoloza was supported by another important 'Chief' – Sam Nyambezi (alias 'Joseph') who, along with his followers, used the Crown Deep Mine compound as a base from which to raid and plunder the black townships to the south-west of the city. East of Johannesburg Note's most trusted follower was one Jan Mtembu who by 1912 was located at the Premier Mine near Pretoria, while within the Cinderella Prison at Boksburg – a nerve centre for the entire organisation – the Ninevites were under the control of Jim Mandende, a Xhosa who had been personally appointed by the Nkosi Nkulu when he had won his spurs back in the days of the South African Republic. In the far south-east Nongoloza was represented by yet another 'Chief', Jacob Xaba, whose gang inhabited the open countryside between the mine compounds of Brakpan and Nigel and lived by robbery and stock theft. The amazing Note not only succeeded in uniting these five important brigand chiefs under his command, but by 1912 he could also rely on the support of at least ten other 'fighting generals' based in the mine compounds all along the line of reef.[52] At the height of his criminal career Nongoloza could count on the support of between 750 and 1,000 strongly committed Ninevites, the large majority of them being Zulus, but also including amongst their number Shangaans, Basutos, Xhosas and Swazis.[53]

That Note possessed extraordinary charisma seems beyond doubt. But even criminal empires are not built on personality alone and they also have more mundane requirements such as the need for communication. Nongoloza made sure that his wishes reached the Ninevite troops through an elaborate system of signals which could reach most corners of the Witwatersrand, and which was ultimately based on the constant ebb and flow of pass offenders. New prison arrivals would pass on information of the organisation's outside activities, while discharged prisoners – usually making their way to one of the half-dozen rickshaw yards in Johannesburg – would convey Note's wishes from prison. These 'rickshaw boys', whose occupation suited them ideally to the task, would then pass the messages on to the communications officers of the various gangs. Thus, Nkuku (alias 'Forage'), 'office boy' in the Number Two gang at Randfontein, apparently used to collect messages from the Nkosi Nkulu via a certain Mpilempile in a Jeppestown rickshaw yard.[54] Not all messages, however, passed via these intermediaries described by the police as 'recognised agents who disseminate orders and instructions to the members of the gangs outside'.[55] 'Top secret' or 'operations' information occasionally passed directly between gang leaders. Promotions within the organisation, for example, were sometimes discussed in letters between 'generals' from different regions,[56] and mere 'office boys' or 'messengers' were not allowed access to such privileged information. Nongoloza's criminal army appears to have made use of a sophisticated two-tier communication system.

But while it was one thing for the Nkosi Nkulu and his 'generals' to issue orders, it was quite another to ensure that they were obeyed and the Ninevite army, as much as any other, had need of a disciplinary code to control its tough and sometimes individualistic troops. In this case, as in that of the communications system, it was the ceaseless flow of urban blacks into the prisons that enabled the army of the underworld to function. Although the organisation operated both inside and outside of the prisons, disciplining of the ranks for the most part took place within the confined space of the communal cells that characterised the Transvaal penal system – here there was no place to hide from Ninevite justice. Nongoloza and his officers could rest assured in the knowledge that, sooner or later an infringement of the pass laws would inevitably deliver any defiant troops to their prison 'court'.

Lesser offences under the Ninevite disciplinary code centred on matters of status, privilege and prison etiquette. Any member who developed a fully fledged homosexual relationship with an *umfana* (boy), before having officially attained the rank of *ikhela* (Zulu male in traditional society with the chief's permission to marry), for example, stood to be tried before a 'magistrate',[57] and to be punished by the withdrawal of prison privileges such as tobacco, food or sex. Those with rank who contravened the code stood to be demoted, and also to sacrifice certain benefits while in prison.[58] More serious offences were immediately referred to superior courts where there were 'judges', 'prosecutors', 'doctors', and 'jurymen'. Charges brought in these higher courts invariably centred on breaches of Ninevite security, and the sentences were harsh and bloody. Those found guilty of passing on trivial information to the police or prison authorities could consider themselves lucky, since they would simply have their front teeth knocked out. But more serious transgressors stood the risk of being stabbed through the shoulder blades with sharpened nails, or of being sentenced to the equally unpleasant alternative of 'ballooning'. This consisted of tossing the victim with the aid of a blanket to greater and greater heights and then, at a pre-arranged signal, removing the blanket and allowing him to plummet to the concrete floor of the cell.[59]

Another form of severe punishment was the dreaded *shaya isigubhu* – the systematic beating of the ribs with clenched fists. 'Tomboek' Umfanawenduku, who was in the Pretoria prison at the time of Nongoloza, offered a first-hand account of this particular Ninevite ritual:

The penalty inflicted as a rule is anything from three to ten blows. But before this penalty is inflicted they call their Doctor who is also a member of the gang, and he feels your pulse and orders the punishment reduced if he thinks the person is not very strong. He will reduce it from ten to five. I have on two occasions been assaulted in this manner, the first time it was at Pretoria. I had already joined their society when I was ordered to be tried as I was a native constable in the Transvaal Police prior to my arrest. I was taken before the Magistrate, a prisoner named 'Toby', and he punished me for being a native constable and sentenced me to be punished by means of the 'sigubu'. I was to receive twenty blows on each side of the ribs with clenched fists. A Doctor named Charlie, also a hard labour prisoner, was called to examine and he ordered the punishment reduced to ten blows only. I was then taken into the middle of the room and told to stand straight up with my hands folded, and four members who rank as private soldiers detailed by the Captain. The four soldiers get around you, one at the rear and front of you, and the Captain then orders them to attention. They then clench their fists and when he orders 'present arms' they extend their arms in a fighting attitude and continue this until he gives the order of 'sigubu' when each of the soldiers starts punching you from side to side until the Captain gives the order 'halt'. This is a very severe punishment and often when you cough a person brings up blood through the effects. . .[60]

But even the coughing of blood that came with shaya isigubhu was considered insufficient punishment for the worst offenders of all – for them only death was enough.

Unfortunately, we have few cases at present available which show precisely what the exact nature of the 'crimes' were that warranted the death sentence under the Ninevite code. One hapless victim, Matshayli Zungu, a Zulu miner from the Cason compound, had the misfortune to accidentally cross the path of a Boksburg branch of the Ninevites – a particularly tough gang composed of fourteen members who included amongst their number several veterans from Pretoria Central and 'Blue Sky Gaol', Cinderella Prison. On being 'invited' to join the gang and choose himself an ikhehla Zungu made the fatal mistake of refusing. The 'Government' and the 'General' conferred briefly for a moment and then the 'General', Elijah Mazinyo, pronounced, 'I sentence you to the rope'. Zungu was promptly strangled with a handkerchief,[61] after which the gang half-concealed the body in a hole in the wall of a nearby slimes dam. The affair ended with the arrest and execution of the fourteen Ninevites.[62]

But the apparently random choice of a victim and the crudity of the execution mark the Zungu murder as exceptional. More frequently, as one of the Witwatersrand detectives most familiar with the organisation noted, 'The orders for murder are ... against natives who have formerly belonged to the gang and afterwards turned police informers.'[63] The police believed that some of these had been killed through having large doses of powdered glass administered to them, a refined procedure when compared with 'the rope',[64] while the same detective described what was perhaps the most cunning Ninevite method of all:

> In prison, the death sentence is carried out in the following manner. The prisoner is strangled with a wet towel. The Executioners then chew mealies (maize) and stuff it down his throat. I am told that natives so found have been certified cause of death [sic] due to choking whilst eating mealies.[65]

Thus in 1912 Nongoloza controlled an army which knew what his directives were, and one which possessed a ruthlessly implemented if not universally understood disciplinary code. Those who are in control of armies, however, have not only to possess power, they also have to be seen to possess and exercise it. How were men who considered themselves to be 'judges', 'generals', 'doctors' and 'captains' to be distinguished from the ordinary mass of prisoners and proletarians herded into the conformity of 'total institutions'? Where did a compound or prison number end, and a Ninevite begin?

In several respects this problem must have been at its most acute within the depersonalised culture of the prisons; nevertheless a new inmate of the communal cells soon learnt who were the Ninevites and who, for example, the 'Scotlanders' were – a rival gang noted for their rejection of homosexuality.[66] The followers of Nongoloza were distinguished from the latter groups by the sacrifices of food and tobacco which the 'troops' made for their 'officers' and by their show trials and rituals. By 1912, however, an even more visible sign was invariably associated with the leaders of Note's army – the large 'I.S.' sign on the prison jacket which distinguished those prisoners serving an indeterminate sentence.[67] This insignia of the underworld elicited its own twisted form of respect in a twisted institution.

It was in the comparatively relaxed compounds and their immediate peri-urban surroundings, however, that the Ninevites could most fully and freely develop many of the more obvious features associated with an army. In the sub-culture of Nongoloza the 'troops' used their own distinctive slang: a 'bird' was an ignorant person, a 'buck' was a victim, the gang was the 'stone' and a person who 'came with the horses' was not to be trusted since he was either a spy or a policeman.[68] Like many soldiers Note's men had a reputation for their indulgences – in this case drinking the powerful working-class concoction called *ukhali* or smoking *dagga*, marijuana. In this connection it was perhaps also significant that the troopers referred to each other as *mgusas*, the flashily dressed members of a drinking society.[69] Outside of the immediate confines of the compound the soldiers of the underworld invariably carried sticks or coshes, and drilled in time to the instructions of an 'officer' who brandished a knife.[70] Up to about 1910 the most distinctive part of the Ninevite uniform was apparently the hat, which was later discarded and by 1912 mgusas could most easily be recognised by the way in which they kept their trousers closely pinned to their ankles by the means of bicycle clips or string.[71]

Unlike some of its modern counterparts Jan Note's 'army' was not all dressed up with nowhere to go and very little to do. Its central concern was crime, and its members knew exactly how to set about that business. The main thrust of that activity, however, seems to have shifted slightly between 1908 and 1912 as a subtle change in the rank-and-file composition of the Ninevite army took place.

Between 1906 and 1910 – but more especially between 1906 and 1908 during which period much of rural Natal was beset by the Bambatha rebellion and the Rand plagued by a serious economic depression – the police described the majority of Ninevite 'soldiers' or *amakhehla* as being recruited from the 'vagrant class'.[72] Many of these 'vagrants', pushed out of the rural economy and unable to be absorbed into the urban labour force, sought refuge in the more inaccessible *kopjes* of the central Witwatersrand area or even further afield in the eastern or western Transvaal, in mountain caves.[73] Working from these strongholds the Ninevites set to work concentrating on the abathelisi trick and various forms of armed robbery. Although the monotony of this pattern was sometimes broken with expeditions of house burglary most of this crime was directed against people – usually fellow Africans. The more urban of these bandits, however, were particularly vulnerable to arrest under the pass laws and as one detective noted:

These vagrants have often told me that they have no fear of gaol, as it is much better than being outside where they are continually harassed by the police and asked for their passes.[74]

While this was perhaps something of an overstatement it was nevertheless true that this particular rural intake of Nongoloza's army soon learnt the need for a more sophisticated defence against the Transvaal pass system.

By 1910–1 many of these Ninevites had discovered that they could keep the police at bay by taking refuge in those large industrial forts which the state itself had assisted in developing – the mine compounds. Designed to keep people in, the compounds also effectively kept the police out.[75] In 1912 a frustrated Deputy Commissioner of Police noted that the continual police harassment of urban 'vagrants' for passes had 'driven [the Ninevites] into the mine compounds where they enlist as labourers and where they can enjoy all protection that is extended to registered mine boys...'.[76] Within this quasi-prison environment Nongoloza's recruiting officers – the so-called *MaSilvers* who took their name from one of Johannesburg's most notorious pimps of the 1890s, Joseph Silver – had a field day. As the economy improved through 1910–1 they steadily recruited new migrant workers into their 'army' and when the drought of 1912 pushed yet more peasants in the direction of the mines the Ninevites consolidated their new industrial base.

As migrant workers in the compounds rather than 'vagrants' in the surrounding hills started to join Note's organisation in greater numbers, so its criminal focus started to shift. By 1912 much of Nongoloza's army concentrated on store and housebreaking as its principal activity. Partly as a result of the shift in base noted above, the organisation's primary objective had become property rather than people. These Ninevite expeditions to acquire property became highly professional and sophisticated. At Randfontein, no burglary would take place until the 'number two gang', composed of juniors under the supervision of a *landdrost* ('magistrate') and a 'lieutenant', had filed its reconnaissance report. Only then would the older men and the senior officers who constituted 'number one gang' go out, usually to burgle an isolated store or home and invariably carrying with them the tools of their trade – screwdrivers, files, crowbars, jumpers, keys and occasionally guns. Thus tools that were employed underground for the benefit of the mine owners by day became instruments for the use of the worker-criminals by night. In addition such Ninevite squads would seek to avoid recognition and spread their operations by working different 'patches', and by swapping passes with units based in neighbouring territories. Nongoloza's followers in Heidelberg, for example, did much of their best work on 'borrowed' passes in the Boksburg North district.

As a result of these criminal sorties substantial quantities of loot, usually in the form of money or clothing, flowed into the mine compounds. How were these goods distributed? At first sight the fragmentary evidence seems promising for the reader in search of 'social bandits'. It is known that members of Nongoloza's army frequently shared clothing, including stolen property;[77] and also that after one Ninevite gang broke into Schwab's Eating House and Mine Store in 1912, the members returned to the compound and 'all the boys in the room were awakened and asked to have some meat as they had a bag full of it'.[78] However, the sharing of clothing is a common practice amongst the poor and the working classes, and in any case this appears to have been confined to gang members. Moreover, as far as the second report is concerned, meat deteriorates rapidly, and the apparent generosity of the Ninevites might have been born of a calculated need to minimise the risk of betrayal. None of this can therefore simply be construed as evidence of a type of 'Robin Hood' generosity.

It is certainly true that the Ninevite leaders did distribute patronage and occasional gifts to their followers, while the fact that they were called 'chiefs' by some also hints at a traditional redistributive function. However, once again there is no real evidence of any major redistribution of goods and it would appear that the leaders kept back a substantial part of the loot for themselves. Jan Note, in what was undoubtedly an exaggeration claimed to have accumulated 'bags of money' but the same could hardly be said for most of his followers.[79] Such minor redistribution as did occur within the organisation appears to have been an incidental function of certain social relationships within the structure of the movement.

The lot of the poorest Ninevites of all – the *abafana* or boys – for example, was only marginally improved by their Ninevite membership.

These, the hundreds of young lads between the ages of thirteen and sixteen who entered the Witwatersrand compounds during this period, constituted the poorest-paid workers in the industry and immediately attracted the attention of the MaSilvers. As an observer of the compounds noted in 1909:

> When new squads of boys came in the picaninnies are watched with anxious eyes, and proposals are made at the earliest opportunity, and 'matches' are made, and 'trueness' and 'fidelity' are demanded, and failure brings about a disturbance, and likely a row.[80]

These boys became the 'wives' of the amakhehla or soldiers in Nongoloza's army and were expected to play a similar role to that of more orthodox Zulu wives. Thus besides being sexual partners, the boys would clean, sew and cook, but no 'wives' would be allowed to participate in the economically more important criminal activities.[81] In return for their domestic services the abafana would receive gifts and money from their Ninevite husbands, and would usually be given their khehla's portion of the loot for safe-keeping.[82] It was to the limited extent that the poorly paid abafana benefited from such gifts that there was a marginal redistribution of goods amongst the Ninevites. But, in general, we can conclude that there is little evidence of a conscious egalitarianism in the Ninevite philosophy and that if anything the criminal spoils were distributed unequally within a hierarchical organisation.

This structured inequality, however, in no way dampened Ninevite enthusiasm for the movement or undermined the members' loyalty to Nongoloza. By mid-1912, when the Ninevite organisation was probably at its most developed, it was said to be gaining 'further adherents daily'.[83] Over two decades, Jan Note and his followers had developed an army with almost 1,000 members, a sophisticated system of communication, rigid discipline, subtle defences and a set of well-defined criminal objectives. From a motley group of peasant marginals who sought refuge from the police in the Klipriversberg had emerged a well organised lumpen–worker alliance that held criminal control in the very heart of industrialised South Africa. Months before politically conscious blacks met to form the African National Congress, a black army on the Witwatersrand with branches as far afield as Bloemfontein, Kimberley and Pietermaritzburg was delivering a serious challenge to a repressive and privileged white state.

Almost predictably, the severity of that challenge was first felt on the East Rand where Cinderella Prison, a major stronghold of Nongoloza's followers, was located. This prison disgorged a steady stream of offenders who had completed medium to long-term sentences – including many Ninevites – into the surrounding areas. An ironic twist in the operation of the pass law system, however, ensured that many of these men in Jan Note's 'army' found it difficult to get any distance beyond 'Blue Sky' on their release, and this in turn meant that the Boksburg and Benoni districts acted as reluctant hosts to some of the country's most hardened professional criminals. Furthermore, as we have noted above, after 1909 many Ninevites made conscious use of the pass laws in order to gain employment in the nearby mine compounds. As a frustrated Minister of Native Affairs was forced to note in 1913, 'it will be recognised that our powers are limited by the provision of Section 40 of the

Pass Regulations [which] requires that the released criminal be given the opportunity of re-engaging himself'.[84] The net result of all of this was that the East Rand experienced what the local Public Prosecutor termed 'frequent waves of crime' – especially housebreaking, robbery and assault.[85]

On 20 June 1912 the officer commanding the Benoni police informed his superior officer that the build-up of Ninevite strength in the district had reached 'most serious' proportions.[86] Two days later the District Commandant for the East Rand, Inspector M. A. Hartigan, brought the matter to the attention of the Secretary of the Transvaal Police, pointing out that Nongoloza's army had 'now attained a numerical strength and organisation sufficient to warrant its receiving prompt and energetic attention',[87] and from there the matter was referred to both the Commissioner of Police and the Attorney General. By the end of the year Nongoloza's army was under ministerial scrutiny and government was examining 'government'. What had galvanised the state into action was not simply the mounting Ninevite attack on property, serious as that was; it was the fear that its law-enforcement capacity in the compounds and cities was being seriously undermined. It had made the unpleasant discovery that it could no longer rely on two of its most important sets of collaborators – the *onongqayi* or black police, and the industrial or compound 'police' – in running a labour repressive economy.

The day-to-day functioning of the Witwatersrand's mining system was secured by specially selected and uniformed black compound 'policemen'. These management lackeys with state support were responsible for the discipline of the African labour force and for supplying the authorities with a constant stream of politico-economic intelligence.[88] Outside the compound gates the pass laws were enforced by their equally unpleasant fellow collaborators – the onongqayi, of whom, in his contemporary account, *Life Amongst the Coloured Miners of Johannesburg*, the black journalist, F. Z. S. Peregrino had this to say:

> For a picture of the average Zulu policeman at Johannesburg I would depict this: A creature, giant-like and large as to proportions, ferocious and forbidding of aspect, most callously brutal of action and irredeemably ignorant.[89]

There was little love lost between these black collaborators and most African miners – and Nongoloza's men singled them out for particular, sometimes unmerciful attention, thereby, albeit in a largely apolitical fashion, helping to paralyse some of the black working class's most immediate oppressors.

The state was both concerned and dismayed by this paralysis. The police were shocked to learn that at the York Mine, Krugersdorp – a West Rand storm centre where, as early as January 1908 a party of 50 armed Ninevites had launched an open attack on three white constables who had attempted to interrupt their manoeuvres – 'everybody in the compound belonged to the society' by 1912, 'including the police boys'.[90] By August 1912 the Deputy Commissioner of Police was seriously considering the possibility of the onongqayi being infiltrated or otherwise demoralised by Nongoloza's army; and in January 1913 he informed his superiors in Pretoria that, 'I do not consider that the native police is at present capable of dealing effectively with native criminals'.[91] At the apex of its power the Ninevite challenge to the black collaborating arms of the state achieved, at very least, a stalemate situation. An increasingly powerful South African state had no taste for stalemate situations.

The decline of the Ninevites, 1912–1920

On 16 December 1910 two prominent Ninevites – 'Chief' George Schoko, alias 'Kleintje', and Jim Ntlokonkulu, known in the underworld as 'The Giant with the Crooked Eyes' – set out for 'work' on the Main Reef Road in time-honoured fashion, assisted by two trusted lieutenants. At about noon they intercepted three black miners making their way to Maraisburg, and immediately went into the abathelisi routine. Posing as detectives they first asked to see the workers' passes and then demanded their purses. When the workers refused to hand over their money, Schoko and his men assaulted them with sticks and overpowered them. They then relieved two of the workers of £28 in gold, and administered a thrashing to the third who was unwise enough to be penniless. The Ninevites then returned to their 'fort' in the prospect holes near Canada Junction.

The victims, however, made their way to the Langlaagte Police Station and reported the robbery to Detective Duffey and Constable King – the latter a veteran of the 1908 attack at the York Mine. Duffey and two of the miners set out towards Maraisburg in pursuit of the attackers, whilst King and the third worker searched the Canada Junction area. King had the misfortune to find what he was looking for. No sooner had he ordered the Ninevites out of their hiding place than he was attacked and fatally stabbed in the head. The terrified worker fled back to Langlaagte and reported the constable's murder.[92] After a nightlong search police eventually discovered King's body thrust into an ant-bear hole.

This brutal attack on a white official aroused widespread European indignation. The black journalist who wrote later that: 'Public and police alike felt that Ninevism, that cynical challenge to authority [had to] be wiped out', was probably only slightly overstating the case.[93] Members of the public, the Fire Brigade, Prisons Department officials, the Police Band and over 300 policemen attended King's funeral.[94] Determined to find the killers of the constable, Major Mavrogordato (C.I.D.) assigned one of his most able officers, Detective A. J. Hoffman, to the case on a full-time basis.

Despite thorough and protracted searches of the usual Ninevite haunts south-west of Johannesburg, Hoffman enjoyed little immediate success in his hunt for Schoko and Ntlokonkulu. This was hardly surprising. Both Ninevites, 'feeling the heat' near Johannesburg, had migrated elsewhere in search of 'work', Schoko choosing Kimberley, the only large city outside the Witwatersrand which offered him the type of prison/compound complex with which he was most familiar and Ntlokonkulu opting for the country life, eventually making his way to the far south-east of the Reef where he placed himself under 'Chief' Jacob Xaba.

But almost a month after King's murder, Hoffman's arrest of 'vagrants' and scouring of criminal haunts started to pay off, when he received information to the effect that the wanted men were in the vicinity of Vlakfontein. On the night of 18 January 1911 he, Detective Probationer H. G. Boy, and a team of black assistants tracked a group of suspects towards Hartley's farm. The first thing that they found was 'a dying heifer from which the hindquarters had been cut' – a sign of Jacob Xaba's catering arrangements for a bandit get-together.[95] Following the trail they came upon a hut, the Indian inhabitants of which 'were bewailing the loss of their money, poultry and clothes'.[96]

Eventually, at about 2 a.m. they came across Xaba, Ntlokonkulu and the main Ninevite party preparing a sheep for roasting. On the approach of the police the Ninevites fled. Hoffman himself gave chase and, assisted by a *nongqayi* arrested Xaba. Boy tracked the remainder of the fleeing Ninevites and towards daybreak arrested the 'Giant with the Crooked Eyes' – Ntlokonkulu – near a mine pumping station.[97]

The capture of Xaba was an achievement for which both Hoffman and Boy received rewards and commendations. Furthermore, within hours of his arrest 'The Giant with the Crooked Eyes' added to the detectives' success when he told them that Schoko had been involved in a fight in Kimberley, and was lying in hospital there recovering from stab wounds in the stomach.[98] 'Kleintje' was arrested soon afterwards. Within 40 days of the King murder three of the most notable Ninevite leaders had been taken into custody and Nongoloza's army was on the defensive.

In March 1911 Jacob Xaba was sentenced in the Johannesburg Supreme Court to three and a half years' imprisonment with hard labour for stock theft. Shortly afterwards Schoko and Ntlokonkulu were sentenced to death for the murder of Constable King and executed in Pretoria. In August David Ganda and Jim Nomkehla, the most prominent remaining members of Xaba's unit, were arrested and prosecuted for housebreaking, attempted murder and murder in the Heidelberg district. Worse was to follow for Nongoloza's army. In a specific attempt to deal with black professional criminals the government legislated for the above-mentioned 'indeterminate sentence',[99] and when Sam Nyambezi appeared in court in February 1912 on seven counts of robbery and public violence, his case was promptly dealt with in terms of the new provision, whilst fifteen members of his gang were sentenced to lengthy periods of imprisonment.

By early 1912 then, the state had already started to make inroads into the Ninevite organisation, and particularly into its leadership. Even so, its success was piecemeal and largely unintentional since the police were as yet unaware of the depth, breadth or extent of the Ninevite army. They were not fully cognisant of the linkages between the gangs controlled by Schoko, Xaba and Nyambezi or of their overriding loyalty to Nongoloza. They were shocked into fuller knowledge by the unsavoury events of May and June 1912.

On the night of 12 May 'Governor' Jim Swazi, 'General' Bill Langalene and 'Colonel' Bill Frisby set out from the Cason Mine compound for a criminal sortie into the Boksburg district. By the end of the evening, for motives that are not clear, this close knit Benoni-based Ninevite squad had murdered a black policeman named Tsobana using a gun they had acquired from one 'Apricot'.[100] Two evenings later, 'General' Charlie Mxotshwa of the New Kleinfontein compound – who it was said could call on as many as a hundred 'soldiers' as far afield as Nigel – marched a squad of Ninevites into the Brakpan district in search of suitable robbery victims. As they approached the railway station they were asked by a white miner, Owen Duffy, who was making his way to the single quarters of the Brakpan mine, to help carry his mattress. The unfortunate Duffy was clubbed to death, however, and his goods ransacked. The Ninevites found only a key and a knife.[101]

These two brutal East Rand killings, within days of each other, jolted the police into action, and it was while enquiring into them that Detectives W. Futter and H. G. Boy first came to appreciate the magnitude of Nongoloza's army. The publicity of the subsequent trials produced further public concern and, by mid-June, the Ninevites were receiving parliamentary attention.[102] In the wake of these events the state started to attack the 'army' in earnest. At first the government looked solely to the police for the destruction of the Ninevites. Some Ninevite notables such as Xaba, Schoko and Nyambezi had already been accounted for, and the police consolidated on this start by building up a sophisticated picture of the organisation and its *modus operandi*, by infiltrating informers into the compounds of several East Rand mines – a precaution that reaped benefits on at least one occasion.[103] But, as senior police officers were quick to point out, what point was there in rounding up Nongoloza's followers in the morning when Cinderella Prison disgorged another squad of committed followers, confined by the pass laws to the area, in the afternoon? What was the purpose of arresting and punishing members of the organisation when it was the very act of imprisonment that brought them into most immediate and disciplined contact with the leadership of the movement? Action was required not only on the Witwatersrand alone, but within the prison system itself.

In September 1912 the Minister of Justice instructed the Director of Prisons, Roos, to convene a conference of Prison Superintendents in Pretoria, to formulate recommendations for dealing with the Ninevites in prison. The resulting resolutions contained a predictable blend of 'stick and carrot' measures – plenty of stick and very little carrot. Amongst the reforms suggested was that the 'best classes' of black prisoners be allowed to associate more freely where exercise yards were available and 'that single cells for separation at nights be provided as far as possible'. The flow of Ninevite intelligence was to be disrupted by removing well-known leaders to Robben Island, and replacing black warders with Europeans; while membership of prison gangs was to become a punishable 'offence' and Prisons Boards were to be asked 'not to recommend remission of sentence to known members of these gangs'.[104]

These measures presaged a sharp decline in the strength and discipline of the Ninevite leadership. Nongoloza was naturally concerned when he found that a growing number of his most able 'generals' were being confined to prison during 1912, and was particularly perturbed by the indeterminate sentence passed on Sam Nyambezi. Jan Note himself was due to appear before the Prisons Board later in the year and stood to forfeit the chance of a remission of sentence if Ninevite activities persisted unabated.[105] Some time after February 1912, therefore, he sent out a message that he 'wanted things kept quiet for a while as he was endeavouring to get his sentence reduced'.[106] Thus Detective Hoffman had only part of the story when he noted in August that: 'Most of the leaders are at present in gaol, and consequently we have a lull in serious crime.'[107]

But the Prisons Board that met on 8 July 1912 decided not to make any recommendation in the case of Jan Note, choosing instead to reconsider the matter in a year's time. This seems to have constituted a serious blow to the hopes and plans of Nongoloza, who had by now been in the Pretoria Prison for at least four years. Moreover it laid the basis for the authorities' most powerful attack of all on the organisation: shortly after the Board met, Nongoloza was 'befriended' by his European gaoler, Warder Paskin, through whom the Prisons Department dangled the prospect of future sentence remission if the King of Nineveh would not only renounce the movement but also work for the state. On 27 December 1912, Nongoloza capitulated. In a statement to the Director of Prisons, he explained:

> The new law and the new prison administration have made me change my heart.... I am quite prepared to go to Cinderella Prison or any other prison where the Ninevites say they get orders and to tell them that I give no orders even if it costs me my life. I would tell them that I am no longer king and have nothing to do with Nineveh.[108]

In late 1913 the man who could at one stage muster a thousand lumpenproletarian troops on the Witwatersrand, and who had the unquestioned support of 'generals', 'captains' and 'lieutenants' over hundreds of square miles in South Africa's industrial heartland, became a 'native warder' in the Department of Prisons. The oppressed became oppressor, the gaoled the gaoler. Note served his time until 1917 as warder first at Cinderella and later Durban Point Prison, and later still, in the mid-1920s, was said to be back in Pretoria working as a 'warder' in the Weskoppies Mental Hospital.[109]

Not even Nongoloza's defection, nor the other measures taken by the state were sufficient to ensure the total disintegration of the Ninevite army. While the nexus of pass law, compound and prison remained intact at the heart of a repressive political economy, there continued to be a host culture more than capable of sustaining such movements.[110] But the state's various measures did cripple and fragment the Ninevites and by late 1914 the Minister of Justice, N. J. De Wet, was confident that the authorities held the upper hand.[111]

During the decade that followed on Nongoloza's 'conversion', however, the state was never able to relax its hold. The effect of the First World War on the Ninevite movement has yet to be studied but it is clear that the remnants of the black underworld army continued their own particular struggle in the compounds and prisons while the Empire's troops were engaged on other fronts. The Ninevites who murdered Matshayeli Zungu in 1915 for example, were drawn from the compounds of four mines – the Angelo, Comet, Cason and Driefontein. In the immediate wake of the Great War a resurgence of the movement took place, for the same reasons that had facilitated its development after the South African War: the value of real wages had dropped markedly and this hardship was felt particularly acutely by the black population; further 'marginalisation' and an increase in crime took place; and the state's apparatus for controlling the pass laws operated more efficiently once the war no longer diverted most of its energy. More Africans became 'criminals' and the prison population expanded proportionately. In 1919 the Ninevites were certainly active both in and outside of the Kimberley prisons,[112] and were also reported to be present, albeit in embryonic form, at the Noordhoek Prison in the Cape. That they were still capable of making ambitious plans is evident from the report of one Prison Superintendent – the officer in charge of the Durban Point Prison – who reported in 1919:

> At the early part of this year a Ninevite affair was discovered, wherein it was planned to throw the European warders overboard from the ferry boat whilst crossing the bay. This was happily nipped in the bud and the ring-leaders punished with salutary effect.[113]

The succeeding years, however, did see a gradual decline in the more broadly based Ninevite movement. As yet, there is no evidence to show that the organisation was present in its original form in the mine compounds after 1919, and it appears to have become increasingly confined to the prisons proper. During the inter-war years its presence continued to attract official notice – at Barberton Prison in 1927 and at Durban Point Prison eight years later in 1935. At some point after the Second World War the prison-bound Ninevites experienced another minor round of re-organisation and today – almost a hundred years after Mzoozepi Mathebula first sought refuge in the hills of the Witwatersrand – the remnants of Nongoloza's army continues to function within the South African prisons as the much-feared '28 gang'.[114]

Conclusion

In his study of 'social banditry' Eric Hobsbawm has noted that it is:

> usually prevalent at two moments of historical evolution: that at which primitive and communally organised society gives way to class-and-state society, and that at which the traditional rural peasant society gives way to the modern economy.[115]

But, he adds: 'the only regions in which it cannot be easily traced are Sub-Saharan Africa and India'. The social historian of South Africa is at once tempted to place the 'Regiment of the Hills' in the context of these observations. There are at least three reasons for this. First, the years between the mid-1880s and 1920 fit Hobsbawm's description rather neatly. The fall of the independent African states, the rise and decline of the black peasantry, Imperial intervention and capitalist expansion, the formation of Union and the Natives' Land Act of 1913 are only some of the historical high-water marks which lap against the processes which Hobsbawm has described so vividly.[116]

Secondly, the Zulu-dominated Ninevites were essentially rural people with ties of kinship and custom – again not unlike the groups which Hobsbawm describes. The presence of a 'chief' at the head of the gang, but more especially of the ikhehla point strongly towards Zulu custom and traditional society; the language of the 'urban' Ninevites was strongly flavoured with rural metaphor and they spoke constantly of 'buck', 'birds', 'farms' and 'men who came with horses'; and, to the extent that they did have a programme at all, the leaders were not unconcerned with rural objectives – something that was especially true of periods of exceptional peasant hardship, such as 1906–8. Umfanawenduka, a one-time Ninevite, told the police that the leaders of the movement constantly tried to 'entice natives to go away into the hills and live with them' and to 'desert from the work on various mines on the Reef'.[117] Jan Note himself, in his 'confession' to Warder Paskin, spoke warmly of this longing and love for cattle and the countryside, and on his release from duty with the Prisons Department in 1917, the government 'rewarded' him with a small 'farm' in Swaziland.[118] The earliest Ninevites can thus partly be seen as landless labourers seeking to return to a peasant life that was being rapidly destroyed; urban bands with a form of rural consciousness resisting proletarianisation.

Thirdly, the age and social groups recruited into the 'social bandits' and the 'Regiment of the Hills' also bear comparison. In the case of the latter, these similarities are brought into even sharper relief if they are set in the light of Mzoozepi's early experiences, the shattered Zulu military system and the rapid expansion of European commercial agriculture in Natal at the turn of the century. Hobsbawm writes of the social bandits:

> Again, certain age groups – most obviously the young men between puberty and marriage – are both mobile and less shackled by the responsibilities of land, wife and children which make the life of the outlaw almost impossible for adult peasants. It is indeed well established that social bandits are normally young and unmarried. Men marginal to the rural economy, or not yet absorbed or re-absorbed into it, will be drawn into banditry, notably ex-soldiers, who, with herdsmen, form probably its largest single occupational component. So will certain occupations which maintain a man outside the framework of constant social control in the community, or the supervision of the ruling group – e.g. herdsmen and drovers.[119]

Although we do not yet know the detailed socio-economic background of the first Ninevites there is an enticingly familiar ring to these words.

But the similarities promptly end when we consider Hobsbawm's outline of what he considers to be the central characteristics of the groups which he has examined:

> The point about social bandits is that they are peasant outlaws whom the lord and State regard as criminals, but who remain within peasant society, and are considered by their people as heroes, as champions, avengers, fighters for justice, perhaps even leaders of liberation, and in any case as men to be admired, helped and supported.[120]

With the possible exception of a brief period during the early 1890s, the Ninevites were no band of peasant outlaws eliciting the admiration, help or support of their people.

In the industrial revolution that engulfed southern Africa after the discovery of diamonds and gold there was a particularly rapid succession of social formations. In the midst of these traumatic changes there was no time for the landless to linger in the countryside. Those suffering most acutely from the ravages of proletarianisation were swept into the migrant labour system and carried to the cities and compounds. South Africa's 'peasant outlaws' – still carrying some of the conceptual baggage of the countryside – came to town with the rest of their kinsmen. There, living literally and figuratively on the margins of industrial society, they were transformed into essentially urban gangs. No wonder they were difficult to trace in this particular part of sub-Saharan Africa – they were living in the prospect holes, abandoned mine shafts, derelict buildings and caves surrounding the towns – far from their rural homelands.

Hounded and harassed by the pass laws in the centre of the 'white' cities, these lumpenproletarian groups struck at the most vulnerable members of the industrialising system – the black migrant workers making their way home with wages. On the geographical margin of the Witwatersrand they stole and plundered from fellow Africans, or terrorised the inhabitants of the urban black 'locations'. As such they were feared, hated and resented by the majority of proletarians or migrant workers. Here there was no room for help, support or admiration. Where the Ninevites did come into close contact with urban institutions they were usually of the most depressing, authoritarian and dehumanising sort – the prisons and the mine compounds. These institutions provided the Ninevites with rich recruiting grounds since in South Africa miserable wages and endless pass law convictions ensured that today's proletarian was tomorrow's prisoner. As exclusively male institutions the prisons and compounds also provided a host culture readily able to sustain organised violence and homosexuality. Perhaps more than anything else it was these institutions that ensured that this part of sub-Saharan Africa produced not social, but profoundly *anti-social* bandits.

But the role of Nongoloza's men should not be minimised simply because they were not 'social bandits' or because most of their activity was directed against fellow Africans. Nor is their part in South African working-class history so unimportant as to warrant only a single cursory line in a standard reference work.[121] Certainly the Ninevite leaders had a low level of political awareness, but they were able to perceive their followers as being in a state of rebellion in an unjust society. To the extent that its activities were directed away from members of the black working class, and towards white property, the organisation saw itself as redressing the balance between the exploiters and the exploited, the haves and the have-nots, the powerful and powerless in a markedly inegalitarian and racist society.[122] Under the leadership of one charismatic man and professional criminals, there developed a powerful and sophisticated organisation which welded together lumpenproletarian elements and part of the working class. At the height of its development before the First World War, the Ninevite army – albeit for essentially non-political motives – succeeded in seriously challenging the black collaborating arm of a white-dominated state. For these reasons, if for none other, we should reassess the resistance and revolutionary potential of the lumpenproletariat in South Africa's historical evolution.

Notes

1 Amongst others see C. Allen, 'Lumpenproletarians and Revolution' *in Political Theory and Ideology in African Society* (Mimeo. Edinburgh University 1970), pp. 91–115; R. Cohen and D. Michael's 'The Revolutionary Potential of the African Lumpenproletariat: A Sceptical View', *Bulletin of the Institute of Development Studies* (Sussex), 5, 2–3 October 1973, pp. 31–42; and P. Worsley, 'Frantz Fanon and the Lumpenproletariat', *Socialist Register 1972* (London 1972), pp. 193–230.

2 See G. Stedman Jones, *Outcast London* (London 1971); G. Rudé, *Paris and London in the 18th Century* (London 1969); and D. Hay, P. Linebaugh and E. P. Thompson (eds.), *Albion's Fatal Tree* (London 1975). See also the following works by E. J.). Hobsbawm: *Primitive Rebels* (Manchester 1959), *Bandits* (London 1972), and 'Social Banditry' *in* H. Landsberger (ed.), *Rural Protest* (London 1974), pp. 142–157.

3 Cohen and Michael are most explicit about this in their essay on 'The Revolutionary Potential of the African Lumpenproletariat', p. 41.

4 The sociological parameters of the prison are best discussed in E. Goffman, 'On the Characteristics of Total Institutions: The Inmate World', *in* D. R. Cressey (ed.), *The Prison* (New York 1961), pp. 68–106. The sociology and functions of the compound system are fully discussed in C. van Onselen, *Chibaro: African Mine Labour in Southern Rhodesia, 1900–1933* (London 1976), pp. 128–194.

5 From 'Jan Note's Life and Introduction to Crime', South Africa, *Department of Justice Annual Report 1912* (Pretoria 1913), pp. 238–240. (Hereafter, 'Jan Note's Introduction to Crime'.)

6 The origins of Mzoozepi's life of crime thus fit the syndrome as outlined by Hobsbawm in his essay on 'Social Banditry', pp. 143–144. Unfortunately we do not know whether peasants viewed Note's life in the same way, but we do know what a noted black journalist – R. V. Selope Thema – thought about it at a later date. 'Scrutator' [Thema] noted in his column in *Bantu World*, 5 December 1942: 'Jan Note (Mzoozepi) was not an agitator. He was just a human being, driven to desperation by the nature of the pass laws, the dishonesty of a white man, and the unsympathetic attitude of the police and the magistrates'. See also R. V. Selope Thema's *The Plight of the Black Man* (Liberty Press, Pretoria n.d.), pp. 6–9.

7 'Jan Note's Introduction to Crime', pp. 238–9.

8 Editorial, *Standard and Diggers' News*, 31 May 1895. (Hereafter *S. & D.N.*)

9 See, for example, the role of this factor in the formation of the white mineworkers' union as reported in the *S. & D.N.*

10 By its very nature much of this evidence is fragmentary, and derives from several sources. A good brief introduction, however, is 'Vagabond's', 'The Streets of Johannesburg by Night', *S. & D.N.*, 19 June 1895. Note too how these groups – especially the soldiers and deserters – conform with those pointed to by Hobsbawm in *Bandits*, pp. 33–5.

11 See, for example, 'Confessions of a Canteen Keeper', *S. & D.N.*, 5 October 1892. For one detailed study of crime, ethnicity and class formation during this period, see Vol. I, Chapter 2, 'Randlords and Rotgut', pp. 44–102.

12 'Jan Note's Introduction to Crime', p. 239.

13 For example, see *S. & D.N.*, 13 April 1895.

14 'Jan Note's Introduction to Crime', p. 239.

15 Jan Note's introduction to crime was thus an almost classic illustration of a process of which the police at the turn of the century were well aware. See, for example, the evidence of T. E. Mavrogordato, Acting Head C.I.D., Johannesburg, in *South African Native Affairs Commission, 1903–5*, 5 vols (Pretoria 1906), iv, pp. 861–3.

16 These wage robberies and inadequate state protection were the source of constant complaint by the mine owners. See, for example, Transvaal, *Report of the Chamber of Mines for 1897* (Johannesburg 1898), p. 394.

17 Newspapers throughout the 1890s abound with reports of such thefts by state officials. For a selection of examples, see incidents reported in the following editions of the *S. & D.N.*: 20 March 1891 (Z.A.R. police), 9 August 1894 (N.Z.A.S.M. railway officials), and 4 January 1895 (Portuguese border officials). Since such robberies tended to hamper the free flow of labour, the Chamber of Mines complained bitterly about them. See Transvaal, *Report of the Chamber of Mines for 1895*, pp. 69–70; and *Report of the Chamber of Mines for 1896* , pp. 170–1.

18 This setting parallels that of many European case studies. See Hobsbawm, 'Social Banditry', p. 149.

19 'Statement by Jan Note', in South Africa, *Department of Justice Annual Report 1912* (Pretoria 1913), pp. 237–8. (Hereafter, 'Statement by Jan Note'.)

20 This, of course, was the era during which other Africans also started to interpret the Bible in a radical way which frightened the established churches. In particular, it was the decade which saw the emergence of 'Ethiopianism' – black independent churches – and Johannesburg was one such centre. See, for example, reports in the *S. & D.N.* of 29 May and 9 July 1895.

21 'Statement by Jan Note', p. 238. The book of Nahum is filled with verses which Note perhaps found to be relevant and inspirational. For example, 'Thy people are scattered upon the mountains', *Nahum* iii. 18; 'Take ye the spoil of silver, take the spoil of gold', *Nahum* ii. 9.

22 'Statement by Jan Note', p. 238.

23 So much so that the Chamber of Mines eventually organised its own police force to cope with highway robbers. See D. M. Wilson, *Behind the Scenes in the Transvaal* (London 1901), pp. 196–7. See also note 17 above.

24 See items reported in *S. & D.N.* of 19 February and 28 March 1890.

25 *S. & D.N.*, 2 August 1892.

26 See, for example, report of a robbery in *S. & D.N.*, 28 June 1895.

27 *S. & D.N.*, 31 January 1890.

28 See especially items reported in *S. & D.N.* of 21 August 1894 and 7 January 1895.

29 'Izigebengu", *The Star*, 16 June 1896.

30 Hobsbawm, *Bandits*, p. 18.

31 Classic feeder groups for bandits. See *ibid.*, pp. 33–5.

32 Hobsbawm, *Primitive Rebels*, p. 33.

33 As Hobsbawm has noted of the Mafia: 'Obviously it was a complex movement, including mutually contradictory elements.' *Ibid.*, p. 41.

34 P. Warwick, 'African Labour during the South African War, 1899–1902', post-graduate seminar paper presented at the Institute of Commonwealth Studies, University of London, October 1975.

35 *Ipepa lo Hlanga*, 20 November 1902. My thanks to Peter Warwick who brought this reference to my attention.

36 See P. Warwick, 'African Labour during the South African War, 1899–1902'.

37 See especially the evidence of W. J. Clarke (Chief Inspector, C.I.D., Pietermaritzburg) to *South African Native Affairs Commission, 1903–1905*, 5 vols (Pretoria 1906), iii, paras. 27,693–27,696, p. 613; and paras. 27,801–27,802, p. 618. See also, H. P. Holt, *The Mounted Police of Natal* (London 1913), pp. 316–27; my thanks to Jeff Guy who drew this source to my attention. For more detailed case histories, however, see South Africa, *Department of Justice Annual Report 1914* (Pretoria 1915), p. 235. Finally, see N. Devitt, *Memories of a Magistrate* (London 1934), p. 144.

38 P. Warwick, 'African Labour during the South African War, 1899–1902'.

39 See J. S. Marwick's evidence in the case of 'Rex *vs* Mkosi Mkemeseni and 15

Others', p. 48, Archbishop Carter's Papers, Archives of the University of the Witwatersrand, Johannesburg. (Hereafter cited as 'Rex vs Mkosi Mkemeseni'.)

40 *Ibid*. See also Marwick's observations as reported in 'Jan Note's Reform', *Sunday Times*, 19 September 1915.

41 See Transvaal Archives Depot, Pretoria, Department of Justice, Vol. 144, File 1 – No. 3/778/12, Statement by 'Forage', 16 June 1912; and Statements by Detective W. W. Futter and Detective Probationer H. G. Boy made on 19 June 1912. (This source hereafter referred to as T.A.D., File 3/778/12.)

42 According to Jan Note sodomy was already a feature of Ninevite life while the izigebengu were still based in the Klipriversberg – see 'Statement by Jan Note', p. 238. There is little reason to doubt that homosexuality was also a feature of compound life in the pre-war years. What is also clear, however, is the fact that such relationships became increasingly formal, organised and acceptable in the immediate post-war period. See below.

43 Archives of the Transvaal Chamber of Mines, Johannesburg, 1889–1910, N. Series, File N. 35, 'Unnatural Native Vice Enquiry, 1907', pp. 1–2.

44 T.A.D., File 3/778/12, M. A. Hartigan, District Commandant, Boksburg, to Secretary, Transvaal Police, 22 June 1912.

45 *Sunday Times*, 16 June 1912. See also T.A.D., File 3/778/12, Detective A. Hoffman to Deputy Commissioner, C.I.D., Johannesburg, 12 October 1911.

46 *Sunday Times*, 16 June 1912.

47 H. P. Holt, *The Mounted Police of Natal* (London 1913), pp. 316–27.

48 *Ibid*., p. 316 and p. 327.

49 See evidence of prisoner 'Bc' to Transvaal, *Report of the Commission appointed to Enquire into the Johannesburg Prison 1904–5*, paras. 1,268–1,310, pp. 61–3.

50 The three preceding paragraphs are based on the following items drawn from *The Star*: 'Native Desperadoes', 7 March 1907; 'Police Exploit', 13 January 1909; and 'Native Criminal Gang', 22 April 1909. See also items relating to the career of Jan Note as reported in the *Sunday Times* of 16 June 1912 and 19 September 1915.

51 See the following items drawn from *The Star*: 'A Gaol Outbreak', 30 April 1908; 'Convicts in Court', 12 May 1908; 'Native Convicts', 14 May 1908; 'Convict Outbreak', 14 January 1910; and 'The Prison Case', 29 January 1910. Also T.A.D., File 3/778/12.

52 This picture is reconstructed from scattered references in T.A.D., File 3/778/12.

53 *Ibid*. See especially, however, D. M. Tomory to the Secretary of Justice, 6 September 1911.

54 T.A.D., File 3/778/12, Statement by Nkuku, 16 June 1912.

55 *Ibid*. Deputy Commissioner of Police, to Secretary, Transvaal Police, 28 August 1912.

56 T.A.D., File 3/788/12, Statement by Tomboek Umfanawenduka, 19 June 1912.

57 The status of ikhehla and its attendant relationships are best described in *ibid*., statements by 'Office' Josimale (age 13), 17 June 1912; and Tomboek Umfanawenduka, 19 June 1912. Contrast this, however, with the evidence led during the 'Rex *vs* Mkosi Mkemeseni' trial.

58 T.A.D., File 3/778/12, Statement by Tomboek Umfanawenduka, 19 June 1912.

59 Illustrations of the various forms of punishment employed by the Ninevites can be found in any of the following sources: Transvaal, *Report of the Commission appointed to Enquire into the Johannesburg Prison, 1904–05*, paras. 1288–9, p. 62; or the following items drawn from *The Star*: ' "Convict Chiefs" ', 27 January 1908; 'A Brutal Assault', 12 February 1908; and 'Convicts in Court', 12 May 1908. See also, T.A.D., File 3/778/12, 'Statement as to Position of Native Criminal Gangs in Prison', 1912.

60 T.A.D., File 3/778/12, Statement by Tomboek Umfanawenduka, 19 June 1912.

61 'Rex *vs* Mkosi Mkemeseni', p. 25.

62 See report in the *Cape Times*, 20 August 1915.

63 T.A.D., File 3/778/12, Detective A. J. Hoffman to Deputy Commissioner, C.I.D., 12 October 1911.

64 *Ibid.*, 'Statement as to Position of Native Criminal Gangs in Prison', 1912.

65 *Ibid.*, Detective A. J. Hoffman to Inspector in Charge, C.I.D., 12 August 1912; and Statement by Tomboek Umfanawenduka, 19 June 1912.

66 For 'Scotlanders' see T.A.D., File 3/778/12, 'Statement as to Position of Native Criminal Gangs in Prison', 1912; and 'Society in Gaol', *The Star*, 4 August 1914. For an example of conflict between the Scotlanders and the Ninevites, see report in the *Diamond Fields' Advertiser*, 23 May 1919.

67 Much later it was claimed that the state had the Ninevites very much in mind when it first introduced the indeterminate sentence. See leader on 'The Native Criminal', *The Star*, 18 June 1932. For a contemporary description of Cinderella Prison and the 'I.S.' inmates see, for example, *Africa's Golden Harvests*, xiv (October 1919), p. 131.

68 For a selection of these terms see 'Rex *vs* Mkosi Mkemeseni'.

69 The importance of the word '*mgusa*' was known to at least some detectives – see, for example, 'Five Natives Charged – Question of Secret Society', *The Star*, 21 August 1913. The importance of drugs within compound culture is discussed in C. van Onselen, *Chibaro*, pp. 166–74.

70 'Rex *vs* Mkosi Mkemeseni', p. 31.

71 T.A.D., File 3/778/12, Statement by Detective Probationer H. G. Boy, 19 June 1912.

72 *Ibid.*, see especially, Detective A. J. Hoffman to Inspector in Charge, C.I.D., 12 August 1912; and Statement by Detective W. Futter, 19 June 1912.

73 See, amongst other items culled from *The Star*, the following: 'Native Vagrants – A "Herd of Jackals" ', 20 August 1908; 'Cave Dwellers', 24 September 1908; 'Cave Dwellers', 20 August 1909; and 'Native Outlaws', 17 November 1909. Perhaps most interesting of all, however, is the 'group of Zulu and other boys who have escaped from the mines' and established themselves in the vicinity of Potchefstroom. See the following items drawn from *The Star*: 'Native Criminals', 9 May 1909; and 'A Mountain Gang', 22 May 1909.

74 T.A.D., File 3/778/12, Detective A. J. Hoffman to Inspector in Charge, C.I.D., 12 August 1912.

75 For precisely this reason 'vagrants' and the unemployed continued to use the compounds as a sort of refuge in the cities. In the case of 'Rex *vs* Mkosi Mkemseni', for example, see the evidence of Matoko Biyela, p. 12, and that of Joe Loqoqoza, pp. 40–1.

76 T.A.D., File 3/778/12, Deputy Commissioner to Secretary, Transvaal Police, 28 August 1912.

77 See, for example, the evidence of Matoko Biyela in 'Rex *vs* Mkosi Mkemeseni', p. 15.

78 T.A.D., File 3/778/12, Statement by 'Office' Josimale, 17 June 1912.

79 'Statement by Jan Note', p. 239.

80 *Black and White: The Black Underworld, How it is Created* (Johannesburg 1909), p. 1.

81 See evidence led in the case of 'Rex *vs* Mkosi Mkemeseni', p. 26.

82 T.A.D., File 3/778/12, Statement by Tomboek Umfanawenduka, 19 June 1912.

83 *Ibid.*, J. E. Donald, O. C. Benoni Police, to District Commandant, Boksburg Police, 20 June 1912.

84 *Ibid.*, Departmental Memo dated 12 February 1913.

85 *Ibid.*, J. W. Goodman, Public Prosecutor, to Attorney General, 12 June 1912.

86 *Ibid.*, J. E. Donald, O. C. Benoni Police, to District Commandant, Boksburg Police, 20 June 1912.

87 *Ibid.*, District Commandant, Boksburg Police, to Secretary, Transvaal Police, 22 June 1912.
88 For a detailed analysis see C. van Onselen, *Chibaro*, pp. 128–57.
89 F. Z. S. Peregrino, *Life Among the Native and Coloured Miners in the Transvaal* (Cape Town 1910), p. 14; quoted by S. T. Plaatje in the *Pretoria News*, 11 February 1911. See also Plaatje's attack on Swazi, Zulu and Shangaan police in *Tsala ea Becoana*, 5 November 1910.
90 T.A.D., File 3/778/12, Statement by Johnson Johannes, 17 June 1912. See also 'Black Hooliganism', *The Star*, 13 January 1908.
91 T.A.D., File 3/778/12, see Deputy Commissioner to Secretary, Transvaal Police, 28 Jan. 1913; and earlier, Deputy Commissioner to Secretary, Transvaal Police, 28 August 1912.
92 See 'Death of Constable King' in *The Star*, 26 April 1911; and a further report in the same newspaper dated 17 December 1912.
93 James Ndlela, 'How the Ninevites were Suppressed', *Umteteli wa Bantu*, 6 January 1934.
94 The King funeral is recalled in *The Star*, 19 December 1912.
95 'How the Ninevites were Suppressed', *Umteteli wa Bantu*, 6 January 1934.
96 *Ibid.*
97 *Ibid.* This account, however, is largely based on T.A.D., Department of Justice, Vol. 117, File 3/780/11, Deputy Commissioner of Police to Secretary, Transvaal Police, 26 January 1911. (Hereafter, T.A.D., File 3/780/11.)
98 *Ibid.*
99 'The Criminal Native', *The Star*, 10 January 1932.
100 See the following items drawn from *The Star*: 'Mysterious Murder', 13 May 1912; 'Foul Murder', 15 May 1912; and 'Native Policeman's Death', 5 September 1912. See also item reported in the *Transvaal Leader*, 22 June 1912.
101 See the following items in *The Star*: 'Charge of Murder', 11 June 1912; 'Murder of Owen Duffy', 3 September 1912; and 'Murder of Owen Duffy', 4 September 1912. See also items relating to the murder reported in the *Transvaal Leader* of 12 and 19 June 1912.
102 *Sunday Times*, 16 June 1912.
103 T.A.D., File 3/788/12, Detective A. J. Hoffman to Inspector in Charge, C.I.D., 12 August 1912. See also 'Rex *vs* Mkosi Mekmeseni'.
104 T.A.D., File 3/778/12, Secretary for Justice to Chief Commissioner of Police, 3 January 1913.
105 *Ibid.*, Secretary for Justice to Director of Prisons, 17 March 1913.
106 *Ibid.*, Statement by Nkuku, 16 June 1912.
107 *Ibid.*, Detective A. J. Hoffman to Inspector in Charge, C.I.D., 12 August 1912.
108 'Statement by Jan Note', pp. 237–8.
109 This information is drawn from the *Cape Times*, 29 May 1917 and N. Devitt, *Memories of a Magistrate* (London 1934), p. 144. See also, however, University of the Witwatersrand, African Studies Institute, Oral History Project, interview conducted with the Rev. Gideon Sivetye by T. J. Couzens and A. van Gylswyk at Groutville, Natal, on 23 October 1978.
110 Amongst the more important of these were the gang of Pondos and Xhosas set up on the West Rand during the early 1930s under the leadership of 'Chief Hlovu'. See University of the Witwatersrand, Records of the Church of the Province of South Africa, Box 1927, Detective Head Constable H. C. Boy to the Divisional Criminal Investigation Officer, C.I.D., Witwatersrand Division, 8 January 1930, re 'Secret Society of Pondo Natives known as the Isitshozi Gang'. See also item reported in the *Sunday Times*, 27 October 1935; and B. Davidson, *Report on Southern Africa* (London 1952), p. 117.
111 T.A.D., File 3/780/11, Minister of Justice to Justice Ward, 5 August 1914.

112 See various reports in the *Diamond Fields' Advertiser* dated: 13 January 1919, 23 May 1919, and 28 May 1919. My thanks to Brian Willan for bringing these items to my attention.

113 South Africa, *Report of the Director of Prisons for 1919* (Pretoria, U.G. 54–20), p. 49.

114 For an insight into modern South African prison gangs – including the descendants of the Ninevites – see the following series of articles in the *Sunday Times Extra* by Brigadier R. Keswa: 'King Nongoloza made Women of Men', 26 September 1976; 'The "King" Recruits New Gang – in Jail', 3 October 1976; 'I Saw a Jail Gang Execution', 17 October 1976; 'Secret Salutes Ex-Cons Give a Jail Boss', 24 October 1976; and 'Rival Spoilers were Recruited in Prison', 7 November 1976. See also E. R. G. Keswa's unpublished manuscript, 'Outlawed Communities' (1975).

115 Hobsbawm, 'Social Banditry', p. 149.

116 See, for example, C. Bundy, 'The Emergence and Decline of a South African Peasantry', *African Affairs*, lxxi (1972), pp. 369–88.

117 T.A.D., File 3/778/12, Statement by Tomboek Umfanawenduka, 19 June 1912.

118 *Cape Times*, 29 May 1917.

119 Hobsbawm, 'Social Banditry', p. 152.

120 Hobsbawm, *Bandits*, p. 17.

121 E. A. Walker, *A History of Southern Africa* (London 1965), p. 548.

122 Even black journalists who were usually hostile to the Ninevites recognised this element in Jan Note's career – albeit in a historically inaccurate and somewhat ideological form. 'Scrutator' (R. V. Selope Thema) thus wrote: 'Although he was helpless and defenceless, he decided to declare "war" against his persecutors. Without arms, he said, he was going to wage a relentless struggle against the white man. He was going to rob him, to break into his stores, burgle his houses and make him uncomfortable in every way possible.' *Bantu World*, 5 December 1942.

Select Bibliography

Manuscript sources

Government archives
Cape Archives Depot, Cape Town
Natal Archives Depot, Pietermaritzburg
National Archives of the United States of America, Washington, D.C.
Registrar of Companies Office, Pretoria
Transvaal Archives Depot, Pretoria

Other archives
Fawcett Library, City of London Polytechnic
Strange Library, Johannesburg Public Library
University of the Witwatersrand Archives

Printed sources

Primary sources
Chamber of Mines Reports
Johannesburg, Official Publications
Newspapers
Publications of Her Majesty's Stationery Office (H.M.S.O.), London
Transvaal Colony, Official Publications
Transvaal Government (1907–1910), Official Publications
Union of South Africa, Official Publications
Zuid Afrikaansche Republiek, Official Publications

Secondary sources
Directories
Select bibliography of secondary sources on the Witwatersrand
Select bibliography of other secondary sources
Theses and unpublished papers

Interviews

Manuscript sources

Government Archives
Cape Archives Depot, Cape Town
  Cape Supreme Court, Criminal Records, September–October 1904, May–July 1904
Natal Archives Depot, Pietermaritzburg
  Colenso Collection, Box 76
  Durban Corporation Collection (uncatalogued), Police Report Book No. 6
  Secretary for Native Affairs, Confidential Papers, 1890–1897, File 668/1895
  Secretary for Native Affairs, File 1/1/216

National Archives of the United States of America, Washington, D.C.
  Department of Commerce and Labor, Bureau of Immigration and Naturalization, File 1–G, 52484
  Despatches from United States Consuls in Pretoria 1898–1906, Vol. I
Registrar of Companies Office, Pretoria
  'The Eerste Fabrieken Hatherley Distillery Ltd.', File T669
  File on 'Crystal Steam Laundry', (1895)
  'Palace Steam Laundry Ltd.', File T1501
  'Transvaal Soap Co. Ltd.', File T1413
Transvaal Archives Depot, Pretoria
  Colonial Secretary: Correspondence, 1901–1911, Vols. 1–1028
  Colonial Secretary: Confidential Correspondence, Vols. 1076–1085
  Colonial Secretary: Confidential correspondence (unregistered), 1901–1907, Vols. 1088–1092
  Colonial Secretary: Private Secretary to Colonial Secretary, 1901–1906, Vols. 1132–1134
  Government Native Labour Bureau: Uncatalogued Archival Material, 1907–1914
  Secretary of the Governor of the Transvaal: 1901–1910, Vols. 1–1371
  Johannesburg Housing Commission 1903: Minutes of Evidence, Report, Correspondence, Extracts from the Minutes of the Johannesburg Town Council, Statements
  Department of Justice: Miscellaneous Files, 1910–1912
  Legal Assistant to the Military Governor 1900–1901: Minute Files L1–L1503
  Johannesburg Landdrost: Administrasie, 1886–1900, Portfolios 1–88
  Johannesburg Landdrost: Spesiale Landdros, 1886–1900, Porfolios 89–173a
  Johannesburg Landdrost: Spesiale Landdros, 1886–1896, Portfolios 604–836
  Johannesburg Landdrost: Dranklisensie Kommissie, 1892–1899, Portfolios 248–276
  Law Department: Attorney General's Correspondence, 1900–1914, Vols. 25–1814
  Lieutenant Governor: General Correspondence, 1902–1907, Vols. 1–164 and 185–233
  Lieutenant Governor: Confidential Correspondence, 1902–1907, Vols. 176 and 234
  South African Constabulary: 1900–1908, Vols. 1–91
  Secretary for Native Affairs: Miscellaneous Files
  Staatsprokureur: Correspondence, 1886–1900, Vols. 1–572
  Staatsprokureur: Geheime Minute, 1886–1900, Vols. 190–196
  Staatsprokureur: Hofpapiere, 1886–1900, Vols. 573–753A
  Staatsprokureur: Gevangeniswese, 1886–1900, Vols. 904–913
  Staatsekretaris: Correspondence, 1886–1900, Vols. 1148–8796

Other archives

Fawcett Library, City of London Polytechnic
  'Early Transvaal Letters', South African Colonisation Society Collection
  South African Colonisation Society Reports, 1903–1904, Mss. Vol. 41
Johannesburg Public Library
  Johannesburg City Archive, Strange Library, Miscellaneous Boxes referring to the period, 1886–1899
University of the Witwatersrand Archives
  Archbishop Carter's Papers
  Church of the Province of South Africa, Diocesan Board of Mission Minutes 1905–1921, A.B. 767
  Records of the Church of the Province of South Africa, Box 1927

Printed sources

Primary sources

Chamber of Mines Reports
  Annual Reports of the Chamber of Mines 1889–1914
Johannesburg Official Publications
  Census 1896
  Mayor's Minutes 1901–1903, 1905–1919
  Minutes of the City Council, 1908–1914
  Minutes of the Public Health Committee, December 1906
  Minutes of the Town Council Meetings, 1902–January 1903
  Report of the Town Engineer 1904
Newspapers
  Standard and Diggers' News, 4 April 1889–31 May 1900
  The Star, January 1902–December 1914
Publications of Her Majesty's Stationery Office, London
  British Parliamentary Papers, Vol. LXVI (Command 5363), 1910
  British Parliamentary Papers, Vol. XXXV (Command 624), 1901
  Correspondence respecting the African Liquor Traffic Convention, signed at Brussels, 8 June 1899 (Command 9335), July 1899, Africa No. 7
  Further Correspondence relating to the Affairs of the Transvaal and Orange River Colonies, Appendix 1 (Command 1895), 1904
  Papers relating to Legislation affecting Natives in the Transvaal (Command 904), 1902
  Report of the Transvaal Concessions Commission, Part I (Command 623), 1901
  Report of the Transvaal Concessions Commission, Part II, Minutes of Evidence (Command 624), 1901
Transvaal Colony Official Publications
  Johannesburg Insanitary Area Improvement Scheme Commission 1902–1903
  Laws of the Transvaal 1901
  Ordinances of the Transvaal 1903
  Report of the Commission to enquire into the Johannesburg Prison 1904–5
  Report of the Commission on Pretoria Indigents 1905
  Report of the Public Health Committee on the Location Question 1904
  South African Native Affairs Commission, 1903–1905, 5 Vols., Pretoria, 1906
  Transvaal Administration Reports for 1905
  Vrededorp Stands Ordinance 1906
Transvaal Government (1907–1910) Official Publications
  Evidence to the Transvaal Indigency Commission 1906–1908 (T.G. 11–08)
  Report of the Liquor Commission 1908 (T.A. 1–1909)
  South African Republic Officials' Pension Commission, January 1909 (T.G. 10–09)
  Report of the Transvaal Indigency Commission 1906–1908 (T.G. 13–08)
  Transvaal Legislative Assembly Debates 1907–1910
Union of South Africa Official Publications
  Annual Report of the Director of Prisons for 1927 (U.G. 42–48)
  Annual Report of the Director of Prisons for 1935 (U.G. 28–36)
  Department of Justice Annual Report 1912, Pretoria 1913
  Department of Justice Annual Report 1914, Pretoria 1915
  Minutes of Evidence of the Natal Natives Land Committee 1918 (U.G. 35–18)
  Relief and Grants-in-Aid Commission 1916 (T.P. 5–16)
  Report of the Commission appointed to Enquire into Assaults on Women in 1913 (U.G. 34–13)
  Report of the Director of Prisons for 1919 (U.G. 54–20)
  Report of the Economic Commission 1913 (U.G. 12–14)

Report of the Small Holdings Commission (Transvaal) (U.G. 51–13)
Report of the Transvaal Leasehold Townships Commission 1912 (U.G. 34–12)
Select Committee on European Employment and Labour Conditions 1913 (S.C. 9–13)
Zuid Afrikaansche Republiek Official Publications
De Locale Wetten de Zuid Afrikaansche Republiek 1897
De Locale Wetten de Zuid Afrikaansche Republiek 1899
Z. A. R. *Executive Committee*, Resolution 16, Article 462, April 1898 and Resolution
17, Article 1251, 14 December 1898

Secondary sources

Directories
Longland's Johannesburg and District Directory 1890
Longland's Johannesburg and District Directory 1896
Longland's Johannesburg and District Directory 1897—1899
Longland's Transvaal Directory, 1903–1908
South African Who's Who 1909
United Transvaal Directory 1908–1914

Select bibliography of secondary sources on the Witwatersrand
Alston, M., *At Home on the Veld*, London, 1906
Amery, L. S., *The Times History of the War in South Africa 1899–1902*, Vols. I and IV,
London, 1909
Anonymous, *Black and White: The Black Underworld, How it is Created*,
Johannesburg, 1909
Appelgryn, M. S., 'Prostitusie in die Zuid Afrikaansche Republiek', *Codicillus*,
XIII, 1, 1972, pp. 26–29
Aubert, G., *L'Afrique du Sud*, Paris, 1897
Bailey, W. F., 'The Native Problem in South Africa', *National Review*, 28, 1896
Blainey, G., 'Lost causes of the Jameson Raid', *Economic History Review*, 2nd series
XVIII, 1965, pp. 350–366
Bovill, J. N., *Natives under the Transvaal Flag*, London, 1900
Bozzoli, B., *The Political Nature of a Ruling Class: Capital and Ideology in South
Africa 1890–1933*, London, 1981
Buchan, J., *The African Colony: Studies in the Reconstruction*, London, 1903
Cleaver, Mrs (ed. 'His Mother'), *A Young South African – A Memoir of Ferrar
Reginald Mostyn Cleaver, Advocate and Veldcornet*, Johannesburg, 1913
Court, S., 'The Progress of Johannesburg', *Addresses and Papers read at the Joint
Meeting of the British and South African Associations for the Advancement of Science
1905*, IV, Appendix 9
Curtis, L., *With Milner in Africa*, Oxford, 1951
Darragh, J. T., 'The Liquor Problem in the Transvaal', *Contemporary Review*, July
1901
Denoon, D. J. N., 'The Transvaal Labour Crisis 1901–1906', *Journal of African
History*, VII, 3, 1967, pp. 481–494
Denoon, D., *A Grand Illusion*, London, 1973
Devitt, N., *Memories of a Magistrate*, London, 1934
Duminy, A. H. and Guest, W. R. (eds.), *FitzPatrick*, London, 1976
Feldman, L. (in Yiddish), *The Jews of Johannesburg*, South African Yiddish Cultural
Federation, Johannesburg, 1965
Fisher, J., *Paul Kruger*, London, 1974
FitzPatrick, J. P., *The Transvaal from Within*, London, 1899
Fourie, J. J. (ed. Stals, E.L.P.), *Afrikaners in die Goudstad*, Deel I, 1886–1924,
Pretoria, 1978

Fox Bourne, H., *The Native Labour Question in the Transvaal*, London, 1901

Fraser, M. and Jeeves, A. (eds.), *All That Glittered*, Cape Town, 1977

Freed, L., *The Problem of European Prostitution in Johannesburg*, Johannesburg, 1949

Gaitskell, D., ' "Christian Compounds for Girls": Church Hostels for African Women in Johannesburg, 1907–1970', *Journal of Southern African Studies*, 6, 1, October 1979, pp. 44–69

Goldmann, C. S., *South African Mining and Finance*, Johannesburg, 1895

Gordon, C. T., *The Growth of Boer Opposition to Kruger 1890–95*, London, 1970

Headlam, C. (ed.), *The Milner Papers*, Vol. II, London, 1933

Hobson, J. A., *The War in South Africa*, London, 1900

Jensen, E., 'Poor Relief in Johannesburg', *The Journal of the Economic Society of South Africa*, 2, 1, 1928, pp. 26–36

Jeppe, F. (ed.), *Jeppe's Transvaal Almanac for 1899*

Katz, E. N., *A Trade Union Aristocracy*, Johannesburg, 1976

Kaye, H., *The Tycoon and the President*, Johannesburg, 1978

Kubicek, R. V., *Economic Imperialism in Theory and Practice: The Case of South African Gold Mining Finance, 1886–1914* (Duke University Press), Durham, N.C., 1979

Lady Knightley of Fawsley, 'The Terms and Conditions of Domestic Service in England and South Africa', *Imperial Colonist*, IV, 48, December, 1905

Marais, J. S., *The Fall of Kruger's Republic*, Oxford, 1961

Marks, S. and Trapido, S., 'Lord Milner and the South African State', *History Workshop*, 8, 1979, pp. 50–80

Mendelsohn, R., 'Blainey and the Jameson Raid: The Debate Renewed', *Journal of Southern African Studies*, 6, 2, 1980, pp. 157–170

Morgan, B. H., *Report on the Engineering Trades of South Africa*, London, 1902

Nimocks, W., *Milner's Young Men: the "Kindergarten" in Edwardian Imperial Affairs* (Duke University Press), Durham, N.C., 1968

Peregrino, F. Z. S., *Life Among the Native and Coloured Miners in the Transvaal*, Cape Town, 1910

Phillips, Mrs L., *Some South African Recollections*, London, 1899

Plaatje, S. T., 'The Mote and the Beam' *in* Couzens, T. J. and Willan, B. (eds.), *English in Africa*, 3, 2, 1976, pp. 85–92

Ploeger, J., 'Die Maatskappy "Eerste Fabrieken in die Zuid Afrikaansche Republiek" ', *Historia*, Jaargang 2, 1957.

Potgieter, F. J., 'Die vestiging van die Blanke in Transvaal 1837–1886', *Archives Year Book for South African History, 1958*, Vol. 2, pp. (vii) 1–208.

Ramsay Macdonald, J., *What I saw in South Africa*, London, 1902

Rathbone, E. P., 'The Problem of Home Life in South Africa, *19th Century Review*, August, 1906, pp. 245–253

Richardson, P. and Van-Helten, J. J., 'The Gold Mining Industry in the Transvaal 1886–99', *in* Warwick, P. (ed.), *The South African War*, London, 1980

Rose, E. B., *The Truth about the Transvaal*, London, 1902

Scoble, J. and Abercrombie, H. R., *The Rise and Fall of Krugerism*, London, 1900

Spoelstra, Rev. C., *Delicate Matters – Open Letter addressed to Dr. F. V. Engelenberg*, Johannesburg, 1896

Streak, M., *Lord Milner's Immigration Policy for the Transvaal 1897–1905*, Rand Afrikaans University Publication, Series B1, January 1969

Tangye, H. L., *In New South Africa*, London, 1896

Thema, R. V. S., *The Plight of the Black Man*, Pretoria, n.d.

Trapido, S., 'Landlord and Tenant in a Colonial Economy: the Transvaal 1880–1910', *Journal of Southern African Studies*, October 1978, 5, 1, pp. 26–58

Trapido, S., 'Reflections on Land, Office and Wealth in the South African Republic, 1850–1900', in S. Marks and A. Atmore (eds.), *Economy and Society in Pre-industrial*

South Africa (London, 1980), pp. 350–68

Vane, F., *Back to the Mines*, London, 1903

Van der Poel, J. and Hancock, W. K. (eds.), *Selections from the Smuts Papers*, Vol. I, Cambridge, 1965

Vivian, W. N., 'The Cost of Living in Johannesburg', *Imperial Colonist*, IV, 39, March 1905

Wilson, D. M., *Behind the Scenes in the Transvaal*, London, 1901

Select bibliography of other secondary sources

Allen, C., 'Lumpenproletarians and Revolution', in *Political Theory and Ideology in African Society*, Conference Proceedings, Edinburgh University, 1970

Blackwell, W. L., *The Beginnings of Russian Industrialisation 1800–1860*, Princeton, 1968

Bristow, E. J., *Vice and Vigilance*, London, 1977

Bundy, C., 'The Emergence and Decline of a South African Peasantry', *African Affairs*, 71, 1972, pp. 369–388

Burnett, J., *Useful Toil*, London, 1974

Clarke, J., Critcher, C., and Johnson, R., (eds.), *Working Class Culture: Studies in History and Theory*, London, 1979

Cock, J., *Maids and Madams: A Study in the Politics of Exploitation*, Johannesburg, 1980

Cohen, R. and Michael, D., 'The Revolutionary Potential of the African Lumpenproletariat: A Sceptical View', *Bulletin of the Institute of Development Studies* (Sussex), V, 1973, pp. 31–42

Colquhoun, A. R., *Dan to Beersheba*, London, 1908

Couper, J. R., *Mixed Humanity*, London, n.d.

Cressey, D. R. (ed.), *The Prison: Studies in Institutional Organisation and Change*, New York, 1961

Davidoff, L., *The Best Circles: Society, Etiquette and the Season*, London, 1973

Davidoff, L. and Hawthorn, R., *A Day in the Life of a Victorian Domestic Servant*, London, 1976

Davies, R. H., *Capital, State and White Labour in South Africa, 1900–1960*, Brighton, 1979

Davis, A., *The Native Problem*, London, 1903

Doyle, B., *The Etiquette of Race Relations: A Study in Social Control*, New York, 1971

Dumont, L., *Homo Hierarchicus*, London, 1970

. Evans, R. J., 'Prostitution, State and Society in Imperial Germany', *Past and Present*, No. 70, 1976, pp. 106–129

Fanon, F., *The Wretched of the Earth*, London, 1965

Fieldhouse, D. K., *Unilever Overseas: The Anatomy of a Multinational, 1895–1965*, London, 1978

Flexner, A., *Prostitution in Europe*, New York, 1914

Forbes Munro, F., *Africa and the International Economy 1800–1960*, London, 1976

Frankel, S. H., *Capital Investment in Africa*, London, 1938

Genovese, E., *In Red and Black: Marxian Explorations in Southern and Afro-American History*, New York, 1968

Ghyre, G. S., *Caste and Class in India*, New York, 1952

Gilbert, M., 'The Jews of Austria-Hungary, 1867–1914', *Jewish History Atlas*, London, 1969

Goffman, E., 'On the Characteristics of Total Institutions – the Inmate World' *in* Cressey, D. R. (ed.), *The Prison: Studies in Institutional Organisation and Change*, New York, 1961

Gutman, H. G., *Work, Culture and Society in Industrialising America*, Oxford, 1977

Hay, D., Linebaugh, P., and Thompson, E. P., *Albion's Fatal Tree*, London, 1975

Haupt, G., 'Why the History of the Working Class Movement?', *Review*, II, 1978, pp. 5–24

Hecht, J. J., *The Domestic Servant Class in Eighteenth-Century England*, London, 1956

Hobsbawm, E., *Primitive Rebels: Studies in Archaic Forms of Social Movement in the 19th and 20th Centuries*, Manchester, 1959

Hobsbawm, E., *Bandits*, Harmondsworth, 1971

Hobsbawm, E. J., 'From Social History to the History of Society', *Daedalus*, 100, 1, 1971–1972, pp. 20–45

Hobsbawm, E., 'Labour History and Ideology', *Journal of Social History*, 7, 4, 1974, pp. 371–381

Hobsbawm, E., 'Social Banditry', *in* Landsberger, H. A. (ed.), *Rural Protest: Peasant Movements and Social Change*, London, 1974

Hobsbawm, E., *Industry and Empire: An Economic History of Britain since 1750*, London, 1980

Horn, P., *The Rise and Fall of the Victorian Domestic Servant*, Dublin, 1975

Hughes, L. (ed.), *An African Tragedy*, New York, 1974

Katzman, D., *Seven Days a Week*, New York, 1978

Kneeland, G. J., *Commercialized Prostitution in New York City*, New York, 1913

Kollontai, A., 'Prostitution and Ways of Fighting It', *in* Kollontai, A., *Selected Writings*, London, 1978

Landsberger, H. A. (ed.)., *Rural Protest: Peasant Movements and Social Change*, London, 1974

le Bourgeois Chapin, A., *Their Trackless Ways*, London, 1931

Lyaschenko, P. I., *History of the National Economy of Russia to the 1917 Revolution*, New York, 1949

Marks, S., *Reluctant Rebellion*, Oxford, 1970

Maud, Sir John, *City Government*, Oxford, 1938

Maugham, R. C. F., *Portuguese East Africa*, London, 1906

Mitrany, D., *The Land and the Peasant in Rumania*, Oxford, 1930

Mouzinho de Albuquerque, J., *Moçambique 1896–98*, Lisbon, 1899

Mphahlele, E., *Down Second Avenue*, London, 1959

McKay, J. P., *Tramways and Trolleys*, Princeton, 1976

Pirenne, H., *The Economy and Society of Medieval Europe*, London, 1936

Pitje, G. M., 'Traditional Systems of Male Education Among Pedi and Cognate Tribes', *African Studies*, 9, 2, 1950, pp. 53–76, and No. 3, 1950, pp. 150–124

Pratt, A., *The Real South Africa*, London, 1913

Preston-Whyte, E., 'Race Attitudes and Behaviour: The Case of Domestic Employment in White South African Homes', *African Studies*, 35, 2, 1976, pp. 71–89

Riis, J. A., *How the Other Half Lives*, New York, 1971

Roberts, R., *The Classic Slum*, London, 1971

Rudé, G., *Ideology and Popular Protest*, London, 1980

Rudé, G., *Paris and London in the Eighteenth Century: Studies in Popular Protest*, London, 1969

Samuel, R., 'The Workshop of the World', *History Workshop*, 3, 1977, pp. 6–72

Scully, S. C., *The Ridge of White Waters*, London, 1911

Semmel, B., *Imperialism and Social Reform: English Social Imperial Thought 1895–1914*, London, 1960

Shepherd, W. C. A., 'Recruiting in Portuguese East Africa of Natives for the Mines', *Journal of the African Society*, 33, July, 1934

Simons, H. J. and R. E., *Class and Colour in South Africa, 1850–1950*, Harmondsworth, 1969

Somerset Bell, W. H., *Bygone Days*, London, 1933

Stedman-Jones, G., *Outcast London: A Study in the Relationship between Classes in Victorian Society*, Oxford, 1971

Stedman-Jones, G., 'Working-Class Culture and Working-Class Politics in London 1870–1900; Notes on the Remaking of a Working Class', *Journal of Social History*, 1974, pp. 461–508

Stedman-Jones, G., 'Class Expression *versus* social control? A critique of recent trends in the social history of "Leisure" ', *History Workshop*, 4, 1977, pp. 163–174

Stolper, G., *The German Economy 1870–1940*, New York, 1940

Thompson, E. P., *The Making of the English Working Class*, London, 1963

Thompson, F., *Lark Rise to Candleford*, London, 1973

Thompson, F. M. L., 'Nineteenth Century Horse Sense', *Economic History Review*, 29, 1

Thompson, L. M., and Wilson, M. (eds.), *The Oxford History of South Africa*, Vols. I and II, Oxford, 1971

Thrupp, S. S., 'The Gilds', *The Cambridge Economic History of Europe*, Vol. III, Cambridge, 1971

Tobias, J. J., *Crime and Industrial Society in the Nineteenth Century*, London, 1972

Turner, G. K. 'Daughters of the Poor', *McClures Magazine 1909*, pp. 45–61

van Onselen, C., *Chibaro: African Mine Labour in Southern Rhodesia, 1900–1933*, London, 1976

Walker, E. A., *A History of Southern Africa*, London, 1965

Warner, S. B., *Streetcar Suburbs*, Cambridge, Mass., 1962

Welsh, T., 'Contrasts in African Legislation', *Journal of the African Society*, 6, January 1903

Whisson, M. G. and Weil, W., *Domestic Servants*, Johannesburg, 1971

Worsley, P., 'Frantz Fanon and the Lumpenproletariat', *Socialist Register*, London, 1972

Zeldin, T., *France, 1848–1945, Ambition, Love and Politics*, Vol. I, Oxford, 1973

Theses and unpublished papers

Bransky, D., 'The Causes of the Boer War: Towards a Synthesis', Unpublished paper, Oxford, 1974

Cooper, C., 'Land and Labour in the Transvaal, c. 1900', M.A., London, 1974

Evans, R. J., 'The Women's Movement in Germany', D.Phil., Oxford, 1972

Fourie, J. J., 'Die Koms van die Bantoe na die Rand en hulle posisie aldaar, 1886–1899', M.A., Randse Afrikaanse Universiteit, 1976

Fourie, J. J., 'Die Geskiedenis van die Afrikaners in Johannesburg, 1886–1900', D.Phil., Randse Afrikaanse Universiteit, 1976

Hallet, R., 'Policemen, Pimps and Prostitutes – Public Morality and Police Corruption: Cape Town, 1902–1904', Unpublished paper presented to the History Workshop Conference, University of the Witwatersrand, 1978

Howarth, W. D., 'Tramway Systems of Southern Africa', Mimeo, Johannesburg Public Library, 1971

Jeeves, A., 'Het Volk and the Gold Mines – The Debate on Labour policy 1905–1910', Seminar Paper, African Studies Institute, University of the Witwatersrand, 1980

Keegan, T., 'Black Peril, Lapsed Whites and Moral Peril: A Study of Ideological Crisis in Early Twentieth Century South Africa', Unpublished paper, January 1980

Krut, R., ' "A Quart into a Pint Pot": The White Working Class and the "Housing Shortage" in Johannesburg, 1896–1906', B.A. Hons. Dissertation, University of the Witwatersrand, 1979

Naidoo, T., 'The Temple at Melrose', Unpublished paper, Johannesburg, 1978

Perry, F., 'The Transvaal Labour Problem', Speech read to the Fortnightly Club, 1906

Richardson, P., 'Coolies and Randlords: The Structure of Mining Capitalism and Chinese Labour, 1902–1910', Unpublished seminar paper, Institute of Commonwealth Studies, Oxford, 1979

Saron, G., 'The Communal Scene, Pathology: The White Slave Trade and Liquor Offences', Unpublished essay for a forthcoming study on the history of South African Jewry

Saron, G., ' "The Morality Question" in South Africa', Unpublished essay for a forthcoming study on the history of South African Jewry

Simonowitz, G., 'The Background to Jewish Immigration to South Africa and the Development of the Jewish Community in the South African Republic between 1890 and 1902', B.A. (Hons.), University of the Witwatersrand, 1960

Van den Berg, G. N., 'Die Polisiediens in die Zuid Afrikaansche Republiek', D. Litt., Potchefstroomse Universiteit vir Christelike Hoër Onderwys, 1972

Warwick, P., 'African Labour during the South African War, 1899–1902', Unpublished seminar paper, Institute of Commonwealth Studies, London, 1975

Interviews

Brummer, W. H., Johannesburg, 31 March 1980

Buthelezi, N. H., Weenen, 25 April 1977

Buthelezi, R., Mpungu River, Weenen District, 27 April 1977

Cohen, P., Johannesburg, 16 November 1976

Gaddie, B., Johannesburg, 10 April 1977

Gumbi, P., Johannesburg, 16 April 1977

Kaluse, E., Johannesburg, 11 February 1977

Mchunu, N., Weenen, 25 April 1977

Naidoo, J., Johannesburg, 16 November 1976

Sagorin, I., Johannesburg, 15 August 1978 (interview conducted by S. Kahn and C. van Onselen)

Sibiya, M., Eshowe, 27 April 1977

Sivetye, G., Groutville, Natal, 23 October 1978 (interview conducted by T. J. Couzens and A. van Gylswyk)

Skhosana, G. K., Lydenburg, 7 and 8 September 1979 (interview conducted by M. S. S. Ntoane)

Index

Waterval, relocation of brickmakers at, 120
Wernher, Beit & Co., 145
  grants to Rand Aid Association, 134
White labour policy, 99, 135, 137–8, 147, 150
white women, *see* women, white
Whitesun, John, 44–5
Wilson, Edward, 99
Windham, W., 99
Witbank washing site, 81–2, 87
  disadvantages, 83–5
  return from, 88
Witwatersrand Boarding-House Keepers' Protection Association, 4, 5
women
  immigration, 10–13
women, black, 10, 21, 87, 105
  domestic service employment, 16–17, 28
  involvement in *Amalaita*, 57
women, coloured, 8, 26, 87, 92, 105
women, white
  Afrikaner, 5, 15–16, 86, 97, 105, 130, 131, 144
  assault by blacks, *see* black peril scares
  domestic service employment (*see also* children's nurse; cook-general; housemaid)
    contracts, 34–5
    demand and supply, 4–5, 9, 10–13, 15, 19, 22, 28

relationships with 'houseboys', 46–7, 52–3
    wages, 4, 9, 15, 19–20
  employment in laundries, 86–7, 97, 102
  English, 4
  German, 4
  Irish, 4, 11
  relationships with 'houseboys', 31, 43, 46–9
  Scottish, 4, 13
  workers, 92, 98
Woolf, H., 87
working class
  blacks as largest part of, 74, 100
  demand for domestic servants, 3, 9, 22
  family (black), 17
  family (white), 9, 22, 31, 51, 57, 59, 77, 98, 100, 144
  marginalisation, 173
  political consciousness, 155–8, 160–61
World War I
  effect on Ninevites, 192–3

York Mine, Ninevite organisation at, 188

Xaba, Jacob, 181, 190

Zulu, Nkulu, 180
Zulus (*see also AmaWasha*; 'houseboys'), 7–8, 10, 20, 28, 43, 47, 55, 56, 76, 79, 91